ANCIENT TAXATION

ISAW MONOGRAPHS

ISAW Monographs publishes authoritative studies of new evidence and research into the texts, archaeology, art history, material culture, and history of the cultures and periods representing the core areas of study at NYU's Institute for the Study of the Ancient World. The topics and approaches of the volumes in this series reflect the intellectual mission of ISAW as a center for advanced scholarly research and graduate education whose aim is to encourage the study of the economic, religious, political, and cultural connections between ancient civilizations, from the Western Mediterranean across the Near East and Central Asia, to China.

Ancient Taxation

The Mechanics of Extraction
in Comparative Perspective

Edited by
Jonathan Valk *and* Irene Soto Marín

INSTITUTE FOR THE STUDY OF ANCIENT WORLD

NEW YORK UNIVERSITY PRESS
2021

INSTITUTE FOR THE STUDY OF THE ANCIENT WORLD

NEW YORK UNIVERSITY PRESS
New York
www.nyupress.org

References to Internet websites (URLs) were accurate at the time of writing. The author, the Institute for the Study of the Ancient World, and the New York University Press are not responsible for URLs that may have expired or changed since the manuscript was prepared.

Library of Congress Cataloging-in-Publication Data
Names: Valk, Jonathan, editor. | Soto Marín, Irene, 1988– editor.
Title: Ancient taxation : the mechanics of extraction in comparative perspective / edited by Jonathan Valk and Irene Soto Marín.
Description: New York : Institute for the Study of the Ancient World/New York University Press, 2021. | Series: Isaw monographs | Includesbibliographical references and index. | Summary: "The studies collected in Ancient Taxation explore the extractive systems of eleven ancient states and societies from across the ancient world, ranging from Bronze Age China to Anglo-Saxon Britain. Together, the contributors explore the challenges of taxation in predominantly agro-pastoral societies, including basic tax strategy (taxing goods vs. labor, in kind vs. money taxes, direct vs. indirect, internal vs. external, etc.), assessment and collection (particularly over wide geographic areas or at large scale, e.g., by tax farming), compliance, and negotiating the cooperation of social, economic, and political elites or other critical social groups. By assembling such a broad range of studies, the book sheds new light on the commonalities and differences between ancient taxation systems, highlighting how studying taxes can shed light on the fiscal and institutional practices of antiquity. It also provides new impetus for comparative research, both between ancient societies and between ancient and modern extractive practices. This book will be of interest to those studying ancient history, economic history, the history of taxation, or comparative politics and economics"—Provided by publisher.
Identifiers: LCCN 2021003094 (print) | LCCN 2021003095 (ebook) | ISBN 9781479806195 (hardcover) | ISBN 9781479806218 (ebook) | ISBN 9781479806225 (ebook other)
Subjects: LCSH: Taxation—History.
Classification: LCC HJ212 .A63 2021 (print) | LCC HJ212 (ebook) | DDC 336.2009/014—dc23
LC record available at https://lccn.loc.gov/2021003094
LC ebook record available at https://lccn.loc.gov/2021003095

Hardcover: 9781479806195
E-book (consumer): 9781479806218
E-book (institutional/libraries): 9781479806225

New York University Press books are printed on acid-free paper, and their binding materials are chosen for strength and durability. We strive to use environmentally responsible suppliers and materials to the greatest extent possible in publishing our books.

Manufactured in the United States of America

10 9 8 7 6 5 4 3 2 1

Also available as an ebook

In furtherance of the study of the interconnected human past

CONTENTS

FIGURES

PREFACE

This volume is the outcome of a conference held at New York University's Institute for the Study of the Ancient World (ISAW) on September 30 and October 1, 2016. The conference was entitled "The Mechanics of Extraction: Comparing Principles of Taxation and Tax Compliance in the Ancient World." It was made possible by the generous support of ISAW, the NYU Center for Humanities, the NYU Center for Ancient Studies, the NYU Classics Department, and an anonymous gift. The conference brought together fourteen scholars from different disciplines to present research on tax systems from across the ancient world. By bringing these different case studies into direct conversation with each other, the conference sought to stimulate new comparative research and to enrich our understanding of what makes each tax system unique. It also sought to promote a holistic approach to extractive practices that moves beyond money and material goods to incorporate labor and the social dimensions of tax compliance.

This volume includes work that was not presented at the conference and does not include some of the work that was. Whether presented at the conference or not, all the research collected here has benefited from substantial reconsideration in light of the discussions that took place at the conference and the subsequent peer review process. The volume is thus much more than a transcript of the conference: it is the product of ongoing scholarly dialogue and collaborative research. From initial conception to presentation before colleagues, and from reworking to peer review, the research in this volume has profited at every turn from the input of a much broader scholarly community. We are especially grateful for the input of more than two dozen anonymous reviewers, who shared their expertise regarding specific contributions and the volume in its entirety. These individuals took the time to share their knowledge without pay or public recognition, vetting and improving the work presented here. Such generosity is an essential and insufficiently acknowledged service to the advancement of scholarship.

Our gratitude extends to all the participants in the conference and the volume, and in particular to Rod Campbell, who helped move the project forward. It also extends to the publication team at ISAW and NYU Press, and notably to David M. Ratzan, who was instrumental in the publishing process.

The journey from the initial planning of the Mechanics of Extraction conference in 2015 to publication in the beginning of this new and fraught decade has been long. In retrospect, there are things that we would do differently—there always are! But we especially regret that we did not make diversity and representation a central goal. Final publication has also been set back by delays and other turbulence, for which we apologize to the contributors who entrusted us with editorial care over their work. We wish this could have been otherwise, but it was not. We learn, and we are committed to doing better.

This volume is indelibly associated with ISAW. At its best, ISAW stimulates the ambitious intellectual vision of an interdisciplinary and comparative approach to the study of the ancient world. We hope this volume reflects that vision.

Jonathan Valk and Irene Soto Marín
Leiden and Basel
June 24, 2020

1

A State of Extraction

Navigating Taxation in Ancient Polities

JONATHAN VALK

In his political treatise *Leviathan*, Thomas Hobbes conceives of the state as an "artificiall man."[1] Just as individual human beings are constituted by various parts working in concert, so too are states constituted by the human beings whose relationships cohere in the state system.[2] In this analogy, the different elements of the human body correspond to different elements in the structure of the state. But this analogy extends still further: humans must eat, and this is as true of Hobbes' artificial man as it is of people of flesh and blood.[3] To function, the state must consume— and it has a tendency toward gluttony. The state consumes the labor and the materials that allow it to achieve its many ends. Such resources can be put to many uses, from building walls to feeding and compensating laborers to acquiring armaments or amassing the valuable goods that serve to confer prestige. To fuel his strains and struggles, Hobbes' artificial man depends on his access to resources.

Systems of taxation are the basis for the collection of resources and the generation of state revenue. In the modern world, such systems are ubiquitous: we pay taxes whenever we go shopping, taxes are deducted when we receive income, and the state even claims its share of our wealth when we die. But the conditions prevailing today are in many respects different from those of the premodern world, when the capacities, capabilities, and aspirations of states were comparatively limited.[4] These differences are fertile ground for studying the deep history of resource extraction and redistribution by polities. Then as now, the artificial man (or in more colloquial modern parlance, simply "The Man") was in the business of collecting and reallocating resources; this was the *sine qua non* of his activities. How did ancient states sate their appetite for resources? How did they assess the availability of resources and determine who would be held responsible for delivering them, and in what quantities? How did the state enforce compliance with its demands? Different types of taxes and forms of tax collection are attested in the ancient world: what conditions determined the preference for certain types and forms over others? How much agency did ancient states possess in the determination of preferred systems of taxation?

By bringing together numerous case studies of taxation in ancient societies, the present volume aims to provide a broader empirical basis for answering such questions. The research presented here comprises a spatially, temporally, and thematically extensive set of case studies. These studies include small polities, regional states, and empires with universal horizons; they range geographically from Britain to China, and extend temporally from the third millennium BCE to the first millennium CE; they cover taxation at every stage of state formation and in times of transition; and they focus on every aspect of the mechanics of extraction, from material and technical constraints to transaction costs, ideological frameworks, and strategies of enforcement. Despite all the differences in content and perspective that this cornucopia of scholarship represents, there are numerous points of intersection that justify a comparative approach and promise rich rewards.

This volume is organized thematically. In addition to the introduction you are now reading, the volume is divided into two broad sections covering tax systems and tax transitions. *Tax Systems* comprises six contributions offering an overview of extractive systems in six different ancient societies. Although these studies are chronologically and geographically disparate, they demonstrate how systems building on common agro-pastoral foundations can produce different extractive outcomes. These outcomes are not merely the result of diverging state capacities and priorities in the collection of goods and services. They are also the products of different social constellations and mediated by extractive ideologies that inform the state's relationship with those social groups that it regards as its constituents. In *Tax Transitions*, five studies focus on how certain tax systems changed. These studies demonstrate the dynamic nature of tax systems, which are impermanent compromises between different social agents. As these agents navigate their interests and the environments in which they operate, inherited extractive practices are continually reconfigured—sometimes gradually, sometimes at great speed. The common thread is idiosyncrasy: even when confronted by the same essential problems, societies develop unique tax practices that are as much the product of economic necessity as they are of historical accident. The constructive work of comparing between the case studies assembled in this volume is left to its readers. Nevertheless, comparison is inescapable for those who read more than one contribution. Reviewing any two studies will produce reflection about commonalities and differences; the hope is that these reflections will stimulate new insights. At any rate, the rest of this introduction aims to provide a foundation for such reflection.

Forerunners

An awareness of the centrality of taxation to the functioning of states is as old as the state itself. Such recognition can be manifest in practice, as it is in the quotidian administrative record of ancient Mesopotamia. Thousands upon thousands of clay tablets have been recovered documenting the movement of goods and people through the state apparatus. Although these texts are an infinitesimal fraction of the total produced, they testify to the intense involvement of ancient Mesopotamian states in taxation.[5] Recognition of the importance of taxation can also be more theoretical in orientation, as in the Aristotelian *Oikonomika*. The *Oikonomika* offers an extended reflection on economics and devotes extensive attention to the state's generation of revenue.[6]

Because states depend on revenue, the means of revenue generation have long featured prominently in the work of scholars occupying themselves with the nature of states. The 14th-century North African proto-sociologist Ibn Khaldun regarded the authority to tax as a large part of the authority of the state (in his analysis, a generic "kingdom"):

> [The ministry of taxation] constitutes a large part of all royal authority.
> In fact, it is the third of its basic pillars. Royal authority requires soldiers,

money, and the means to communicate with those who are absent. The ruler, therefore, needs persons to help him in the matters concerned with "the sword," "the pen," and finances. Thus, the person who holds the office (of tax collections) has (a good) part of the royal authority for himself.[7]

The state's authority to tax has itself been the subject of vigorous contestation. Disputes over this authority abound in the historical record, instigating major episodes of unrest. It was precisely parliament's authority to raise taxes that enabled it to challenge the English king Charles I in the 17th century, ushering in the English civil war and ultimately costing Charles his head. A century later, colonists in North America challenged the authority of a parliament in which they were not included to levy taxes from them. They came together under the slogan "no taxation without representation" to embark on a struggle that culminated in the independence of the United States of America. It is no wonder that the Scottish economist Adam Smith—writing in a climate informed by these conflicts—echoes Ibn Khaldun's focus on the centrality of revenue to the very existence of the state. In *The Wealth of Nations* Smith stresses the essential role of taxation in supporting the state and develops four maxims for effective and sustainable extraction.[8] Edmund Burke, writing in much the same milieu, is blunter: "the revenue of the state is the state."[9]

Taxation has commanded the attention of more recent thinkers as well. In 1918 Joseph Schumpeter published "Die Krise des Steuerstaats" ("The Crisis of the Tax State"), a paper that has inspired a movement in sociohistorical inquiry that has since been called "the new fiscal sociology."[10] Schumpeter himself emphasizes the importance of fiscal systems—tax regimes, essentially—in the study of human societies:

> The spirit of a people, its cultural level, its social structure, the deeds its policy may prepare—all this and more is written into its fiscal history, stripped of all phrases. He who knows how to listen to its message here discerns the thunder of world history more clearly than anywhere else.[11]

Regardless of the actual novelty of the new fiscal sociology, Schumpeter's vision is consistent with that of many other 20th-century scholars. Historians of the early modern period have been especially active in placing taxation at the center of their analyses. This is in large part due to their interest in identifying the causes of the so-called "Great Divergence," the process whereby the different developmental paths of several European states positioned them to dominate the world in the course of a few centuries. In the work of the late Charles Tilly and many others, it was precisely the need to increase revenue in order to wage war that stimulated the development of the modern tax state: "war made the state, and the state made war."[12]

The idea that extractive practices are at the heart of every state-system is now at the heart of research throughout the social sciences. This literature is vast, but some examples are particularly noteworthy. Margaret Levi explores the relationship between resource distribution in polities and resulting sociopolitical structures,[13] while John L. Campbell synthesizes a number of empirical studies concerning the influence of fiscal systems on social organization.[14] More recently, I. W. Martin, A. K. Mehrotra, and M. Prasad have argued that "the future of fiscal sociology points beyond the study of taxation as an index or symptom of other changes, and toward an understanding of taxation as the central element in the social, political and economic development of the modern world: the actually existing social contract, the renegotiation of which transforms the relationship between state and society."[15] Philip Hoffman asserts that the capacity to tax is foundational to stateness, writing that states "come into existence when in addition to being able to use force they also gain the capacity to impose and collect significant tax revenue, not just temporarily during emergencies but for the foreseeable future."[16] Such insights are still percolating through the study of ancient taxation systems.

The application of these insights to antiquity is an essential complement to a longer scholarly tradition that is concerned primarily with identifying the genealogy of the modern tax state. This tradition tends to exclude a multitude of ancient societies, which rarely fit well in the reconstructed developmental trajectories of modern fiscal systems. The recent volume edited by Andrew Monson and Walter Scheidel, *Fiscal Regimes and the Political Economy of Premodern States*,[17] is a notable exception to this exclusionary tendency. It assembles various case studies of the fiscal regimes of ancient polities that venture beyond the teleological shadow of the modern tax state, instead approaching their subjects on their own terms, but in the context of broader scholarship on fiscal systems. Crucially, this engagement with big questions does not come at the price of forcing the case studies into a narrative framework that is interested first and foremost in the Quixotic search for the origins of the modern tax state—as though it has a single fountainhead, hidden away somewhere, patiently awaiting discovery.

The study of ancient or premodern societies has great potential to improve our understanding of fiscal regimes.[18] It can also be of value when applied more narrowly to particular taxes or tax-systems.[19] Like their modern counterparts, all ancient states are obliged to navigate the same fundamental challenge: how to extract the resources necessary to sustain themselves and pursue their ends. Collectively, ancient societies constitute an incredibly rich dataset of the many different solutions to this problem. This is precisely because of their sometimes radically different constitutions and capabilities, as well as the different cultural and environmental contexts in which they functioned. The comparative study of their extractive solutions is not only instructive on account of its ability to illuminate the (sometimes quite different) economic rationales and priorities of states, but also because it can help us identify basic patterns and parameters of extraction. Securing a better grasp of these patterns and parameters can in turn highlight precisely where we should look for discontinuities both between ancient states and between the premodern and the modern. We can then inquire after the character of any discontinuities: are they differences in substance or degree?

Defining Taxation

Taxes can be levied from any person, social unit,[20] or corporate body[21] within a state's power. The levying of taxes can take a bewildering variety of forms, from property taxes to taxes on particular goods, transactions, or services; from taxes on the use of infrastructure to taxes on particular activities; from a poll tax to income taxes or taxes predicated on social rank—to name only a few. Such taxes can be levied arbitrarily or systematically, at different rates or quantities, regularly or irregularly, and at different moments in time. Sometimes, taxes are raised for a specific public purpose.[22] Sometimes, they are raised for no apparent purpose beyond aggrandizing the state. Hugh Dalton, the British economist and post-second world war Chancellor of the Exchequer, defined taxation as "a compulsory contribution imposed by a public authority, irrespective of the exact amount of service rendered to the taxpayer in return, and not imposed as a penalty for any legal offence."[23] Dalton's definition is derived from the modern world. It is nevertheless applicable across time and space, even if allowances must be made for how best to identify a "public authority" in different historical and cultural contexts. Indeed, it is almost exactly parallel to the less concise but more expressive definition of Richard Bonney:

> For the ordinary citizen, the power to tax is the most familiar manifestation of the government's ability to coerce. This power to tax involves the power to impose, on individuals and private institutions more generally, charges that can be met only by a transfer to government of economic resources, or financial claims to such resources—charges that carry within them effective means of enforcement under the very definition of the taxing authority. The power to tax, *per se*, does not carry with it any obligation to use the tax revenue in any particular way. Seen in this light, the power to "tax" is simply the power to "take."[24]

The equation of taxation with the state's ability to take is apt. It allows taxation to encompass not only the taking of material resources, but also labor.[25] Of equal importance, the expansive definitions of Dalton and Bonney make no claim about the justification for taxation or about the extent to which taxes are delivered freely and willingly.

It is important to stress that there are significant differences between many of the phenomena that are here subsumed collectively under the rubric "taxation." Scholars have proposed multiple competing classificatory schemes through which to understand revenue extraction in premodern states.[26] Among the more recent examples, Martin Rössler recognizes three broad extractive avenues, namely taxes on subjects of the state, the exaction of tribute from conquered peoples, and the imposition of tolls on trade.[27] Richard Blanton and Lane Fargher opt instead for a division between internal and external categories of resource extraction, with an eclectic selection of what sorts of taxes fall under each heading.[28] Richard Bonney and W. M. Ormrod identify four basic fiscal systems with distinct characteristics. These serve almost as developmental stages, through which taxation transitions from being infrequent, irregular, simple, and largely in kind, to being pervasive, regular, complex, and monetized.[29] Each of these approaches has strengths and weaknesses, but none of them gives as full a sense of the major distinctions between different forms and types of taxation in the ancient world as the evidence appears to require. I propose instead four classificatory axes, though these are intended only as elementary guidelines. Their purpose is to facilitate consideration of some of the major contrasts between the varieties of taxation attested in antiquity. They are:

Material Resources and Labor

The state can tax not only tangible things like grain or gold, but also the time and energy of its subjects. Extractable material resources can range from unprocessed agro-pastoral produce like barley and wool to processed goods like beer and textiles; in lieu of such resources, the state can demand payment in a recognized medium of exchange (money, for which see axis 2 below). Labor can likewise be demanded in many forms. The key is that certain categories of people are obliged to perform certain tasks on behalf of the state at certain times. Such obligations can cover the performance of manual labor, from seasonal agricultural work on state lands to service in mobile labor battalions. Labor on behalf of the state is frequently directed toward the development or maintenance of public infrastructure, from dredging canals to building pyramids. Labor obligations can also cover military service, a compulsory contribution that is still common today. Although labor obligations outside of the military sphere are now rare and therefore not generally included in contemporary analyses of taxation, they are fundamental to the extractive practices of many premodern polities.

Collection in Kind and in Money

Taxes can be collected in kind or in money. Collection of taxes in kind involves delivery by the taxpayer of a certain quantity or share of a material resource that is gathered or produced within the jurisdiction of a given taxing authority. Most commonly, agro-pastoral producers are expected to part with a share or fixed quantity of their crops, flocks, or the byproducts of either. The output of other producers can be subjected to taxation of this kind, so that the state can demand the textiles of weavers or the stones and metals of miners and smelters. Instead of (or in addition to) demanding a share of output, the state can also demand payment in a recognized monetary medium. This obliges producers to convert their output into money, which is not always easy and enables the state to insist on special, favorable conversion rates. Because of these difficulties, it is not uncommon for different economic actors to be subject to different kinds of payment—some in kind, others in money. While labor obligations are in theory always delivered in kind, in some systems it is possible for those with means to provide a substitute to perform the service, or to provide a monetary payment in lieu of service. In the latter case, we can say that the tax on labor is being paid in money rather than in kind.

Direct and Indirect Taxation

Direct taxes are payments that are levied directly from taxpaying persons, social units, or corporate bodies. Such taxes can be imposed on taxpayers for a multitude of reasons, from an assessment of production, income, or wealth to ascription to a particular social category like "citizen" or "adult male." Indirect taxes are instead levied on transfers of goods and property. Taxes can be collected every time particular goods are moved or sold.[30] They can also be levied when the state registers a change in the status of persons, such as when slaves are manumitted or when people are elevated to the nobility or some other social rank.

Internal and External Taxation

Taxes can be levied internally or externally.[31] Internal taxes are extracted from people and territories that are under the technical jurisdiction of the extractive authority, like subjects of the state or territories administered by the state's officials. External taxes are extracted from people and territories that are notionally independent of the extractive authority, like other states or otherwise autonomous social formations. External taxation is often described as tribute, but its imposition by an outside authority complies with Dalton's definition of a tax. There can be much ambiguity in determining whether a people or territory should be regarded as being under the "technical" jurisdiction of an extractive authority. Such determinations must be made on a case-by-case basis. Where possible, helpful indicators can be sought among the claims made by the taxing authority itself, in the sustainability of its extraction of resources from the relevant taxpayers, and in the extent to which those who collect the taxes are agents of the state or autonomous social actors. Another source of ambiguity concerns the extraction of booty and plunder in war. Unlike the payment of tribute, such practices tend to be *ad hoc*: the proceeds are not so much delivered by the taxpayer as confiscated by the collectors. Because of the irregularity of such extractive practices and their lack of formalization, they are difficult to qualify as taxes *per se*.[32] It is not always immediately clear how systematic or regular plunder has to be to qualify as a tax, or, indeed, if external taxation is so rapacious and arbitrary that its formal veneer should be regarded as insufficient to elevate it above the act of plundering.[33]

* * *

The taxation systems of different polities manifest different constellations of extraction along these four axes.[34] Each state's fiscal system features unique and constantly developing combinations of extractive practices, relying on a balance of human and material resources, collection in kind or in money, direct and indirect taxes, and internal and external taxes. Occasionally, as in pre-monetary economies, a taxation system can find itself on one of the extremes of a given axis. Much more common, however, is a place at some point between the extremes, combining elements of both. Precisely where a state's fiscal system sits along these four axes is determined by its own social reality: the different interests that shape it, geographical constraints, administrative capacities, economic patterns, and assorted serendipities dictating movements in one direction or another. Taxation systems are also rarely uniform, so that the balance of taxation prevailing in one region need not be identical or even particularly similar to the extractive balance elsewhere in the same state. Indeed, each form and type of taxation offers different advantages and meets different needs. The maximization of these advantages and needs informs distinct preferences and choices in line with the priorities of the taxing authorities.

The Question of Evidence

In modern societies there is an overabundance of evidence for the mechanics of extraction. These include tax codes that are so complex that making sense of them has spawned whole industries dedicated to guiding the perplexed—the British tax code, for example, is currently over 10 million words in length.[35] Such evidence is supplemented by vast amounts of readily available data of other sorts, from precise statistics concerning the collection of taxes to extensive information about their socioeconomic context and innumerable records of social attitudes and philosophical perspectives. Students of modern tax systems are thus confronted with a task that is distinct from that of the ancient historian. When studying the ancient world, we encounter the opposite problem: not a surfeit of evidence, but its dearth. Scholars are obliged to make do with whatever materials the vicissitudes of history have preserved and chance has allowed to be recovered. While certain sorts of data can survive in vast quantities—like clay tax receipts from Mesopotamia or equivalent papyri from Egypt—they still represent a limited and fragmentary body of evidence. The materials available to scholars vary dramatically across different contexts, and the results are invariably patchy. In some cases, there might be administrative texts recording the collection of taxes. In others, there might be references to taxation in letters or assorted narrative texts. In still others, there might be archaeological material that sheds light on extractive practices. Scholars must work with a combination of sources of varying kinds and quality that even in the best case offer an incomplete portrait of the mechanics of extraction.[36] As the papers in this volume demonstrate, it is a tribute to the investigative skills of historians of the ancient world that with due diligence so much can nevertheless be said about ancient taxation.

What to Tax and How to Do So

Preindustrial agro-pastoral economies are the common foundation of all ancient states. Consequently, the bulk of the material resources available for taxation are the commodities typical of such economies, namely agricultural produce, livestock, and their byproducts. Resources like metals, wood, and precious stones, as well as finished products like textiles, tools, and luxury goods, can also be taxed, particularly at the strategic points through which they pass, be they the site of production, important transit nodes, or markets—if not all three. Before the monetization of economies, resources are necessarily collected in kind, which imposes practical constraints and additional expenses relating to transit, storage, and convertibility. Each of these constraints presents high transaction costs.[37] Because of the costs associated with extraction in kind, taxation in a standard medium of exchange often supplants taxation in kind when it becomes a viable option—and when whatever is being taxed is available in sufficient quantities and at acceptable prices in the open market. This has the advantage of greatly reducing storage and transit costs while eliminating the problem of convertibility. Insofar as there is widespread trust in the value and convertibility of the currency, monetization is thus a critical transitional stage in the development of fiscal systems.

Besides agro-pastoral produce, the other major and widely available taxable resource in premodern economies is human labor. Obligatory contributions of labor enable polities to pursue labor intensive projects like the maintenance and expansion of complex irrigation systems and the erection of public buildings, like ziggurats and fortresses. As is the case for material resources, the advent of monetization is a critical transitional stage in the realm of human resource extraction. The rise of sophisticated labor markets that enable the state to secure access to sufficient manpower in exchange for payment often results in the elimination or reduction of labor obligations or their commutation to cash payments.

For all that monetization is a critical economic development, it is not without its complications. Monetization involves complex problems that relate to the standardization of currency, fluctuating monetary values, and control over the production of money. In metal currencies, for instance, changes in access to the metal(s) of exchange can result in changing currency values or even in changes to the ability of the available currency to fulfill its intended economic function. Liquidity is a perennial concern; when not enough currency is available, many transactions are forced to revert to in kind. Monetization is therefore reversible and need not be distributed evenly across all sectors of the economy or all forms of tax collection.[38] There are also problems associated with counterfeiting: people can dilute more valuable metals with less valuable ones, profiting from the difference in value while undermining trust in the currency as a whole. States can counteract such behaviors, notably by minting coins and monopolizing the process, but here too counterfeiters can find space to operate. While monetization can solve the problem of convertibility between different economic goods, it comes with risks and costs of its own. Often, these are borne by taxpayers who are obliged to pay taxes in money and solve the problem of conversion themselves—sometimes at considerable added cost. The convenience of tax collectors is not identical with the convenience of taxpayers.

One of the key obstacles faced by taxation systems involves assessing what to tax—and how much. This depends on evaluating what can be taxed profitably, from whom such taxes should be levied, and how much should be extracted. This is a complex task that necessitates substantial administrative capabilities, as well as detailed knowledge of local conditions. Because agro-pastoral productivity is based in large measure on unpredictable environmental factors, determining in advance how much to tax and planning accordingly is not easy. Such determinations can be made on the basis of past experience or with the continual input of local informers; in both cases, decision-making improves in proportion to the knowledge available to those making the decisions. Effective extraction of resources is thus utterly dependent on the development of an administrative apparatus that can obtain and process relevant data. Beyond the local level, such an apparatus must also be able to coordinate and communicate reliably over large distances. Accordingly, the administrative capacity of ancient polities must be identified as an essential constraint on the efficiency and sophistication of the mechanics of extraction.[39]

Maintaining and cultivating an administrative capacity is itself a significant challenge. Administration is largely the preserve of trained professionals; indeed, writing developed in no small measure as a tool in the service of greater administrative efficiencies.[40] Employing scribes is expensive and administration is difficult, so much so that the high costs of effective taxation systems often preclude their extension to less profitable or secure areas within a state's nominal jurisdiction. The obvious alternative is the establishment or preservation of decentralized modes of government, particularly in larger polities. Local élites with detailed knowledge of local conditions are entrusted with the responsibilities of taxation in their territories in exchange for a share of the spoils. In this way, the state can escape the burdens of administration and governance at the expense of some of the revenue it might otherwise have collected.[41] In other cases, high transaction costs and the challenge of maintaining an adequate administrative capacity can induce states to opt for tax farming, which effectively outsources the task of taxation to third parties in exchange for a fee.[42] Tax farming can also have the further benefit of transferring the risk of fluctuating income to these same third parties. At any rate, the challenges and costs of effective administration in ancient polities regularly encourage reliance on local élites and result in the development of decentralized and non-uniform systems of taxation.

Taxation and the Social Order

One area of ambiguity with broad implications for how states work concerns the practice of slavery. Because enslaved people are classified as property, they cannot be taxed directly. Instead, their productivity must be taxed through levies imposed on the assets or income of the slave-owner. The exclusion of servile laborers from the community of direct taxpayers suggests that direct taxes can only be levied from "free" people, though in different societies this status can denote individuals from the top of the social pyramid to those whose social situation is only formally distinguishable from that of the enslaved. The payment of direct taxes by free people often implies a form of belonging to the extracting authority. In this model, a community of taxpayers opts into a fiscal regime (at least notionally) in order to participate in the common project of the state; paying taxes then comes with certain rights as well as responsibilities, such as legal protections from various abuses and a stake in the material and social dividends of the state project. In this context, it is worth noting that it is precisely those subject populations that are or can be taxed directly by the state that should be regarded as its actual or potential constituent base: it is on these tax-payers that states depend, and it is the interests of these taxpayers that states often seek to represent.[43]

The relationship between taxes and inclusion in the state tends to be especially stark when it involves military service. Extracting manpower for the armed forces is a central concern in many of the extractive sys-tems of ancient polities. Unlike ordinary labor service, however, military service has a more pronounced ability to forge political communities.[44] Those who are entrusted with the security of the state are also to a sig-nificant degree the people on whose behalf the polity is supposed to function. This correlation is reflected in the prominence of hierarchies of military service, with those toward the top of the social pyramid—the greatest stakeholders in the sociopolitical system embodied by the polity—expected to contribute most in terms of materiel and expertise.[45] Simultaneously, some social groups are excluded from military service, marking their exclusion from participation in the state—like the helots of Sparta. The relationship between military service and representation in the polity is underscored by the occasional preference of states for mercenaries or sources of military manpower beyond the state's core constituents. Such preferences are pursued precisely in order to create an instrument of force that is distinct from and independent of these central constituents—and thus more amenable to being deployed against them.

Yet the obligation to pay direct taxes need not create community. It can also be a simple marker of subjection without a commensurate sense of participation in or ownership of the state. The payment of taxes as a marker of subjection to a state rather than participation in the com-munity that it represents is exemplified by Jesus' answer to the question posed to him in three of the gospels of the New Testament. Because pay-ing taxes to the Roman authorities is regarded as a tacit acknowledge-ment of the legitimacy of these authorities, Jesus is asked: "is it lawful to pay taxes to the emperor, or not?" He famously responds: "Render unto Caesar the things that are Caesar's, and unto God the things that are God's" (Matthew 22: 15–22; Mark 12: 13–17; Luke 20: 20–26). Mun-dane authority does not, in other words, operate on the same plane as spiritual authority, and need not interfere with it: one can pay taxes to the pagan Roman emperor without accepting the imperial project and worldview that he represents. Paying taxes does not necessarily mean identifying with the taxing authority. On the contrary, the anarchist P.-J. Proudhon views taxation as one of the many humiliating subjections that a governed person—a subject of the state—must endure:

> To be GOVERNED is to be kept in sight, inspected, spied upon, directed, law-driven, numbered, enrolled, indoctrinated, preached at, controlled, estimated, valued, censured, commanded, by creatures who have neither the right, nor the wisdom, nor the virtue to do so. . . . To be GOVERNED is to be at every operation, at every transaction, noted, registered, enrolled, taxed, stamped, measured, numbered, assessed, licensed, authorized, admonished, forbidden, reformed, corrected, punished. It is, under pretext of public utility, and in the name of the general interest, to be placed under contribution, trained, ransomed, exploited, monopolized, extorted, squeezed, mystified, robbed; then, at the slightest resistance, the first word of complaint, to be repressed, fined, despised, harassed, tracked, abused, clubbed, disarmed, choked, imprisoned, judged, condemned, shot, deported, sacrificed, sold, betrayed; and, to crown all, mocked, ridiculed, outraged, dishonored. That is government; that is its justice; that is its morality.[46]

No taxation as identification with the state project for Proudhon, then.

In some systems, it is precisely exemption from some or all taxes that marks partnership in the state, to be contrasted with the subjection and exclusion inherent in taxation. In pre-revolutionary France of the *Ancien Régime*, two of the three estates were largely free of taxes: the nobility and the clergy. This marked their superior status within the state, so that they served as partners rather than simple taxpaying subjects of the king—unlike the common folk of the third estate (*le tiers état*). In the Neo-Assyrian empire too, entire urban communities and leading functionaries could be rewarded by the state with various tax-exemptions, signaling their favored position within the state system, to be contrasted with that of ordinary taxpayers. Returning again to classical Sparta, the notable social division is between helots who pay considerable material taxes, and Spartan citizens, who contribute military labor: one form of taxation marks inclusion, whereas the other marks subjection. Comparable phenomena are attested in many societies.[47] In our own time, the low to non-existent rates of taxation for major corporations indicate their privileged partnership with the state, not their exclusion from the state project. Although tax exemptions mark a privileged position within the state system, they also signal the autonomous position of those who are exempted. Exemptions can thus frequently be understood as an indication of the weakness of the state relative to the exempted. This weakness results in the state's decision to coopt exempted persons, social units, and corporate bodies through privileges rather than by the (sometimes prohibitively costly) expedient of asserting their own authority. Sometimes the state becomes the vehicle of those it privileges, rendering it unwilling to assert itself against these selfsame privileged bodies.

Tax Compliance

Taxation is redistributive in nature: it involves the collection and reallocation of resources, a process that can quickly lead to grievances and the entrenchment of special interests. In the modern world, we expect to reap benefits from the taxes that we pay. We assume that the same state that collects our taxes will collect our rubbish, police our streets, maintain public infrastructure, and—in many countries—educate our children and provide health care. Of course, all the particulars vary across states and produce a bewildering spectrum of possible configurations for raising taxes and spending revenues. This profusion of possibilities is not simply the product of practical considerations, of objective bookkeeping conducted by impartial civil servants in pursuit of the common good. Every decision pertaining to taxation is ultimately a political choice.[48] Each such political choice has immediate implications for the economic wellbeing and socio-political standing of individuals and social groups, as well as for shaping broader economic patterns, so that it is automatically invested with socioeconomic significance. The political dimensions of taxation thus raise the question of legitimacy: who has the right to impose taxes, on whom, and on what basis?[49] Where does one draw the line between unjust despoliation and just extraction—and who gets to draw it? It is the function of ideology to mediate between the redistributive practices of the state and the cooperation of the taxpayers. Taxation is not merely a question of the practicalities of collecting and distributing resources, but is rooted in broader ideological and socio-political systems that continually negotiate the limits of "legitimate" tax practice.

For all that there are disagreements about the finer points of taxation—and notwithstanding the philosophical opposition of certain parties[50]—there is today remarkable social consensus regarding the very fact of taxation. As the US Supreme Court Justice Oliver Wendell Holmes Jr. observed in 1927, "taxes are what we pay for civilized society."[51] People might grumble about this or that tax, or complain about wasteful use of tax monies, or lament the fact that taxes are being misdirected in pursuit of misguided priorities. But when all is said and done, taxes are paid, and the machinery of the state rumbles on. True, some taxpayers shirk, or cheat, or embezzle, yet even they will generally acknowledge that taxes should be paid in principle—by others, of course.[52] Like the office worker who takes office supplies home on permanent loan, such tax dodgers tend to doubt that their evasions, being of no obvious harm to anyone, could possibly challenge the system itself; their failure to pay their taxes in full will not prevent the fire service from coming to their rescue or keep the pothole on the road from being filled—that only happens when others do not pay *their* taxes. The assumed inevitability of taxation, and the nigh on universal acceptance of taxation in theory if not in practice, is itself a testament to the extent to which taxation is embedded in our social structures.

Effective tax enforcement rests on two pillars: coercion and compliance. At its most basic, coercion entails being in a position to credibly threaten those being taxed with onerous penalties for noncompliance,[53] and such penalties rest ultimately in the ability to resort to greater force.[54] This is a significant challenge for taxation systems, as projecting a credible threat of violence depends on the maintenance of an effective system of enforcement that comes with costs of its own.[55] In larger polities, this challenge tends again to benefit local élites. Their knowledge of and power in particular regions or over particular social groups enables them to maintain order and enforce compliance more efficiently than agents brought in by a distant central authority. They are therefore often entrusted with regional tax-collecting obligations and privileges, reinforcing their local power.

Coercion alone cannot sustain tax systems in the long run. Without cooperation from those being taxed, the credible projection of force quickly becomes prohibitively expensive; infinitely greater efficiencies can be secured through consent.[56] The question is then why anyone would consent to being taxed, and the modern view is familiar to all: taxes are paid in exchange for the provision of public goods. Ancient polities can and often do claim to have provided stability and security—the preconditions for the flourishing of justice and economic development—as well as to have invested in public infrastructure. In the nearly four millennia old inscriptions of Mesopotamian potentates from the Old Babylonian period, these ancient rulers present themselves as fulfilling the basic functions of kingship. Depending on the immediate context of the inscriptions, they emphasize the king's role in placating the gods, defeating enemies, keeping the peace at home, developing infrastructure, ensuring economic prosperity, or providing justice.[57] An inscription commemorating the construction of an irrigation canal, for instance, presents the king in his capacity as guarantor of tranquility, development, and agricultural plenty:

> I, Rīm-Sîn, king of Larsa, king of Sumer and Akkad, made firm the foundation of my extensive land. I restored the cities and villages. I established there, for my numerous people, food to eat (and) water to drink. I made Sumer and Akkad peaceful and contented the god Enlil.[58]

In a similar vein, the preamble to the Babylonian king Hammurabi's famous law code presents this king as the gods' chosen vehicle for the dispensation of justice:

> At that time the gods Anu and Enlil called me by my name to enhance the wellbeing of the people: Hammurabi, the faithful sovereign, the one who venerates the gods, me! To make justice prevail in the land, to abolish the wicked and the evil, to prevent the strong from oppressing the weak, to rise over humankind like the sun-god Šamaš and illuminate the land![59]

A perennial favorite in Mesopotamian royal inscriptions—as indeed in the rhetoric of kingship in many cultural horizons—is the pastoral metaphor of the good shepherd. In this metaphor, the king is identified as the shepherd of his human flock, leading his people to good pastures. In the 18th century BCE, Hammurabi often refers to himself as "the shepherd";[60] the 13th-century Assyrian king Tukultī-Ninurta I is "the one who shepherded his land in good pastures";[61] the 8th-century Assyrian king Tiglath-Pileser III asserts that "I increased the territory of Assyria by taking hold of (foreign) lands (and) added countless people to its population. I constantly shepherd them in good pastures."[62] Yet the inverse of this metaphor has long been obvious to critics of kingship: shepherds only look after their flocks so they can fleece and otherwise exploit them.

The provision of services in ancient states is altogether different in scale and extent from that of their modern counterparts. At their best, ancient states could maintain domestic order, keep hostile forces at bay, and stimulate public welfare through economic development programs. To do this, they needed to collect the necessary resources and reallocate them. But the primary beneficiaries of the redistributive practices of ancient polities often appear to have been the same élites that profited most from the established division of resources: as those with the greatest investment in the sociopolitical order, it was the élite who prospered most from the provision of stability and it was by and large their property that was protected through the provision of security. If that were not enough, economic development was of disproportionate benefit to these very élites. Of what interest is the expansion of agriculture to the peasant if it means more land for them to work without keeping any more of the surplus?

The need for direct coercion by the state can be lessened by giving taxpayers a stake in the state project beyond the promise of stability and security. Certain social groups can be empowered relative to others, not only through material returns like favorable rates of taxation but through the promise of enhanced social status or access to positions in the state apparatus. By privileging certain groups over others, states can engineer a social hierarchy with predetermined winners and losers. In *Utopia*, Thomas More offers a vivid description of the process whereby the state's chosen winners—in this case "the rich"—use the machinery of the state to secure their privileges:

> The wretched earnings of the poor are daily whittled away by the rich, not only through private dishonesty, but through public legislation. As if it weren't unjust enough already that the man who contributes most to

society should get the least in return, they make it even worse, and then arrange for injustice to be legally described as justice. In fact, when I consider any social system that prevails in the modern world, I can't, so help me God, see it as anything but a conspiracy of the rich to advance their own interests under the pretext of organizing society. They think up all sorts of tricks and dodges, first for keeping safe their ill-gotten gains, and then for exploiting the poor by buying their labor as cheaply as possible. Once the rich have decided that these tricks and dodges shall be officially recognized by society—which includes the poor as well as the rich—they acquire the force of law. Thus an unscrupulous minority is led by its insatiable greed to monopolize what would have been enough to supply the needs of the whole population.[63]

The logic of divide and rule incentivizes the privileged to safeguard their interests from the unprivileged.[64] In pursuit of their own interests, the privileged help the state exert its coercive pressure over unenfranchised populations, strengthening the existing extractive framework and their own social position. Coopted taxpayers who feel represented by or included in the state extend the state's projection of force and are more likely to comply with its demands. Coopting elements of the social order thus reduces the overall level of state coercion necessary to levy taxes. Coopted groups can, however, feel emboldened to challenge the state when they feel it is working against their privileges. Giving people a stake in the state is a double-edged sword: at the same time that it buys increased compliance, it also creates or bolsters powerful interest groups that can effectively limit, resist, or seek to dictate the state's policy choices.

As we saw when discussing tax exemptions, the state can itself be little more than a vehicle through which the interest groups that have captured it pursue their ends. Although consent to taxation on the part of élites and other circumscribed groups who profit directly from their relationship with the state can be readily explained in terms of material and social interests, this is not true of other taxpayers. For them, different inducements must prevail. In this light, it is essential to keep in mind that as in the present, people in the past were not the purely rational, self-interested creatures of the *homo economicus* type that serve as the model for classical economic theory.[65] While there is certainly an important dimension of self-interest in the tax compliance calculations of a given taxpayer, the processes whereby such calculations are made are not necessarily based on maximizing economic self-interest, however that might be defined. These calculations rely, moreover, on limited information about the likely consequences of compliance or evasion, resulting in unpredictable behaviors. And indeed, perception of one's self-interest is not necessarily material in nature; the social implications of tax compliance are sometimes of greater import than its material costs. Even then, it is possible that a major element in accounting for general tax compliance might simply be social inertia. More charitably, this essentially passive philosophical demeanor can be construed as a recognition or calculation by individuals that, for all its costs, participation in the extractive framework of a state is familiar and preferable by default to an unknown and unpredictable alternative. In other words, stability is preferable to the risk of chaos—an outlook known in psychological literature as the status quo bias. Of course, this kind of passive acquiescence to taxation declines in proportion to the extent to which the tax system is perceived as working against one's interests.[66]

A more complex factor informing acquiescence to extractive systems is ideological in character. Societies are structured by ideologies that demarcate the place of individuals of a given social category in the social order. These ideologies give shape to social relationships and configure social expectations, such that people are socialized to behave in certain ways. This socialization can exert strong pressure toward tax compliance. Belief systems have a role to play, too: where the state presents itself as the agent of the divine, for instance, failure to comply with the demands of the state can be framed as defiance of the heavens; in other systems, membership in a political community with its attendant benefits can be predicated on the contribution of various resources. The successful diffusion of ideological systems that incorporate the social expectation of tax compliance is critical to manufacturing consent to taxation, regardless of any tangible returns for taxpayers or any inequalities in the distribution of the tax burden.[67] This consent is often framed as "legitimacy," a valuable commodity for states.

Despite the existence of such ideological superstructures, there is widespread evidence that many of the claims propounded by state propaganda could be recognized as little more than pretense. In *City of God*, Augustine illustrates this position with an apocryphal tale:

> It was an elegant and true reply that was made to Alexander the Great by a certain pirate whom he had captured. When the king asked him what he was thinking of, that he should molest the sea, he said with defiant independence: "The same as you when you molest the world! Since I do this with a little ship I am called a pirate. You do it with a great fleet and are called an emperor."[68]

Augustine's tale exemplifies the predatory or bandit model of the state, in which the mechanics of extraction are ultimately a scaled-up equivalent of those of any group of robbers, pirates, or gangsters.[69] A similar view of the extractive policies of states is attested in the Hebrew Bible, where the Israelites are warned that the machinery of the ancient state is little more than the machinery of systematic exploitation:

> 11 This is what the king who will reign over you will claim as his rights: He will take your sons and make them serve with his chariots and horses, and they will run in front of his chariots. 12 Some he will assign to be commanders of thousands and commanders of fifties, and others to plow his ground and reap his harvest, and still others to make weapons of war and equipment for his chariots. 13 He will take your daughters to be perfumers and cooks and bakers. 14 He will take the best of your fields and vineyards and olive groves and give them to his attendants. 15 He will take a tenth of your grain and of your vintage and give it to his officials and attendants. 16 Your male and female servants and the best of your cattle and donkeys he will take for his own use. 17 He will take a tenth of your flocks, and you yourselves will become his slaves. 18 When that day comes, you will cry out for relief from the king you have chosen, but the Lord will not answer you in that day. (1 Sam. 8: 11–18)

Nevertheless, the Israelites demand a king "to go out before us and fight our battles" (1 Sam. 8: 20). For them, apparently, the promise of security is reason enough to submit to the extractive practices of the state.

The predatory model of the state represents a cynical interpretation of the function of ancient polities. It chooses to confront and expose the ideology of states, but neglects to consider the extent to which this ideology is more than a mere veneer: state ideology is not simply a plaything for élites to manipulate willy-nilly. Along with social inertia, state ideology structures the outlook and behavior of both taxpayers and tax collectors.[70] It is not always clear where consent ends and exploitation begins, and the boundary between conscious and unconscious manipulation can be indistinct. By emphasizing the tyranny of state power, the predatory model of the state undercuts the state's claims to providing security and stability, which in ancy case serve disproportionately to benefit (and make) élites. But this model dwells less on the extent to which tyrannical use of state power is offset by the elimination of other tyrannical actors from the social stage and the harnessing of collective resources for the public good.[71] Yet even if one favors a more benign reading of states, there is certainly scope for considering the extent to which the central purpose of a given polity should be understood as the aggrandizement of the central authority and its associated élites and the perpetuation of established privileges:[72] in other words, to what extent do the central authority and its associated élites comprise a coercive kleptocracy?

Conclusion

The artificial man must eat, and taxes are his supper. Stripped bare, bereft of its long historical and social baggage, taxation is essentially a way for the state to extract and redistribute resources as it—or the dominant interest groups that it represents—sees fit. Collective action on any scale is predicated on the extraction and redistribution of resources, without which there can be no society, much less a state. Whatever one's view of states, their very existence is inextricably bound up in the mechanics of extraction. Without the ability to extract resources, a state cannot support itself; without the ability to establish enduring systems of extraction, a state cannot sustain itself over time. It is therefore appropriate to speak of the state as dependent on its extractive mechanisms, and to approach the ancient state as a state of extraction. In different contexts and with different emphases and approaches, the papers assembled in this volume all address one central question: how do state structures secure the resources that underwrite their operations? Phrased differently, what *are* the mechanics of extraction? Progress is well served by a clearer sense of the universal in light of the particular, as well as by a deeper appreciation of the historical development of systems of taxation. Through its broad sample of case studies, this volume aspires to be a next step on the road to advancing our understanding of the past, present, and future of the mechanics of extraction.

NOTES

1 Hobbes 2003 [1651]: 9: "For by Art is created that great LEVIATHAN called a COMMON-WEALTH, or STATE, (in latine CIVITAS) which is but an Artificiall Man; though of greater stature and strength than the Naturall, for whose protection and defence it was intended; and in which the *Soveraignty* is an Artificiall *Soul*, as giving life and motion to the whole body; The *Magistrates*, and other *Officers* of Judicature and Execution, artificiall *Joynts*; *Reward* and *Punishment* (by which fastned to the seate of the Soveraignty, every joynt and member is moved to performe his duty) are the *Nerves*, that do the same in the Body Naturall; The *Wealth* and *Riches* of all the particular members, are the *Strength*; *Salus Populi* (the *peoples safety*) its *Businesse*; *Counsellors*, by whom all things needfull for it to know, are suggested unto it, are the *Memory*; *Equity* and *Lawes*, an artificiall *Reason* and *Will*; *Concord*, *Health*; *Sedition*, *Sicknesse*; and *Civill war*, *Death*. Lastly, the *Pacts* and *Covenants*, by which the parts of this Body Politique were at first made, set together, and united, resemble that *Fiat*, or the *Let us make man*, pronounced by God in the Creation."

2 The concept of the "state" is the subject of a vast literature, much of it building on Max Weber's famous definition of the state as (successfully) claiming "the monopoly of the legitimate use of force within a given territory." Among the compelling critiques of this model are that of Abrams 1988, who argues that the state is not an empirical reality, but rather an ideological "thing" whose purpose is to legitimate an existing political structure, to represent its norms, conventions, and procedures as "natural" and "just," and to institutionalize its distribution of power. For the present purposes, we can do without a meticulous definition of the state and leave the argument to others. It is sufficient to observe that more often than not, we know a state when we see it, and this is true both on Weber's and on Abrams' terms.

   For an overview of the various approaches to understanding the ancient state, see Scheidel 2013. Campbell 2009 offers a thoughtful new way of thinking about ancient polities. For an extended critique of the use of the state category in antiquity, see Osiander 2007.

3 As noted and discussed in Hobbes 2003 [1651]: 170–76 (Chapter XXIV). This analogy has been picked up by others, such as Furnivall 1991 [1939]: 116 *apud* Scott 2009: 75–76.

4 An excellent introductory account of the essential differences between modern and premodern polities can be found in Crone 2003. Ando and Richardson 2017

offer a valuable collection of studies on the limits of the infrastructural power of ancient states, by which the editors mean the ability of ancient states to project their power and act upon the world. This builds in part on Richardson 2012, an extended meditation on the limits of state power in second millennium BCE Mesopotamia. Scott 2009 offers an overview of the relationship between pre-modern states and non-state peoples and spaces in the Southeast Asian highlands ("Zomia"), while Scott 2017 is in turn a broader attempt to make sense of the earliest states. Scott's work stresses the ancient state's extractive function. Note also Giddens (1985: 58), who observes that in premodern societies "the main overall link connecting the state with the mass of its subjects, i.e. the peasantry, was its requirement for taxation."

5 See Steven Garfinkle's contribution the present volume.

6 See Andrew Monson's contribution to the present volume.

7 Ibn Khaldûn 1980: 23.

8 Smith 1954 [1776]: 306–9.

9 Burke 2003 [1790]: 192.

10 Martin, Mehrotra, and Prasad 2009: 2: "We think that the field may be poised to rewrite conventional accounts of modernity itself by placing the social relations of taxation at the center of any historical or comparative account of social change. We call this emerging field *the new fiscal sociology.*"

11 Schumpeter 1991 [1918]: 101. For an overview of the context and ideas of Schumpeter's "Die Krise des Steuerstaats," see Musgrave 1992: 90–93.

12 See Tilly 1975: 42 for this simplified formulation. See also Tilly 1990: Chapter 3 for a more developed account of his ideas about the relationship between warfare and the increasing power of European states, notably manifest in their ability to extract resources, viz. to tax. Tilly's arguments have prompted a vast deal of further discussion and research with a correspondingly vast bibliography. See the edited volume of Kaspersen and Strandsbjerg 2017 for a critical introductory foray into this literature with further bibliography. One of the virtues of this volume is its attempt to apply Tilly's thinking to contexts outside of Europe and beyond the chronological parameters of Tilly's own work.

13 See for instance Levi 1981 and Levi 1988.

14 Campbell 1993.

15 Martin, Mehrotra, and Prasad 2009: 26.

16 Hoffman 2015: 307.

17 Monson and Scheidel 2015.

18 As indicated by the assembled studies in Monson and Scheidel 2015. See Hoffman 2017 for an assessment of how these ancient case studies can contribute to economic history and a call for more data to feed into formal models. Hoffman's call for data is optimistic for many ancient societies, and much of this data will perforce consist of informed estimates. The study of ancient economies will remain a largely qualitative rather than quantitative project.

19   There are numerous examples of this in the valuable edited volume of Klinkott, Kubisch, and Müller-Wollermann 2007, which brings together studies of revenue generation in ancient Mediterranean and Near Eastern societies (Mesopotamia, Egypt, the Levant, Greece, Asia Minor, and Rome: precisely those societies that are often associated genealogically with the modern West).

20   By "social unit" I mean any group of persons who are collectively liable for the payment of a given tax. This might be a family unit, a city, a pastoral community, or some other collection of human beings.

21   By "corporate body" I mean any institution, association, or commercial enterprise that is recognized as having legal personality.

22   One example of such a public purpose is fending off hunger: the earliest states have at times been explained as vehicles for the redistribution of food, acting as bulwarks against food insecurity for the community as a whole. For a study that demonstrates that this function was rhetorical rather than practical in early Mesopotamia, see Richardson 2016.

23   Dalton 2003 [1922]: 32.

24   Bonney 1999: 5–6. Interestingly, as pointed out to me by David Ratzan, the etymology of the English word tax, coming from Greek, points to the state's authority to measure, order, and control, rather than "take." This ties in neatly with James C. Scott's emphasis on the state's need to create "legible" landscapes that facilitate extraction and control, for which see Scott 1998: Part 1.

25   The need to include compulsory labor in any consideration of ancient fiscal systems has also been noted by Monson and Scheidel 2015: 7: "The important role of compulsory services in some early states . . . ultimately enriches our understanding of fiscal regimes. These include forced labor, conscription for military duty, and various other public liturgies. States that rely heavily on them in lieu of taxes or other payments may seem deficient in their fiscal capacity. The case of Egypt and early Mesopotamia, however . . . shows an accounting system by which state officials could convert any sort of revenue into its equivalent value in one of the three media—labor time, grain, and money—as well as these into one another in order to determine total revenue and collect amounts due. Thus labor time was conceived as revenue and integrated into a sophisticated system of state finance."

26   There is a relevant discussion of taxonomies of revenue collection in Monson and Scheidel 2015: 16–19.

27   Rössler 2007: 17–18: "Die Finanzierung von Verwaltung, Religionsausübung und Militär im frühen Staat wurde folglich hauptsächlich durch das Erheben von Steuern und Pachtzahlungen unter den Bürgern, Tributen von den Eroberten und Zollabgaben im Rahmen des Handels sichergestellt."

28   Blanton and Fargher 2009: 139–40.

29   Bonney and Ormrod 1999: 4–8, table 0.2. See in particular the row on "Methods of financing" on page 5 and the row on "Revenues" on page 6.

30 An exceptional body of evidence concerning the taxation of trade comes from the Anatolian settlement of Kaneš (modern Kültepe), the central node in the extensive Old Assyrian trade network. For an analysis of the relevant evidence, see Dercksen 2007.

31 This distinction is highlighted in Blanton and Fargher 2009: 139–40.

32 As is the case in numerous extreme historical examples, among them Spanish claims to tribute during the early colonization of the Americas and the extractive practices applied in the Belgian Congo before its formal subjection to the Belgian state. For a popular account of the extractive model applied in the Congo, see Hochschild 1999. The fictionalized description of this extractive model in Joseph Conrad's novella *Heart of Darkness* is particularly evocative. In one illuminating passage, Conrad describes the Congolese model in the following terms: "Their administration was merely a squeeze, and nothing more, I suspect. They were conquerors, and for that you want only brute force—nothing to boast of, when you have it, since your strength is just an accident arising from the weakness of others. They grabbed what they could get for the sake of what was to be got. It was just robbery with violence, aggravated murder on a great scale, and men going at it blind—as is very proper for those who tackle a darkness" (1990 [1899]: 4).

33 Marx is unsparing in his assessment of European extractive practices in Africa, Asia, and the Americas, identifying them as a colossal episode of organized expropriation that lies at the origin of modern capitalism: "The discovery of gold and silver in America, the extirpation, enslavement and entombment in mines of the indigenous population of that continent, the beginnings of the conquest and plunder of India, and the conversion of Africa into a preserve for the commercial hunting of blackskins, are all things which characterize the dawn of the era of capitalist production. These idyllic proceedings are the chief moments of primitive accumulation" (1976 [1867]: 915.)

34 The complexity of each such configuration can be immense, as emerges clearly from Rod Campbell's contribution to the present volume.

35 As claimed in a polemic in favor of its simplification; see Heath 2016.

36 For an exceptional extended study of an ancient economy based on a large but difficult body of evidence, see the survey of the Babylonian economy of the first millennium BCE in Jursa 2010; see Bresson 2016 for an account of the ancient Greek economy that builds on very different evidence.

37 Building on the work of Douglass North, the standard economic definition of transaction costs is captured succinctly by Acheson 2002: 29: "the time, effort, and expense of obtaining the information necessary to make an exchange, negotiate the exchange, and enforce the exchange agreement once made."

38 The gradual and piecemeal process of monetization is documented in Maxim Korolkov's contribution to the present volume; the place of monetization in the collection of one particular tax also surfaces in Irene Soto Marín's contribution.

39 A similar point is made by Levi 1981: 455: "The third major kind of constraint on any ruler is his ability to measure the economic value of what is produced and traded in his domain . . . Historically, one of the first acts of states has been to standardize weights and measures. Money is another mechanism for standardizing the relative value of taxable goods."

40 See, for instance, Woods 2010: 18 and Postgate, Wang, and Wilkinson 1995.

41 The possible implications for the state of reliance on local élites for tax collection are apparent in Juan Carlos Moreno García's contribution to the present volume.

42 This point is also developed by Kiser 1994: 290: "The type of agency relation that rulers will use for tax collection is a function of the control capacities of rulers. When rulers can adequately monitor and sanction the actions of their agents, they will use state administration with fixed salaries. When direct control of agents is not possible or too costly, rulers will use tax farming to give agents higher incentives to collect taxes . . . In short, principals will choose to have market relations with their agents when low control capacities make hierarchies inefficient."

43 Blanton and Fargher 2009: 134 posit a direct correlation between the extent to which the state depends on its taxpaying constituent base for its revenues and its advancement of that base's interests: "When taxpayers or other civil society groups are endowed with few resources with which to bargain, rulers are predicted to provide few public goods, to exercise a more coercive domination of state and society, and to lack accountability in society. States that are more collective are predicted to develop if rulers are forced to strike bargains with other civil society groups, especially when rulers are strongly dependent on taxpayers for state revenues, including labor."

44 Krebs 2006: chapters 1 and 2 explores the socially integrative potential of military service in modern times.

45 Such models are known from many times and places and are a prominent feature in Richard Payne's contribution to the present volume.

46 Proudhon 1969 [1851]: 294. More to the point, Proudhon writes in the context of France in 1851 that "the President and the Representatives, once elected, are the masters; all the rest obey. They are subjects, to be governed and to be taxed, without surcease" (Proudhon 1969 [1851]: 159).

47 The politics of tax exemptions features in James Tan's contribution to the present volume.

48 As Bonney 1995: 432 writes, "there is inevitable tension between rulers and taxpayers, even if the members of the governing class are themselves taxpayers or profit from the handling of tax receipts. All fiscal policy is politicized and involves a greater or lesser degree of political conflict."

49 For more on the conceptualization of legitimacy and its utility in government, see the useful synthesis with further bibliography of Levi, Sacks, and Tyler 2009.

50 There are those whose opposition to the state leads them to question the very legitimacy of taxation itself, notably in the anarchist and libertarian political

traditions. See for instance Bastiat 1998 [1850], rediscovered in the last few decades as an intellectual hero for libertarians in the USA.

51 Compania General de Tabacos v. Collector, 275 U.S. 87 (1927): Page 275 U.S. 100.

52 Note the negative connotations of the constellation of terms used to describe the
act of tax evasion, along with the inescapable moral condemnation they convey.
Tax evasion is generally depicted as a failure to fulfill an essential social responsibility and is portrayed as contrary to the naturally prosocial tendencies of human
beings.

53 In the words of Levi 1998: 91, "the willingness to pay taxes quasi-voluntarily or
to give one's contingent consent to conscription often rests on the existence of
the state's capacity and demonstrated readiness to secure the compliance of the
otherwise noncompliant."

54 Bartolomé de las Casas provides a graphic account of methods of extraction
based entirely on the threat (and use) of force in the early stages of the Spanish
colonization of the Americas. De las Casas relates of one episode of extraction
that a colonial governor "ordered that as many of the locals as possible should be
seized, including women and children, and driven into a stockade which he had
built expressly for this purpose. He then let it be known that the prisoners would
only be released if they arranged for a ransom to be paid directly to the unspeak-
able governor: so much for a man, and then so much for his wife and so much
for each child. To ensure that his victims were responsive to his demands, he also
decreed that no prisoner should be fed until his or her ransom had been paid"
(1992 [1542]: 98–99)

55 On the ability of taxpayers to resist the demands of the state even in the face of
superior force, see Scott 1985.

56 This point is stressed by Hoffman 2015: 307: "Successfully establishing a monopoly
of violence is difficult. It requires resources and (at the very least) popular acquiescence, both of which took time for states to get. So, by sticking to Weber's definition, we overlook the centuries of work that states did both to acquire resources
and to win people over so that the cost of ruling (including the political risks and
the expenses involved in collecting tax revenue from a recalcitrant population)
would not be prohibitive."

57 The contextually bound depiction of rulers fulfilling the various tasks of rulership
can be found in the contemporary propaganda of many dictatorial regimes; see
Valk and Pongratz-Leisten 2015: 650–51 for this analogy.

58 *RIME* 4: 293 (E4.2.14.15: 48–54); I have slightly modified Frayne's translation.

59 Roth 1997: 77 (i 27–49); I have modified Roth's translation.

60 Roth 1997: 77 (i 50).

61 *RIMA* 1: 271 (A.0.78.23: 6–7). The phrase is *ir-te-ʾ-ú a-bu-riš*, and the term
aburriš—derived from *aburru* (pasture, meadowland)—is variously translated as
"in green pastures" or "in safe pastures." Here and in the following example I prefer
instead "good pastures."

62 *RINAP* 1: 86 (Tiglath-Pileser III 35: ii 15–17).

63 More 1965 [1516]: 129–30.

64 For more on these dynamics, see Valk 2018: 79–97.

65 For an accessible synthesis of psychological studies that undermine the *homo economicus* model, see Kahneman 2011: Part 4. The concept of rationality is itself problematic: what is "reasonable" is not static and is informed by different aims and outlooks, often within the same social system.

66 The importance of confidence and trust in the intentions of rulers is discussed in Blanton and Fargher 2009: 143, and Levi 1998: 88–89.

67 As emphasized in Tyler 2011: 81–82: "the effectiveness of legal authorities, law, and government depends upon the widespread belief among citizens that these are legitimate and entitled to be obeyed. The classic argument of political and social theorists has been that for authorities to perform effectively those in power must convince everyone else that they 'deserve' to rule and make decisions that influence the quality of everyone's lives. It is the belief that some decision made or rule created by these authorities is 'valid' in the sense that it is entitled to be obeyed by virtue of who made the decision or how it was made that is central to the idea of legitimacy. While some argue that it is impossible to rule using only power, and others suggest that it is possible but more difficult, it is widely agreed that authorities benefit from having legitimacy, and find governance easier and more effective when a feeling that they are entitled to rule is widespread within the population."

68 Augustine 1963: 16–17 (Book IV, Chapter IV). Augustine's work here is probably based directly on the similar passage from Cicero's *De res publica*, on which see Harding 2008: n13.

69 This aligns with the view of the state as an exercise in organized crime considered in Tilly 1985, or indeed Scott's definition of "the successful pre-modern state" as "a monopolistic protection racket that keeps the peace and fosters production and trade while extracting no more rents than the traffic will bear" (Scott 2009: 151). In his very popular recent history of human beings, Yuval Harari expresses the same view of premodern states, writing that "many kingdoms and empires were in truth little more than large protection rackets. The king was the *capo di tutti capi* who collected protection money, and in return made sure that neighbouring crime syndicates and local small fry did not harm those under his protection. He did little else" (Harari 2014: 358).

70 Establishing a rhetoric of reciprocity or embedding extractive mechanisms in ritual practices can promote compliance, while "feasting" can serve to negotiate relationships between resource contributors and the state. Such relationships are explored in several contributions to the present volume, notably those of Dimitri Nakassis and Lorenzo d'Alfonso and Alvise Matessi.

71 The space for growth created by state systems is apparent in Pam Crabtree's contribution to the present volume.

72 This does not always refer narrowly to material privileges. As Campbell 1993: 172 notes, "some political élites may be more inclined to maximize revenues than others for ideological reasons." This is exemplified by James Tan's contribution to the present volume.

WORKS CITED

Abrams, Philip. 1988. "Notes on the Difficulty of Studying the State (1977)." *Journal of Historical Sociology* 1: 58–89.

Acheson, James M. 2002. "Transaction Cost Economics: Accomplishments, Problems, and Possibilities." In K. Ensminger (ed.), *Theory in Economic Anthropology* (Walnut Creek, CA: AltaMira Press), 27–58.

Ando, Clifford, and Seth Richardson (eds.). 2017. *Ancient States and Infrastructural Power: Europe, Asia and America*. Philadelphia: University of Pennsylvania Press.

Augustine. 1963. *City of God, Volume II: Books 4–7*. Loeb Classical Library 412. Trans. W. M. Green. Cambridge, MA: Harvard University Press.

Bastiat, Frédéric. 1998 [1850]. *The Law*. Trans. Dean Russell. Irvington-on-Hudson, New York: Institute of Economic Affairs.

Blanton, Richard E., and Lane F. Fargher. 2009. "Collective Action in the Evolution of Pre-Modern States." *Social Evolution & History* 8.2: 133–66.

Bonney, Richard. 1995. "Revenues." In R. Bonney (ed.), *Economic Systems and State Finance* (New York: Clarendon Press), 423–505.

Bonney, Richard. 1999. "Introduction: The Rise of the Fiscal State in Europe, c. 1200–1815." In R. Bonney (ed.), *The Rise of the Fiscal State in Europe, c. 1200–1815* (Oxford: Oxford University Press), 1–17.

Bonney, Richard, and W. M. Ormrod. 1999. "Crises, Revolutions and Self-Sustained Growth: Towards a Conceptual Model of Change in Fiscal History." In W. M. Ormond, M. Bonney, and R. Bonney (eds.), *Crises, Revolutions and Self-Sustained Growth: Essays in European Fiscal History* (Stamford, UK: Shaun Tyas), 1–21.

Bresson, Alain. 2016. *The Making of the Ancient Greek Economy: Institutions, Markets, and Growth in the City-States*. Trans. S. Rendall. Princeton: Princeton University Press.

Burke, Edmund. 2003 [1790]. *Reflections on the Revolution in France*. Ed. Frank M. Turner. New Haven: Yale University Press.

Campbell, John L. 1993. "The State and Fiscal Sociology." *Annual Review of Sociology* 19: 163–85.

Campbell, Roderick B. 2009. "Toward a Networks and Boundaries Approach to Early Complex Polities: The Late Shang Case." *Current Anthropology* 50(6): 821–48.

Conrad, Joseph. 1990 [1899]. *Heart of Darkness*. New York: Dover Publications.

Crone, Patricia. 2003. *Pre-Industrial Societies: Anatomy of the Pre-Modern World*, Oxford: Oneworld.

Dalton, Hugh. 2003 [1922]. *Principles of Public Finance*. London: Routledge.

De las Casas, Bartolomé. 1992 [1542]. *A Short Account of the Destruction of the Indies*. Trans. N. Griffin. London: Penguin.

Dercksen, Jan Gerrit. 2007. "Die Altassyrischen Handelsabgaben in Nordmesopotamien und Anatolien im 19.–18. Jh. V.Chr. in Verträgen und Praxis." In H. Klinkott, S. Kubisch and R. Müller-Wollermann (eds.), *Geschenke und Steuern, Zölle und Tribute: Antike Abgabenformen in Anspruch und Wirklichkeit* (Leiden: Brill), 187–211.

Furnivall, John S. 1991 [1939]. *The Fashioning of Leviathan: The Beginnings of British Rule in Burma.* Ed. Gehan Wijeyewardene. Canberra: Department of Anthropology, Research School of Pacific Studies, Australian National University.

Giddens, Anthony. 1985. *The Nation-State and Violence: Volume Two of a Contemporary Critique of Historical Materialism.* Cambridge: Polity Press.

Harari, Yuval N. 2014. *Sapiens: A Brief History of Humankind.* Toronto: Signal Books.

Harding, Brian. 2008. "The Use of Alexander the Great in Augustine's *City of God.*" *Augustinian Studies* 39(1): 113–28.

Heath, Allister. 2016. "The Chancellor Must Make It His Mission to Simplify Our Crazy Tax System." *The Telegraph.* Telegraph Media Group, 27 Jan. 2016. Web. 07 Dec. 2016.

Hobbes, Thomas. 2003 [1651]. *Leviathan.* Revised Student Edition, Cambridge Texts in the History of Political Thought. Ed. R. Tuck. Cambridge: Cambridge University Press.

Hochschild, Adam. 1999. *King Leopold's Ghost: A Story of Greed, Terror, and Heroism in Colonial Africa.* New York: Mariner Book.

Hoffman, Philip T. 2015. "What Do States Do? Politics and Economic History." *The Journal of Economic History* 75(2): 303–32.

Hoffman, Philip T. 2017. "Public Economics and History: A Review of *Fiscal Regimes and the Political Economy of Premodern States.*" In A. Monson and W. Scheidel (eds.), *Journal of Economic Literature* 55(4): 1556–69.

Ibn Khaldûn. 1980. *The Muqaddimah: An Introduction to History.* Volume 2. Trans. Franz Rosenthal. Princeton: Princeton University Press.

Jursa, Michael. 2010. *Aspects of the Economic History of Babylonia in the First Millennium BC: Economic Geography, Economic Mentalities, Agriculture, the Use of Money, and the Problem of Economic Growth.* Münster: Ugarit-Verlag.

Kahneman, Daniel. 2011. *Thinking, Fast and Slow.* New York: Farrar, Straus & Giroux.

Kaspersen, Lars Bo, and Jeppe Strandsbjerg (eds.). 2017. *Does War Make States? Investigations of Charles Tilly's Historical Sociology.* Cambridge: Cambridge University Press.

Kiser, Edgar. 1994. "Markets and Hierarchies in Early Modern Tax Systems: A Principal-Agent Analysis." *Politics & Society* 22(3): 284–315.

Klinkott, H., S. Kubisch, and R. Müller-Wollermann (eds.). 2007. *Geschenke und Steuern, Zölle und Tribute: Antike Abgabenformen in Anspruch und Wirklichkeit.* Leiden: Brill.

Krebs, Ronald R. 2006. *Fighting for Rights: Military Service and the Politics of Citizenship.* Ithaca: Cornell University Press.

Levi, Margaret. 1981. "The Predatory Theory of Rule." *Politics and Society* 10: 431–65.

Levi, Margaret. 1998. "A State of Trust." In V. Braithwaite and M. Levi (eds.), *Trust and Governance* (New York: Russell Sage Foundation), 77–101.

Levi, Margaret, Audrey Sacks, and Tom Tyler. 2009. "Conceptualizing Legitimacy, Measuring Legitimating Beliefs." *American Behavioral Scientist* 53(3): 354–75.

Martin, Isaac William, Ajay K. Mehrotra, and Monica Prasad. 2009. "The Thunder of History: The Origins and Development of the New Fiscal Sociology." In I. W. Martin, A. K. Mehrotra, and M. Prasad (eds.), *The New Fiscal Sociology: Taxation in Comparative and Historical Perspective* (Cambridge: Cambridge University Press), 1–28.

Marx, Karl. 1976 [1867]. *Capital: A Critique of Political Economy, Volume I.* Trans. B. Fowkes. London: Penguin.

Monson, Andrew, and Walter Scheidel (eds.). 2015. *Fiscal Regimes and the Political Economy of Premodern States.* Cambridge: Cambridge University Press.

More, Thomas. 1965 [1516]. *Utopia.* Trans. P. Turner. London: Penguin.

Musgrave, R. A. 1992. "Schumpeter's Crisis of the Tax State: An Essay in Fiscal Sociology." *Journal of Evolutionary Economics* 2: 89–113.

Osiander, Andreas. 2007. *Before the State: Systemic Political Change in the West from the Greeks to the French Revolution.* Oxford: Oxford University Press.

Postgate, Nicholas, Tao Wang, and Toby Wilkinson. 1995. "The Evidence of Early Writing: Utilitarian or Ceremonial?" *Antiquity* 69: 459–80.

Proudhon, Pierre-Joseph. 1969 [1851]. *General Idea of the Revolution in the Nineteenth Century.* Trans. John Beverley Robinson. New York: Haskell House Publishers.

Richardson, Seth. 2012. "Early Mesopotamia: The Presumptive State." *Past & Present* 215(1): 3–49.

Richardson, Seth. 2016. "Obedient Bellies: Hunger and Food Security in Mesopotamia." *JESHO* 59(5): 750–92.

RIMA 1 = Grayson, A. Kirk. 1987. *The Royal Inscriptions of Mesopotamia, Assyrian Periods Volume I: Assyrian Rulers of the Third and Second Millennia BC (to 1115 BC).* Toronto: University of Toronto Press.

RIME 4 = Frayne, Douglas. 1990. *The Royal Inscriptions of Mesopotamia, Early Periods, Volume 4: Old Babylonian Period (2003–1595 BC).* Toronto: University of Toronto Press.

RINAP 1 = Tadmor, Hayim, and Shigeo Yamada. 2011. *The Royal Inscriptions of the Neo-Assyrian Period Volume 1: The Royal Inscriptions of Tiglath-pileser III (744–727 BC), and Shalmaneser V (726–722 BC), Kings of Assyria.* Winona Lake: Eisenbrauns.

Rössler, Martin. 2007. "Von der Gabe zur Abgabe: Transaktionen im politischen Kontext." In H. Klinkott, S. Kubisch, and R. Müller-Wollermann (eds.), *Geschenke und Steuern, Zölle und Tribute: antike Abgabenformen in Anspruch und Wirklichkeit* (Leiden: Brill), 3–27.

Roth, Martha T. 1997. *Law Collections from Mesopotamia and Asia Minor.* 2nd edition. Atlanta: Scholars Press.

Scheidel, Walter. 2013. "Studying the State." In P. F. Bang and W. Scheidel (eds.), *The Oxford Handbook of the State in the Ancient Near East and Mediterranean* (Oxford: Oxford University Press), 5–57.

Schumpeter, Joseph Alois. 1991 [1918]. "The Crisis of the Tax State." In R. Swedberg (ed.), *The Economics and Sociology of Capitalism* (Princeton: Princeton University Press), 90–140.

Scott, James C. 1985. *Weapons of the Weak: Everyday Forms of Peasant Resistance.* New Haven: Yale University Press.

Scott, James C. 1998. *Seeing Like a State: How Certain Schemes to Improve the Human Condition Have Failed.* New Haven: Yale University Press.

Scott, James C. 2009. *The Art of Not Being Governed: An Anarchist History of Upland Southeast Asia.* New Haven: Yale University Press.

Scott, James C. 2017. *Against the Grain: A Deep History of the Earliest States.* New Haven: Yale University Press.

Smith, Adam. 1954 [1776]. *The Wealth of Nations. In Two Volumes: Volume Two.* London: J. M. Dent & Sons Ltd.

Tilly, Charles. 1975. "Reflections on the History of European State-Making." In C. Tilly (ed.), *The Formation of National States in Western Europe* (Princeton: Princeton University Press), 3–83.

Tilly, Charles. 1985. "War Making and State Making as Organized Crime." In P. B. Evans, D. Rueschemeyer and T. Skocpol (eds.), *Bringing the State Back* (Cambridge: Cambridge University Press), 169–91.

Tilly, Charles. 1990. *Coercion, Capital, and European States, AD 990–1990.* Cambridge, MA, and Oxford: Basil Blackwell.

Tyler, Tom R. 2011. *Why People Cooperate: The Role of Social Motivations.* Princeton: Princeton University Press.

Valk, Jonathan. 2018. "Assyrian Collective Identity in the Second Millennium BCE: A Social Categories Approach." Unpublished Ph.D. Dissertation, New York University. ProQuest.

Valk, Jonathan, and Beate Pongratz-Leisten. 2015. "Representations of Power: Shaping the Past and the Present (Response)." In R. Rollinger and E. van Dongen (eds.), *Mesopotamia in the Ancient World: Impact, Continuities, Parallels. Proceedings of the Seventh Symposium of the Melammu Project Held in Obergurgl, Austria, November 4–8, 2013,* (Münster: Ugarit-Verlag), 643–51.

Woods, Christopher. 2010. "Visible Language: The Earliest Writing Systems." In C. Woods with E. Teeter and G. Emberling (eds.), *Visible Language: Inventions of Writing in the Middle East and Beyond* (Chicago: The University of Chicago), 15–25.

TAX SYSTEMS

2

Taxing Questions

Financing the Chinese Bronze Age

RODERICK B. CAMPBELL

Introduction

Taxation presupposes both an extracting entity as well as a population from which extractions come. Moreover, as the nature of both the polity and the subject/citizen is constituted in their relationship of authority and compliance, extraction and service, duty and right, taxation is not merely an economic issue but also one of relational political economy. For this reason, I believe that the study of taxation, especially in ancient polities where knowledge is fragmentary, should proceed holistically. In the case of Bronze Age China, or to be more accurate, the Central Plains polities of the second millennium BCE, where even the nature of the political economies in question are controversial and almost no direct taxation evidence exists, the need for a holistic approach is all the more pressing. By "holistic" I mean not only to cast a wide net and synthesize the contents, but more specifically to consider the nature of the polity, its economic networks, its social formations, and the linkages between them.

My paper will begin with a brief critical survey of the literature on Bronze Age Chinese political economy. After illustrating some of the conceptual shortcomings of previous approaches, including the idea that the Chinese Bronze Age is a useful analytical category, I will focus on one specific time and place: Anyang (contemporaneously known as "The Great Settlement Shang") and its polity during the last centuries of the second millennium BCE. This polity, frequently conflated with Shang civilization or even the Chinese Bronze Age, has the widest array of (albeit scanty) information with which to sketch the outlines of the polity, its social structure, the size and distribution of settlements, the nature, scale and organization of production, and what little is known or can be conjectured about the population that supplied its labor, skill, and resources.

In an effort to organize and interpret this scattering of empirical data, estimates, and inferences concerning the political economic networks of the Great Settlement Shang and its hinterland, I will use two comparative models of ancient political economies: an idealized redistributive model based on the Inka and an idealized tributary-market model based on the Aztecs. Both of these models have a series of features that should have more or less testable ramifications. It is hoped that through a comparison with these distinct ideal types a clearer perspective on the Shang political economy will emerge, as well as a better sense of where future empirical and theoretical work needs to be done.

What, Where, When?

What was the Chinese Bronze Age? For older scholarship (Chang 1983, 1986; Thorp 2005; Allan 2007) it covers the period between the beginning of second millennium to the middle of the first millennium BCE and corresponds explicitly or implicitly with the Three Dynasties period of traditional Chinese historiography (Table 2.1). More accurately, however, this time/place ought to be termed "the Central Plains Bronze Age," or even better, "the Central Plains Metropolitan Tradition" (Campbell 2014). The Central Plains Metropolitan Tradition certainly did not come close to encompassing the territory within the People's Republic of China, and was, in any case, but one of the many contemporaneous traditions of East Asia (Figure 2.1). An even more important objection, however, is that "the Bronze Age" is a fundamentally misleading term when taken to mean a developmental epoch—especially in East Asia (Campbell 2014). More to the point, from the perspective of economic history, societies and polities have economies, "ages" do not.

TABLE 2.1. Historiographic and Archaeological Chronology of Ancient China

Historiographic Dynasty	Dates (BCE)	Archaeological Period	Dates (BCE)
Xia	2070–1600	Erlitou	1800–1600
Shang (Early)	1600–1400	Erligang	1600–1400
Shang (Middle)	1400–1250	Xiaoshuangqiao-Huanbei	1400–1250
Shang (Late)	1250–1046	Anyang	1250–1050
Western Zhou	1046–771	Western Zhou	1050–771
Eastern Zhou	771–256	Eastern Zhou	771–221

The dynastic dates are derived from Duandai 2000; the archaeological dates from Campbell 2014.

Nevertheless, K. C. Chang influentially described the period in almost exactly these terms:

> The Three Dynasties are treated as a single unit . . . This is permissible . . . because the characteristics of the political culture in ancient China were in many important respects common throughout the period . . . Profound changes in ancient Chinese society took place around 500–600 B.C., when the Iron Age began to replace the Bronze Age. (1983: 8)

For Chang, Bronze Age cities were "king's cities" lacking the markets and merchants that would characterize urbanism in the Eastern Zhou (Chang 1985; see also von Falkenhausen 2008 and Shen Chen 1994). It was a central premise of Chang's delimitation of Chinese civilizational difference that, unlike the Ancient Near East, the Chinese Bronze Age was built on the foundations of an economy unchanged from the Neolithic (Chang 1989; Von Glahn 2016). Wealth was concentrated not through technological innovation or trade, but rather politico-religious organization (Chang 1980, 1983, 1989).

Arguably, all of the major Western approaches to the economies of the Central Plains Bronze Age are built on the basis of these assumptions.[1] They have all taken Chang's point that bronze was used not for tools of production, but for ritual vessels, and that bronze is key to understanding the political economies of the Central Plains polities between ca 1850–500 BCE. Thus, Liu and Chen (2000, 2001, 2003, 2012) based their political economic analysis of early Chinese states on the assumption that the

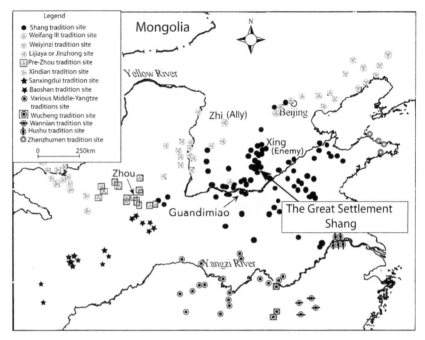

Figure 2.1. Material Culture Map of North China, Anyang Period. Map by author, based on Campbell 2014, Fig. 5.2.

production of ritual bronzes and the securing of their resource flows was *the* central concern of China's first "states."[2] Underhill and Fang (2004)'s account of the Anyang political economy, while nuancing Liu and Chen's monolithic model by considering other political actors and taking into account élite gifting of prestige goods, still ends up with a bronze-centric, centralized, tributary model.[3] Bagley (1999), while not specifically addressing the issue of political economy, nevertheless asserts that the bronze of the Chinese Bronze Age is key to understanding the period, going so far as to say that it is "indexical of civilization" in China due to the organizational needs of multi-component mold bronze casting. Li (2003) in his pioneering study of bronze casting at Anyang, also assumes that bronze was crucial to Shang political economy, and that being so, must have been tightly controlled by the court.[4] In the most recent and economically sophisticated account of "the economy of the Bronze Age," von Glahn (2016) approvingly cites Bagley on the unique importance of bronze to the Chinese Bronze Age, K.C. Chang on the unchanging "Stone Age" nature of the agricultural base, and maintains that the Western Zhou political economy was redistributive, estate-based, and patrimonial.[5]

All of these approaches have focused on élite production, exchange, and consumption; assumed a direct relationship between production and political organization; and based themselves on élite-biased sources, whether archaeological, paleographic, or received textual. In so far as there is a consensus model, it is that "the Chinese Bronze Age" political-economy was élite-redistributive with centralized control of key industries, tributary relations with subordinate polities, and some long-distance trade for valuable raw materials. Villages were self-sufficient and the urban-hinterland relationship was characterized by simple extraction of agricultural surplus. It is my contention that this consensus view is at best only part of the picture, and at worst, a fundamental distortion.

First of all, it is far from clear that the political economies of the various Central Plains polities were organized the same way. Indeed, we know next to nothing about the fiscal administration of Erlitou or Erligang, the relationships between commoners and élites, the integration of urban and non-urban settlements, the ways in which surplus labor or goods were extracted by the polity, or how the mega-centers themselves were provisioned. What evidence we do have for the development of Central Plains political economies suggests, instead, a great deal of change. For one thing, site size (and presumably urban population) showed dramatic change between Erlitou (300 ha), Erligang (1500 ha) and Anyang (3000 ha), even while the scale and organization of craft production reached ever greater size and complexity. At the same time, the agro-pastoral regimes of the Central Plains did *not* remain unchanged from the third millennium BCE, but underwent a series of developments. The late Longshan trend toward crop diversity and agricultural intensification continued over the second millennium BCE, with the traditional north China multi-cropping package of millet, wheat, and rice in place by Erligang times (Lee et al. 2007). Sheep, goat and cattle were added to Central Plains economies during the late Longshan, and became increasingly prominent down to the Anyang period, when beef overtook pork in some Shang diets (Li et al. 2014). Sometime during the second millennium BCE, possibly as early as Erlitou, and certainly by Anyang times, cattle traction was added to the economy, most probably in the form of the oxcart. As consumers of an otherwise untapped resource (grass), sheep and cattle served to expand the capture of energy from the environment, even while their transportability over long distances created novel affordances for provisioning networks. Thus, even if the stone, bone, and shell tools of the late second millennium BCE look much the same as agricultural tools of the third millennium BCE, they suggest an intensified, broadened, and integrated agro-pastoral economy, one worlds away from the simpler pig, dog, and millet economies of the north Chinese Neolithic. As Trigger (2003: 280) notes, agricultural intensification cross-culturally generally has little to do with bronze.

Thus, not only is it untrue that the Shang economy was unchanged from the Neolithic, but it is also unlikely that the Erlitou, Erligang, and Anyang economies were identical as well. Due to the greater abundance of evidence for the Anyang period, it will form the focus of this paper, as I attempt to piece together what is currently known about the political economy of the Shang hegemony and the nature of its sovereign extractions.

Models

Before attempting to describe the Shang political economy and its forms of taxation, I would like to set up two ideal-types at either end of the market-redistributive spectrum, both based on pre-modern, non-Western examples and inspired by Feinman and Nichols 2004. I will call these the Inka and Aztec models, though I make no claims that the simplified constructs I will be presenting are accurate representations of those political economies. Their realities were messier and more complex, but the advantage of simple models with logically coherent components is that they allow for the derivation of straightforward hypotheses (Hopkins 2002 [1980]). The goal then, will be to try to capture some of the variation between different early complex political economies and, through the exercise, come to a better understanding of that of the Shang polity during the Anyang period.

The Inka model is an ideal type drawn and simplified from a variety of authors' depictions of Inka political economy (D'Altroy 2002; Costin 2004; Earl and D'Altroy 1989). It is a classic redistributive model, where the chief form of extraction is labor—whether on state fields, in government building projects, or royal workshops. In this model the key economic factor is people, and the Inka polity is known to have undertaken large-scale resettlement for both political and economic reasons. Craft production occurred in centralized or at least government-controlled workshops through either a labor tax or by permanently attached craftspeople. Textiles, beer, seeds, and other things from government stores were distributed to corvée laborers as redistribution dressed up as reciprocity. The polity thus needed a well-developed storage and administrative system to organize labor, store surpluses, and oversee redistribution. The basic social unit (the *allyu*) was self-sufficient, with crops cultivated in different environmental niches and basic craft and community infrastructure needs met through rotational assignment. There are no markets and no large-scale trade in this model: the needs of the people are met through local production or state redistribution, and the needs of élites though state and estate workshops, fields, and herds.

Abstracting further, political economies of this ideal, redistributive type are fundamentally concerned with people rather than things— their labor, their organization, their location. A further corollary is a relatively large investment in infrastructure to lower the transaction costs of managed redistribution—transportation (roads, bridges), storage (granaries, storehouses), and administration (corvée supervisors, storehouse officials, redistribution organizers). If the conditions of this model obtain, there should be no evidence of markets or the distribution of market products. While both of these conditions are difficult to verify archaeologically, logically, if craft production is either domestic/ local or government-controlled, then non-local, non-centralized workshop products should be absent or rare, especially in non-élite contexts. On the other hand, a wide distribution of everyday goods of non-local origin would naturally suggest some form of market. Agriculturally, there should be evidence of collective labor, such as tool caches and large granaries. Where élite economic records are available, one would expect to see records of labor mobilization and the accounting of stores, but not of money taxes or taxes in kind. In fact, in a redistributive economy there should be no need of money at all (whether as unit of exchange or value).

The Aztec model is also a simplification derived from the writings of different authors (Feinman and Nichols 2004; Smith 2015). This model is a market-taxation political economy, where the nature of sovereign extraction is largely in things. Taxes are levied on subordinate political entities, which in turn extract from subordinate units down to those who actually produce the agricultural or craft goods extracted. Taxes are paid in money and in kind. The horizontal circulation of goods in the economy is through trade and markets are well developed. Craft production is largely domestic and villages economically specialize for regional markets (Feinman and Nichols 2004). Trade is also important for élites and there are professional traders. Bulk agricultural products are taxed and consumed locally, obviating the need for large storage facilities. This model implies a less managed economy—less intensive infrastructurally, requiring no central organization of production or redistribution, allowing existing market and trade institutions to perform those functions instead. This model also predicts the existence of money, both in terms of units of exchange and of value (though not necessarily coinage).

Archaeologically and historically, the evidentiary correlates of the Aztec model are the inverse of the Inca model. There should be no evidence of large-scale storage or centralized workshops. Markets and traders should be attested through the broad distribution of non-local goods, market spaces, or textual evidence. We should find indications of standardized units of value and exchange. To the extent that the economy adheres to this ideal type, transportation or other economic infrastructure investment should be locally sponsored and directed from the the bottom up.

The Political Economy of the Great Settlement Shang

What was the nature of the Shang polity at Anyang? As I have argued elsewhere (Campbell 2009, 2018), the Shang polity network was a hegemonic (cf. Lin 1982) skein of élite kinship, alliance, and ritual (cf. Keightley 1983, 2000)—a lineage polity (see also Li 2008) combining both direct and indirect rule. Put another way, multiple lines of evidence suggest that Shang sovereignty had at least three zones—a zone of direct rulership, of commands, expropriations, and levies; a zone of indirect sovereignty, of alliance, gifting, and tribute; a zone of enemies, military campaigns, and booty (Campbell 2018). The political economy of the polity as a whole therefore had different components and should

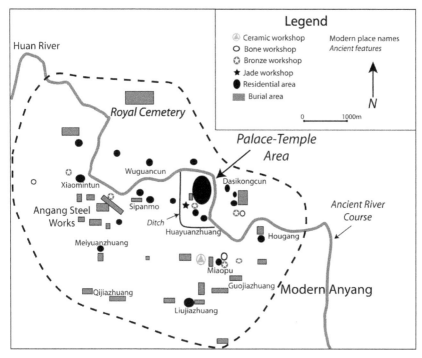

Figure 2.2. Map of Anyang, the Great Settlement Shang. Map by author, based on Campbell 2014, Fig. 5.2.

probably be thought of in terms of the political economy of the core, the zone of indirect rule, and the networks that linked them. Several facts complicate this picture. First, the size and nature of these components are not at all clear. Second, the Shang polity underwent reorganization halfway through the Anyang period, but most of the inscriptional evidence comes from the period before this process. Finally, the political valence of many of the actors seen in the oracle-bones changed over the course of the period—from subordinate, to ally, to enemy and back again—with the heave and toss of the political sea.

At the center of the royal demesne was the Great Settlement Shang— one hundred times larger than the next largest contemporaneous Shang site and, at 30 km², one of the largest centers in the world at its time (Figure 2.2). Having been perhaps the longest and most intensively excavated site in China, Anyang archaeology is key to understanding the

Shang polity. While older scholarship had underestimated Anyang's size and interpreted it as merely a ritual and political center (Chang 1980, Wheatley 1971) or as just one of the many Shang capitals (Chen 1988), it is now known to have been a massive center of industry and population in addition to royal residence and burial.

The population of the Great Settlement Shang has been estimated to have been as high as 300,000 (Song 1994) and as low as 30,000 (Flad 2016); but more rigorous estimates extrapolated from burials and houses within large area excavations at Anyang, and average population densities from other contemporaneous sites (ca. 30–50/ha), converge on a conservative estimate of around 100,000 at Anyang's peak (Campbell, forthcoming). How this massive population and Anyang's huge workshops (bronze, bone and others) were provisioned is a key question.

With 100,000 people and the overly optimistic estimate of 0.5 ha/person supported for growing food, the Great Settlement would have needed at least 50,000 ha under cultivation, and probably much more (Campbell, forthcoming). Given that settlements of this period hugged waterways and that no more than about a third of produce could be sustainably extracted in taxes (assuming that much of Anyang itself was under cultivation), more than 200 km^2 (and likely far more) of river valley would have been needed to provision the center (Campbell, forthcoming). All of this leads to the conclusion that Anyang would have to have been tightly and transformatively integrated into its extensive economic hinterland and not merely an adjunct atop a pre-existing landscape of self-sufficient farmers. The question is, how?

Agriculture

How was this massive agricultural enterprise managed? Sadly, we have little direct archaeological evidence concerning Shang farming practices beyond stone, bone, and shell tools putatively identified as agricultural on the basis of form. So, while recent archaeometric work has revealed evidence concerning crop and domestic animal ratios (e.g., Lee et al. 2007), animal husbandry practices (Li et al. 2014), and human diet (Cheung et al. 2017), the issue of provisioning and agricultural economic organization has only begun to be studied. The oracle-bone inscriptions are a little more helpful, but, being royal divinations and not administrative records, they are not ideal sources. Nevertheless, in these records inscribed on bone (bovine scapula and turtle plastrons and carapaces), Shang kings (though mostly Wu Ding) sometimes made charges concerning agriculture. The key issue divined about in the vast majority of cases is whether or not a good harvest would be received. What is not divined about is the grain itself, or its transportation. Moreover, the king took a personal interest in agriculture on a number of levels and in a variety of places. At its most expansive, the king's divinatory interest encompassed the agriculture of the polity as a whole as can be seen in the following series of divinations from the end of the Anyang period.

1a) 己巳王卜，貞：〔今〕歲商受〔年〕。王占曰：吉。
On Jisi day (day 6) the King cracked and tested: [this] season Shang will receive [harvest]. The King prognosticating said: "auspicious."

b) 東土受年。
The Eastern lands will receive harvest.

c) 南土受年。吉。
The Southern lands will receive harvest. Auspicious.

d) 西土受年。吉。
The Western lands will receive harvest. Auspicious.

e) 北土受年。吉。
The Northern lands will receive harvest. Auspicious. (Heji 36975)[6]

Here we can see the king personally divining either about the polity's agriculture in general before referring to individual lands within it, or, about the central Shang lands and then about lands beyond the core. In either case, the concern is for the state of the harvest in the polity writ large. Given that the land was considered to be populated by numinous entities and the harvest subject to their whims, it is not surprising that the king, as key mediator between the living and the spirits, would be concerned about the agricultural welfare of the realm in general.

2) 貞：禱年于岳燎三小牢卯三牛 (Heji 385)
Tested: (we should) pray for harvest to the mountain spirit, liao-burning three specially reared sheep and mao-splitting three head of cattle.

In this example we can see the king sacrificing to the spirit of the mountain in prayer for harvest. While the context does not allow us to be sure whether it is the harvest of specific lands or the harvest in general for which the sacrifice and prayer are being offered, nevertheless, the king's ritual role in ensuring successful agriculture is clear from this and many other examples (Keightley 2000: 15–16).

On a less encompassing level, a number of inscriptions indicate that the king had a more direct role in agricultural practices—levying laborers, participating personally or ordering officials to manage field preparation, planting, and harvesting.

3) [王] 大令眾人曰：劦田，其受年。十一月 (Heji 1)
   [The King] greatly ordered the masses saying: "Work together in the fields; we should receive harvest." Eleventh month.

4) 庚戌卜，殸鼎：王立黍，受年。(Heji 9525)
   On Gengxu day cracked, (diviner) Ke tested: The King should plant millet, (for if he does, we) will receive harvest.

5) 貞：叀小臣令眾黍。一月。(Heji 12)
   Tested: it should be a minor official that orders the masses to plant millet. First month.

In these inscriptions we can see that at least some Shang agriculture is managed and that the king, or his officials, have a direct role. An obvious next question is whether the entire agricultural economy was managed or simply certain royal fields or estates.

6) 貞：我北田受年 (Heji 9750)
   Tested: My/our northern fields will receive harvest.

7) . . . 卜，古貞：我在南奠从龍受年。(Heji 9770)
   . . . day cracked, (diviner) Gu tested: When I (the King) am in the southern colony (or: colonies) we will receive harvest from Long.

8) 王固卜曰："我其受甫耤在姐年"。(Heji 165)
   The King read the cracks and said: "We/I can expect to receive the harvest that (Prince) Fu cultivates at Zi."

From examples such as these it is apparent that at least King Wu Ding had agricultural concerns in a wide variety of locations, from colonies to places (estates?) managed by consorts, princes, subordinate lords and officials. While it has been previously noted that the most common harvest place divined about is some version of self-reference (i.e., my, our, king, Shang or the Great Settlement; cf. Keightley 1983), in a quantitative study of oracle-bone political geography (Campbell 2018: chapter 4, appendix A), I showed that the places for which the king most commonly divines about the harvest ranks high in terms of affiliation with the Shang polity, even while the self-referential harvest inscriptions make up around 60% of the total (Appendix A, table 2). In other words, of the hundreds of places mentioned in the oracle-bones, only a handful are named in harvest inscriptions—nearly two-thirds of which are self-referential and the majority of the rest refer to places strongly affiliated with the king. This suggests that royally-managed agriculture was but a small part of the overall agricultural picture. The further association in many of these inscriptions with colonies suggests that their establishment in conquered areas or with vanquished people moved from other places (Qiu 1993) could have been one avenue through which Shang kings received agricultural produce. Given the indirect nature of much of Shang rule, it seems likely then that other élites mentioned in the oracle-bones whose harvest is not divined about, had their own colonies and fields, farmed with locally levied labor.

Given the focus on labor rather than things, the Shang agriculture that we have evidence for seems to comport with the Inka model, with farmers (who presumably had their own fields) called upon to render labor tax on the king's or their local lord's fields. In some places this labor was probably undertaken by attached dependents such as colonists or slaves rather than free farmers, although we know precious little about the lives of the lower strata of Shang society.

Naturally, with royal and élite fields and colonies scattered across the land, the question of how grain was stored and transported arises. While there is no convincing archaeological evidence of large-scale grain storage,[7] the oracle-bone inscriptions do mention granaries, as in this inscription below.

9) . . . 有𡚒在𢿢，𠂤在□其林農亦焚廩三。(Heji 583)
   . . . there is trouble in X, Y is there . . . (did something to) its forests, agriculture and burned granaries, three.

This and other inscriptions show that not only were there granaries at places outside of the capital, but their inspection and protection was a royal concern. Taken together these strands of evidence—the widespread royally-administered fields, the granaries, and the lack of references to grain itself—tentatively suggest a network of royal fields and storage spread across the Shang domain, interspersed with the fields of other lords and lineages. The scale of the king's agriculture is unclear and while it may have only supplied the royal household, it is also possible that the scattered granaries were to supply the king's hunts and campaigns. Nevertheless, the evidence does not seem to support the idea that the Great Settlement itself was provisioned by royally-managed agriculture, much less the polity as a whole, but more likely that each lineage had own its fields and settlements.

Animal Husbandry

Turning to livestock, an interesting distinction emerges when compared with agricultural divinations. Unlike agriculture, where, as mentioned above, preparing fields, planting, and harvesting are mentioned, but never grain itself, the king frequently divines about livestock, but almost never about their husbandry, with the following example constituting a rare exception.

10) 貞：呼王牧十羊。(Heji 774+778)
    Tested: (we should) call upon the King's herdsmen (for) ten sheep.

This example would seem to indicate that the King owned herds, but that, unlike agriculture, the Shang animal economy involved neither levying labor, nor (generally) royal management. Instead, the oracle-bone inscriptions show that cattle, sheep, and dogs (but not pigs), like people, were themselves "levied," "taken," "requested," as well as "brought" or "sent in" (Campbell 2018; Campbell, forthcoming).

11) 癸亥貞：危方以牛，其叙于來甲申。(Heji 33191)
    Cracked on Guihai day, (unnamed diviner) tested (the following charge): the cattle that the Wei Fang [Shang enemies] brought should be offered up (in sacrifice) on the coming Jiashen day.

12) 戊午卜，宾貞：呼取牛百，以。王占〔曰〕："吉。以，其至。"
(Heji 93 reverse)
Cracked on Wuwu day, Bin tested (the following charge): call upon
[someone contextually understood] to take cattle, one hundred, and bring
them. The King (then) read the cracks and [said], "Auspicious." "He will
bring them, they should arrive."

13) 甲午卜，宾貞：令周乞牛多 . . . (Heji 4884)
Cracked on Jiawu day, Bin tested (the following charge): Command Zhou
to request cattle, many . . .

14) 貞：冒牛百。(Heji 9041)
Tested: levy cattle, one hundred.

15) . . . 烄羊三百 . . . (Heji 8959)
. . . levy sheep, three hundred.

In example 11 we can see the acquisition of livestock through indirect, sporadic gifts from erstwhile enemies, while in example 12 we can see the uncertainty of at least some royal requisitions. Not only is the taking of the cattle a matter for divination, but also whether the agent in question will actually bring them. Example 13 is another interesting inscription about the auspiciousness of commanding the Zhou (who roughly 150 years after this divination overthrew the Shang) to "request" many cattle—perhaps indicating an informal, even voluntary(?), but indirectly administered levy.[8] Much more typical are examples 14 and 15 where the animals are directly "levied" or "raised," just as with human agricultural or military resources.

Taken together, these divinations suggest sporadic flows of movable resources as gifts or tribute from beyond the polity, informal extractions from allies, and levies and expropriations from areas under direct governance. While the divinatory nature of this body of evidence precludes its being unambiguous evidence for routine economic flows, it is suggestive of the range of forms that royal livestock provisioning may have taken. An unanswered question concerning the levying divinations is whether they refer to something entirely ad hoc or whether there were some customary limits on the obligations to the king. Since it seems unlikely that any lasting government could simply arbitrarily and without limit extract manpower and resources from its populace, it seems more likely, that, as in later times, there was a customary quantity of human and animal resources that each household, or perhaps each lineage, owed the king. Thus, these inscriptions perhaps reveal something analogous to households in later times having to provide and equip one adult male for war (if called upon)—only the obligation extended to livestock as well as people and the occasion was sacrifice rather than war.

Summarizing the oracle-bone inscription evidence, the agricultural inscriptions suggest direct royal participation in some agriculture, but no mention of the grain itself. The situation is reversed in the livestock provisioning inscriptions, where there are almost no divinations about husbandry, but hundreds concerning animals coming from a wide variety of contexts. A systematic study of oracle-bone political economy likewise showed that while agricultural divinations were almost exclusively about places securely within the Shang orbit, livestock came from far and wide through both indirect and direct political economic networks (Campbell 2018). These lines of evidence together suggest that a fundamental variable was transportation costs, with bulk items stored and consumed locally, while mobile resources like people and livestock were brought from near and far, both through tax and tribute/gifting. Together, this both suggests the existence of agricultural estates and labor corvée rather than taxes in kind, and, at the same time, an animal levy or tax that extended beyond the king's own estates, analogous to human resource mobilizations for labor or war.

From the perspective of the economic models introduced above, the agricultural situation seems more akin to the Inka system—privileging the control and mobilization of labor rather than direct taxation in kind. The livestock provisioning, on the other hand, seems more like the Aztec model of tax and tribute imposed on existing husbandry rather than direct state management. If the Inka model suggested the need for infrastructural investment, the Shang evidence suggests only a limited investment in royal grain storage combined with a concern for minimizing transportation costs.

Craft Economies

Turning to craft production and its chains of distribution and consumption, aside from bronze casting, which largely underpins the élite redistributive consensus, recent work has shone light on other aspects of the Shang crafting economy. Thus, while there were several large-scale bronze casting workshops at Anyang producing ritual vessels and weapons for élites, work on the Tiesanlu bone-working site has shown that large-scale bone workshops at Anyang were producing everyday goods for wide distribution (Campbell et al. 2011, Li et al. 2011). The most common products of these workshops were hairpins, which were produced in vast quantities outstripping local (Anyang) consumption by as much as 4 to 1 (Campbell et al. 2011). Preliminary research has shown that production at Tiesanlu was divided into stages which took place in different parts of the site, while the tools, methods, and products were highly standardized compared to bone working in other contexts. Essentially, Tiesanlu should be understood as a factory, where a small range of artifacts in an even smaller range of styles were mass produced for broad consumption. The provisioning and control of the workshop remains controversial though given the lineage-settlement nature of the capital (Tang and Jing 2009), the distribution of workshops in several industrial areas each with its own associated residential and mortuary areas suggests that workshops were controlled by different crafting lineages or clans (Li et al 2011, Campbell et al. 2011).

The hypothesis that the Anyang bone workshops were producing for distribution beyond Anyang received dramatic support with a recent study of bone-working at Guandimiao, the only well excavated Anyang period village in North China (Hou et al. 2018). Work at this village, located 200 km from Anyang, has shown not only that nearly a quarter of the bone artifact assemblage recovered was of a high-skill, labor-intensive, specialized tool and manufacture type associated with Anyang's large-scale bone workshops, but also that the most common artifact type amongst this group was a hairpin that exactly matches hundreds of wasters, semi-finished and finished pins from the Tiesanlu workshop. Moreover, a comparison with Guandimiao locally manufactured artifacts clearly shows the exogenous nature of the specialized bone workshop products (Hou et al. 2018). The lack of tell-tale worked bone waste of the large-scale workshop type with its bronze saw cuts and standardized cut patterns on large mammal bones and antler not only shows that Guandimiao was not the site of specialized bone-working, but the lack of such assemblages from other Anyang period sites outside of Anyang also further strengthens the argument that certain categories of artifacts were only being produced at the capital for widespread distribution.[9]

To summarize: it appears as if large-scale bone workshops at the Great Settlement Shang, where cattle bone resources were concentrated through royal and élite sacrifice, produced huge batches of hairpins in just a few styles (or grades) for widespread distribution. Interestingly, other than hairpins, no other mass-produced bone workshop products were found at Guandimiao, suggesting that different categories of artifacts had different distributions. Superficially at least, the large workshops in the capital appear to match the Inka model more closely than the Aztec one. On closer look, however, the multiple, simultaneous workshops distributed around the capital argue against centralized control, even while the siting of workshops near the source of raw materials (cattle bone) could explain their location in the capital. This then begs the question of the mechanisms through which the hairpins were distributed. If the production was in the hands of independent crafting lineages, then it is possible that they were producing for market and the presence of the pins at Guandimiao and concentration of specialized bone working in the capital suggest both an extensive market system and a monopoly based on access to bronze saws, raw materials, and economies of scale. If, on the other hand, the workshops were producing for the king, then the presence of the pins in a remote village means that royal redistributive systems were far more expansive and locally penetrating than hitherto suspected. If it were analogous to Inka cloth workshops, the pins may have been used to recompense in part the corvee laborers and perhaps to mark status.

Another interesting piece of the puzzle is the fact that Guandimiao was itself a craft-specialized village with more kilns than houses (Henan 2008, 2009; Li et al. 2018).[10] Preliminary observations of the kilns and associated features show that not only were different kilns used for producing different ceramic types, but that the majority of the wasters are of fine-paste serving ware that is conspicuously absent from the residences and associated middens (Li et al. 2018). It appears then, that Guandimiao was a pottery production village focused on producing fine-ware for use elsewhere. Other facts relevant to Guandimiao's wider political economic context is the apparent poverty of the site—as seen in ceramic assemblage, animal bones, residences, and burials—and the near total lack of weapons (Li et al. 2018). Compared to even non-élite areas of Anyang, Guandimiao villagers were poor and unarmed, suggesting that they were dependent on local élites (who lived elsewhere) for protection.

Given that Guandimiao ceramics do not look exactly like those found at Anyang, it seems likely that ceramic production at the site was for distribution within the local region. At the same time, however, their integration into the wider Anyang political economy can be seen through the mass-produced hairpins discovered at the site. At first glance, the presence of crafting villages suggests the Aztec model, with regional trade leading to product specialization. If, on the other hand, the situation was more of a managed, redistributive type, one could postulate that Guandimiao was part of an extended élite estate, producing ceramics for their lord's household and perhaps redistribution in the region, while the hairpins were given to the villagers by their local lord (or official), who in turn received them from the workshops in the capital. Nevertheless, while the defenseless villagers of Guandimiao were certainly not politically independent, they could have been economically independent—producing for a local market while paying taxes to their local lord (perhaps in kind) and buying what they could not produce locally. In this model, the regional and inter-regional market systems would have to have been sufficiently well integrated such that the products of Anyang workshops could travel 200km to a tiny village of no more than 10–20 families (Li et al. 2018), while at the same time such communities could afford to specialize in a single craft.

Without more work on rural sites and smaller centers it is difficult to be certain which model fits best, but drawing on other periods and larger contexts suggests a mixed model. While it is true that very few small Central Plains sites have been excavated for the second millennium BCE, all those that have been published fit the specialized production pattern seen at Guandimiao. The Erlitou-period (ca. 1800–1600 BCE) site of Huizui, for instance, was a specialized stone tool-making village located near raw material sources and produced tools for exchange both before and during the rise of the Erlitou center in the area (Liu et al. 2007; Chen 2005). As Chen (2005) points out, this suggests pre-existing, non-élite exchange systems. Another well-published small site, Gaocheng Taixi, dating to the Huanbei-Xiaoshuangqiao period (ca. 1400–1250 BCE), shows evidence of having been a settlement specialized in fermenting alcohol (Hebei 1985). While it is not entirely clear how that site was related to wider political economic networks in its time, the fact that all of the small sites known from the Central Plains Bronze Age (ca. 1800–1050 BCE), including the temporary salt-working sites in Shandong (Shandong et al. 2010a, 2010b), appear to have a specialized economic function, suggests a high degree of economic integration. At the same time, the fact that some crafts, like stone tool manufacture, seem to have been exchanged independently of political élites suggests the existence of markets and trade rather than a completely managed economy.

Money

While it has long been claimed that cowrie shells served as money in the Shang and Western Zhou periods, recent Western and Japanese scholarship (Kakinuma 2011; Li 2006; von Glahn 2016) has argued that cowries served merely as a unit of account, and only from the Middle Western Zhou (ca. 10th century BCE), with "the value imputed to cowries undoubtedly derived from their ritual uses in sacrifice and as mortuary goods, rather than any abstract notion of monetary value" (von Glahn 2016: 39). Li Yung-ti, citing mid-20th century monetary theory states, "for something to circulate as money and to be accepted in every transaction, there has to be universal agreement among individual agents in the function and value of the item . . . once the agreement is in place, money as an object disappears. It becomes a universally recognized symbol independent of what the object actually is" (Li 2006: 4). He then goes on to argue that there is only inscriptional evidence from the Middle Western Zhou of cowries being used as a unit of account and, following evolutionary and absence of evidence arguments (i.e., primitive money is first a unit of account and only secondarily exchange, so Mid-Western Zhou inscriptions must be an early stage in the development), he claims that cowries could not have been used as currency in the Shang or Early Western Zhou. Thus, the fundamental arguments are that cowries were used in ritual and as ornaments, and as such they could not also have functioned as a perfectly abstract and universal units of value and exchange. The issue with this argument is that it confuses what money is ideally with what it can and has been in history. If we discard the universality and total abstraction from the definition (most modern currencies are neither perfectly universal or entirely abstract, never mind ancient coinage systems, much less historical examples of commodities of exchange), and focus on money as unit of account and, or, exchange, we can then begin to capture the diversity of things that served as money through history.

Substantively, the argument from absence of evidence is extremely weak: the Shang and Early Western Zhou bronze inscriptions are not the sort of texts in which one would expect to find economic transactions. Their earliest records are of ancestral dedications followed nby memorializations of gifts received from superiors. To arrive at the conclusion that the Shang and Western Zhou economies revolved fundamentally around élite gifting because this is what élite commemorative gifting texts describe is entirely circular. It is only in the latter half of Western Zhou that bronze inscriptions occasionally take on a function analogous to legal records (as opposed to simply claims to ancestral merit) (Shaughnessy 1999; Li 2006, 2008). This only means that our first glimpse of élite disputes over land and the exchange of valuable commodities dates from the Mid-Western Zhou, not that élites did not have land disputes or exchange things in earlier times or have units of account or exchange to facilitate them.

To summarize: the arguments against cowries being money are merely arguments that there is no evidence that they were such before the ninth century BCE, and, given the primitivist assumptions of the authors in question, the redistributive patrimonial economies of the Bronze Age were not the sort of economies that would have developed money in any case.

If use in ritual and ornamentation do not automatically rule out cowries as money (like precious metals in other cultures, or coins in later Chinese history), what are the arguments in favor of their use as units of exchange and/or of account? The first, as has been long-pointed out (including by Li 2006) is that later tradition has it that cowries were used as money before coinage and that nearly all of the graphs for words referring to value or exchange use the graph for cowrie as a signific, including contemporaneous Shang graphs such as bao寶 (treasure, precious), mai 買 (to buy) and jia賈 (trader, to trade). Archaeologically, though it is true that the vast majority of Anyang-period cowries are recovered from mortuary contexts (there are scattered cowries recovered from middens and house remains as well), this is also true of all valuable Shang material culture. There is relatively little evidence, on the other hand, archaeological or inscriptional, for the use of cowries as sacrificial offerings. By and large, the Shang offered consumables in sacrifice, especially livestock. The argument that cowries were used primarily as ornament also rests on shaky ground: while it is true that some of the horses recovered from Anyang chariot pits had bridles decorated with cowries (in addition to tooth, bronze, bone, turquoise, and gold foil), cowries were never the main decorative element, nor were chariot ornaments ever more than a tiny élite fraction of Anyang material culture.[11] In mortuary contexts, cowries are either found in small numbers, often (but not always) in the hand or mouth of the tomb occupant, or in strings. The largest quantity of cowries recovered were the ca. 6000 from the tomb of the royal consort Fu Hao. If these strings of cowries are to be understood as ornamental, it means that Fu Hao had dozens of long cowrie necklaces. What makes this interpretation unlikely is the fact that we know cowries were counted in double strings peng朋 (so, a pile of cowries found in a tomb is not necessarily a necklace), and what contemporaneous string-like decorative assemblages we do have (e.g., horse bridles, necklaces, bracelets, etc.) tend to combine varieties of ornament (bead, shell, jade, bronze, bone, etc.). Since the overwhelming majority of cowries are found unassociated with other ornaments, but with holes for a string to tie them together, it seems much more likely they were carried on strings just as coins were in later times.

The argument that the fundamental purpose of cowries was for death ritual is also problematic for a number of reasons. The most obvious issue is that the logic of Shang mortuary ritual was to equip the dead for the afterlife (Campbell 2018: 341). This being so, everything in a Shang tomb—from ceramic vessels and food offerings to ritual bronzes, weapons and jades—bore some relationship to things used in life or those required for the next one. Why then should we assume that cowries, roughly as ubiquitous in Anyang burials as ceramic vessels, had no non-mortuary function just because we find them mostly in tombs?[12] Another line of evidence is their poor correlation with tomb size, an otherwise reliable marker of Shang mortuary status. Thus, while bronze and jade artifacts show significant correlations with tomb size in Anyang tombs, cowries do not (Campbell 2018: Appendix C, table 4). In other words, the quantity of cowries in tombs does not reliably correlate with the mortuary status of the deceased. At the same time, some élite burials, like Fu Hao's, have enormous numbers of cowries. This means that cowries, while deemed necessary for the dead, were not part of the ritual sumptuary system that employed bronze vessels, weapons, jades, and sacrificial victims to mark status. Cowries were rather an article of value that proper burial required in minimum quantities but not to mark ancestral status, even while some tombs could afford to be equipped with large quantities. Thus, if small quantities of cowries served a broad purpose in mortuary ritual (cash for the afterlife?), and large quantities of them were not likely ornament, then their significance in large quantities was not merely for death ritual or marking sumptuary status, but rather part of the general logic of equipping the dead as completely and richly as possible—the same logic which underwrote the inclusion of food offerings, personal ornaments, tools, and sometimes even raw materials of craft, despite the fact these were not part of the main, status-marking assemblage (Campbell 2018: 356–59).

If, then, there is no theoretical contradiction between the use of cowries in sacrifice, ornament or burial on the one hand, and as money on the other; and if cowries do not pattern with other types of ornament or ritual artifacts in mortuary assemblages, we are left with the conclusion that there is no good empirical or theoretical reason why Shang cowries could not have been used as units of exchange and/or of value. On the positive side of the equation, cowries feature in nearly every early Chinese graph denoting value or exchange, including in Shang inscriptions, and cowries are nearly the only thing given as rewards by the king or other superiors in the Shang bronze inscriptions. While Li (2006) claims these are simply status-marking gifts, which in the Western Zhou develop into larger lists of precious things (chariots, horses, weapons, cloths, bronze, jade, etc.), to assume that the Shang political economy was more primitive than that of the Western Zhou is to adopt the position of later Chinese historiography's teleological narrative. It would be strange indeed, considering the limited scope of uses for cowries inferred from their patterns of archaeological recovery, if they were nearly the only thing offered as rewards for meritorious service and yet could not be exchanged for the bronzes, jades, chariots, horses, and other precious things that figure so prominently in Shang élite self-fashioning. Put another way, if the Shang élite economy was based on gifting, how were Shang nobility supposed to obtain their ritual and status enabling assemblages if the only thing their superiors gave them were cowries and cowries could not be exchanged for anything?

Could cowries have been a form of élite money, restricted to aristocratic interactions and high-value exchanges, while the common people either did not possess money or used something else? The broad distribution of cowries argues against this. Cowries can be found not only in the poorest grade of Anyang tombs but even in the tiny crafting village of Guandimiao in otherwise impoverished tombs (which lack even ceramics in most cases). At a minimum, this demonstrates that cowries had a broad distribution—broader by far than jade or even bronze. At the same time, the holes in the Guandimiao cowry shells indicate they were strung together, as at Anyang.

Taken together, numerous indirect lines of evidence not only support the idea that cowrie shells were used as commodities of exchange and likely units of value in the Shang, but also that they were part of the broader economy that I have been attempting to outline here. Along with stone, shell, and some bone artifacts at Guandimiao, the cowries represent yet another type of non-local material culture that the villagers of Guandimiao had to acquire somehow. The simplest explanation is that cowries were money, placed in tombs as basic offerings (as in later Chinese custom), and that the Guandimiao villagers had access to cowries because the economy of the Shang polity was at least partially monetized. This conclusion is predicted by the Aztec ideal type while being contrary to the Inca model. This, in turn, minimally suggests that there were significant portions of the Shang economy that were not redistributive. The existence of commodities in addition to cowries that could serve as units of exchange or account, such as bales of cloth, ingots of metal, measures of grain or salt, or heads of livestock seem likely, but remain to be demonstrated.

Conclusion

Bringing all of the (admittedly weak and disparate) strands of evidence together, three facts clearly emerge: (1) the Shang political economy was built around a minimization of transportation costs; (2) there was a high degree of economic specialization and integration even in the countryside that likely long predated the Anyang period; and (3) the economy was at least partially monetized (assuming a broad definition of money). The first fact fits the observations that Shang agricultural taxes seem to be labor levies rather than grain taxes and that élites were supported through managed agriculture. The combination of direct and indirect rule, however, meant that this managed agriculture was likely segmentary, with each lord having his or her own lands and labor taxes, and free commoners their own fields (whether individually or lineage owned). Mobile resources like people and livestock, on the other hand, seem to have been taxed in kind, making the basic mechanism for royal extraction the levy (whether in people or animals). The second fact (specialization) can be reconciled with the first insofar as the Inka redistributive model implied an investment in transportation and storage infrastructure that is significantly missing from the Central Plains archaeological record and contrary to the logic of segmentary organization and the avoidance of bulk good shipments. Though we have no direct evidence of taxes in craft goods or for managed craft production, the Aztec model suggests that in situations with traditions of rural craft specialization and exchange, local polities could simply apply taxes in kind (routinized tributes) on crafting communities and/or tax markets, especially where non-strategic crafts were concerned. These two facts, moreover, fit with the observation that production sites seem to be located near resources, both minimizing transportation costs and promoting the existence of numerous small-scale craft specialized communities.

The large-scale bronze and bone workshops in the capital are interesting exceptions. It has long been noted that bronze-casting workshops set apart major Central Plains Bronze Age settlements from minor ones. Nevertheless, mining sites were scattered far and wide with smelting inevitably located near the mines (Golas 1999). Thus, in being a strategic, élite industry, bronze metallurgy, its infrastructure and its craftspeople, was relocated every time a new center of power was created. This is seen clearly with the Zhou conquest of the Shang and is strongly indicated in the seamless continuity and development of élite crafting despite the rise and fall of Central Plains centers over the course of the second millennium BCE. The siting of large-scale bone-working, on the other hand, may have had more to do with the location of resources—cattle bone and deer antler—the former deriving from élite sacrificial feasting, the latter from élite hunting activities. It is notable that there is only evidence for this kind of bone-crafting at Anyang, which also sees a dramatic jump in the quantity of cattle consumed compared with Erlitou and Erligang. With access to bronze saws unavailable in smaller centers without adjacent bronze foundries and massive quantities of bone, the bone-crafting lineages of Anyang were able to specialize in and mass-produce the most common and widely demanded bone artifact—the hairpin. While awls, spatulas, arrowheads and spades could be and were manufactured of bone domestically and in smaller local workshops, hairpins are the only common Shang article of apparel made in bone. Unlike tools and utensils, they were visibly worn and, like other articles of personal ornamentation, part of the extended self and an immediate register of social standing. Thus, even the lowest end (least labor-consuming) hairpin produced in the Anyang workshops—a smoothly polished cylindrical pin made from cattle bone, lustrous and white like the nephrite preferred by Anyang élites, was worlds away from the dog fibulas or bone splinter awls sometimes used as ad-hoc hairpins. The presence of Anyang workshop-produced pins at Guandimiao thus implies that it was easier to acquire them than to replicate them locally without the proper tools or skills. This, in turn, indicates a relatively efficient exchange system of some kind. In a market and trade scenario, the Guandimiao villagers would have had to pay taxes in kind and in labor to their local lord, who in turn gave taxes in transportable goods and mobile resources to the king. At the same time, they would also have been producing ceramics for regional exchange while trading for metal, shell, bone and stone artifacts not locally produced (Li et al. 2018).

In summary, then, the comparison of Shang evidence with ideal type Inka and Aztec models suggests a focus on people and labor, like the Inka, but segmentary in organization and lacking the infrastructure of a general redistributive political economy. Complementing the managed aspects were a myriad economically specialized rural sites and a deep-time tradition of regional exchange in non-élite goods, as in the Aztec model. The Shang king drew taxes in mobile or non-bulk commodities and local lords likely did the same in a form of commodity and labor tax-farming. Thus, from this preliminary examination of the evidence concerning Anyang period Shang taxation and political economy it appears that the Shang polity had elements of both redistributive and market models. Future work is needed especially on rural trade and regional political economies, but also on the archaeology of agriculture at and around the capital.

NOTES

1 The Chinese language literature generally either avoids discussing political economic models (e.g., ZSKY 2003) or overtly or covertly employs vulgar Marxist ones (e.g., Yang and Ma 2010). Nevertheless, as the audience for this volume is an international one, I will direct my argument at the English-language literature.

2 Salt also appears as a strategic resource in their narrative, making the putative Erlitou and Erligang states' salt and bronze monopolies Bronze Age precursors to the salt and iron monopolies briefly instated in the Western Han.

3 Although to be fair, the authors do stress the insufficiency of the evidence, and the tentative nature of their account—especially for inter-polity economic interaction and urban-hinterland integration.

4 Actually, when confronted with the fact that there are multiple large-scale foundries outside of the palace-temple area simultaneously producing the same types of artifacts, Li is forced to admit that bronze production itself does not appear to have been centralized even if the raw materials and products *must* have been under state control.

5 Since the Western Zhou is said to have largely continued Shang industries and ritual with some additional innovations in administrative organization, we are left to assume that Anyang's political economy was similar but more primitively organized.

6 Heji refers to the oracle-bone inscription corpus *Jiaguwen Heji* (ZSLY 1982).

7 This is not to say that some scholars (eg. Yu and Ye 1982–1983) have not speculated that some of the larger and more regular pits found at Shang sites might have been used for grain storage, but to date this issue has not been systematically investigated for any Shang sites.

8 Although the verb translated as "request" (乞), means "to beg" in later Chinese, it mostly appears in administrative notes on the margins of oracle-bones concerning the supply of osteomantic materials and seems to indicate some kind of internal transfer of resources. Given this, "requisition" might give a better sense of the nature of the transaction.

9 It should be noted that for each hairpin made, a much larger volume of bone debitage is produced. Thus, large-scale bone working using large mammal bones is among the most archaeologically visible crafting activities. Coupled with the fact that animal bone preserves well in North China, and dozens of Anyang

period sites have been excavated, the absence of evidence, in this case, approaches evidence of absence.

10 Roughly three-quarters of the Anyang period village at Guandimiao survived, and almost all of this was entirely excavated, making it hard to argue for discovery bias.

11 Chariots were rare, and the cowries found in horse-chariot ornament contexts likely numbers in the low hundreds. If we consider that over 60 pits have been recovered and most of the élite cemeteries dug at Anyang, this is likely a considerable portion of the depositional record, and accounts for a very small proportion of the tens of thousands of cowries recovered from Anyang alone.

12 By this logic, jades and bronzes (including weapons), and indeed all Shang élite material culture, should be considered to have only a mortuary function since we find them nearly exclusively in tombs.

WORKS CITED

Allan, Sarah. 2007. "Erlitou and the formation of Chinese civilization: Toward a new paradigm." *Journal of Asian Studies* 66: 461–96.

Bagley, Robert. 1999. "Shang Archaeology." In M. Lowe and E. Shaughnessy (eds.), *The Cambridge History of Ancient China*. (Cambridge: Cambridge University Press), 124–231.

Campbell, Roderick. 2014. *Archaeology of the Chinese Bronze Age: from Erlitou to Anyang*. Los Angeles: Cotsen Institute of Archaeology Press.

Campbell, Roderick. 2018. *Violence, Kinship and the Early Chinese State: the Shang and their World*. Cambridge: Cambridge University Press.

Campbell, Roderick. Forthcoming. "Feeding the Great Settlement: Preliminary Notes on the Shang Animal Economy." In L. Atici and B. Arbuckle (eds.), *Food Provisioning in Complex Societies* (Boulder, CO: University of Colorado Press).

Campbell, Roderick, Li Zhipeng, He Yuling, Yuan Jing. 2011. "Consumption and Production at the Great Settlement Shang: Bone working at Tiesanlu, Anyang." *Antiquity* 85: 1279–97.

Chang, K. C. 1980. *Shang Civilization*. New Haven: Yale University Press.

Chang, K. C. 1983. *Art, Myth and Ritual: The Path to Political Authority in Ancient China*. Cambridge: Harvard University Press.

Chang, K. C. 1985. "Guanyu Zhongguo chuqi 'chengshi' zhege gainian" ["On the Concept of 'City' in Ancient China"]. *Wenwu* 1985.2: 61–67.

Chang, K. C. 1986. *The Archaeology of Ancient China*. 4th ed. New Haven and London: Yale University Press.

Chang, K. C. 1989. "Ancient China and its Anthropological Significance." In C. C. Lamberg-Karlovsky (ed.), *Archaeological Thought in America* (Cambridge: Cambridge University Press), 155–66.

Chen, Mengjia. 1988. *Yinxu buci zongshu* (A Complete Description of the Yinxu Divinatory Inscriptions). Reprint. Beijing: Zhonghua shuju. 2004.

Chen, Xingcan. 2005. "Lithic Production of Early States in China—An Examination of the Development of Craft Specialization." Paper presented at *Workshop on Early Chinese Civilization*, March 10-12, 2005, University of British Columbia.

Cheung, Christina, Zhicun Jing, Jigen Tang, Darlene Weston and Michael Richards. 2017. "Diets, social roles, and geographical origins of sacrificial victims at the royal cemetery at Yinxu, Shang China: New evidence from stable carbon, nitrogen, and sulfur isotope analysis." *Journal of Anthropological Archaeology* 48: 28–45. DOI: 10.1016/j.jaa.2017.05.006.

Costin, Cathy. 2004. "Craft Economies of Ancient Andean States." In G. Feinman and L. Nichols (eds.), *Archaeological Perspectives on Political Economies* (Salt Lake City: University of Utah Press), 189–222.

D'Altroy, Terrence. 2002. *The Inkas*. Malden: Blackwell Publishers.

Earl, Timothy and Terrence D'Altroy. 1989. "The Political Economy of the Inca Empire: The Archaeology of Power and Finance." In C. C. Lamberg-Karlovsky (ed.), *Archaeological Thought in America* (Cambridge: Cambridge University Press), 183–204.

von Falkenhausen, Lothar. 2008. "Stages in the Development of 'Cities' in pre-Imperial China." In Joyce Marcus and Jeremy Sabloff (eds.), *The Ancient City: New Perspectives on Urbanism in the Old and New World* (Santa Fe, NM: School of Advanced Studies Press), 209–28.

Feinman, Gary and Linda Nichols. 2004. "Unraveling the Prehispanic Highland Mesoamerican Economy: Production, Exchange and Consumption in the Classic Period Valley of Oaxaca." In G. Feinman and L. Nichols (eds.), *Archaeological Perspectives on Political Economies* (Salt Lake City: University of Utah Press), 129–44.

Flad, Rowan. 2016. "Urbanism as Technology in Early China." *Archaeological Research in Asia*. https://doi.org/10.1016/j.ara.2016.09.001.

von Glahn, Richard. 2016. *The Economic History of China: From Antiquity to the Nineteenth Century*. Cambridge: Cambridge University Press.

Golas, Peter. 1999. *Part XIII: Mining*. In *Volume 5: Chemisty and Chemical Technology. Science and Civilization in China*, ed. Joseph Needham. Cambridge: Cambridge University Press.

Hebei Province (Hebei Provincial Institute of Cultural Relics). 1985. *Gaocheng Taixi Shangdai Yizhi* [The Shang Period Site of Gaocheng Taixi]. Beijing: Wenwu chubanshe.

Henan Sheng Wenwu Kaogu Yanjiusuo. 2008. "Henan Xingyangshi Guandimiao yizhi Shangdai wanqi yicun fajue jianbao (A Preliminary Report on the Excavation of the Late Shang Remains from Guandimiao, Xingyang municipality, Henan)". *Kaogu* 7: 32–46.

Henan Sheng Wenwu Kaogu Yanjiusuo. 2009. "Henan Xingyangshi Guandimiao yizhi kaogu faxian yu renshi (The Archaeological Discovery and Understanding of the Guandimiao Site, Xingyang municipality, Henan)". *Huaxia Kaogu* 3: 8–13.

Hopkins, Keith. 2002 [1980]. "Rome, Taxes, Rents and Trade." In W. Scheidel and S. von Reden *The Ancient Economy* (New York: Routlege), 190–230.

Hou Yanfeng, Roderick Campbell, Li Zhipeng, Zhang Yan, Li Suting, and He Yuling. 2018. "The Guandimiao Bone Assemblage (and What it Says about the Shang Economy)," *Asian Perspectives* 57.2: 281–310.

Kakikuna Yōhei. 2011. *Chūgoku kodai kahei keizai shi kenkyū* [The Economic History of Coinage in Ancient China]. Tokyo: Kyūko shoin.

Keightley, David. 1983. "The Late Shang State: When, Where, and What?" In D. Keightley (ed.), *The Origins of Chinese Civilization*. (Berkeley: University of California Press), 523–64.

Keightley, David. 2000. *The Ancestral Landscape: Time, Space, and Community in Late Shang China*. Berkeley: IEAS & CCS.

Lee, Gyoung-ah, Gary Crawford, Li Liu, and Xingcan Chen. 2007. "Plants and people from the Early Neolithic to Shang periods in north China." *Proceedings of the National Academy of Sciences* 104(3): 1087–92.

Li, Feng. 2006. *Landscape and Power in Early China: The Crisis and Fall of the Western Zhou 1045–771 BC*. Cambridge: Cambridge University Press.

Li, Feng. 2008. *Bureaucracy and the State in Early China: Governing the Western Zhou*. Cambridge: Cambridge University Press.

Li Suting, Roderick Campbell, and Hou Yanfeng. 2018. "Guandimiao: A Shang Village Site and its Significance." *Antiquity* 92: 1511–29.

Li, Yung-ti. 2003. "The Anyang Bronze Foundries: Archaeological Remains, Casting Technology and Production Organization." Unpublished PhD dissertation, Department of Anthropology, Harvard University, Cambridge, MA.

Li, Yung-ti. 2006. "On the Function of Cowries in Shang and Western Zhou China." *Journal of East Asian Archaeology* 5: 1–26.

Li Zhipeng, He Yuling, Jiang Yude (Roderick Campbell). 2011. "Yinxu wan Shang zhigu zuofang yu zhigu shougongye de yanjiu huigu yu tantao" [Research on Late Shang bone workshops and the bone working industry at Yinxu]. *Sandai Kaogu* 4: 471–80.

Li, Zhipeng, Roderick Campbell, Katherine Brunson, Jie Yang and Yang Tao. 2014. "The Exploitation of Domestic Animal Products from the Late Neolithic Age to the Early Bronze Age in the Heartland of Ancient China" in H. Greenfield (ed.), *New Perspectives on the Secondary Products Revolution* (Oxford: Oxbow), 56–79.

Lin Yun 1982. "Jiaguwen zhong de Shangdai fangguo lianmeng" [The Shang Dynasty Hegemonic Polity in the Oracle-bone Inscriptions]. *Guwenzi yanjiu* 6: 69–74.

Liu, Li and Chen Xingcan. 2000. "Cheng: Xia Shang shiqi dui ziran ziyuan de kongzhi wenti" ["Cities: Control of Natural Resources in the Xia and Shang Period"]. *Dongnan Wenhua* 3: 45–60.

Liu, Li and Chen Xingcan. 2001. "Cities and Towns: The Control of Natural Resources in Early States, China." *Bulletin of the Museum of Far Eastern Antiquities* 73: 5–47.

Liu, Li and Chen Xingcan. 2003. *State Formation in Early China*. London: Duckworth.

Liu, Li and Chen Xingcan. 2012. *The Archaeology of China: From the Late Paleolithic to the Early Bronze Age*. Cambridge: Cambridge University Press.

Liu Li, Chen Xingcan, and Li Baoping. 2007. "Non-state Crafts in the Early Chinese State: An Archaeological View from the Chinese Hinterland." *Indo-Pacific Prehistory Association Bulletin* 27: 93–102.

Qiu, Xigui. 1993. "Shuo Yinxu buci de 'dian': Shilun Shang ren chuzhi fushuzhe de yizhong Fangfa" [Concerning the word '*dian*' in the Oracle-bones: A Preliminary Discussion of a Shang Method of Disposing of Subjugated Peoples]. *Bulletin of the Institute of History and Philology, Academia Sinica* 64.3: 659–86.

Shandong Sheng Wenwu Kaogu Yanjiusuo, Beijing Daxue Zhongguo Kaoguxue Yanjiu Zhongxin, Shandong Shifan Daxue Qi-Lu Wenhua Yanjiu Zhongxin, and Binzhou Shi Wenwu Guanlichu. 2010a. "Shandong Yangxin Xian Liwu yizhi Shang dai yicun fajue jianbao." *Kaogu* 3: 3–17.

Shandong Sheng Wenwu Kaogu Yanjiusuo, Beijing Daxue Zhongguo Kaoguxue Yanjiu Zhongxin, and Shouguang Shi Wenwuju. 2010b. "Shandong Shouguang Shi Shuangwangcheng yanye yizhi 2008 nian de fajue." *Kaogu* 3: 18–36.

Shaughnessy, Edward. 1999. "Western Zhou History." In M. Loewe and E. Shaughnessy (eds.), *The Cambridge History of Ancient China: From the Origins of Civilization to 221 B.C.* (Cambridge: Cambridge University Press), 292–351.

Shen Chen. 1994. "Early Urbanization in the Eastern Zhou in China (770–221 B.C.): An Archaeological View." *Antiquity* 68: 724–44.

Smith, Michael. 2015. "The Aztec Empire." In A. Monson and W. Scheidel (eds.), *Fiscal Regimes and the Political Economy of Premodern States* (Cambridge: Cambridge University Press), 71–114.

Song Zhenhao. 1994. *Xia Shang shehui shenghuoshi*. 2 vols. Beijing: Zhongguo shehuikexue chubanshe.

Tang Jigen and Jing Zhicun. 2009. "Anyang de 'Shang yi' yu 'Da Yi Shang'" [Anyang's 'Shang settlements' and 'Great Settlement Shang']. *Kaogu* 9: 70–80.

Thorp, Robert. 2006. *China in the Early Bronze Age: Shang Civilization*. Philadelphia: University of Pennsylvania Press.

Trigger, Bruce. 2003. *Understanding Early Chinese Civilizations*. Cambridge: Cambridge University Press.

Underhill, Anne and Fang Hui. 2004. "Early State Economic Systems in China." In G. Feinman and L. Nichols (eds.), *Archaeological Perspectives on Political Economies* (Salt Lake City: University of Utah Press), 129–44.

Wheatley, Paul. 1971. *Pivot of the Four Quarters: A Preliminary Inquiry into the Origin and Character of the Ancient Chinese City*. Chicago: Aldine Publishing Company.

Yang Shengnan and Ma Jifan. 2010. *Shang dai jingji yu keji* [Shang dynasty economy and technology]. *Shang dai shi—juan liu*. Beijing: Zhongguo shehuikexue chubanshe.

Yu Fuwei and Ye Wansong. 1982–1983. "Zhongguo gudai dixia chuliang zhi yanji" [Research into China's ancient underground grain storage]. *Nongye kaogu* 1982: 2, 1983: 1, 2.

ZSKY = Zhongguo Shehuikexueyuan Kaogu Yanjiusuo. 2003. *Zhongguo Kaogu: Xia, Shang Juan* [Chinese Archaeology: the Xia and Shang]. Beijing: Zhongguo shehuikexue chubanshe.

ZSLY = Zhongguo Shehuikexueyuan Lishi Yanjiusuo. 1982. *Jiaguwen Heji*. Beijing: Zhonghua shuju.

3

Co-Option and Patronage

The Mechanics of Extraction in Southern Mesopotamia under the Third Dynasty of Ur

STEVEN GARFINKLE

Introduction: The Third Dynasty of Ur and State Power

The era of the Third Dynasty of Ur (2012–2004 BCE) in early Mesopotamia is generally known both for the abundance of its records and the supposed power of its centralized administration. This era witnessed an experiment in secondary state formation as the kings of Ur created and managed a territorial state that encompassed all of the traditional urban centers of southern Mesopotamia. More than 100,000 clay tablets survive from the Ur III period, and the great majority of these document the activities of the state and provincial administrations that managed the economy on behalf of the crown.[1]

The state that the kings built in this period was broadly extractive and directed the bulk of the goods produced by an active agrarian economy for use by élites who also managed much of the labor force through a ration system that bound many workers to the great institutional households. One consequence of this was the growth of tax farming as the crown used local professionals, especially merchants, to create greater efficiencies in the collection and distribution of resources and revenue. A second consequence of this was the creation of a parallel system of patronage, especially among military officials, to extract additional resources, largely through military campaigns, and further build up both the wealth of the crown and the new royal constituency.[2]

Using the copious textual record from both institutional and non-institutional households, this chapter explores the ways in which the state co-opted local systems and hierarchies and created new ones in order to direct resources towards the royal household. In this process, the royal family gained agency over a much broader community in southern Mesopotamia while also granting agency to traditional regional élites as well as to a new statewide élite bound directly to the royal family.

The Third Dynasty of Ur marked the second time in the late third millennium BCE that the many city-states of southern Mesopotamia were united into a single political community. The first experiment in larger state building, under the kings of Akkad in the 23rd century BCE, collapsed only a few generations after its creation by Sargon. The Third Dynasty of Ur was a similarly short-lived experiment in complex secondary state formation. From the time of its creation under Ur-Namma, the kingdom lasted 108 years and foundered during its third generation of rulers. In spite of its relatively short duration, the kingdom of the Third Dynasty of Ur occupies a significant place in our reconstructions of the history of early Mesopotamia. First, later rulers of Mesopotamia emulated the patterns of rule established by this kingdom. Echoes of the kings of Ur are found in the literature and actions of subsequent kings down to the end of the cuneiform tradition. Second, the abundant record keeping of the Ur III dynasts makes the century of their rule one of the best documented eras in all of antiquity. This period is famous for the vast number of its surviving texts. We have access to tens of thousands of texts from this kingdom in modern museums, libraries, and private collections; and this is but a fraction of the original number. Thousands of texts from this era continue to appear as a result of ongoing looting, as well as new excavations in Iraq today.

The tens of thousands of clay tablets that survive from the vast administrative archives of the Third Dynasty of Ur have made the study of this era central to examinations of the political economy of early Mesopotamia. The kings of Ur created a territorial state that extended from the Persian Gulf up through most of southern Mesopotamia. These kings also increased their influence over neighboring regions to the east, including Susa in modern Iran.

The sheer volume of extant texts from this era has convinced us not only that this was a highly organized state, but also that the central power of the state was absolute.[3] This view of the Third Dynasty of Ur greatly overestimates the nature of state control and its permanence. As I will detail below, the texts instead highlight the boundaries placed on the expansion of that authority. A first step towards understanding the limits of state power in this period is to recognize the character of the surviving archives and their limitations. The chronological distribution of the texts is not evenly spaced throughout the century of this dynasty's reign, but is instead concentrated in the middle years.[4] This period also coincided with the years during which the military power of the dynasty and its ability to extract tribute were at their height.

The texts are certainly evidence for the wealth of the royal household and its appropriation of resources for the crown and its clients, at least for a couple of generations.[5] This process relied on a charismatic royal élite working with literate administrators to exert control over materiel and people from both inside and outside of the borders of the fledgling state. This development was also part of the state-building process, as the production of texts allowed the kings of Ur to assert control over different parts of their kingdom and bring them together for the benefit of the royal élite. The tablets that document this work illustrate a multi-layered process to ensure the flow of goods into royal hands. At the same time, the archives from large provincial centers, like Umma and Girsu, reveal the ongoing importance of local and regional actors who continued to exercise power in the heartland of the kingdom, but whose efforts were co-opted by the crown.

In spite of the survival of such a rich documentary record, we are, of course, missing some crucial pieces, especially for the subject of our current investigation. The bulk of the surviving Ur III texts were found at the significant provincial centers of the kingdom, especially Umma, Girsu, and Nippur. Almost 70% of the tablets with a secure provenance originated in the institutional archives from Umma or Girsu. These records, demonstrate the state's efforts to extract wealth from the old urban centers and their hinterland; however, the sources from the provinces offer few specifics about the royal institutions that supervised these efforts.[6]

Significant archives also survive from some of the hubs of royal activity away from the capital, for example, from Puzriš-Dagan, which was established as a livestock distribution and storage center late in the reign of Šulgi, and from Iri-Sağrig, which was likely the staging point for the kingdom's frequent military forays into the eastern periphery.[7] The institutions of the newly forming territorial state can best be seen at these sites of state-directed activity and in the archives of wealthy estates created by court functionaries.[8] Records from the capital city of Ur, however, remain comparatively rare.[9] We lack the core royal archives that tracked the economy, and especially the military economy, from the perspective of the central administration. Therefore, even with the abundance of records to which we have access, our conclusions about the methods of extraction undertaken by the Ur III kings remain somewhat tentative.

The good news is that the abundance of records extensively documents the state's interactions with its core provinces, with its élites, and with a variety of professionals who accomplished the goals of the kingdom. These administrative records were so exhaustive that we can follow the activity of a specific craft workshop over the entirety of a given year, or we can follow a particular animal from its capture in the periphery to its slaughter in the kitchens of the king. Below, I will discuss the impetus for this extraordinary level of recordkeeping, but it would be a mistake to regard this as part of the growth of a state bureaucracy. The absence of rational bureaucratic mechanisms was one of the hallmarks of early states in Mesopotamia and elsewhere. At the same time, the crown and other large institutions in early Mesopotamia needed access to significant resources in order to fund state directed activities and maintain the infrastructure of the state. This infrastructure, which included canal maintenance as well as monumental building activity, was essential both to the economic viability of the urban communities of Mesopotamia and to the ideological goals of the state.

A key question is whether the growth of centralized power in Mesopotamia in the latter half of the third millennium BCE also expressed itself in the form of a state-directed economy. Our assumptions about the development of the state in Mesopotamian antiquity ordinarily call for the presence of a coercive authority that was able to exploit the economy ruthlessly for the benefit of the royal authority. Below, I will highlight not only the power of the Ur III state, but also the limitations on that coercive and extractive authority. In order to examine these processes, the remainder of this chapter is divided into two parts. First, we will examine the manner in which the kings of Ur redirected the existing redistributive economy of the provinces to allow the crown to centralize control of resources within the state. In this effort, the kings relied on local élites and professionals. Second, we will look at the ways in which the kings used patronage to create a parallel tributary economy to fund and maintain their goals.

Taxation and Local Professionals under the Third Dynasty of Ur

The kings of Ur created a large territorial state comprised of the numerous, and previously independent, city-states of southern Mesopotamia.[10] One of the characteristic features of this socio-political environment was the way in which local élites were already embedded in the administration of the key urban institutions, especially temples that controlled so much of the labor and land on which the subsistence economy depended. From the beginning of our historical records in the third millennium BCE, it is clear that Mesopotamian society placed great emphasis on family control and inheritance of positions and professions.

The early Mesopotamian economy also relied heavily on a large pool of dependent laborers that served the community both in the fields and as corvée labor to accomplish monumental projects such as canal maintenance and wall building.[11] This redistributive economy created the expectation that it was normative for the state to receive the lion's share of the agricultural produce. This was true for the earlier city-states, and they had developed mechanisms to handle this extraction of resources, but the scale increased dramatically with the growth of larger territorial kingdoms. Moreover, the state had to address the problem of collection and storage of bulk agricultural commodities. Merchants provided some of the solutions to these challenges, and their work was especially well documented. Merchants (Sumerian *dam-gar₃*) have attracted significant scholarly attention among Assyriologists.[12] They engaged in a wide range of activities, but trade was their primary professional responsibility. The merchants arranged for the purchase or sale of commodities on behalf of their clients, and the agrarian economy of Mesopotamia made them indispensable.

Merchants are an important category of people for any discussion of taxation in the Ur III period because of their role as intermediaries on behalf of the growing power of the state. Merchants were deeply engaged in transactions on behalf of the *bala*, which was the chief instrument for the collection of "taxes" from the provinces.[13] The import of copper and other strategic materials was also left in the hands of merchants and other traders throughout early Mesopotamia. The reliance of the state on these individuals demonstrates the value of their specialized knowledge and the symbiotic relationship between their enterprise and the growth of the kingdoms of early Mesopotamia. Long distance trade was a critical arena for commercial activity, but in spite of its cultural, and even literary, significance, the scale of such trade was always dwarfed by local exchange.[14]

In order to function effectively, the households of ancient Mesopotamia had to be able to dispose of their surplus in exchange for necessary goods. This was the case for all but the smallest households under the Third Dynasty of Ur. Hence, we find merchants acting on behalf of fisherman, handling the sale of their catch and the payment of their taxes to the central authority, and we see merchants acting on behalf of large institutions, such as the temples and the palace, selling their excess produce and acquiring necessary goods. Often, the institutions relied on the merchants for the continued operation of their workshops as well as their agrarian endeavors. This was especially the case for workshops that required raw materials not locally available in Mesopotamia. The merchants were able to exercise a great deal of autonomy, despite growing centralization, because their hierarchies were the result of regional and traditional professional organizations that operated beyond the direct control of the crown.

As the size of the state expanded under the kings of Ur, so did its interest in the economy. In order to manage their growing economies more efficiently, the central authorities used the merchants not only to procure necessary trade goods and exchange products grown on their estates, but also to collect the taxes owed to the crown.[15] The activities of these merchants on behalf of the palace in the late third millennium BCE can be described as tax farming. Tax farming is an arrangement in which the state sells the right to collect taxes to individuals or groups. Much of the evidence for this comes from the provincial archives at Umma and Girsu. The *damgars* were intimately involved with the *bala* system. The *bala* functioned in the broadest sense as an office of central taxation for the Ur III state.[16] The Sumerian word *bala* has the meaning "term of office" and it was used to describe the periods for which a province of the state owed resources to crown.[17] In general, the provinces of the Ur III kingdom were assigned a month during which they had to deliver their produce. This produce was often in the form of bulk commodities like barley, but it could include regionally specific products as well.[18] Girsu, as a very large and prosperous region, was assigned two *bala* months. The merchants, as a result of their professional responsibilities, were involved with the *bala* system at both the local and the state levels. At the local level, the merchants helped the provincial authorities arrange for their *bala* payments, and at the state level the merchants collected the *bala* resources and in some cases administered accounts on its behalf.[19]

There is direct evidence that the merchants of Girsu were involved in making collections for the *bala*. A group of Girsu documents lists transactions undertaken for the *bala* (*bala-še₃* in Sumerian).[20] In these texts, merchants delivered silver for the *bala*, and other merchants most often made the collections. The merchants then delivered the silver to the central administration. For the best documented year from which we find these texts, Amar-Suen 5, the merchants of Girsu appear to have provided a set amount that was due in the twelfth month of the year. The regularity of the payments made for the *bala* in Amar-Suen 5 may represent a negotiated fee owed by the merchants that corresponded to their tax farming role. Numerous other texts document the delivery by merchants of silver or commodities to their clients, but these payments appear to be the delivery of a fixed commitment. Moreover, the size of the payments made by individual merchants paralleled their placement within the organization of merchants. Most of the merchants who delivered larger payments were elsewhere identified in texts as overseers (*ugula* in Sumerian) supervising the work of other merchants.[21] The silver most often passed from one merchant to another more senior merchant. The management of this system was in the hands of the merchants themselves within a professional hierarchy most often organized along familial lines.

Unfortunately, the brevity of the *bala-še₃* texts makes it difficult for us to establish the precise nature of the transactions that they record, but the prosopographic connections in these texts allow us to draw some further conclusions. A prominent individual named Lu-Utu was a frequent recipient of silver for the *bala* from the merchants. We encounter Lu-Utu in a number of additional texts that recorded significant deliveries of silver by merchants.[22] The amounts of silver in these texts may indicate a consolidation of smaller deliveries or the results of larger transactions undertaken on his behalf by the merchants. Lu-Utu occupied a significant place in the provincial administration at Girsu organizing the activity of the merchants on behalf of the governor. Numerous texts record Lu-Utu's receipt of significant amounts of grain from the governor and his transfer of that grain to merchants in exchange for silver.[23]

Current data do not allow us to state definitively what was really meant by *bala-še$_3$*; but these documents are likely evidence for tax farming by the Ur III merchants. In an environment in which most of the payments made to the *bala* were paid in kind, the crown needed the merchants to collect some of these commodities and convert them to silver. The expertise and cooperation of these local professionals was required in order for the royal household to extract resources efficiently from the local economies.

Patronage and Royal Authority under the Third Dynasty of Ur

Above I have discussed the manner in which the royal household used the pre-existing local networks to divert significant resources from the provincial agricultural economies for centralized use through the *bala*. At the same time, an enormous amount of wealth was created through the military activities of the crown. Indeed, the capture of tribute and booty from the periphery was essential to the state building activities of the kings of Ur. This process was also directly related to a system of patronage that allowed the kings to extract even more resources from this process.

As we have seen, the imposition of centralized authority by the royal household did not displace local and regional hierarchies and mechanisms of extraction. This posed two problems for the crown. First, the royal household needed to find ways to create larger notions of community that would bind élites to the new, larger idea of political community rather than to their traditional city-states.[24] Second, the scale of the economy and the new economic endeavors of the crown required the creation of new administrative structures to guarantee the kings their share of this revenue. The new economic endeavors to which I am referring arose from the kingdom's regular campaigns in the periphery that generated enormous wealth from booty and tribute during the heyday of the dynasty.

The effort to create a statewide community loyal to the crown focused on the same groups that helped the kings to collect resources. These were chiefly merchants and members of the military, along with royal officials, like messengers. Some of the key attributes of these groups were their mobility, i.e., they traveled more regularly both within the kingdom and out into the periphery, and the fact that they owed some of their prominence and wealth to the favor they received from the crown. Quite often these individuals already occupied privileged positions in their regional hierarchies, but they enjoyed much greater prominence as a result of their connection to the royal household. Perhaps the best example of this is the figure of Šu-kabta, who controlled a large agricultural estate at Garšana in Umma province.[25] Šu-kabta came from a family of doctors, but he ultimately comes to our attention as a general and a spouse of the royal princess Simat-Ištaran.[26] The process by which real space was carved out of the kingdom for its functionaries was also made clear in the prologue to the Laws of Ur-Namma, in the course of which, the king proclaimed, "I settled (in independent settlements?) my generals, my mothers, my brothers, and their families . . ."[27]

This expansion of the power of the king and his functionaries came at some expense to local officials and aided in the increased extraction of resources for the crown. In a well-documented case, the authority of these royal officials trumped that of governors and other provincial élites. A text from Umma records a dispute between the governor of Umma and Šu-Kabta's estate at Garšana concerning the harvesting of timber in a forest in Umma province.[28] In this case the governor sought to assert his control over the resources within his province against the interests of the general's estate. The general's lieutenants were apparently able to shield the suspected thief within his household and retain the timber.

The kings of Ur oversaw the creation of a new royal élite that became invested in a tributary economy in which they sought royal patronage, were rewarded with offices, and in turn transferred great wealth to the royal household. This process is especially visible in the texts that document the military activities of the kings of Ur. Numerous royal inscriptions and year names attest to the importance that the dynasty assigned to its wars. The Ur III kingdom as we know it was a consequence of the social and economic effects of a state of near constant warfare.[29] The militarism of the kings led to the creation of great wealth and great responsibilities, and to an increased role for the army both abroad and at court.

The regularity with which the armies of Ur campaigned in the east was both an ideological and economic imperative for the kings of the dynasty. The kings and their administrators devoted a great deal of attention to the results of their military adventures. These raids across the frontier played a critical role in the emerging view of the territorial kingdom put forward by Ur-Namma, Šulgi, and their successors. Creating a statewide community of élites bound not to their local political community but to the household of the king ultimately relied on both the projection of martial success and the acquisition of resources that came with that success. In this way, as I will detail below, the kings or Ur not only extracted significant wealth from peripheral areas beyond their frontier, but they also levied tribute within the kingdom from the élites who profited from these campaigns alongside the king.[30] Therefore, the constant warfare of the kingdom achieved multiple goals. First, the defeat of outside forces reinforced key aspects of royal self-representation. Second, military victories, especially in the east, ensured greater access to, and control over, key trade routes and pasture lands.[31] Finally, and perhaps most significantly for the purposes of this examination, the emphasis on military success gave wealth and opportunity to the growing statewide élite tied directly to the royal court at Ur. The extraction of resources from this emerging group was also a significant source of wealth for the crown, which oversaw the delivery of goods in a tributary economy that also allowed royal functionaries to provide direct evidence of their loyalty.

Late in the reign of Šulgi, the crown established Puzriš-Dagan as the primary depot and redistribution center that handled much of the tribute, primarily in livestock, delivered to royal authority. The royal administrators recorded several types of deliveries related to royal military activity: booty texts;[32] the delivery of tribute from dependent areas;[33] and the frequent offerings of often single animals by individuals associated with the royal and military sector.[34] This has left behind a dense historical record documenting the tributary economy that ran parallel to the extraction of resources from the provinces and their traditional redistributive networks. The third category of delivery, in which a group of people,[35] from a handful to several dozen, each delivered animals, most often one lamb, provides rich evidence for the extraction of wealth from the royal élite and its documentation by officials at Puzriš-Dagan. Over a thousand examples of these deliveries survive in the extant archives, and most of these can be correlated with the military activities of the kingdom.[36] *Ontario* 1 128 is a representative example of this category of text:

Obverse

1. 3 sila$_4$ Lugal-a$_2$-zi-da sabra
2. 2 sila$_4$ da-da ensi$_2$
3. 1 sila$_4$ Zu-hu-tum nu-banda$_3$
4. 1 sila$_4$ Lu$_2$-^{d}Nanna dumu Inim-^{d}Šara$_2$
5. 1 sila$_4$ Nam-ha-ni sabra
6. 1 sila$_4$ Lu$_2$-^{d}Suen dam-gar$_3$
7. 1 sila$_4$ A-ab-ba-mu dam-gar$_3$
8. 1 sila$_4$ Ku$_3$-^{d}Nanna dam-gar$_3$
9. 1 sila$_4$ Lugal-an-ne$_2$ dam-gar$_3$
10. 1 sila$_4$ Lu$_2$-^{d}En-lil$_2$-la$_2$ dam-gar$_3$
11. 1 sila$_4$ Lu$_2$-^{d}Nin-šubur

Reverse

1. 1 sila$_4$ Ku$_5$-da-mu
2. 1 sila$_4$ Hu-un-^{d}Šul-gi
3. 1 sila$_4$ Šu-Eš$_4$-tar$_2$
4. 1 sila$_4$ Lugal-a$_2$-zi-da
5. 1 maš$_2$ Lu$_2$-ama-na di-ku$_5$
6. mu-ku$_x$ lugal
7. In-ta-e$_3$-a i$_3$-dab$_5$
8. giri$_3$ Nu-ur$_2$-^{d}Suen dub-sar
9. u$_4$ 13-kam
10. iti a$_2$-ki-ti

11. mu us$_2$-sa ^{d}Šu-^{d}Suen
12. lugal Uri$_5^{ki}$-ma-ke$_4$
13. bad$_3$ mar-tu Mu-ri-/iq-Ti-id-ni-im mu-du$_3$

Left Edge
    19 udu

TRANSLATION

3 lambs from Lugalazida, šabra;[37] 2 lambs from Dada, the governor; 1 lamb from Zuhutum, the captain; 1 lamb from Lu-Nanna, son of Inim-šara; 1 lamb from Namhani, šabra; 1 lamb from Lu-Suen, the merchant; 1 lamb from Ku-Nanna, the merchant; 1 lamb from Lugalanne, the merchant; 1 lamb from Lu-Enlila, the merchant; 1 lamb from Lu-Ninšubur; 1 lamb from Kudamu; 1 lamb from Hun-Šulgi; 1 lamb from Šu-Eštar; 1 lamb from Lugalazida; 1 goat from Luamna, the judge; delivery for the king, received by Intaea, conveyed by Nur-Suen, the scribe, the thirteenth day of the seventh month, year after the year: Šu-Suen, king of Ur, built the Amorite wall "Muriq-Tidnim" (ŠS 5). 19 sheep (total).

The individuals on these delivery lists represent some of the most significant professions associated with royal activity in the Ur III period. Often, the lists bring together courtiers from all over the kingdom who were connected through their service directly to the crown. These texts illustrate several important developments. First, the royal court was creating new paths to status and wealth, and we see this with the appearance on these lists of military officers, judges, royal messengers, and merchants alongside traditional urban élites, like governors and estate managers.[38] These individuals gained access to the spoils of foreign campaigns either in the course of the campaigns themselves or in their roles as processors of those spoils. Therefore, their service to the crown was rewarded through access to resources. Second, these officials, in turn, dedicated some of these resources to the crown through the delivery of animals documented in these texts. Their participation here reinforced their allegiance to the royal household and justified their privileged status. The fact that these deliveries connected them with the sacred, sacrificial economy of offerings also involved them directly in pious economic activity intended to aid the state. Finally, all of these factors combined to provide the kings of Ur with an additional avenue of resource extraction.

We find these same groups of people appearing together not only at Puzriš-Dagan, but also in other locales directly related to the establishment of statewide royal authority, such as the royal estate at Garšana and at Iri-Saĝrig, which was likely the staging point for many of the campaigns into the east. Our texts suggest that these places were filled with soldiers, royal messengers, captains, generals, merchants, and other personnel whose professional careers provided them with new opportunities outside of the old urban centers and their established local economies. Significantly, these lists show an additional important manner in which the kings extracted resources from their community. The foreign raids brought significant booty directly into the hands of the crown.

The requirement that élites also regularly donated livestock to the king meant that the royal household could lay claim to the fruits of military adventures more than once in an ongoing fashion. While each of these lists may document a modest contribution from élite households, the sum total of the group donations indicates an enormous extraction of tribute by the kings from the Mesopotamian élite. This was an arrangement in which these households also exercised some socio-economic agency as they became clients of the royal household and ensured their continued enjoyment of privilege. Of course, this system relied not only on the continued participation of the élite, but also, perhaps more importantly, on the ability of the kings to continue to campaign effectively beyond the kingdom's frontiers. For this reason, we find our evidence for this tributary economy drying up late in the reign of Šu-Suen as the kings of Ur struggled to maintain their military ascendancy across the Zagros mountains and their control of the cities of southern Mesopotamia.

My analysis has focused on evidence for the mechanics of resource extraction under the Third Dynasty of Ur. At the level of the individual household, this evidence primarily records élite activity, as those were the individuals whose transactions required documentation. As I have made clear, this was a two-way process. Not only did the texts detail delivery of wealth to the crown, but they also enshrined the participation of élites in this process in ways that clearly conveyed both social and economic benefits to those notables as part of the kingdom's efforts to create loyalty and community on a scale that incorporated all of the historic urban centers in southern Mesopotamia. The great numbers of dependent laborers who toiled on behalf of the kingdom seldom appear in discrete ways in our texts. Of course, we must remember that most of these individuals had their work and labor taxed through the traditional redistributive mechanisms at work in the provinces. At the same time, our focus mirrors that of the Ur III kings since the wealth created by the expansion of the state was concentrated in the hands of the royal élite. The administrative record from this era indicates that real wages, both distributed as rations and for hired labor, remained essentially constant throughout this period.[39]

The crown in this era was good at extracting resources from the populace, both at home and abroad, and at diverting those resources to the growing royal family and its clients. Clearly, the royal household showed considerable energy and enjoyed great success in directing these endeavors; however, the kings still relied on local and regional élites who could be co-opted as clients. A large scribal administration came into existence to document these activities. These administrators had to ensure that the resources were being registered and properly distributed and that clients received appropriate credit for their contributions. The vast extant archives are proof of the success of the court and its patronage in this tributary economy, but this success was temporary.

The ability of the crown to extract resources in this way was based on the power of the institution of kingship and on the military successes of those kings. In the end, it relied more on their personal agency than on the creation of new centralized agencies and institutions to directly oversee important state functions like taxation. I am suggesting that the provincial economies remained broadly redistributive and regional, and that the Ur III kings used existing mechanisms to redirect this system to benefit the court at Ur. At the same time, these kings introduced a parallel tributary economy to fund their larger statewide goals and build a statewide royal (and loyal) constituency. The enormous administrative archives of the Third Dynasty of Ur are evidence for the success of these endeavors as well as indications of their limited scope and endurance.

What we find, in the end, is a "low power" state whose ability to extract resources was tied to its dexterity in creating and controlling access to resources.[40]

NOTES

1 For a detailed description of the corpus, see Molina 2008 and see the database of Neo-Sumerian texts at: http://bdtns.filol.csic.es. The period of the Third Dynasty of Ur is unique in early Mesopotamia for the large number of administrative texts that survive along with a literary corpus and royal inscriptions. More administrative texts are coming to light from the preceding eras of the Third Millennium, but the numbers available for the last century of that long era dwarf any comparable early corpora.

2 Taxation is difficult to define in modern terms in the context of early efforts at secondary state formation in Mesopotamia. Here I consider taxation to be the process by which the crown used compulsory systems to extract resources from the state's inhabitants in order to transfer wealth to the royal household and to fund state activities. Numerous mechanisms of extraction were used including those based on the traditional redistributive economies of the earlier city-states out of which the rulers of Ur formed their kingdom. This was in addition to the extraction of enormous amounts of labor through the corvée system (see Steinkeller 2013 and 2015). I will also suggest below that the kings of Ur created a vast system of patronage in which élites bound themselves to the royal household in a reciprocal process that allowed for the crown's élite clients to gain access to wealth and office in the new statewide community. In turn, those élite clients then dedicated a portion of their newly acquired wealth back to the crown.

3 This image of the Ur III state continues to dominate more general treatments of Mesopotamia, but it is increasingly being questioned by specialists; see Yoffee 2005 and 2013, and Michalowski 2004 and 2013. This view results not only from the appearance of power demonstrated by the tens of thousands of surviving administrative documents, but also, as Michalowski (see 2011 and 2013) notes, from the representations—or better, self-representations—of power in the surviving royal inscriptions and hymns. Yoffee (2005: 147) summed this up as follows: "The quantity and quality of these sources from the royal house of Ur motivate scholarship today in roughly inverse proportion to the stability and normative character of the Ur III state."

4 See, for example, Molina 2008: 47. The surviving archives overwhelmingly date from the second half of Šulgi's reign down to the first years of the reign of Ibbi-Suen, a period of roughly 50 years.

5 The term "clients" refers both to élites within the kingdom and along its boundaries who sought the patronage of the kings of Ur.

6 See Sharlach 2004 for a detailed description of the *bala* system through which the central administration extracted resources from the provinces for crown use; see also Sigrist 1992.

7 For Drehem, see Sigrist 1992; for Iri-Saĝrig see Owen 2013. In the view of this author, the concept of the capital was somewhat fluid. Ur was the dynasty's home and the ideological center of the community.

8 The best example of such a wealthy estate is Garšana, a large household established in Umma province for a royal princess and her husband, a general in the crown's military establishment. For Garšana, see Owen and Mayr 2007; Kleinerman and Owen 2009; Heimpel 2009; and Owen 2011.

9 In practical terms, the capital was wherever the king and the court resided. Numerous royal officials maintained estates and residences in other important urban centers, such as Nippur. As the military activity of the kings of Ur increased in the east, royal staging centers, such as Iri-Saĝrig, took on even greater importance as the sites of royal activity.

10 The kings of Ur presided over the second attempt at such a unification of the southern Mesopotamian city-states in the second half of the third millennium BCE. The dynasty created by Sargon of Akkad had collapsed roughly a century earlier. For a recent treatment of Sargon's dynasty, see Foster 2016.

11 Many of the urban professionals, such as merchants and smiths, were also subject to periodic corvée obligations alongside the dependent laborers. On corvée labor in the Ur III period, see Steinkeller 2013 and 2015.

12 There is a long bibliography on merchants in early Mesopotamia, see, for example, Leemans 1950; Oppenheim 1954; Curtis and Hallo 1959; Foster 1977, 1985, and 1997; Powell 1977; Snell 1977, 1982, 1988, and 1991; Neumann 1979, 1992, 1993, and 1999; Englund 1990: 13–55; Zettler 1992: 220–6; Steinkeller 2002 and 2004; Garfinkle 2004, 2008, and 2010; Feuerherm 2010. Discussions of merchants typically include related professions, such as the Sumerian *ga-raš*, who likely traveled abroad on trade missions, and the Akkadian *alik Telmun* of the early Old Babylonian period who traveled to the Persian Gulf. The merchants themselves were more closely associated with the trade that took place within Mesopotamia and involved the exchange of bulk commodities for silver and other goods.

13 Below I will suggest that some of this activity constituted tax farming. On the bala system, see the following discussion, and see Sharlach 2004. The bala was system based on existing forms of administration in the core provinces of the kingdom (made up of the previously independent city-states like Umma and Girsu), that allowed the state to draw upon those resources in rotation as they were fed from the provincial economies into the state's storehouses and coffers. Significantly, the booty and tribute acquired through the kings' campaigns to the east added greatly to the wealth directed towards the crown's administration, for which see section 3 below.

14 See Foster 1977 and Van De Mieroop 2002.

15 This situation has long been recognized for the succeeding Old Babylonian
period: "The material from Larsa shows that under the Babylonian occupation of
the south the palace used the merchants extensively to collect taxes and to market
the surpluses produced on palace owned land" (Van De Mieroop 1992: 203).

16 See Sharlach 2004.

17 See *PSD* B 65.

18 We find this regional specialization already in the Sargonic period; see Foster
1977: 38–39.

19 This process is made apparent, for example, in the archive of Turam-ili, who was
an overseer of merchants heavily involved with transactions on behalf of the bala.
Turam-ili's archive indicates contacts throughout the Ur III state; see Garfinkle
2002 and 2008.

20 See Sharlach 2004 and Garfinkle 2010.

21 For more on the regional organizations of the merchants in the Ur III period, see
Garfinkle 2008 and 2010.

22 In *BPOA* 1 148 (AS 4), Lu-Utu received 1 *mana* and 10 *gin*$_2$ of silver from Lu-
Kinunir; in *BPOA* 1 190 (AS 4), Lu-Utu received nearly 4 *mana* of silver from
Ur-Bau and Ibni-ili; and in *SNAT* 24 (AS 6), Lu-Utu received 1 *mana* 11 2/3 *gin*$_2$
from Ur-guenna. The latter text includes a notation that this delivery covered six
months of Amar-Suen 6.

23 See, for example, *MVN* 6 159 (Š 36), which recorded Lu-Utu's receipt of 270 *gur*
of grain from the governor. *ITT* 5 6760 (ŠS 4) and 6776 (ŠS 4) both show Lu-Utu
receiving silver for grain from merchants.

24 This was a pressing concern in light of the earlier failure of Sargon and his successors to disrupt the local allegiances in southern Mesopotamia that re-emerged
with the collapse of the kingdom of Akkad. Moreover, the kings of Ur had to
do this without undermining the traditional views of inheritance and property
rights, since the continuation of their own dynasty relied on the same mechanisms.

25 See note 8 above.

26 For Šu-kabta's family, see Kleinerman 2011. Šu-kabta came from a prominent family that included royal courtiers.

27 Roth 1997.

28 Molina 2010: 210.

29 For a discussion of constant warfare in the Ur III state, see Michalowski 2011 and
Garfinkle 2014. All of our sources send a consistent message about the importance
of warfare, and we find extensive evidence for the prominence of warfare, and
its economic significance, in royal inscriptions, year names, and administrative
texts. Between Šulgi 20 and Ibbi-Suen 8, 24 years were named directly for military
activity. During this same era, a further 20 years were named for previous campaigns (the mu-us$_2$-sa "year after the year" formulae). For a list of the year names,
see Sigrist and Gomi 1991: 319–29; an online version of this list can be found at the
Cuneiform Digital Library Initiative: www.cdli.ucla.edu. The majority of years Be-

tween Šulgi 20 and Ibbi-Suen 8 refer to the defeat of foreign cities and lands. Text production increased alongside the annual campaigns of the kings and reached its peak between Šulgi 44 and Ibbi-Suen 2, when the kingdom was accustomed to regular success in its raids across the state's frontier to the east and northeast. This pattern of surviving texts correlated with increased military activity may result from the accident of discovery, but Adams (2009: 2) noted that this picture is not likely to be radically altered by new discoveries. The chronological distribution of texts in newly discovered archives, like those of Garšana and Iri-Saĝrig, also accords well with the patterns previously observed in the corpus.

30 Soldiers and functionaries returned from campaigns with significant amounts of booty and tribute, especially in small cattle. The crown was able to further extract resources from these groups when they were required to dedicate some of these animals to the kings, see below and see Garfinkle 2015.

31 Virtually all references to the kings of Ur noted their status as mighty warriors. Success in the wild lands beyond the frontier made these claims real. Moreover, the emerging motif of the king as shepherd was doubly reinforced through the annual campaigns as the kings not only protected their lands (and pasturelands) from the outside world, but they also brought back more sheep as booty.

32 See Lafont 2009 and Garfinkle 2014.

33 See Michalowski 1978, Steinkeller 1991, and Maeda 1992.

34 For delivery of animals, acquired through military activity, to Puzriš-Dagan, see also Allred 2006: 67–72.

35 I avoid using gendered language here since women also featured among the notables delivering animals to the king. The overwhelming majority of people listed on these texts were men, but this was not always the case; see Sigrist 1995: 86–7.

36 The greatest concentration of these texts comes from the latter part of Šulgi's reign, the reign of Amar-Suen, and the early years of Šu-Suen. These years correspond directly to significant campaigns documented in the year names, and to the greatest eras of the dynasty's military successes.

37 Šabra was a title held by the chief administrator of a household, often temples or other institutions.

38 Indeed, this process included "foreigners" who were allies of the crown, (Amorites, for example) and members of the royal family. For example, the list recorded on *BIN* 3 538 (Amar-Suen 5) began with several prominent Amorites, including Naplanum, followed by a collection of governors, *šabras*, merchants, etc.; *Ontario* 1 135 (Šu-Suen 2) included deliveries from merchants, a governor, a *šabra*, a captain, and two prominent figures at court and on campaign: Babati and Ṣilluš-Dagan.

39 Labor was often in short supply during the bottlenecks in the agricultural cycle, but there is little evidence that this allowed the laborers themselves to benefit. The antichretic loans of this period (loans in which property or service, most often labor, was provided as debt service) make clear that the real beneficiaries were

the élites, occasionally military officers, who controlled access to laborers; see Garfinkle 2012: 60–65.

40 On "low power" states in early Mesopotamia, see Richardson 2012 and 2017.

WORKS CITED

Adams, Robert McC. 2009. "Old Babylonian Networks of Urban Notables." *CDLJ* 2009: 7. http://www.cdli.ucla.edu/pubs/cdlj/2009/cdlj2009_007.html. Last accessed October 5, 2020.

Allred, Lance. 2006. "Cooks and Kitchens: Centralized Food Production in Late Third Millennium Mesopotamia." PhD dissertation. Johns Hopkins University. Baltimore, MD.

Ando, Clifford and Seth Richardson (eds.). 2017. *Ancient States and Infrastructural Power: Europe, Asia, and America*. Philadelphia: University of Pennsylvania Press.

Curtis, John B. and William W. Hallo. 1959. "Money and Merchants in Ur III." *HUCA* 30: 103–39.

Englund, Robert K. 1990. *Organisation und Verwaltung der Ur III-Fischerei*. Berlin: Dietrich Reimer Verlag.

Feuerherm, Karljürgen. 2010. "The Tamkar Network from Ur III to Rim-Sîn." *Journal of the Canadian Society for Mesopotamian Studies* 5: 5–12.

Foster, Benjamin R. 1977. "Commercial Activity in Sargonic Mesopotamia," *Iraq* 39: 31–44.

Foster, Benjamin R. 1985. "Selected business Documents from Sargonic Mesopotamia." *Journal of Cuneiform Studies* 35: 147–75.

Foster, Benjamin R. 1997. "A Sumerian merchant's account of the Dilmun trade." *Acta Sumerologica* 19: 53–62.

Foster, Benjamin R. 2016. *The Age of Agade*. London: Routledge.

Garfinkle, Steven J. 2002. "Turam-ili and the Community of Merchants in the Ur III Period." *Journal of Cuneiform Studies* 54: 29–48.

Garfinkle, Steven J. 2004. "Shepherds, Merchants, and Credit: Some Observations on Lending Practices in Ur III Mesopotamia." *JESHO* 47: 1–30.

Garfinkle, Steven J. 2008. "Silver and Gold: Merchants and the Economy of the Ur III State." In P. Michalowski (ed.), *On Ur III Times: Studies in Honor of Marcel*. Journal of Cuneiform Studies Supplementary Studies 1. (Boston: American Schools of Oriental Research), 63–70.

Garfinkle, Steven J. 2010. "Merchants and State Formation in Early Mesopotamia." In A. Slotsky and S. Melville (eds.), *Opening the Tablet Box: Near Eastern Studies in Honor of Benjamin R. Foster* (Leiden: Brill), 185–202.

Garfinkle, Steven J. 2012. *Entrepreneurs and Enterprise in Early Mesopotamia: A Study of Three Archives from the Third Dynasty of Ur (2112–2004 BC)*. CUSAS Volume 22. Bethesda, MD: CDL Press.

Garfinkle, Steven J. 2014. "The Economy of Warfare in Southern Iraq at the End of the Third Millennium BC." In H. Neumann et al (eds.), *Krieg und Frieden im Alten*

Vorderasien, Proceedings of the 52ᵉ Rencontre Assyriologique Internationale. Alter Orient und Altes Testament Band 401 (Münster: Ugarit-Verlag), 353–62.

Garfinkle, Steven J. 2015. "Ur III Administrative Texts: Building Blocks of State Community." In P. Delnero and J. Lauinger (eds.), *Texts and Contexts* (Berlin: De Gruyter), 143–65.

Heimpel, Wolfgang. 2009. *Workers and Construction Work at Garšana.* CUSAS 5. Bethesda, MD: CDL Press.

Kleinerman, Alexandra and David I. Owen. 2009. *Analytical Concordance to the Garšana Archives.* CUSAS 4. Bethesda, MD: CDL Press.

Kleinerman, Alexandra. 2011. "Doctor Šu-Kabta's Family Practice." In D. I. Owen (ed.), *Garšana Studies.* CUSAS 6. (Bethesda, MD: CDL Press), 177–81.

Lafont, Bertrand. 2009. "The Army of the Kings of Ur: The Textual Evidence." *CDLJ* 2009.

Leemans, W. F. 1950. *The Old-Babylonian Merchant, His Business and His Social Position.* Leiden: Brill.

Maeda, Tohru. 1992. "The Defense Zone During the Rule of the Ur III Dynasty." *ASJ* 14: 135–172.

Michalowski, Piotr. 1978. "Foreign Tribute to Sumer in the Ur III Period." *ZA* 68: 34–39.

Michalowski, Piotr. 2004. "The Ideological Foundations of the Ur III State." In W. Meyer and W. Sommerfeld (eds.), *2000 v. Chr. Politische, wirtschaftliche und kuturelle Entwicklung im Zeichen einer Jahrtausendwende. 3 Internationales Colloquium de Deutschen Orient-Gesellschaft 4.–7. April 2000 in Frankfurt/ Main und Marburg/ Lahn* (Saarbrücken: SDV), 219–35.

Michalowski, Piotr. 2011. *The Correspondence of the Kings of Ur: An Epistolary History of an Ancient Mesopotamian Kingdom.* Winona Lake, IN: Eisenbrauns.

Michalowski, Piotr. 2013. "Networks of Authority and Power in Early Mesopotamia." In S. Garfinkle and M. Molina (eds.), *From the 21st Century BC to the 21st Century AD. Proceedings of the International Conference on Neo-Sumerian Studies held in Madrid, July 22–24, 2010* (Winona Lake, IN: Eisenbrauns), 169–205.

Molina, Manuel. 2008. "The Corpus of Neo-Sumerian Tablets: an overview." In S. J. Garfinkle and J. C. Johnson (eds.), *The Growth of an Early State in Mesopotamia: Studies in Ur III Administration* (BPOA 5. Madrid: CSIC), 19–54.

Molina, Manuel. 2010. "Court Records from Umma." In A. Kleinerman and J. Sasson (eds.), *Why Should Someone Who Knows Something Conceal It? Cuneiform Studies in Honor of David I. Owen on his 70ᵗʰ Birthday* (Bethesda, MD: CDL Press), 201–17.

Neumann, Hans. 1979. "Handel und Handler in der Zeit der III. Dynastie von Ur." *AoF* 6: 15–67.

Neumann, Hans. 1992. "Zur privaten Geschäftstätigkeit in Nippur in der Ur III-Zeit." In M. de Jong Ellis (ed.), *Nippur at the Centennial: Papers Read as the 35ᵉ Rencontre Assyriologique Internationale, Philadelphia, 1988* (Philadelphia: Occasional Publications of the Samuel Noah Kramer Fund), 161–76.

Neumann, Hans. 1993. "Zu den Geschäften des Kaufmanns Ur-Dumuzida aus Umma." *AoF* 20: 69–86.

Neumann, Hans. 1999. "Ur-Dumuzida and Ur-Dun: Reflections on the Relationship between State-Initiated Foreign Trade and Private Economic Activity in Mesopotamia towards the End of the Third Millennium BC." In *Trade and Finance in Ancient Mesopotamia* (Istanbul: Nederlands Historisch-Archeologisch Institut), 43–53.

Oppenheim, A. Leo. 1954. "The Seafaring Merchants of Ur." *Journal of the American Oriental Society* 74: 6–17.

Owen, David I. (ed.). 2011. *Garšana Studies*. CUSAS 6. Bethesda, MD: CDL Press.

Owen, David I. 2013. *Cuneiform Texts Primarily from Iri-Saĝrig/ Āl-Šarrākī and the History of the Ur III Period, Volume I Commentary and Indexes*. Bethesda, MD: CDL Press.

Owen, David I. and Rudolf H. Mayr. 2007. *The Garšana Archives*. CUSAS 3. Bethesda, MD: CDL Press.

Powell, Marvin A. 1977. "Sumerian Merchants and the Problem of Profit." *Iraq* 39: 23–30.

Richardson, Seth. 2012. "Early Mesopotamia: The Presumptive State." *Past & Present* 215: 3–49.

Richardson, Seth. 2017. "Before Things Worked: A 'Low-Power' Model of Early Mesopotamia." In *Ancient States and Infrastructural Power: Europe, Asia, and America*, edited by C. Ando and S. Richardson. Philadelphia: University of Pennsylvania Press: 17–62.

Roth, Martha T. 1997. *Law Collections from Mesopotamia and Asia Minor*. 2nd Edition. Atlanta: Scholars Press.

Sharlach, Tonia. 2004. *Provincial Taxation and the Ur III State*. Leiden: Brill.

Sigrist, Marcel. 1992. *Drehem*. Bethesda, MD: CDL Press.

Sigrist, Marcel. 1995. *Neo-Sumerian Texts from the Royal Ontario Museum, I*. Bethesda, MD: CDL Press.

Sigrist, Marcel and Tohru Gomi. 1991. *The Comprehensive Catalogue of Published Ur III Tablets*. Bethesda, MD: CDL Press.

Snell, Daniel C. 1977. "The Activities of some Merchants of Umma." *Iraq* 39: 45–50.

Snell, Daniel C. 1982. *Ledgers and Prices: Early Mesopotamian Balanced Accounts*. New Haven: Yale University Press.

Snell, Daniel C. 1988. "The Allocation of resources in the Umma Silver Account System." *JESHO* 31: 1–13.

Snell, Daniel C. 1991. "Marketless Trading in Our Time." *JESHO* 39: 129–41.

Steinkeller, Piotr. 1991. "The Administrative and Economic Organization of the Ur III State: The Core and the Periphery." In M. Gibson and R. D. Biggs (eds.), *The Organization of Power, Aspects of Bureaucracy in the Ancient Near East*. SAOC 46. (Chicago: The Oriental Institute), 15–33.

Steinkeller, Piotr. 2002. "Money Lending Practices in Ur III Babylonia: The Issue of Economic Motivation." In M. Hudson and M. Van De Mieroop (eds.), *Debt and Economic Renewal in the Ancient Near East* (Bethesda, MD: CDL Press), 109–37.

Steinkeller, Piotr. 2004. "Towards a Definition of Private Economic Activity in Third Millennium Babylonia," in R. Rollinger and C. Ulf (eds.), *Commerce and Monetary Systems in the Ancient World* (Stuttgart: Franz Steiner Verlag), 91–114.

Steinkeller, Piotr. 2013. "Corvée Labor in Ur III Times." In S. Garfinkle and M. Molina (eds.), *From the 21st Century BC to the 21st Century AD. Proceedings of the International Conference on Neo-Sumerian Studies held in Madrid, July 22–24, 2010* (Winona Lake, IN: Eisenbrauns), 347–424.

Steinkeller, Piotr. 2015. "The Employment of Labor on National Building Projects in the Ur III Period." In P. Steinkeller and M. Hudson (eds.), *Labor in the Ancient World.* International Scholars Conference on Ancient Near Eastern Economies 5 (Dresden: ISLET-Verlag), 137–236.

Van De Mieroop, Marc. 1992. *Society and Enterprise in Old Babylonian Ur.* Berlin: Dietrich Reimer Verlag.

Van De Mieroop, Marc. 2002. "In Search of Prestige: Foreign Contacts and the Rise of an Elite in Early Dynastic Babylonia." In E. Ehrenberg (ed.), *Leaving No Stones Unturned: Essays on the Ancient Near East and Egypt in Honor of Donald P. Hansen* (Winona Lake, IN: Eisenbrauns), 125–38.

Van De Mieroop, Marc. 2004. "Economic Theories and the Ancient Near East." In R. Rollinger and C. Ulf (eds.), *Commerce and Monetary Systems in the Ancient World* (Stuttgart: Franz Steiner Verlag), 54–64.

Yoffee, Norman. 2005. *Myths of the Archaic State, Evolution of the Earliest Cities, States, and Civilizations.* Cambridge: Cambridge University Press.

Yoffee, Norman. 2013. "The Limits of Power." In S. Morton and D. Butler (eds.), *It's Good to be King: The Archaeology of Power and Authority. Proceedings of the 41st (2008) Annual Chacmool Archaeological Conference, University of Calgary, Alberta, Canada* (Calgary: University of Calgary, Chacmool Archaeological Association), 253–60.

Zettler, Richard L. 1992. *The Ur III Temple of Inanna at Nippur. The operation and organisation of urban religious institutions in Mesopotamia in the late third millennium B.C.* Berlin: Dietrich Reimer Verlag.

4

The Extractive Systems of the Mycenaean World

DIMITRI NAKASSIS

This chapter surveys the means by which the Late Bronze Age polities of Mycenaean Greece acquired goods and services, with a focus on regular extractive transactions.[1] The Mycenaean world is typically defined as the central and southern Greek mainland, as well as much of the Aegean basin, during the Late Bronze Age (ca. 1700–1050 BCE according to the high chronology, ca. 1600–1050 BCE according to the low).[2] In the 14th and 13th centuries BCE, a number of small, independent palatial centers operated on the Greek mainland and the island of Crete. Administrators at these centers composed documents in the Linear B script, used to write an early form of the Greek language (see Figures 4.1 and 4.2). These Linear B texts form the main source of evidence for our understanding of palatial systems of finance. I argue in this paper that Mycenaean extractive regimes are composed of complex systems of internal exchanges characterized by reciprocity.

Linear B documents can be a frustrating source for the scholar of extractive systems for at least two reasons.[3] Because writing in the Mycenaean world is a practice that is thoroughly associated with the institution of the palace and its administrative systems, almost all of our documents relate to the extraction of goods and services, broadly defined. Yet the extremely specialized application of writing in the Mycenaean world produced very laconic documents, written by and for a limited number of administrators. While the tablets are more than just aides-mémoires, they often do not provide much contextual information, and consequently there can be legitimate debate about whether a document records the extraction or allocation of material.[4] It is this extreme lexical economy of the Linear B tablets, coupled with the lack of all textual genres other than the administrative, that encouraged

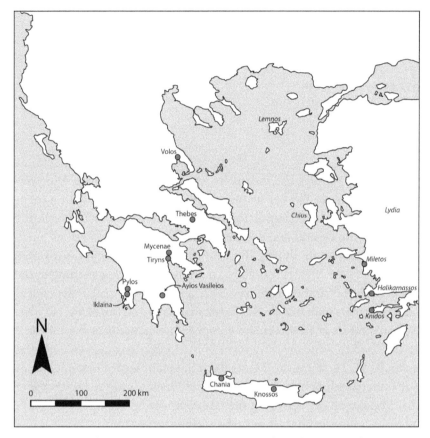

Figure 4.1. Map of the Late Bronze Age Aegean. Drawn by author. Sites with Linear B tablets are labeled in roman font; sites and regions mentioned in the text without Linear B tablets are labeled in italics.

the derogatory description of them as "laundry lists."[5] Second, all of these texts were temporary, with a probable shelf-life of a year or so at most, and they belong to specific chronological horizons associated with fire destructions. Thus, at Pylos virtually all of the records were preserved by the final destruction of the palace, yielding a snapshot of administrative activity in the polity's final months.[6] Most Mycenaean sites preserve texts from multiple destructions,[7] but in no case is the material full enough to meaningfully analyze how extractive procedures changed over time.[8] Consequently, it can be difficult to ascertain whether particular imposts represent ordinary transactions or extraordinary requests at moments of crisis.[9]

The nature of the texts is both a blessing and a curse. On the one hand, their association with the palace, their administrative function, and the preservation bias towards those texts composed annually means that they preserve a large quantity of direct evidence for Mycenaean mechanics of extraction. Much scholarly energy has been devoted to increasing our understanding of the internal organization of the documents, especially the identification of individual scribes on the basis of handwriting and of coherent sets or dossiers of documents, known as in the secondary literature as "series."[10] On the other hand, the lack of non-palatial and non-administrative texts limits our vision to internal institutional receipts, stripping us of much of the texture (social, economic, and political) of Mycenaean finance and its constituent parts. It is difficult to talk about the legal and ideological bases of extractive practices, how they were enforced and complied with, and so on.

To a large extent, the loss of that texture has been mitigated by the way that these texts have usually been interpreted. Up until recently, it was standard to assume that "the role which the palaces played in the economy of Mycenaean states was not merely significant, but central and dominant."[11] This perspective ensured that Mycenaean taxation

0   5   10 cm

Figure 4.2. "Leaf-shaped" Linear B tablet, PY Ma 393. Photograph by the Pylos Digital Tablets Project. Courtesy of the Classics Department, University of Cincinnati. All Linear B texts are referred to by a two-letter uppercase prefix that indicates where it was found, a one- or two-letter text prefix that indicates the series (set or dossier) to which the text belongs, and a number. For example, PY Ma 393 has the site prefix PY (for Pylos), the text prefix Ma (indicating the series to which it belongs) and the number 393 (unique to the tablets at Pylos).

records have been among the most analyzed, but from a perspective that emphasizes top-down palatial control. Scholars understood these texts in mathematical terms through the quantities listed, with the goal of understanding the underlying tax system designed and enforced by palatial authorities. Researchers even tried to find a "fiscal law": a large-scale tax structure that operated across multiple domains and polities.[12] If palatial control was a virtual monopoly, then issues of enforcement and compliance were basically unimportant in any case: all that was required was to determine the underlying system as it was devised by the ruling authorities.

Two recent developments make a reassessment of Mycenaean extractive regimes timely. First, there has been a large amount of scholarly work on Mycenaean taxation in the past ten years that has challenged, largely on technical and methodological grounds, older studies that emphasized the top-down and systematic aspects of extractive systems.[13] Second, the traditional image of total state control has been contradicted on empirical and theoretical grounds, generating significant debate over the past thirty years about the extent and nature of palatial interests and oversight. Some scholars believe that the "central and dominant" role of the palaces best fits the available evidence, with the primary economic mode of exchange best characterized as redistribution, whereas others prefer to see palatial involvement as more limited in scope and focused on particular goods and activities in a mixed economic system.[14] The latter position has been steadily gaining ground, and it seems increasingly likely that the role of regular extractive systems was much less important than other economic elements for the Mycenaean political economy.[15] These two scholarly developments are largely independent of each other, but in combination they open up a space to reconsider Mycenaean extractive systems.

The Language of Extraction

As mentioned above, Linear B texts are extremely economical in their use of language. Most texts that deal with the extraction of goods and labor do not give an indication of how, or under what conditions, the extraction takes place, but in some cases specific terms do designate particular extractive modalities. These terms can be opaque, but their meanings have been gradually revealed through careful study of administrative context and etymology.[16]

Exchanges of all kinds can be indicated by various forms of the verb "give" (Greek δίδωμι), but the verb and the nouns derived from it are used especially for payments of various commodities to the central authority, whether these payments have actually taken place or are prospective.[17] Shortfalls are described as debts or deficits, using forms of the verb "owe" (Greek ὀφείλω).[18] Scheduled non-payments are either indicated by the verbal phrase "they do not give" or the adjective "free" (presumably understood as "free from the obligation to pay").[19] Thus, for example, one of the Ma tablets from Pylos (Ma 393; see Fig. 2 and further below) records for a particular district that a group of people called the *ma-ra-ne-ni-jo* "do not give." Documents with this language are typically understood as indicating taxation or some other obligatory payment, such as rent (see below). Another term governing the extraction of goods, indicating the payment or assessment of a fine or penalty (*qe-te-o*), is a verbal adjective formed from the root *k^wei-, from which we get the first millennium verb τίνω, meaning "pay a penalty/debt."[20] Exchanges in which the palatial authority apparently purchases goods are indicated by a different term (*o-no*).[21]

Specific expressions for the extraction of labor are less commonly attested in the texts, and are associated with the preparation of material goods. One term (*o-pa*) refers to work on materials or livestock that involves bringing them "to a full state of readiness or completion."[22] It is likely that a similar meaning is indicated by *wo-ka* (probably "work"), but the precise difference between the two is uncertain.[23] The manufacture of crafted goods from raw materials, on the other hand, is indicated by a separate term (*ta-ra-si-ja*),[24] which refers to a system of production in which materials are weighed out and distributed to individuals or groups of artisans who are expected to transform them into finished goods and render them to the central authority.[25]

As useful as these terms are to our understanding of Mycenaean extraction, it is important to note that they are comparatively rare: many Linear B tablets that apparently refer to extractions of labor or material do not include such terms at all. There is also typically not a one-to-one correspondence between extractive modalities and material goods. That is to say, the same principle may apply to the acquisition of more than one product: *ta-ra-si-ja* can be used to produce both textiles and chariots. Moreover, the same product may be acquired in more than one way: textiles can be produced by the *ta-ra-si-ja* system or acquired via an *o-no* transaction.[26]

The Objects of Extraction

As the discussion above indicates, Mycenaean economic systems extracted both labor and goods. Labor recruitment was variously arranged and put to a variety of purposes. For instance, it seems likely that some contingents of military coastguards and rowers at Pylos were expected to serve because of specific landholdings in a series of documents (the Na series) that records quantities of flax that the palace expected to receive. This hypothesis is based on the observation that the numbers of men in specific contingents in one set of documents (the An series) are sometimes equal to the numbers of units of flax associated with men of the same description in the Na series.[27] It also seems certain that other labor recruitment systems were in place, since most of the labor recorded in the texts cannot be accounted for in terms of landholding; there is also evidence that labor was recruited through the intermediation of high-ranking individuals.[28] It is less clear how non-military labor was drawn up; some texts (the Ac series) record deficits in the number of men provided to the palace, suggesting that their service might have been compulsory, probably corvée, labor.[29]

Another form of labor extraction that has been much discussed is fully dependent labor, especially slavery. The Greek word for enslaved person (masculine δοῦλος, feminine δούλα) is present in Linear B, but its precise meaning in its Mycenaean context is uncertain, and it might be preferable to translate "servant."[30] "Slaves" of deities and of high-status persons appear in important contexts (e.g., landholding texts) alongside individuals of apparent high standing suggesting that appellations like "slave of the god" might well be honorific titles. Unnamed "slaves," on the other hand, usually appear in groups and in labor contexts. Four texts at Knossos appear to record the purchase of a single enslaved individual.[31] The overall numbers are small: at Pylos there are some 140 persons identified explicitly as enslaved, out of over

4,000 persons tracked by the administration.[32] Other groups of dependent laborers who are not explicitly designated as enslaved have been hypothesized to be servile, however. The best example of this are groups of women at Pylos who receive monthly payments of grain and dried figs, usually understood as subsistence rations, from the palace.[33] These women (and their children) are sometimes referred to by profession—primarily relating to textile working, but there are also grain-grinders and attendants—and sometimes by ethnics, some of which are local, but others of which seem to cluster along the western coast of Anatolia: there are groups of Knidian, Milesian, and Lemnian women, as well as possibly Lydian, Halikarnassian, and Chian women (see Figure 4.1).[34] The presence of one group described by an adjective that might mean "plundered" has suggested to many that these women, especially those of apparently non-local origin, were enslaved persons acquired by trade or raiding.[35]

A great deal of energy has been put into understanding the sources of palatial labor in terms of top-down structures through which the palace either exerts complete control over fully-dependent labor or conscripts it directly from subject communities. There has been a focus, understandably, on determining whether labor was conscripted as a kind of tax, i.e., in which each community is required to deliver corvée laborers on the basis of its population (or some other value), or whether another system applies, most often that groups are required to deliver corvée laborers on the basis of landholdings.[36] This has sometimes involved assuming relatively simple, flat systems of labor extraction. For instance, the "women of Pylos" have been treated as a homogeneous group with respect to their status and relation to the palatial authority, such that one may argue that they are *all* hired labor, *all* corvée laborers, or *all* enslaved.[37] But similarities in the way that different groups are treated administratively need not indicate similarities in social status, legal status, or how their labor was extracted. In the case of the "women of Pylos," much attention has been paid to the women described as "plundered": this group has served as one pillar of the argument that *all* the women in these texts were enslaved.[38] It is universally agreed, however, that two groups of women at Pylos receiving monthly rations are described as "wage-earners."[39] Although this might suggest that all the other women receiving rations are *not* wage-earners, it certainly illustrates not only that workers could be hired, but also that wages and rations are virtually indistinguishable.

In fact, much of the labor recorded in the texts cannot be understood in terms of top-down palatial structures. The evidence points instead to various regimes of labor recruitment, including the direct hiring of labor and the indirect recruitment of labor through élite intermediaries. Within a single text or set of texts, there can be multiple modes of labor extraction in use.[40] All this is to say that labor extraction in the Mycenaean world was, from what we can see in the texts, complex and multi-faceted. And, as Paul Halstead has pointed out, there is quite a lot of labor that is entirely missing from the texts.[41]

Even more than labor, the Linear B texts are focused on the extraction of goods. The documents most associated with regular extraction, normally understood as taxation or tribute, are the Pylos Ma series and the Knossos Mc series. The former is a probably complete set of eighteen documents, each of which records the targets for the payment of six commodities, always listed in the same order, in a fixed proportion, from each of the major towns in the kingdom.[42] Four of these tablets record payments, and in the three cases where the payment is not yet complete, the remaining deficits are noted. Some texts refer to "last year's deficit" and the scheduled non-payment of particular groups.[43] Unfortunately, only three of the six commodities can be identified: a simple textile (*146), linen thread (RI), and an animal hide (*152); the three unknown commodities are indicated by signs with the syllabic values of KE, O, and ME. Some of these six commodities are also extracted by the palaces at Thebes and Knossos, suggesting that these goods were assembled for a specific purpose, perhaps military.[44] This remains very tentative, however, due to the uncertainty in exactly what was being collected. Similar problems plague the Mc series at Knossos, which record contributions of four commodities, two of which are known: female goats (CAP^f) and goat horns (CORN); the other two (*142, *150) are unknown (perhaps also goat products).[45] Although the Knossos Mc series lacks the language of taxation present in the Pylos Ma series, the rough proportionality between the four commodities suggests extraction. Indeed, a fiscal law was proposed by Jean-Pierre Olivier that accounted for the proportions that governed both sets of tablets (Pylos Ma and Knossos Mc), but it has been shown to be implausible by subsequent research.[46]

Although these M- series documents at Pylos and Knossos are most closely associated with taxation or fiscality, in truth they comprise a very small portion of the extractive forces of the central authority. Agricultural goods, unsurprisingly, are the focus of Mycenaean extractive regimes. Agricultural commodities in texts which indicate payments and/or deficits include grain and linen (on which, more below), spices of various kinds, olive oil, and honey.[47] Fines are largely paid in agricultural goods (grain, olives, wine, olive oil, and animals), but also textiles.[48]

At Pylos and probably at Knossos, quantities of linen are expected to be delivered to the palace from specific places (and, in some cases, individuals) on the basis of landholdings.[49] The same relationship between landholding and payments also appears in certain series: the Es series at Pylos records the annual contributions (*do-so-mo*) of grain to be made by thirteen individuals on the basis of their landholdings.[50] In the case of the Es series, the context is religious: the chief recipient of the grain is the deity Poseidon. Another pair of landholding documents at Pylos, Er 312 and 880, are connected to a third tablet (Un 718) that records four contributions (*do-so-mo*) of mixed agricultural commodities to Poseidon in the context of a feast.[51] Other landholding series do not record contributions, but presumably have the same purpose: to monitor the basis for future extractions.[52] Other than this, however, almost all else is uncertain, including how exactly these extractions were made and on what basis.[53] Virtually all of the land in the Linear B tablets seems to be connected with an institution called the *dāmos* (*da-mo*).[54] This organization appears in the tablets as a local administrative entity concerned with agricultural matters,[55] but there are good reasons to believe that the Mycenaean *dāmos* had a broader sense of "community," as it does in the first millennium (δῆμος, δᾶμος).[56] Paul Halstead has argued that "'palatial' grain production involved a 'share-cropping' arrangement, whereby the palace provided plough animals and perhaps their fodder, while local communities provided human labor and, ostensibly, land."[57] This is probably true for *some* grain production, but the evidence is hardly consistent with the notion that this is true for *all* of it; as we have seen above, palatial systems for acquiring goods are typically complex. But Halstead's hypothesis suggests at least one way that the palatial authority extracted agricultural goods from *dāmos* landholdings. On the other hand, it is noteworthy that where contributions of foodstuffs on the basis of landholdings are preserved in our documents, they always occur in a religious context; other landholdings at Pylos also have religious associations, sometimes very strong ones.[58] This adds yet another layer of complexity: we seem to have religious contributions, apparently within the purview of palatial authorities, on the basis of plots on *dāmos* land.

Non-agricultural products—such as wood, deer hides, and perhaps weapons—are much less commonly extracted in texts which indicate payments and/or deficits.[59] Metals are also occasionally extracted in this way: one Pylos text (Jn 829) records that various officers, including one clearly religious functionary, in each of the sixteen districts of the Pylian polity "will give" (-*do-so-si* /*dōsonsi*/) temple bronze as points for javelins and spears, a uniquely explicit statement of a levy's purpose.[60] The quantities in this text are almost equally balanced between the two provinces of the Pylian polity, suggesting a top-down assessment.[61] Gold is also probably assessed in a single text at Pylos (Jo 438).[62]

Outside of these contexts that scholars of Linear B normally associate with taxation, there are a number of goods that flow through the written documentation in other ways. The most outstanding of these is wool, for textile production was a major interest of Mycenaean administrators. Wool was acquired directly from flocks of sheep that were allocated to individual shepherds to maintain: some 80,000–100,000 sheep are recorded in the Knossos tablets, ca. 10,000 at Pylos.[63] As Paul Halstead has pointed out, the administration was primarily concerned with the numbers of sheep and quantities of wool owed and delivered, so that individuals tasked with herding palatial sheep were free to move animals between institutional and "private" flocks.[64] This fluidity seems to have benefited the shepherds, who could swap in their own yearlings to remove fat palatial wethers (for consumption) or ewes (for breeding), and implies large-scale "private" herding: at least 150,000 head of sheep in central and western Crete alone.[65] At Knossos, we have sets of documents that record the composition of flocks and the corresponding production targets of wool, or of wool and lambs: the total quantities of raw wool collected by the central authority is in the region of 30–50 tons.[66] This wool was assigned to groups of workers to be woven into textiles of different types; at Knossos these workers largely operated under the *ta-ra-si-ja* system of production (see above).[67] Many of the "women of Pylos" discussed above were involved in textile production.[68] Palatial records also document arrangements for the production of perfumed olive oil, chariots, weapons and other bronze objects, and furniture.[69] In some cases the extraction of the raw materials for these productive fields have already been discussed, but in others it is uncertain how they were acquired. Bronze, for instance, was levied on occasion at Pylos, but only ca. 50 kg is recorded in the levy of PY Jn 829, whereas the total quantity of bronze worked by smiths at Pylos certainly exceeded 500 kg (and probably 1,000 kg).[70] Neither copper nor tin are locally available, and would have needed to be imported, yet there is virtually no evidence for trade in our texts.[71]

This lacuna brings us to two important, interrelated observations. First, the extractive regimes of Mycenaean polities were certainly more extensive than what is presented in the texts, which represent only a fraction of the totality of all economic activity.[72] Paul Halstead has pointed out that the texts do not mention, or barely mention, commodities that we know from archaeological evidence or analogy must have been used or extracted by the palaces.[73] This lacuna is presumably due to the fact that the textual evidence is biased towards regular, obligatory transactions, and only rarely betrays evidence of other types of exchanges. As Bennet and Halstead point out, records of exchanges between the central authority and individuals that use the term *o-no* (literally "benefit" but meaning something like "payment") are rare, but were probably contingent documents with short life-spans, discarded soon after the transaction was complete.[74] These exchanges typically involved payment in agricultural products or simple textiles for various goods and services. In two *o-no* texts from Pylos, the central authority even acquires an imported good, alum, from named individuals in exchange for agricultural goods (wool, goats, wine, and figs) and simple cloth.[75] We have also seen above that two groups of women at Pylos who are allocated staples (grain and dried figs) are referred to as "wage-earners." Many scholars now believe that exchanges such as those indicated in the texts with *o-no*, as well as textually invisible gift-exchanges, explain the goods and services missing from our texts, including most ceramics, imported goods (metals, glass, ivory, semi-precious stones, etc.), a wide variety of agricultural goods (such as pulses), human labor for various activities, and so on.[76] In sum, it seems likely that regular extractions attested in our texts are much less important than they have typically been considered, and that reciprocal and other exchanges were crucially important to the functioning of the palatial economy.[77]

Such exchanges have until recently been downplayed in Linear B scholarship for at least two reasons. One, as we have seen, is that they are minimally attested in the textual evidence. The other is the presumption that the palace held a virtual monopoly on economic activity. This view, expressed by Moses Finley in the late 1950s, proved to be extremely influential, especially among textual scholars.[78] Work since the 1990s, beginning with a series of articles by Paul Halstead, began to show quite the opposite, namely that "palaces exercised only partial control over economic activity within their territories."[79] As the palatial monopoly has been shown to be illusory, the importance of non-redistributive exchanges to the functioning of the political economy has become correspondingly clear.[80]

The Rhetoric of Extraction

As we have seen, research on Mycenaean extractive regimes has tended to focus on texts interpreted as documenting taxation: regular, obligatory payments to the center.[81] Certainly from the perspective of the composers of these texts, it was important to record the total quantities expected, the anticipated exemptions of payment, how much had been paid, and how much material was still missing; but it hardly follows that such procedures were understood in the same way that we now understand taxation. As Perna has observed, and as was noted above ("The language of extraction"), the terms used in these documents are generally not technical. Indeed, the language of Mycenaean extraction is largely composed of terms that in first millennium BCE Greek are generic and belong to the vocabulary of reciprocity, both compactual and compensatory.[82] Payments in Mycenaean texts are indicated by terms formed from the generic verb of giving (δίδωμι), the verbal root that characterizes reciprocal gift-giving in the first millennium.[83] Mycenaean fines are indicated with various formations from the verbal root *$k^w ei$- (cf. τίνω), which is generative of later terms for ransom (ἄποινα), revenge (τίσις) and reparations (ποινή).[84] The receipt of payments in

Mycenaean texts is indicated using the same verb (δέχομαι) that is later used generically for the receipt of goods, including gifts.[85] Shortfalls in the Bronze Age are indicated by terms from a generic verb of owing (ὀφείλω) that is regularly associated in Homer for debts (χρεῖος) for damages.[86] These connections suggest the possibility that the terminology of Mycenaean extraction was animated by a rhetoric of reciprocity.[87]

A critic would surely object at this point that these words need not have a specific connection to reciprocity. Michel Lejeune concluded from a contextual analysis of the Mycenaean use of δίδωμι that it always indicated the fulfillment of an obligation.[88] Of course, words can (and did) radically change their meanings over the course of the half millennium (or more) that separates the Mycenaean world and the earliest Greek literary texts. Yet Lejeune's analysis is problematic insofar as it focuses on the way that a particular verb is used in specific administrative contexts, which are understood from the beginning as reflecting taxation. That is to say, the interpretation of the documents, which is analytically prior to the interpretation of the terminology, leads Lejeune to conclude that δίδωμι in the Late Bronze Age is exclusively associated with formal obligations, and therefore that it has an exclusive meaning consonant with that use. Function and meaning are thereby collapsed.[89] Yet this is a dubious way to treat a data set whose function is so circumscribed. In fact, where our evidence allows, we can see that these verbs retain their general meaning.[90] For example, the term qe-te-o /kʷeiteʰon/ indicates a fine, and seems to be entirely administrative in function. Yet the middle participle of the same verb, qe-ja-me-no /kʷeiamenos/ is used to describe a man who has taken land in compensation for manslaughter (e-ne-ka , a-no-qa-si-ja /(h)eneka anorkʷʰasiās/), demonstrating that the verb has retained its general meaning and function outside of, and within, the narrow confines of administrative documents.[91] Likewise, we have seen that dāmos appears in the tablets as an administrative body narrowly associated with agricultural pursuits, but its use in personal names and official titles is suggestive of a non-administrative meaning of "community."[92]

Another objection might be that these terms were simply common verbs with flexible semantic fields. Yet a broader view of Mycenaean palatial language suggests that a rhetoric of reciprocity was active. Each of the two provinces of the Pylian state was administered by an official called a *da-mo-ko-ro* /*dāmokoros*/, literally "he who nourishes/satiates the *dāmos*."[93] The titles of the district administrators, governors (*ko-re-te* /*korētēr*/) and vice-governors (*po-ro-ko-re-te* /*prokorētēr*/) were almost certainly derived from the same verbal root in *dāmokoros*, thus reinforcing the rhetoric that these officials—one of whose main jobs was organizing the extraction of goods from local communities—were "agents of increase or satiety."[94] Many plots of land are referred to as an *o-na-to* /*onāton*/, literally a "benefit," even though, as I argued, these plots are recorded for the extractive benefit of the center.[95] Likewise, what seem like straightforward exchanges of goods are marked by the term *o-no* /*onon*/, "benefit."

The extractive regimes of Mycenaean palaces do, in fact, involve real reciprocities. In the case of grain production, it seems that the palace (at least occasionally) provided plow animals.[96] Paul Halstead has also convincingly suggested that the plots of land recorded in the Pylos Na series were much larger than they needed to be in order to provide the flax expected by the center, so that the holders of plots in the Na series would have also grown crops that were not extracted.[97] As mentioned above, herders of palatial flocks would have benefited from their ability to swap animals between their own flocks and those of the palace.[98] Additionally, it seems that herders were allowed to keep any surplus wool and other secondary animal products.[99] Workers in the *ta-ra-si-ja* system may also have benefited from their participation: Marie-Louise Nosch has pointed out that the quantities of wool allocated to textile workers at Knossos seem much greater than necessary for the products expected by the center, in which case the extra wool might have constituted a form of payment.[100]

The central authority also seems to have allocated benefits to specific groups in recognition of their service. Select groups are exempted from the obligation to make payments in the Pylos Ma tablets, the most common of which are smiths (*ka-ke-we* /*kʰalkēwes*/, cf. singular χαλκεύς).[101] In the Pylos Na tablets there are exemptions granted to various groups: smiths, shipbuilders, hunters, planters, the king, and others.[102] Smiths are the largest group of *ta-ra-si-ja* workers at Pylos, and so it seems likely that these exemptions are granted as a kind of reward for their service.[103] Plots of *dāmos* land were also allocated to some craftsmen, presumably for the same reason. Many plots were taxable, but some apparently had special statuses, as mentioned above. Many scholars have also suspected that the palace gave gifts to individuals and groups as rewards for their service.[104] To a large extent, this hypothesis is based on the fact that the palaces were heavily involved in the manufacture of high-quality craft products, whose recipients must have included members of the élite, broadly speaking. Most of this gift-giving is textually invisible, but not all of it. There is the occasional mention of goods (olive oil, textiles) that are described as *ke-se-ni-wi-jo* /*ksenwion*/ (cf. ξείνιον), probably meaning "guest gift."[105] One text from Pylos (On 300) apparently allocates animal hides (*154*) to palatial officials, and another set of Pylos tablets (the Qa series) possibly records the allocation animal skins (*189*) to individuals, among whom religious officials are prominent; it is even possible that these skins were considered γέρα, "prizes of honor."[106] Finally, the prominent role of state-sponsored feasting should be mentioned. One of the main activities of Mycenaean administration was the organization and provision of large-scale feasts; indeed, at Pylos most of the staples recorded in the texts are destined for consumption at such events.[107] These feasts were opportunities for the palatial authority to display their generosity and thereby to promote solidarity and reproduce hegemony.[108]

The Mechanics of Extraction

The details of how goods were extracted are extremely hazy, largely due to the extreme economy of Mycenaean writing. For example, the Pylos Ma tablets, which are the main focus of any study of Mycenaean taxation, say nothing about the process of extraction beyond indicating what has been paid, what is still owed, and what payments have been exempted or deferred.[109] For instance, one of these texts reads as follows (see Figure 4.2 above):

PY Ma 393

TRANSLITERATED TEXT (UNDERLINED TEXT INDICATES UNCERTAIN [I.E., DOTTED] READINGS):

.1]za-ma-e-wi-ja *146* 28 *RI* M 28 *KE* M 8 *152* 12 *O* M 5 *ME* 600

.2]a-pu-do-si *146* 20 a-ne-ta-de *146* 1 *RI* M 21 *KE* M 5 *O* M 1 *152* 8 *O* M 6 *ME* 450

.3 o-da-a$_2$, ma-ra-ne-ni-jo , o-u-di-do-si *146 7 RI M 7 KE M 2 *152
3 O M 2 ME 150

TRANSLATION:

.1 *za-ma-e-wi-ja* [a place-name]: 28 textiles, 28 kg of linen thread,
8 kg of KE, 12 animal hides, 5 kg of O, 600 units of ME

.2 payment: 20 textiles (remitted: 1 textile), 21 kg of linen thread,
5 kg of KE, deficit: 1 kg, 8 animal hides, 6 kg of O, 450 units
of ME

.3 And also: the *ma-ra-ne-ni-jo* [a group of people in the plural]
do not give: 7 textiles, 7 kg of linen thread, 2 kg of KE, 3 animal
hides, 26 kg of O, 150 units of ME

Other texts in related series have been persuasively interpreted as
detailed breakdowns of the Ma tablets, demonstrating that the administration did track payments at the level of the individual.[110] These
payments have been almost universally interpreted as taxation or tribute. Many attempts have been made to abstract this system and apply
it to other documents.[111] On the other hand, nothing requires us to
interpret the Ma tablets as the payment of taxes: they could equally
be rents. Massimo Perna has recently argued precisely this: he points
out that a number of the exemptions constitute a large percentage of
the total owed, as in Ma 393, where one quarter of the total is exempt
from payment, and he asks whether it is reasonable that one group of
people (the *ma-ra-ne-ni-jo*) should be responsible for a full quarter of
the amount due for an entire district.[112] This is a reasonable question,
and it is also reasonable to suggest, as Perna does, that the Ma tablets
and other texts interpreted as taxation documents actually record goods
or services due to the palace in respect of land that has been allocated
to them.[113] Unfortunately none of the Ma texts make reference to land,
so Perna's suggestion cannot be substantiated.[114] This predicament illustrates how little we actually know about the mechanics of extraction in
the Mycenaean world.

There are occasional windows in the texts that do shed some light on
extractive practices. One celebrated text, Pylos Jn 829, has a heading that
is carefully composed by the scribe to indicate specifically how taxes will
be collected in this particular case:

PY Jn 829

TRANSLITERATED TEXT:

.1   jo-do-so-si , ko-re-te-re , du-ma-te-qe ,

.2 po-ro-ko-re-te-re-qe , ka-ra-wi-po-ro-qe , o-pi-su-ko-qe , o-pi-ka-pe$^{-e\text{-}we\text{-}qe}$

.3 ka-ko , na-wi-jo , pa-ta-jo-i-qe , e-ke-si-qe , a$_3$-ka-sa-ma

TRANSLATION:

.1 Thus will give the governors (*ko-re-te-re*) and the masters (*du-ma-te*)

.2 and the vice-governors (*po-ro-ko-re-te-re*) and the key-bearers (*ka-ra-wi-po-ro*) and the fig-supervisors (*o-pi-su-ko*) and the digging-supervisors (*o-pi-ka-pe-e-we*)

.3 temple bronze as points for light javelins and spears

What follows these headings are specific weights of metal—technically "bronze" (*ka-ko* /*kʰalkos*/, cf. χαλκός) could also indicate copper—that the governors and vice-governors will render to the central authority.[115] These governors and vice-governors administer the same sixteen districts that are taxed in the Ma series.[116] Indeed, the method of composing Jn 829 seems to be similar to that of the Ma series in that the assessment was made from the top down.[117] Thus this text is organized and shaped by similar administrative structures as the Ma tablets discussed above.[118]

In this case, however, the author of Jn 829—Hand 2, one of the most active of the scribal hands and the author of the Ma series—takes care to create a parallelism in the heading. By erasing and re-writing the sentence, he intentionally associated the governors with the masters whereas the vice-governors were associated with the key-bearers, the fig-supervisors and the digging-supervisors.[119] This detail cannot tell us what we would like to know, namely the precise process(es) whereby this temple bronze was collected and the roles played by these particular officials, but it does suggest that this extraction was about more than simply setting targets at some office within the palatial center. It seems likely that local palatial administrators (the governors and vice-governors) had to work together with local religious and (apparently) agricultural officials to determine how the assessments would be fulfilled.[120]

Mycenaean Extractive Regimes in Context

It has been traditional to understand Mycenaean financial systems in systematic terms, understood from the perspective of the palace. I have argued, however, that the rhetoric employed, as well as the few windows that we have into the processes whereby materials were extracted, is suggestive of complex systems in which reciprocities and exchanges between individuals and institutions were extremely important. Indeed, it seems that complexity is the rule: where the evidence allows us to understand the processes of extraction, they are heterogeneous. Thus, for instance, the condition of the "women of Pylos" seems to run the gamut from fully dependent (perhaps even enslaved) labor, all the way to wage-earners, and textiles are acquired by the center in a number of different ways, ranging from direct production to their purchase from craft specialists. This observation that extraction is characterized by complex sets of exchanges is an especially striking result because the Linear B texts focus overwhelmingly on routine, regular transactions, underrepresenting non-routine exchanges.[121]

From a comparative perspective, Mycenaean extractive practices are distinctive in a number of ways. In the introduction to this volume, Jonathan Valk suggests that extractive regimes can be usefully characterized using four major classificatory axes: (1) material and human resources, (2) collection in kind and in money, (3) direct and indirect taxation, and (4) internal and external taxation. While Mycenaean extractive regimes are, like many others, based on the acquisition of a complex mix of material and human resources (axis 1), for the other three axes (2–4), Mycenaean systems fall firmly on one side of each continuum. Extracted goods are paid in kind, directly, and internally. Indeed, the texts concentrate primarily on staples: payments are always made with agricultural products and simple textiles rather than wealth items such as crafted products or valuable raw materials. These agricultural staples were also used to support laborers of various kinds and to provision religious ceremonies, especially large-scale feasts.[122] Especially surprising from a comparative perspective is the apparent absence of large institutional estates that financed state operations. Such estates are characteristic of the Inka and Aztec, as well as of the contemporary and near-contemporary kingdoms of the ancient Near East and Egypt.[123] Although earlier studies thought that such estates were a significant feature of the Mycenaean palatial economy, recent work has shown that virtually all holdings recorded in the texts were on *dāmos* land.[124] Certainly royal lands do exist and are recorded, but they constitute a small percentage of the total holdings monitored in the Linear B tablets.[125]

Other external revenues, i.e., those "derived primarily from sources other than a broad population of taxpayers," are difficult to find in Linear B texts.[126] Revenues from warfare or imperial tribute are conspicuously absent from the textual evidence.[127] A handful of craft producers and workshops are designated as royal, but the evidence is certainly not consistent with extensive royal control over labor.[128] External trade is virtually absent from the textual documentation, so it seems unlikely that taxation of such exchanges contributed significantly to state revenue. It has usually been thought that Mycenaean palaces exerted significant control over, or even monopolized, international trade, and that only the palaces would have been able to acquire imported high-value goods.[129] Yet the empirical basis for this claim is weak, and a complex model of exchanges in which the palaces were "player[s] on a diverse stage of commerce and interaction" seems a much likelier alternative.[130] Indeed, it is probable that international exchange was for Mycenaean palaces largely handled through élite intermediaries.[131]

Mycenaean polities, so far as we can tell from the available evidence, were largely financed through staples and internal revenues. As Richard Blanton and Lane Fargher have pointed out, polities that rely on internal revenues tend to have complex administrative procedures in place to collect them, as well as "policies that promote quasi-voluntary taxpayer compliance."[132] These expectations are met by the Mycenaean textual data, which provide both extensive evidence for an elaborate system to track targets, payments, deficits and exemptions, as well as a rhetoric and practice of reciprocity that pervades even regular, apparently obligatory, exchanges. These two aspects of Mycenaean extractive regimes come together in the feast: state-sponsored feasts were the product of complex administrative processes that collected and distributed these staples in a ritual that at once reproduced community solidarity and political hierarchies.[133] Reciprocity, rhetorical and practical, must lie at the heart of this system.[134] Indeed, we might understand the widespread use of reciprocity as a form of "symbolic violence" *sensu* Bourdieu: modes of domination that are disguised as such, that in fact deny that they are such, like the generous gift that subordinates.[135]

The image of the Mycenaean political and economic order as described in this chapter is a significant departure from the traditional one in which oppressive palaces overexploited their territories in respect to both agricultural production and labor,[136] or even the more balanced position that the palaces were dominant centers of an economy that was selective in its coverage.[137] The human objects of Mycenaean extractive regimes have typically been marginalized in this discussion: sometimes they are understood as the passive recipients of a palatial system imposed upon them;[138] but more often there has been an attempt to understand the relationship between the palace and the individuals, communities, and institutions in its territory in a more dynamic way, even if the precise nature of that relationship is obscured by the nature of the evidence.[139] To a large extent, debate has centered on the issue of economic and political control, especially the extent of palatial control over various socioeconomic fields; but control itself has been treated as unproblematic, a kind of black box, no doubt because the dry administrative content of the tablets makes it difficult to interrogate the specifics of how control was exerted.[140] Difficult, but not impossible: as recent studies of Mycenaean feasting have shown, careful attention to specific practices has allowed us to retrieve some of the social texture that the Linear B texts conceal from us. So too can the restudy of the extractive regimes provide us with insights into the conceptual structures that gave shape to Mycenaean social, political, and economic orders.

NOTES

1 I thank the editors for inviting me to participate in the workshop, which I unfortunately missed, and the published volume. Sarah James and Ruth Palmer graciously lent their expertise to me; Susan Lupack and two anonymous referees substantially improved the text. I have tried, less successfully than I would have liked, to keep the number of citations to a reasonable number; I hope that specialist readers will forgive me.

2 Manning 2010.

3 I avoid using the term "taxation" in this chapter because it is debatable whether any of the documents preserved do record taxes *stricto sensu*. I will instead focus

on how Mycenaean states acquire goods and services, with more of a focus on those records that document regular and obligatory transactions.

4 On the texts as more than *aides-mémoires*, see Bennet 2001: 27–29. On the difficulties of studying Mycenaean fiscality, see Perna 2016: 453.

5 Cf. Chadwick 1976: ix, who calls them "drab and lifeless documents."

6 Zurbach 2016: 678.

7 Usefully discussed by Driessen 2008, with references.

8 The tendency has been for textual scholars to emphasize the homogeneity of the texts across space and time; while this can be an extremely productive way to proceed, it has also been the object of legitimate criticism (Parkinson 2007: 88).

9 Palaima 1995; Killen 2006a.

10 Palaima 2011.

11 Killen 2008b: 180.

12 Olivier 1974, 2014.

13 See Perna 2016, 2017 (with references to earlier work).

14 This literature is immense: Bennet 2007, Zurbach 2016, and Nakassis 2020 provide useful reviews; see too Galaty et al. 2011, Parkinson et al. 2013, and Nakassis et al. 2016.

15 Bennet and Halstead 2014: 279. It has been usual to associate regular systems with redistribution, and irregular transactions with reciprocity or market-type exchanges.

16 See recently Varias 2006 and Luján 2011.

17 "Give": verbal forms are *di-do-si* /*didonsi*/, *di-do-to* /*didotoi*/, *do-se* /*dōsei*/, *-do-so-si* /*dōsonsi*/, *do-ke* /*dōke*/, *de-do-me-na* /*dedomena*/, and the suffixed *a-pu-do-ke* /*apudōke*/, *a-pe-do-ke* /*apedōke*/; nominal forms are *do-so-mo* /*dosmos*/ and *a-pu-do-si* /*apudosis*/; adjectives formed from the nominal forms are *do-si-mi-jo* /*dosmios*/. The fragmentary *a-pu-do-so*[is probably the nominal / *apudosmos*/ (alternatively, verbal /*apudōsonsi*/). Duhoux (1968: 93–96, cf. Lejeune 1975: 3–9) has shown that there is a difference between *do-so-mo* /*dosmos*/ and *a-pu-do-si* /*apudosis*/. The latter always indicates an actual payment, whereas the former does not include the sense of the realization of the payment and is used rather for the imposition of payment. The word for "gifts," *do-ra* /*dōra*/, also appears on one text in a religious context (PY Tn 316).

18 "Debts/deficits": *o-pe-ro* /*opʰelos*/ (cf. ὄφελος, ὀφείλω), which can be abbreviated by the syllabogram *o*. Verbal forms ("owe") are also attested: *-o-pe-ro-si* /*opʰellonsi*/, *-o-po-ro* /*opʰlon*/, *o-pe-ro* /*opʰellōn*/, *o-pe-ro-sa* /*opʰellonsa*/, and *o-pe-ro-te* /*opʰellontes*/.

19 "Do not give": *o-u-di-do-si* /*ou didonsi*/. "Free": *e-re-u-te-ro* /*eleutʰeros*/ (cf. ἐλεύθερος).

20 Fine/penalty: *qe-te-o* (also *qe-te-jo* and plural *qe-te-a*, *qe-te-a₂*) /*kʷeiteʰon*/, normally understood as a verbal adjective of the type ending in -τέον, which expresses necessity, from a verbal root **kʷei-* (cf. τίνω). See Hutton 1990.

21 Exchange: *o-no* /*onon*/, cf. the verb ὀνίνημι, "profit, benefit." See Killen 1995: 217–24; Bennet and Halstead 2014.

22 Refurbishment: *o-pa* /ʰopā/, a *nomen actionis* from a verbal root *ʰep- (cf. ἕπω). See Killen 1999. The definition is taken from Palaima 2001: 152. Older scholarship thought that *o-pa* might mean "workshop" (e.g., Duhoux 1976: 82).

23 Work: *wo-ka*, probably /worgā/, a *nomen actionis* (cf. ἔργω), although some prefer to render it as /wokʰā/, "chariot" (Aura Jorro 1993: 441, s.v. *wo-ka*). I prefer the former interpretation because the term *wo-ka* (with a personal name in the genitive, indicating the person responsible for the work in question) appears exclusively in the Pylos Sa series with chariot wheels that are serviceable (*we-ke-ke-a₂*) and never with wheels that are not serviceable (*no-pe-re-a₂*); see too Duhoux 1976: 126–28.

24 This term is commonly understood as /tala(n)siā/. Cf. Greek ταλασία, "wool-spinning."

25 Killen 2001; Nosch 2006. Cf. the Middle Assyrian *iškāru* system (Postgate 2010).

26 For a probable *o-no* transaction involving textiles, see PY Un 1322.4, discussed by Chadwick 1964.

27 See discussion in Killen 2006a: 74. If, however, Perna (2016: 476–78) is right that the Na texts mentioning these groups have a different purpose from the rest of the Na series, then the relationship between landholding and military service is called into question. In one other case it is also possible to argue that landholding in the Na series is associated with non-military labor (De Fidio 1987: 136; Nakassis 2012a: 273).

28 Nakassis 2012a, 2015.

29 Killen 2006a: 77.

30 Slave: masculine *do-e-ro* /do⁽ʰ⁾elos/, feminine *do-e-ra* /do⁽ʰ⁾elā/. The classic work remains Lejeune 1959; more recently, Garlan 1988: 25–29, Hiller 1988, Shelmerdine 2008: 138–39. On the translation "servant," see Nakassis 2013: 14–15.

31 Olivier 1987; the verb in question ("he purchased") is *qi-ri-ja-to* /kʷriato/ (cf. πρίατο).

32 Hiller 1988: 54; Garlan 1988: 26.

33 Palmer 1989.

34 Chadwick 1988.

35 Chadwick 1988: 92–93. The term in question is *ra-wi-ja-ja*, understood by Chadwick and others as /lāwiaiai/, cf. λεία from *λαϝ-ία, "plunder" (Beekes 2010: 842, s.v. λεία).

36 For a classic demonstration that labor can be required as a kind of tax, see Killen 1983; a broader discussion is provided by Killen 2006b.

37 Most recently, Olsen 2014: 109–14. It is legitimate to hypothesize that a group might be enslaved despite the lack of an explicit label; because Mycenaean scribes tend to be laconic, they would not feel the need to indicate the servile status of groups unless it were necessary or useful information for the composition of the document. As Chadwick (1988: 90) puts it, "The fact that they are not specifically described as *do-e-ra* is of little consequence, for anyone handling these documents would have known their status."

38 It has often been assumed that the staples assigned to the women are subsistence rations, so that these women would be totally dependent on the palace for their sustenance, but this is an assumption that may not be reasonable, considering the clear presence of "wage-earners" (see below).

39 Wage-earners: *e-ke-ro-qo-no* /*egkʰērokʷoinoi*/, cf. ἐπίχειρα, ποινή (Aura Joro 1985: 211–12, s.v. *e-ke-ro-qo-no*; Chadwick 1988: 79). Cf. KN Am(2) 821, which contains the phrase *e-ne-ka e-mi-to* /⁽ʰ⁾*eneka emmisthōn*/, "for salaries" (see also Luján 2011: 28).

40 Nakassis 2012a.

41 Halstead 1999a; Bennet and Halstead 2014. See too Jörg Weilhartner's (2017) argument that there is evidence in the Linear B texts for work feasts.

42 The literature is immense; see most recently Perna 2016: 456–61, with earlier references.

43 Killen 1984b on the deficits from the previous year. Smiths are exempted from payment on ten tablets (see further below); other groups that are exempted are perhaps leatherworkers (*ku-re-we* /*skulēwes*/), and two groups identified with probable ethnics (*ma-ra-ne-ni-jo, pe-ra₃-qo*). In one case (PY Ma 365), it is specified that the smiths will pay in the following year (*ka-ke-we, a₂-te-ro, we-to, di-do-si* /*kʰalkēwes ʰateron wetos didonsi*/).

44 Killen 2008a; Perna 2016.

45 Perna 2004: 273–85; 2016: 484–85. Perna (1996) has argued that one of the unknown commodities is goat hair. Melena (2014: 140, 145) suggests that *142 represents a bundle, possibly of tendons/sinew of the *agrimi*, the wild Cretan goat, and that *150 might indicate the hide of a male *agrimi*.

46 Olivier 1974, defended also in Olivier 2014; Perna 2004: 140–52.

47 Killen 2008b: 189–91 provides a useful overview; olives too are recorded at Knossos in contexts that are suggestive of extraction (KN F series).

48 Aura Jorro 1993: 201–2, s.v. *qe-te-jo*.

49 Foster 1981; Perna 2004: 209–61; 2006.

50 The classic study is de Fidio 1977; see too Perna 2008a.

51 Nakassis 2012b.

52 Killen 2008b: 163–64; Del Freo 2017; see too Zurbach 2006, 2016.

53 See, e.g., Del Freo 2017 for a recent review of landholding at Pylos.

54 Killen 1998.

55 Lejeune 1965: 6: "une entité administrative locale à vocation agricole."

56 Lupack 2011. A general (non-technical) meaning for the word may be suggested by personal names and titles compounded with *dāmos*; see below (p. 105 and n92), and cf. Nakassis 2013: 12–13 n66, with bibliography and discussion.

57 Halstead 2001: 41.

58 Del Freo 2017: 117–18. In a famous dispute recorded in Eb 297 and Ep 704.5–6, the priestess Eritha claims that she holds an *e-to-ni-jo* for the god, a claim contested by the *dāmos*. It has been plausibly argued that *e-to-ni-jo* land had a special status, either total exemption from payment, or perhaps a lower rate compared to other

types of landholdings (Deger-Jalkotzy 1983: 99–100; Lupack 2008: 65–67; 2011: 213). If this interpretation is correct, then this dispute illustrates the intimate relationship between religion and payments made from *dāmos* land.

59 Wood: PY Vn 10. Deer hides: PY Ub 1316, 1317. Perhaps weapons: KN U 7507 (see Olivier 1965). On chariot wheels at Knossos described as "given," see Killen 2001: 165–69, 177–78.

60 Varias 2016.

61 Killen 1996. The western "Hither Province" is assessed 99 N units of bronze, and the eastern "Further Province" 101 N units. Killen's (1996) suggestion that there is a relationship between the quantities on Jn 829 and those in the Ma series have not met with agreement (Perna 2004: 261–73).

62 Chadwick 1998–1999.

63 For references, see Nosch 2012: 43–44 n5. Some shepherds are also associated with individuals commonly known in the scholarly literature as "collectors." The precise role of these individuals is unclear, and indeed their activities and responsibilities may have been diverse (Bennet 1992; Nakassis 2013: 18–19, 174–75); Killen (1995: 213) has suggested that "they are prominent members of the ruling élite . . . who have been assigned part of the productive capacity of the kingdoms for their own benefit."

64 Halstead 2001: 41–44.

65 Halstead 1999b: 166.

66 Killen 1984a: 360.

67 Nosch 2006. There is also evidence that textile production is associated with *ta-ra-si-ja* at Mycenae (Nosch 2006: 162) and Pylos (Killen 1984a: 361).

68 Killen 1984a, Chadwick 1988.

69 Killen 2008b: 192–93.

70 PY Ja 749, perhaps the totaling tablet of the Jn series, records a total of ca. 1,046 kg of bronze; the individual quantities of allocated bronze in the Jn series total 594 kg (not counting bronze recorded in the preliminary documents Jn 693 and Jn 725). On Ja 749 as a totaling text for the Jn series, see Ventris and Chadwick 1973: 508–9, not entirely accepted by Smith 1992–1993: 171–72 n4.

71 Killen 2008b: 181–89; Murray 2017: 162–65.

72 Schon (2014) estimates that only 3% of the territory of Pylos would have been required to maintain palatial operations.

73 Halstead 1992.

74 Bennet and Halstead 2014. On *o-no* as "payment" see Palmer 1994: 91–94; Killen 1995: 217–24.

75 The texts are An 35 and Un 443; see Bennet and Halstead 2014 and Nakassis 2010.

76 Halstead 1992; Whitelaw 2001.

77 Bennet and Halstead 2014: 279. As Zurbach (2017: 160) points out, many documents (Un 718, the Ma series) seem not to directly extract agricultural production on lands held, but involve payment to the center in some mix of commodities on

the basis of landholdings, which suggests that such "redistributive" extractions presuppose market exchanges.

78 Finley 1957; for its application to the Linear B evidence, see Killen 1985, 2008b. For discussion, see Galaty and Parkinson (eds.) 2007; Nakassis et al. 2011; and Zurbach 2016.

79 Halstead 1992: 72. See also Halstead 1988.

80 Galaty et al. 2011; Parkinson et al. 2013; and Nakassis et al. 2016.

81 Perna 2004: 7–9.

82 "Compensatory balanced exchanges are: debts, dues, fines, wages and rewards, blood-price, recompense for injury or insult" (Donlan 1982: 143), whereas compactual are "peace-making and friendship agreements, marital alliances, hospitality, gift-giving and gift-exchange" (Donlan 1982: 145).

83 Chantraine 1999: 279–81, s.v. δίδωμι; Benveniste 1951.

84 Cook 2016: 99–102, with references.

85 Aura Jorro 1985: 164, s.v. de-ka-sa-to. For δέχομαι used for the receipt of gifts, ransom (ἄποινα) or reparations (ποινή) in Homer, see Il. 1.20, 7.400, 9.633, 11.124, 22.340, 24.429, 24.434, Od. 8.483, 11.327 (ironically), Homeric Hymn to Hermes 549, cf. Il. 2.420, Od. 2.186. See too Sappho 1.22. Further discussion at Conover 2013.

86 Perna 2017: 141. On debts and reciprocity, see Donlan 1982: 143–44; on the Homeric usage, see West 1988: 183 ad Od. 3.367; see too Od. 8.332.

87 As Sahlins (1972: 134 n. 16) notes, "redistribution is conceived and sanctioned as a reciprocal relation, and is in form but a centralization of reciprocities."

88 "Le verbe δίδωμι, dans nos textes, signifie partout 's'acquitter d'un dû'" (Lejeune 1975: 2, emphasis in original).

89 As Liverani (2001: 5–9) has demonstrated, reciprocity is a cultural representation, not an objective reality.

90 For instance, Mycenaean personal names compounded with the root *dō are consistent with its general sense and difficult to explain using Lejeune's definition: a-pi-do-ro /Ampʰidōros/, a-pi-do-ra /Ampʰidōrā/, te-o-do-ra /Tʰeodōrā/, a-wi-to-do-to /Awistodotos/, i-su-ku-wo-do-to /Iskʰu(w)odotos/. On the final two names, see García Ramón 2005.

91 García Ramón 2007.

92 Killen 1998. The complete personal names compounded with dāmos are a-ko-da-mo /Arkʰodāmos/, a-ko-ro-da-mo /Akrodāmos/, e-ke-da-mo /Ekʰedāmos/, e-u-da-mo /E⁽ʰ⁾udāmos/, and e-u-ru-da-mo /Eurudāmos/, all of which are difficult to render if dāmos retains only a technical meaning.

93 Palaima 2012: 349; García Ramón 2010. The verbal element is related to the later Greek verb κορέννυμι, "satiate," from IE *kerh₃- "feed, grow." The term da-mo-ko-ro is also attested as an official title at Knossos.

94 Palaima 2012: 350.

95 Aura Jorro 1993: 26–27, s.v. o-na-to. This status is not simply rhetorical, for some plots are described as "without benefit," a-no-no /anonon/ (Zurbach 2017: 53–54, 61).

96 Halstead 2001: 40–41.

97 Halstead 2001: 45–46.

98 Halstead 2001: 41–44.

99 Lupack 2006: 93–96.

100 Nosch 2012: 51, who estimates that ca. 400 g of yarn would be required per *pa-wo* (/*p^{h}arwos*/) textile, which is "less than 10% of the raw wool allocated for 1 *pa-wo*."

101 Perna 2004: 71–93. See discussion above (n43).

102 Killen 1992–1993; Perna 2016: 472–73.

103 Nakassis 2013: 174.

104 Nakassis 2010: 127–33, 138–39, with references; Bennet and Halstead 2014: 278.

105 Killen 2008b: 182–84. Alternative spellings include *ke-se-nu-wi-ja* and *ke-se-ne-wi-ja* (neuter plural).

106 Melena 2000–2001: 380–84, on the basis of PY Un 1482, where the ideogram *189 is apparently described as *ke-ra-e-we*, perhaps /*gera^{h}ēwes*/; but Killen 2000–2001 makes the argument that the word is better understood as /*kera^{h}ēwes*/, "horn workers."

107 Nakassis 2010.

108 Nakassis 2012b. We might also include in this discussion religious offerings (Weilhartner 2012), made by the center on behalf of the community as a whole.

109 Perna 2004: 63–102.

110 Killen 1996; Shelmerdine 1998–1999; Perna 2016: 463–67. See too the individual breakdown on Pylos Nn 831 (discussed recently by Del Freo 2017: 108–9).

111 Shelmerdine 1973: 275; Olivier 1974; de Fidio 1982; Shelmerdine 1989; Killen 1996.

112 Perna 2016: 467–68.

113 On the Na tablets, Perna 2004: 249–51.

114 Del Freo 2017: 106–7.

115 "Temple bronze" could also be rendered "ship bronze"; while this is formally possible, it has been rightly rejected by most scholars; see Palaima 1991: 288, 295.

116 The differences in toponyms between Jn 829 and the Ma series are fairly small; of the 16 main centers in Jn 829, 14 (or perhaps 15) appear in the Ma series. The toponyms *a-si-ja-ti-ja* and *e-re-e* in Jn 829 are replaced in the Ma series by *a-[.]-ta$_2$* (an alternative spelling for *a-si-ja-ti-ja*?) and *a-te-re-wi-ja* and *e-sa-re-wi-ja* (for *e-re-e*).

117 Killen 1996.

118 Perna (2008b) argues, however, that the administrative structures of Jn 829 and the Ma series are not identical.

119 Palaima 2001: 159. The scribe (Hand 2) initially wrote *ko-re-te-re, po-ro-ko-re-te-re-qe* ("the governors and the vice-governors"), erased the second word, and wrote *du-ma-te-qe* above the erasure. The remainder of the tablet records payments of metal from the governors and vice-governors from each of the 17 districts of the Pylian kingdom.

120 They may also have determined to what extent assessments would be fulfilled; there are taxation documents that refer to "last year's deficit" (Killen 1984b), implying that not all assessments were paid in a timely fashion.

121 Bennet and Halstead 2014.

122 Nakassis 2010.

123 D'Altroy 2015; Smith 2015; Jursa and Moreno García 2015.

124 Killen 1998; earlier work by Halstead (1988, 1992) suggested the importance of such estates, but modified his view in light of Killen's 1998 article (Halstead 1999a, 2001). See the recent review by Zurbach 2017: 118–29.

125 The royal temenos recorded in PY Er 312 constitutes ca. 5.5% of all the land measured by seed grain at Pylos. The estate of $e\text{-}ke\text{-}ra_2\text{-}wo$, which is perhaps the personal name of the Pylian *wanax* (Nakassis 2012b), constitutes ca. 17.2% of all such land at Pylos. The flax land of the *wanax* at Pylos constitutes only ca. 1.1% of all such land. Of course, our texts do not represent a complete sample, but on the basis of the material that we do have, royal estates can hardly have financed a great deal of state operations.

126 Blanton and Fargher 2008: 112.

127 The possible exception is some of the "women of Pylos," who might represent plunder from military raids. As argued above, however, this interpretation is hardly certain, and a number of other interpretations are possible (Nikoloudis 2006: 115–117).

128 Palaima 1997.

129 E.g., Bennet 2007: 191.

130 Murray 2017: 248–54 (quotation from 254).

131 Nakassis 2020: 281–82.

132 Blanton and Fargher 2008 (quotation from 112).

133 Palaima 2004; Nakassis 2010, 2012b.

134 Nakassis 2012b: 23–25.

135 Bourdieu 1977: 191–92; 1990: 125–29.

136 E.g., Deger-Jalkotzy 2008: 387–90; see in contrast the judicious summary of Dickinson 2006: 35–43.

137 Bennet 2007: 188–90, 206–7.

138 E.g., Bendall 2004: 128, cf. Shelmerdine 2008: 145.

139 De Fidio 1987; Halstead 2001; Shelmerdine 2008: 146; 2011.

140 See the papers in Voutsaki and Killen 2001.

WORKS CITED

Aura Jorro, Francisco. 1985. *Diccionario micénico (DMic.)* I. Madrid: Consejo superior de investigaciones científicas.

Aura Jorro, Francisco. 1993. *Diccionario micénico (DMic.)* II. Madrid: Consejo superior de investigaciones científicas.

Beekes, Robert S. P. 2010. *Etymological Dictionary of Greek*, 2 volumes. Leiden: Brill.

Bendall, Lisa M. 2004. "Fit for a King? Hierarchy, Exclusion, Aspiration, and Desire in the Social Structure of Mycenaean Banqueting." In P. Halstead and J. Barrett (eds.), *Food, Cuisine, and Society in Prehistoric Greece*. Sheffield Studies in Aegean Archaeology 5 (Oxford: Oxbow Books), 105–35.

Bennet, John. 1992. "'Collectors' or 'owners'? An examination of their possible functions within the palatial economy of LM III Crete." In J.-P. Olivier (ed.), *Mykenaïka. Actes du IXe Colloque international sur les textes mycéniens et égéens*. BCH Supplement 25 (Paris: de Boccard), 65–101.

Bennet, John. 2001. "Agency and Bureaucracy: Thoughts on the Nature and Extent of Administration in Bronze Age Pylos." In Voutsaki and Killen (eds.) 2001: 25–37.

Bennet, John. 2007. "The Aegean Bronze Age." In W. Scheidel, I. Morris, and R. Saller (eds.), *The Cambridge Economic History of the Greco-Roman World* (Cambridge: Cambridge University Press), 175–210.

Bennet, John, and Paul Halstead. 2014. "O-no! Writing and Righting Redistribution." In D. Nakassis, J. Gulizio, and S. A. James (eds.), *KE-RA-ME-JA: Studies Presented to Cynthia W. Shelmerdine* (Philadelphia: INSTAP Academic Press), 271–82.

Benveniste, Émile. 1951. "Don et échange dans le vocabulaire indo-européen." *L'Année Sociologique* (3ème série) II: 7–20.

Blanton, Richard, and Lane Fargher. 2008. *Collective Action in the Formation of Pre-Modern States*. New York: Springer.

Bourdieu, Pierre. 1977. *Outline of a Theory of Practice*. Translated by Richard Nice. Cambridge: Cambridge University Press.

Bourdieu, Pierre. 1990. *The Logic of Practice*. Translated by Richard Nice. Stanford: Stanford University Press.

Chadwick, John. 1964. "Pylos Tablet Un 1322." In E. L. Bennett, Jr. (ed.), *Mycenaean Studies: Proceedings of the Third International Colloquium for Mycenaean Studies Held at "Wingspread," 4–8 September 1961* (Madison: University of Wisconsin Press), 19–26.

Chadwick, John. 1976. *The Mycenaean World*. Cambridge: Cambridge University Press.

Chadwick, John. 1988. "The Women of Pylos." In J.-P. Olivier and T. G. Palaima (eds.), *Texts, Tablets and Scribes: Studies in Mycenaean Epigraphy and Economy Offered to Emmett L. Bennett, Jr*. Minos Supplement 10 (Salamanca: Universidad de Salamanca), 43–95.

Chadwick, John. 1998–1999. "Pylian Gold and Local Administration: PY Jo 438." In J. Bennett and J. Driessen (eds.), *A-NA-QO-TA. Studies Presented to J. T. Killen*. Minos 33–34 (Salamanca: Universidad de Salamanca), 31–37.

Chantraine, Pierre. 1999. *Dictionnaire étymologique de la langue grecque: histoire des mots*. New ed. with a supplement. Paris: Klincksieck.

Conover, Kellam. 2013. "The First Athenian Law Against Bribery." *SSRN*. DOI: 10.2139/ssrn.2231641.

Cook, Erwin. 2016. "Homeric Reciprocities." *Journal of Mediterranean Archaeology* 29: 94–104.

D'Altroy, Terence N. 2015. "The Inka Empire." In Monson and Scheidel (eds.) 2015: 31–70.

De Fidio, Pia. 1977. *I dosmoi pilii a Poseidon: Una terra sacra di età micenea*. Roma: Edizioni dell'Ateneo e Bizzarri.

De Fidio, Pia. 1982. "Fiscalità, redistribuzione, equivalenze: per una discussion sull'economia micenea." *Studi Micenei ed Egeo-Anatolici* 23: 93–136.

De Fidio, Pia. 1987. "Palais et communautés de village dans le royaume mycénien de Pylos." In P. Ilievski and L. Crepajac (ed.), *Tractata Mycenaea* (Skopje: Macedonian Academy of Sciences and Arts), 129–49.

Deger-Jalkotzy, Sigrid. 1983. "Zum Charakter und zur Herausbildung der mykenischen Sozialstruktur." In A. Heubeck and G. Neumann (eds.), *Res Mycenaeae* (Gottingen: Vandenhoeck & Ruprecht), 89–111.

Deger-Jalkotzy, Sigrid. 2008. "Decline, Destruction, Aftermath." In C. W. Shelmerdine (ed.), *The Cambridge Companion to the Aegean Bronze Age* (Cambridge: Cambridge University Press), 387–415.

Del Freo, Maurizio. 2017. "Quelques réflexions sur les possessions foncières et les obligations à Pylos." *Pasiphae* 11: 105–19.

Dickinson, Oliver. 2006. *The Aegean from Bronze Age to Iron Age: Continuity and Change between the Twelfth and Eighth Centuries BC*. London and New York: Routledge.

Donlan, Walter. 1982. "Reciprocities in Homer." *The Classical World* 75: 137–75.

Driessen, Jan. 2008. "Chronology of the Linear B Texts." In Duhoux and Morpurgo Davies (eds.) 2008: 69–79.

Duhoux, Yves. 1968. "Le groupe lexical de δίδωμι en mycénien." *Minos* 9: 81–108.

Duhoux, Yves. 1976. *Aspects du vocabulaire économique mycénien (cadastre—artisanat—fiscalité)*. Amsterdam: Adolf M. Hakkert.

Duhoux, Yves, and Anna Morpurgo Davies (eds.). 2008. *A Companion to Linear B: Mycenaean Greek Texts and their World. Volume I*. Leuven: Peeters.

Finley, Moses I. 1957. "The Mycenaean Tablets and Economic History." *Economic History Review* 10: 128–41.

Foster, Ellen D. 1981. "The Flax Impost at Pylos and Mycenaean Landholding." *Minos* 17: 67–121.

Galaty, Michael, Dimitri Nakassis, and William Parkinson (eds.). 2011. "Forum: Redistribution in Aegean Palatial Societies." *American Journal of Archaeology* 115: 175–244.

Galaty, Michael, and William Parkinson (eds.). 2007. *Rethinking Mycenaean Palaces II. Revised and expanded second ed.* Cotsen Institute of Archaeology at UCLA Monograph 60. Los Angeles: UCLA Press.

García Ramón, José Luis. 2005. "Anthroponymica Mycenaea: 5. *a-wi-to-do-to* /Awistodotos/ und die unsichtbaren Götter im Alph.-Griechischen. 6. *we-re-na-ko* /Wrēnāgos/ oder /Wrēn-ắkos/ und Myk. /wrēn-/ *: alph.-gr. °ρρην-, ἀρήν 'Lamm.'" *Živa Antika* 55: 85–97.

García Ramón, José Luis. 2007. "Mykenisch *qe-ja-me-no* und *e-ne-ka a-no-qa-si-ja*, alph.-gr. τεισάμενος und ἀνδροκτασία 'Mord' und der PN Τεισίφονος." In F. Lang, C. Reinholdt, and J. Weilhartner (eds.), *Στέφανος Αριστείος. Archäologische Forschungen zwischen Nil und Istros: Festschrift für Stefan Hiller zum 65. Geburtstag* (Vienna: Phoibos Verlag), 113–23.

García Ramón, José Luis. 2010. "Reconstructing IE Lexicon and Phraseology: Inherited Patterns and Lexical Renewal." In S. W. Jamison, H. C. Melchert, and B. Vine (eds.),

Proceedings of the 21st Annual UCLA Indo-European Conference (Bremen: Hempen Verlag), 69–106.

Garlan, Yvon. 1988. *Slavery in Ancient Greece*. Revised and expanded edition. Translated by Janet Lloyd. Ithaca: Cornell University Press.

Halstead, Paul. 1988. "On Redistribution and the Origin of Minoan-Mycenaean Palatial Economies." In E. B. French and K. A. Wardle (eds.), *Problems in Greek Prehistory* (Bristol: Bristol Classical Press), 519–30.

Halstead, Paul. 1992. "The Mycenaean Palatial Economy: Making the Most of the Gaps in the Evidence." *Proceedings of the Cambridge Philological Society* 38: 57–86.

Halstead, Paul. 1999a. "Surplus and Share-croppers: The Grain Production Strategies of Mycenaean Palaces." In P. Betancourt, V. Karageorghis, R. Laffineur, and W.-D. Niemeier (ed.), *Meletemata: Studies presented to Malcolm H. Wiener as he enters his 65th year*. Aegaeum 20. (Liège and Austin: Université de Liège and the University of Texas at Austin), 319–26.

Halstead, Paul. 1999b. "Missing Sheep: On the Meaning and Wider Significance of *o* in Knossos Sheep Records." *Annual of the British School at Athens* 94: 145–66.

Halstead, Paul. 2001. "Mycenaean Wheat, Flax and Sheep: Palatial Intervention in Farming and its Implications for Rural Society." In Voutsaki and Killen (eds.) 2001: 38–50.

Hiller, Stefan. 1988. "Dependent Personnel in Mycenaean Texts." In M. Heltzer and E. Lipiński (eds.), *Society and Economy in the Eastern Mediterranean (c. 1500–1000 B.C.)* (Leuven: Peeters), 53–68.

Hutton, William F. 1990. "The Meaning of *qe-te-o* in Linear B." *Minos* 25: 105–31.

Jursa, Michael, and Juan Carlos Moreno García. 2015. "The ancient Near East and Egypt." In Monson and Scheidel (eds.) 2015: 115–65.

Killen, John T. 1983. "PY An 1." *Minos* 18: 71–79.

Killen, John T. 1984a. "The Textile Industries at Pylos and Knossos." In C. W. Shelmerdine and T. G. Palaima (eds.), *Pylos Comes Alive: Industry and Administration in a Mycenaean Palace* (New York: Fordham University Press), 49–63.

Killen, John T. 1984b. "Last Year's Debts on the Pylos Ma Tablets." *Studi Micenei ed Egeo-Anatolici* 25: 173–88.

Killen, John T. 1985. "The Linear B Tablets and the Mycenaean Economy." In A. Morpurgo Davies and Y. Duhoux (eds.), *Linear B: A 1984 Survey* (Louvain-la-Neuve: Cabay), 241–305.

Killen, John T. 1992–1993. "Ke-u-po-da e-sa-re-u and the Exemptions on the Pylos Na Tablets." *Minos* 27–28: 109–23.

Killen, John T. 1995. "Some Further Thoughts on 'Collectors.'" In R. Laffineur and W.-D. Niemeier (eds.), *Politeia: Society and State in the Aegean Bronze Age*. Aegaeum 12. (Liège and Austin: Université de Liège and the University of Texas at Austin), 213–26.

Killen, John T. 1996. "Administering a Mycenaean Kingdom: Some Taxing Problems." *Bulletin of the Institute of Classical Studies* 41: 147–48.

Killen, John T. 1998. "The Rôle of the State in Wheat and Olive Production in Mycenaean Crete." *Aevum* 72: 19–23.

Killen, John T. 1999. "Mycenaean *o-pa*." In S. Deger-Jalkotzy, S. Hiller, and O. Panagl (ed.), *Floreant Studia Mycenaea* (Vienna: Verlag der Österreichischen Akadmie der Wissenschaften), 325–41.

Killen, John T. 2000–2001. "A Note on Pylos Tablet Un 1482." *Minos* 35–36: 385–90.

Killen, John T. 2001. "Some Thoughts on *ta-ra-si-ja*." In Voutsaki and Killen (eds.) 2001: 161–80.

Killen, John T. 2006a. "Conscription and Corvée at Mycenaean Pylos." In M. Perna (ed.), *Fiscality in Mycenaean and Near Eastern Archives* (Paris: De Boccard), 73–87.

Killen, John T. 2006b. "The Subjects of the *wanax*: Aspects of Mycenaean Social Structure." In S. Deger-Jalkotzy and I. S. Lemos (eds.), *Ancient Greece: From the Mycenaean Palaces to the Age of Homer* (Edinburgh: Edinburgh University Press), 87–99.

Killen, John T. 2008a. "The Commodities on the Pylos Ma Tablets." In A. Sacconi, M. Del Freo, L. Godart, and M. Negri (eds.), *Colloquium Romanum* (Rome: Fabrizio Serra), 431–47.

Killen, John T. 2008b. "Mycenaean Economy." In Duhoux and Morpurgo Davies (eds.) 2008: 159–200.

Lejeune, Michel. 1959. "Textes mycéniens rélatifs aux esclaves." *Historia* 8: 129–44.

Lejeune, Michel. 1965. "Le *damos* dans la société mycénienne." *Revue des Études Grecques* 78: 1–22.

Lejeune, Michel. 1975. "Δοσμός et ἀπύδοσις." *Museum Helveticum* 32: 1–11.

Liverani, Mario. 2001. *International Relations in the Ancient Near East, 1600–1100 BC*. London: Palgrave.

Luján, Eugenio R. 2011. "Payment and Trade Terminology on Linear B Tablets." In M. P. García-Bellido, L. Callegarin, and A. Jiménez Díaz (eds.), *Barter, Money and Coinage in the Ancient Mediterranean (10th—1st centuries BC)* (Madrid: Consejo Superior de Investigaciones Científicas), 25–32.

Lupack, Susan. 2006. "Deities and Religious Personnel as Collectors." In M. Perna (ed.), *Fiscality in Mycenaean and Near Eastern Archives. Proceedings of the Conference Held at Soprintendenza Archivistica per la Campania, Naples, 21–23 October 2004.* Studi Egei e Vicinorientali 3 (Paris: De Boccard), 89–108.

Lupack, Susan. 2008. *The Role of the Religious Sector in the Economy of Late Bronze Age Mycenaean Greece*. British Archaeological Reports, International Series 1858. Oxford: Archaeopress.

Lupack, Susan. 2011. "A View from Outside the Palace: The Sanctuary and the Damos in Mycenaean Economy and Society." *American Journal of Archaeology* 115: 207–17.

Manning, Sturt. 2010. "Chronology and Terminology." In E. C. Cline (ed.), *The Oxford Handbook of the Bronze Age Aegean (ca. 3000–1000 BC)* (Oxford: Oxford University Press), 11–28.

Melena, José Luis. 2000–2001. "63 Joins and Quasi-Joins of Fragments in the Linear B Tablets from Pylos," *Minos* 35–36: 371–84.

Melena, José Luis. 2014. "Mycenaean Writing." In Y. Duhoux and A. Morpurgo Davies (eds.), *A Companion to Linear B: Mycenaean Greek Texts and their World. Volume 3* (Leuven: Peeters), 1–186.

Monson, Andrew, and Walter Scheidel (eds.). 2015. *Fiscal Regimes and the Political Economy of Premodern States.* Cambridge: Cambridge University Press.

Murray, Sarah M. 2017. *The Collapse of the Mycenaean Economy: Imports, Trade, and Institutions, 1300–700 BCE.* Cambridge: Cambridge University Press.

Nakassis, Dimitri. 2010. "Reevaluating Staple and Wealth Finance at Mycenaean Pylos." In D. J. Pullen (ed.), *Political Economies of the Aegean Bronze Age* (Oxford: Oxbow Books), 127–48.

Nakassis, Dimitri. 2012a. "Labor Mobilization in Mycenaean Pylos." In P. Carlier et al. (eds.), *Études mycéniennes 2010* (Pisa/Rome: Fabrizio Serra), 269–83.

Nakassis, Dimitri. 2012b. "Prestige and Interest: Feasting and the King in Mycenaean Pylos." *Hesperia* 81: 1–30.

Nakassis, Dimitri. 2013. *Individuals and Society in Mycenaean Pylos.* Leiden: Brill.

Nakassis, Dimitri. 2015. "Labor and Individuals in Late Bronze Age Pylos." In P. Steinkeller and M. Hudson (eds.), *Labor in the Ancient Near East* (Dresden: ISLET-Verlag), 583–615.

Nakassis, Dimitri. 2020. "The Economy." In I. S. Lemos and A. Kotsonas (eds.), *A Companion to the Archaeology of Early Greece and the Mediterranean. Volume 1.* (Hoboken: Wiley-Blackwell), 271–91.

Nakassis, Dimitri, Michael Galaty, and William Parkinson. 2011. "Redistributive Economies from a Theoretical and Cross-Cultural Perspective." *American Journal of Archaeology* 115: 177–84.

Nakassis, Dimitri, Michael Galaty, and William Parkinson (eds.). 2016. "Discussion and Debate: Reciprocity in Aegean Palatial Societies: Gifts, Debt, and the Foundations of Economic Exchange." *Journal of Mediterranean Archaeology* 29: 61–132.

Nikoloudis, Stravroula. 2006. "The *ra-wa-ke-ta*: Ministerial Authority and Mycenaean Cultural Identity." PhD thesis, University of Texas at Austin.

Nosch, Marie-Louise B. 2006. "More Thoughts on the Mycenaean *ta-ra-si-ja* System." In M. Perna (ed.), *Fiscality in Mycenaean and Near Eastern Archives* (Paris: De Boccard), 161–82.

Nosch, Marie-Louise B. 2012. "From Texts to Textiles in the Aegean Bronze Age." In M.-L. Nosch and R. Laffineur (eds.), *Kosmos: Jewellery, Adornment and Textiles in the Aegean Bronze Age.* Aegaeum 33 (Leuven/Liège: Peeters), 43–53.

Olivier, Jean-Pierre. 1965. "L'idéogramme *249 du linéaire B." *Kadmos* 4: 58–63.

Olivier, Jean-Pierre. 1974. "Une loi fiscal mycénienne." *Bulletin de correspondence hellénique* 98: 23–35.

Olivier, Jean-Pierre. 1987. "Des extraits de contrats de vente d'esclaves dans les tablettes de Knossos." In J. T. Killen, J. L. Melena, and J.-P. Olivier (eds.), *Studies in Mycenaean and Classical Greek Presented to John Chadwick.* Minos 20–22 (Salamanca: Universidad de Salamanca), 479–98.

Olivier, Jean-Pierre. 2014. "Une 'loi fiscale mycénienne' et le tableau des prix du boucher de Malia en 1972." Κρητικά χρονικά 34: 83–88.

Olsen, Barbara A. 2014. *Women in Mycenaean Greece: The Linear B Tablets from Pylos and Knossos*. London: Routledge.

Palaima, Thomas G. 1991. "Maritime Matters in the Linear B Texts." In R. Laffineur and L. Basch (eds.), *Thalassa: L'Égée prehistorique et la mer*. Aegaeum 7 (Liège and Austin: Université de Liège and the University of Texas at Austin), 273–310.

Palaima, Thomas G. 1995. "The Last Days of the Pylos Polity." In R. Laffineur and W.-D. Niemeier (eds.), *Politeia: Society and State in the Aegean Bronze Age*. Aegaeum 12. (Liège and Austin: Université de Liège and the University of Texas at Austin), 623–33.

Palaima, Thomas G. 1997. "Potter and Fuller: The Royal Craftsmen." In R. Laffineur and P. P. Betancourt (eds.), *TEXNH: Craftsmen, Craftswomen and Craftsmanship in the Aegean Bronze Age*. Aegaeum 16 (Liège and Austin: Université de Liège and the University of Texas at Austin), 407–12.

Palaima, Thomas G. 2001. "The Modalities of Economic Control at Pylos." *Ktema* 26: 151–59.

Palaima, Thomas G. 2004. "Sacrificial Feasting in the Linear B Documents." *Hesperia* 73: 217–46.

Palaima, Thomas G. 2011. "Scribes, Scribal Hands and Palaeography." In Y. Duhoux and A. Morpurgo Davies (eds.), *A Companion to Linear B: Mycenaean Greek Texts and their World. Volume 2* (Leuven: Peeters), 33–136.

Palaima, Thomas G. 2012. "Security and Insecurity as Tools of Power in Mycenaean Palatial Kingdoms." In P. Carlier et al. (eds.), *Études mycéniennes 2010* (Pisa/Rome: Fabrizio Serra), 345–56.

Palmer, Ruth. 1989. "Subsistence Rations at Pylos and Knossos." *Minos* 24: 89–124.

Palmer, Ruth. 1994. *Wine in the Mycenaean Palace Economy*. Aegaeum 10. Liège and Austin: Université de Liège and the University of Texas at Austin.

Parkinson, William. 2007. "Chipping Away at a Mycenaean Economy: Obsidian Exchange, Linear B, and 'Palatial Control' in Late Bronze Age Messenia." In Galaty and Parkinson (eds.) 2007: 87–101.

Parkinson, William, Dimitri Nakassis, and Michael Galaty (eds.). 2013. "Forum: Crafts, Specialists, and Markets in Mycenaean Greece." *American Journal of Archaeology* 117: 413–59.

Perna, Massimo. 1996. "Le tavolette delle serie Mc di Cnosso." In *Atti e memorie del secondo Congresso internazionale di micenologia. Volume 1: Filologia*. Incunabula Graeca 98. (Rome: Gruppo editorial internazionale), 411–19.

Perna, Massimo. 2004. *Recherches sur la fiscalité mycénienne*. Étudies anciennes 28. Paris: Association pour la diffusion de la recherche sur l'antiquité.

Perna, Massimo. 2006. "Les tablettes de la série Na de Pylos." In M. Perna (ed.), *Fiscality in Mycenaean and Near Eastern Archives* (Paris: De Boccard), 189–97.

Perna, Massimo. 2008a. "Le tavolette della serie Es di Pilo." In M. Perna and F. Pomponio (eds.), *The Management of Agricultural Land and the Production of Textiles in the Mycenaean and Near Eastern Economies* (Paris: De Boccard), 89–98.

Perna, Massimo. 2008b. "A proposito di alcuni documenti 'fiscali' in lineare B." In A. Sacconi et al. (eds.), *Colloquium Romanum* (Rome: Fabrizio Serra), 659–68.

Perna, Massimo. 2016. "Testi che trattano di procedure fiscali." In M. del Freo and M. Perna (eds.), *Manuale di epigrafia micenea: Introduzione allo studio dei testi in lineare B. Volume 2* (Padova: Webster SRL), 453–89.

Perna, Massimo. 2017. "Quelques réflexions sur la fiscalité mycénienne." *Pasiphae* 11: 141–50.

Postgate, Nicholas. 2010. "The Debris of Government: Reconstructive the Middle Assyrian State Apparatus from Tablets and Potsherds." *Iraq* 72: 19–37.

Sahlins, Marshall. 1972. *Stone Age Economics.* New York: Aldine.

Schon, Robert. 2014. "The Political Ecology of the Pylian State." In G. Touchais, R. Laffineur, and F. Rougemont (eds.), *Physis: l'environnement naturel et la relation homme-milieu dans le monde égéen protohistorique.* Aegaeum 37 (Leuven and Liège: Peeters), 547–53.

Shelmerdine, Cynthia W. 1973. "The Pylos Ma Tablets Reconsidered." *American Journal of Archaeology* 77: 261–75.

Shelmerdine, Cynthia W. 1989. "Mycenaean Taxation." In T. G. Palaima, C. W. Shelmerdine, and P. Hr. Ilievski (eds.), *Studia Mycenaea (1988)* (Skopje: University of Skopje), 125–48.

Shelmerdine, Cynthia W. 1998–1999. "The Southwestern Department at Pylos." In J. Bennet and J. Driessen (eds.), *A-NA-QO-TA: Studies Presented to J.T. Killen.* Minos 33–34 (Salamanca: Universidad de Salamanca), 309–37.

Shelmerdine, Cynthia W. 2008. "Mycenaean Society." In Duhoux and Morpurgo Davies (eds.) 2008: 115–58.

Shelmerdine, Cynthia W. 2011. "The Individual and the State in Mycenaean Greece." *Bulletin of the Institute of Classical Studies* 54: 19–28.

Smith, Joanna S. 1992–1993. "The Pylos Jn Series." *Minos* 27–28: 167–259.

Smith, Michael E. 2015. "The Aztec Empire." In Monson and Scheidel 2015 (eds.): 71–114.

Varias, Carlos. 2006. "The Mycenaean Fiscal Vocabulary." In M. Perna (ed.), *Fiscality in Mycenaean and Near Eastern Archives* (Paris: De Boccard), 241–53.

Varias, Carlos. 2016. "Testi relativi ai metalli." In M. del Freo and M. Perna (eds.), *Manuale di epigrafia micenea: Introduzione allo studio dei testi in lineare B. Volume 2* (Padova: Webster SRL) 403–19.

Ventris, Michael, and John Chadwick. 1973. *Documents in Mycenaean Greek,* 2nd edition. Cambridge: Cambridge University Press.

Voutsaki, Sofia, and John Killen (eds.). 2001. *Economy and Politics in the Mycenaean Palace States.* Cambridge Philological Society Supplementary Volume 27. Cambridge: Cambridge Philological Society.

Weilhartner, Jörg. 2012. "Religious Offerings in the Linear B Tablets: An Attempt at their Classification and Some Thoughts about their Possible Purpose." In C. Varias (ed.), *Actas del Simposio Internacional: 55 Años de Micenología (1952-2007)*. Faventia Supplementa 1 (Bellaterra: Universitat Autònoma de Barcelona), 207–31.

Weilhartner, Jörg. 2017. "Working for a Feast: Textual Evidence for State-Organized Work Feasts in Mycenaean Greece." *American Journal of Archaeology* 121: 219–36.

West, Stephanie. 1988. "Books I–IV." In A. Heubeck, S. West, and J.B. Hainsworth (eds.), *A Commentary on Homer's* Odyssey. *Volume I: Introduction and Books I–VIII* (Oxford: Clarendon Press), 51–245.

Whitelaw, Todd. 2001. "Reading between the Tablets: Assessing Mycenaean Palatial Involvement in Ceramic Production and Consumption." In Voutsaki and Killen (eds.) 2001: 51–79.

Zurbach, Julien. 2006. "L'impôt pesant sur la terre dans le royaume de Pylos." In M. Perna (ed.), *Fiscality in Mycenaean and Near Eastern Archives* (Paris: De Boccard), 267–80.

Zurbach, Julien. 2016. "L'economia dei regni micenei." In M. del Freo and M. Perna (eds.), *Manuale di epigrafia micenea: Introduzione allo studio dei testi in lineare B. Volume 2* (Padova: Webster SRL), 677–89.

Zurbach, Julien. 2017. *Les hommes, la terre et la dette en Grèce, c. 1400—c. 500 a.C.* Bordeaux: Ausonius Éditions.

5

Extracting Cohesion

Fiscal Strategies in the Hittite Staple Economy

LORENZO D'ALFONSO AND ALVISE MATESSI[1]

Hittite history covers the approximately five centuries between the 17th and the end of the 13th century BCE.[2] At the beginning of this period, the Hittite kingdom emerged in North-Central Anatolia in the bend of the Kızıl Irmak river (Hitt. *Marrassantiya*). During an initial phase, termed the Old Kingdom, Hittite supremacy gradually spread over much of Anatolia; but it was in the following phase, beginning in the early 15th century, that the Hittite polity became a cross-regional empire, expanding its hegemony from Western Anatolia to Upper Mesopotamia and the Northern Levant. As a result of this expansion, the Hittite empire rose to prominence within the "circle of great powers" of the Late Bronze Age, establishing diplomatic relations on equal terms with Egypt, Babylonia, and Assyria.

Yet, as far as environmental conditions and land use practices are concerned, Anatolia is by no means comparable with the Nile valley, Mesopotamia, or the Syrian interface.[3] The broad alluvial plains characteristic of these regions allowed for the accumulation of large surpluses through irrigated agriculture that facilitated the development of highly centralized extractive systems. No such plains are present in Anatolia. The Anatolian plateau, the heartland of the Hittites, rises between 800 and 1,500 m above sea level and is enclosed by two imposing barriers, the Taurus Mountains to the south and the Pontic Mountains to the north. Today, average precipitation in this region rarely exceeds 600 mm per year and in some areas, especially south of the Salt Lake (Tuz Gölü), precipitation peaks at less than 300 mm. Recent paleo-environmental studies have demonstrated that, except for micro-variations, average climatic conditions have not changed substantially over the last 6,000 years. Under such conditions and lacking the potential for extensive canalization systems, Anatolian populations down to the Ottoman period have had to rely upon dry farming, generally combined with horticulture and livestock breeding as a means of diversifying their resources and thus counterbalancing the unpredictability of precipitation rates.

As we shall see in more detail, under pre-industrial conditions Anatolian fields produced very low yields compared to contemporary counterparts in Mesopotamia and Egypt. Without a supplementary infrastructure, farming could support little more than a subsistence economy.

Even though acquiring more arable land could have increased production, its effects would have been null without the necessary manpower to till the new fields. For this reason, preserving and, where possible, increasing the supply of manpower was a primary concern for the Hittite state, surfacing almost everywhere in available texts. For example, international treaties set obligations for client states to return runaways from Hatti. "Historiographic" texts refer repeatedly to deportations of prisoners of war (Sum. NAM.RA; Hitt. $^{LÚ(.MEŠ)}arnuwala$) and to the repopulation of Hittite cities. Normative documents prescribe the redistribution of the labor force among different branches of the economic administration. The endemic climatic instability in Anatolia complicated this labor system, however, as it presented a constant risk of demographic shifts, especially at the interface between different environmental niches, and often caused political stakeholders to switch their allegiances, thus undermining the power base of the court at *Hattusa*. In sum, Bronze Age Central Anatolia lacked the pristine conditions for the "social cage" that Mann (1986: 73–104) argues was instrumental to the emergence of complex societies in the Fertile Crescent. In this environment, the "social cage" had to be forged and maintained through ad hoc organizational means, a challenge that the Hittite state was able to address with considerable success for almost five centuries. It did this by maintaining a delicate balance between the extraction of resources from its subjects, the development of infrastructure, and the cultivation of ideological motivation.

In this chapter, we will begin with an evaluation of the first part of this triad and then analyze its interplay with the other two. Hittite authorities employed multiple strategies to maintain sovereignty over their vast domain. The area formally controlled directly by the Hittite king through various functionaries comprised Hatti, the core of the Hittite domain in North-Central Anatolia, and most of Southern Anatolia. This was also the main catchment area for the extraction of the primary resources upon which the empire subsisted.

Recent studies have revealed the prominence of private patrimony accumulated by most of the chief officials of the empire through tribute from rich, peripheral regions like Western Anatolia and Syria, as well as some instances of embezzlement. These studies have demonstrated that the accumulation of luxury goods helped bind élites to the ruling authority, both in the imperial core—North-Central Anatolia—and in the imperial peripheries.[4] It is probably because of the central importance of wealth accumulation in the Hittite political system that it is more visible in extant textual sources than the staple economy. This is true, for example, in the so-called Hittite inventory texts (CTH 241–250), long lists of finished luxury goods and raw materials, especially metals, assigned to craftsmen, institutions, and officials linked to the royal family (Siegelová 1986). Spectacular finds like the hoard of the officer Taprammi uncovered in Kastamonu province also provide concrete manifestations of this phenomenon.[5] Despite the significance of wealth accumulation in terms of prestige and its cultic associations, it is unlikely that this wealth could be monetized and transformed into improvements in the staple economy that was the economic basis of Hittite power.

Since it has recently been studied in some detail, the modalities and social implications of wealth accumulation will not be dealt with in this contribution. Due to the difficult nature of the sources, we also omit the slippery topic of conscription from the present study.[6] Within these limits, we will introduce the evidence for Hittite taxation and endeavor to make sense of it from an emic perspective. Building on a long series of studies that reached its apex in the social history movement of the 1960s and 1970s, we will show that the modes and strategies of extraction in the Hittite world were highly fluid and can therefore not be encapsulated by a single model of political economy.[7] The result is a more flexible and certainly an altogether different reconstruction of Hittite taxation than the traditional ones based on theoretical models valid for Classical and modern political economies.

Sources

Unlike other contemporary archives of the Eastern Mediterranean, those found in the Hittite capital *Hattusa* (mod. Boğazköy) and other find-spots in Anatolia have yielded very few documents relating to everyday administrative practice, which otherwise constitute the traditional basis for socio-economic analyses of the so-called "palatial systems." The paucity of administrative texts is nonetheless complemented by a very rich corpus of other types of sources that offer important clues regarding taxation. These sources are chiefly represented by a number of normative texts, including a law collection, several treaties, the so-called "instructions and oath impositions" for different categories of officials, and edicts and royal land grants (Archi 2008; d'Alfonso 2008; Mora 2008; and Miller 2013). In addition, documents relating to religious practice, namely festival descriptions and cult inventories, are increasingly being understood as evidence of an "economy of religion" parallel to and perhaps constitutive of the Hittite "political economy."[8] Finally, letters, lists of land plots, and a small number of highly illuminating registers of land production complete the suite of textual evidence relevant to Hittite taxation.[9]

None of these sources informs us directly concerning the functioning of taxation. More specifically, they do not define the quantity and nature of items subject to taxation, nor the social status or the overall percentage of the population required to pay taxes. We do not have here "Solonian" normative formulations of any fiscal reform and, conversely, not a single note of a tax payment contributed by an individual, group, or institution to the royal palace or its local representatives. Extant evidence clearly indicates the existence of variable means for extracting resources and sometimes provides deep insights into specific, and often controversial, matters of taxation. Such evidence offers very few and intermittent clues on the overall needs and expenditures of the empire, so that it is unclear precisely which expenditures the empire covered with its tax revenues.

The Norms of Taxation

The Hittite law collection is by far the most important and most investigated source on Hittite taxation (CTH 291–92).[10] It is preserved in numerous versions, and internal references testify to an ongoing process of textual revision. There are two main manuscripts: A, which is Old Hittite (17th–15th century BCE), and B, which is New Hittite (14th century BCE). There is also a very late version (end of the 13th century BCE) that is known as the *Parallel Text* (PT).[11] We have no direct evidence that the collection had normative value, as it does not appear to have been employed in judicial praxis. Nevertheless, the existence of successive stages of formulation, including references to actual reforms, indicates that the collection was very much in use, incorporating new legislation that derived from legal praxis.[12] The question of the law collection's territorial reach is not a trivial one. Certainly, the collection comprised laws applied in the capital Hattusa and in the rest of the land of Hatti that formed the core of the Hittite domain in North-Central Anatolia.[13] Occasional paragraphs deal with cases involving peripheral regions or their people, but the scope of the collection does not generally extend to laws and rights beyond the borders of Hatti proper.[14]

Some 25 paragraphs of the law collection subdivided between the two manuscripts are indirectly concerned with taxation. They do not explicitly address tax revenues but instead adopt four *termini technici* defining service obligations toward the Hittite crown and its administration: two are Hittite words (*saḫḫan* and *luzzi-*), one is an Akkadogram (*ILKU*), and one is a Sumerogram (GIŠTUKUL). All of them appear in connection with land parcels assigned to specific categories of people. Here is an example:

> § 40. If a man who has a GIŠTUKUL-obligation disappears, and a man owing *ILKU*-services is assigned (in his place), the man owing *ILKU*-services shall say: "This is my GIŠTUKUL-obligation, and this other is my **saḫḫan-services**." He shall secure for himself a sealed deed concerning the land of the man having a GIŠTUKUL-obligation. He shall both hold the GIŠTUKUL-obligation and perform the **saḫḫan-services**. But if he refuses the GIŠTUKUL-obligation, they shall declare the land of the man having the GIŠTUKUL-obligation to be that of (a person) who has disappeared, and the men of the village (LÚ.MEŠ URU-*LIM*) will work it. If the king supplies a deportee (NAM.RA^HI.A), they will give him the land, and he will become a GIŠTUKUL-(man).

§ 41. If a man owing *ILKU*-service (LÚ *IL-KI*) disappears/dies, and a man having a ^{GIŠ}TUKUL-obligation (LÚ ^{GIŠ}TUKUL) is assigned in his place, the man having the ^{GIŠ}TUKUL-obligation shall say: "This is my ^{GIŠ}TUKUL-obligation, and this other is my **saḫḫan-services**."[15] He shall secure for himself a sealed deed concerning the land of the *ILKU*-man. He shall hold the ^{GIŠ}TUKUL-obligation and perform the **saḫḫan-services**. But if he refuses (to do) the **saḫḫan-services**, they will take the (deed concerning the) land of the *ILKU*-man to the Palace. And the obligation for **sahhan-services** shall cease.

(Based on Hoffner 1997: 48–50)

The interpretation of the terms *saḫḫan*, *luzzi-*, *ILKU* and ^{GIŠ}TUKUL is not straightforward. Scholarly debate about these terms extends back to the infancy of Hittitological research, with the most important contributions made by experts in Roman law.[16] Scholars have generally tried to reconstruct the specific kinds of taxes designated by each term. This is reflected in one of the most important and recent papers on the management of agricultural land in Hittite Anatolia, in which Marazzi (2008: 64–65) assumes that the four terms correspond to obligations that are different in nature and apply to specific sectors of the population. Marazzi understands *luzzi-* and *saḫḫan* as harvest taxes, the first imposed on family plots, the latter on land plots assigned by the state; *ILKU* is the leasehold of a plot of land and ultimately the rent; and the ^{GIŠ}TUKUL is a labor obligation (corvée) owed to the state.

The scholars who produced the main editions of the law collection, namely Friedrich (1959), Imparati (1964), and Hoffner (1997), had to confront the superimposition and interchangeability of these *termini* between the earlier redactions and the latest one preserved in PT. For example:

A=B (Old Kingdom and early Empire period)

§ 47b. If anyone buys all the land of a man having a ^{GIŠ}TUKUL-obligation, he shall render the **luzzi-services**. But if he buys only the largest portion of the land, he shall not render the **luzzi-services**. But if he carves out for himself fallow land, or the men of the village give (him land), he shall render the **luzzi-services**.

PT (late Empire period)

§ 37. If anyone buys all the land of a ^{GIŠ}TUKUL-man, and the (former) owner of the land dies, (the new owner) shall perform whatever *saḫḫan*-services the king determines. But if the (former) owner is still living, or (there is) an estate of the (former) owner of the land, whether in that country or another country, (the new owner) shall not perform *saḫḫan*-services.

§ 39b. If anyone buys all the land of a ^{GIŠ}TUKUL-man, they shall ask the king, and he shall render whatever *luzzi*-services the king says. If he buys in addition someone else's land, he shall render (any additional) *luzzi*-services. If the land is fallow (*ḫarkant-*: Marazzi 2008: 75), or the men of the village give him (other land), he shall perform the *luzzi*-services (on it).

(Adapted from Hoffner 1997: 56–58)

It is not only in these and other passages of the law collection that the terms *saḫḫan* and *luzzi-* seem to overlap. In the royal edicts and in late documents they actually tend to merge, becoming either interchangeable or appearing together in hendiadys; they are also often confused with *ILKU*. Examining the occurrence of the two terms demonstrates that even if *saḫḫan* and *luzzi-* referred to distinct taxes in the early stage of the Hittite period, by the early Empire they designated a general and never-specified obligation to the Hittite royal court and its administration (d'Alfonso 2010; most recently Lorenz 2017).

It is noteworthy that the Hittite laws explicitly adopt these four terms for obligations *only* to address specific categories of people, who are defined either by the very same terms of obligation—the ^{GIŠ}TUKUL-men, the ILKU-men—or were already bound to the Hittite administration through land assignments or as deportees and prisoners. The same categories of people are indeed the main target of state-led policies for administering and monitoring land use practices. This impression is conveyed both in the Laws and by the so-called *Feldertexte* (CTH 239) and *Landschenkungsurkunden* (CTH 222), which together represent the bulk of direct sources on the Hittite agricultural economy.

The *Feldertexte* are long lists of fields recorded by dimension, quantities of grain, the name of their owners or usufructuaries, and sometimes by vague indications of their location.[17] The exact function of these texts is not clear, but they are the product of state-led surveys of the productivity of fields that were likely conducted to assess tax burdens and in order to plan for the following sowing season. When their status is disclosed, land plot tenants can be grouped in three main categories. One is represented by the [GIŠ]TUKUL-men, people bound to a local "palace" through a [GIŠ]TUKUL-service obligation. The remaining groups of fields are either directly associated with a local "palace," (e.g. É.GAL [URU]Hattina), or with the muškēnu, a term that in Hittite texts seems to denote a precise category of personnel, possibly employed in the military and/or in the cult.[18]

The *Landschenkungsurkunden* (LSU) were royal grants registering the transfer of substantial estates, labor forces, and, sometimes, livestock from one subject, often an institution, to another. These documents were issued between the Old Kingdom and the early Empire period, more specifically in the century and a half from the reign of Telipinu (16th century BCE) to the reigns of Tuthaliya I and Arnuwanda I (late 15th century BCE).[19] The legal formulation of the transfer is that of a "royal gift" (log. NÍG.BA), through which the king intended to secure the loyalty of officials of high rank and compensate them for extraordinary administrative and military services. The LSU do not offer any specific information on the taxation of the land plots in question, but there are references in the Hittite Laws:

A=B (Old Kingdom and early Empire period)

§ 47a. If someone holds land as a royal grant (NÍG.BA), [he shall] not [have to render] *saḫḫan-* and *luzzi*-services. Furthermore, the king shall provide him with food at royal expense.

(Adapted from Hoffner 1997: 56)

The Old Kingdom and early Empire period formulations of the law thus grant tax exemptions for land assigned by the king as a gift and even add the provision of food. This is not true of the latest version of this paragraph, which clearly states that lands assigned by the king were not "duty-free" by default; specific tax exemptions had to be applied by the king through ad hoc decrees:

PT (late Empire period)

§ 39a. If someone holds land by a royal grant (NÍG.BA), he shall perform the *luzzi*-services. But if the king exempts him, he shall not perform the *luzzi*-services.

(Adapted from Hoffner 1997: 57)

This change is also reflected in practice. Drafts and copies of royal decrees of land donation to powerful officials or cultic institutions dating to the Late Empire (mid 13th century BCE) focus precisely on specific exemptions from *saḫḫan* and/or *luzzi*- obligations.[20] As argued by Imparati (1988), both the LSU and these later decrees were meant not only to reinforce royal authority by establishing client relations, but also to put the acquisition of extensive *latifundia* (landed estates) under royal control. By making such *latifundia* dependent on royal decree, dignitaries and courtiers could be prevented from becoming decentralized regional potentates. But there is a further aspect that both types of land grants share with the other texts mentioned so far regarding taxation patterns: they reveal robust intervention by the state to keep the land productive and thus to maintain the inflow of state revenues through the allotment of resources to various stakeholders and through the distribution of manpower. The same seems to apply to the management of pastoral resources, at least judging from the little positive evidence we have in this respect: livestock "belonging to Hatti" were entrusted to specialized herdsmen ([LÚ.MEŠ]SIPAD) working for the palace or even to foreign clients (e.g. subjugated Kaska tribes in the Pontus region), who tended them alongside their own herd animals.[21]

The Infrastructure of Taxation and Accumulation

The collected staple revenues in rural districts were mainly overseen by the storehouse-keeper ([LÚ.MEŠ]AGRIG), whose office was based in the É[ḪI.A] [NA4]KIŠIB (lit. "houses of the seal"), i.e., storehouses dispersed in various towns of the Hittite domain.[22] In addition to houses of the seal, Hittite sources refer to other decentralized administrative facilities whose mutual interrelationships and division of responsibilities escape clear definition. We know, in particular, of several local "palaces" (É.GAL) that, besides serving as temporary residences for the king and his entourage during their visits, also collected local revenues.[23] The functions of such "palaces" overlapped in part with those of the storehouse network; perhaps a sort of hierarchy existed between the two institutions, with the latter subordinate to the former. For example, the city of Tapikka (mod. Maşat Höyük) was the seat of an É [NA4]KIŠIB, but the local authorities were also accountable to different É.GALs situated in the region.[24]

We do not know if, and to what extent, the territorial distribution of such administrative facilities, their relative status, and their functions evolved through time. According to Singer (1984b), the AGRIGs may have enjoyed a prominent position in the Hittite state hierarchy during its formative stages (17th century BCE), but their status likely declined afterwards. This would have been due to a reform introduced by king Telipinu (16th century BCE) in response to the frequent cases of corruption and embezzlement in local administration that allegedly characterized the reigns of his predecessors.[25] Nonetheless, the recently published LSU Bo 90/671 proves that the AGRIGs continued to represent a recognizable office in the civil administration at least down to the end of the Old Kingdom, while festival texts copied down throughout the Empire period attribute a prominent role to them within the cultic administration (see below).[26] Matessi (2016: 134–42) has shown that some seats of storehouses during the Old Kingdom were later subsumed into extensive regional provinces, namely the Lower and the Upper Land. There is some hint that this reorganization affected methods of military conscription—e.g., we know of contingents from the Upper Land (Beal 1992: 87–89)—and we can suppose that something similar transpired in the field of taxation.

Once amassed by and stored in the administrative infrastructure, the proceeds of taxation in kind, and seeds in particular, entered an economic cycle the ultimate goal of which was to facilitate and improve their own generation. This was done by securing sufficient sowing seed for the following season(s) and, where possible, for the cultivation of new, previously untilled terrain. This is consistent with the textual evidence presented above, in which Hittite political institutions directly regulate rural life only in order to keep non-private land productive. A text known as the *Instructions for the Governor of the frontier post* (CTH 261.I) demonstrates this principle. In §§ 41–44 of this text, the addressee is required to supervise the centralized distribution of sowing seed for fields assigned to deportees and to oversee irrigation and other agricultural infrastructure.

CTH 261, III 36–65'

(36-39) You (governor of the frontier post), must devote attention to the deportee who has been settled in the province with regard to provisions, seed, cattle (and) sheep; further, you must provide him with cheese, sourdough, (and) wool. Whoever remains in place of a deportee who leaves your province, though, (40) you yourself must sow seed for him. Furthermore, he must be satisfied with regard to fields, (41) s[o] they shall promptly assign him a plot.

III 42–59': fragmentary passages mainly concerning the maintenance of irrigation facilities and pasture lands.

(60') When, however, they sow seed for deportees, the governor of the post (61'-64') must keep his eyes on all of them as well. But if someone speaks as follows: "Give me seed, and I will sow it in my field, then I will heap up stores (of grain)," then the governor of that very post must keep (his) eyes on (him). (65') When the harvest arrives, then [he shall ha]rvest that field.

(Adapted from Miller 2013: 230–31)

The supervisory role of the Governor of the frontier post implies that there were estimates of the quantities of seed needed for sowing non-private land, as well as an accurate estimate of the incoming harvest. An administrative text found at Maşat Höyük/Tapikka, HKM 109, represents the only known source that sheds light on how these estimates were calculated.[27] It records a three-year plan for cultivation, indicating types and quantities of sowing seed for each year. The first year is dealt with in two paragraphs: the first records the quantity of seed corn of each species for planting in the sowing season, and the second provides the estimated seed growth for the next harvest. The third and the fourth paragraphs are devoted to the second and third years respectively, recording the quantities of seed corn estimated for each year. Finally, the last two paragraphs, mostly lost, likely provided overall figures and additional notes. The following table synthesizes the data from this document:

TABLE 5.1. Sowing and Harvest Estimates Recorded in HKM 109

	1st Year		2nd Year	3rd Year
	Seed Corn	Harvest (Estimate)	Seed Corn (Estimate)	Seed Corn (Estimate)
barley (ŠE)	900	2100	1300	500
wheat (ZÍZ^HI.A)	300	900	400	[ ]'
small emmer? (šeppit-)	100	100	50	[ ]'
emmer (KUNAŠU)	100	100	60	-
karši-grain	70	90	30	-
Rye (ZÍZ^HI.A KALAG.GA)	-	80	-	-
peas (GÚ.GAL)	-	30	10	-
broad beans (GÚ.GAL.GAL)	-	30	5	-
lentils (GÚ.TUR.TUR)	-	20	10	-

Numbers refer to capacity measures as given in the text (PARĪSU).

As Marazzi has argued (2008: 78–79), the division into a three-year timespan and the complex articulation of the qualities and quantities of seeds planted per year may well reflect a three-year rotation of crops, according to instructions issued by the local administration.

The uniqueness of HTM 109 within the Hittite corpus precludes any possibility of extrapolating general rules from it.[28] It is also difficult to identify a rationale for the figures in the text, especially when comparing the number provided for the first-year harvest with the seed crop estimates for the following years. It is nonetheless readily apparent from the available figures for the first year how low the estimated crop yield is: e.g., quantities relating to barley and wheat point to seed crop:harvest ratios ranging between a mere 1:2 and 1:3. As a rule, one can assume that quantities were underestimated to account for possible crop failures or losses during storage. Indeed, there were quite good reasons for this practice: annual climatic conditions in Central Anatolia display a high degree of variability, with precipitation rates often shifting +/– 50% from one year to another. The barley and wheat seed crop:harvest ratio observable in HKM 109 is thus consistent with the productivity of many areas of the Anatolian plateau that generated similar yields in years with low precipitation rates prior to the introduction of modern fertilizers (Castellano 2018).

Considering that parallel ratios in Lower Mesopotamia could reach peaks exceeding 1:30, the Hittites must have devised a tremendous administrative system of production and extraction to overcome the gap in agrarian productivity and sustain a major polity able to compete with contemporary Babylonia, Assyria, and Egypt.[29] Schachner has elaborated on this in several articles (e.g. 2009; 2011b) and in his monograph (2011a), concluding that the Hittites were able to build an Empire in a low-productivity landscape by developing sophisticated storage installations that enabled the conservation of very large quantities of grain in and around each of the main urban centers of their territory; they also invested in an advanced infrastructure for storing and supplying water. Several storage structures were found in the Hittite capital Böğazköy/ Hattusa, among which the largest by far is an underground granary made up of two rows of sixteen elongated rooms built along the inner side of the southern fortification wall of the Lower City. In addition, several silo pits were found close to the fortification wall of Büyükkaya, the northern peak of Böğazköy/Hattusa. Granaries of this kind feature in other Hittite centers, such as Kaman-Kalehöyük (ca. 100 km south of Hattusa) and, most prominently, Kusaklı/Sarissa (ca. 200 km south-east of Hattusa) with its impressive triangular silo, again located close to the fortification wall. In addition to imposing storage facilities, Hattusa, Sarissa, and other Hittite centers of North-Central Anatolia hosted large dams and reservoirs, situated either inside or outside the town (most recently d'Alfonso in press, with further references). The peak in their construction seems to have been reached in the mid-16th century BCE (Schachner 2009).

Seeher (2000) and Mielke (*apud* Müller-Karpe 2001: 241) have provided insights into the grain capacity of some of the storage facilities. According to their analysis, the silo of Sarissa could store ca. 700 tons of grain, and the granary in Hattusa's Lower City ca. 4,200 tons. Considering that 100 tons of grain are sufficient to supply ca. 550 people year-round with daily rations of 500g, the grain stored at Sarissa could feed just under 4,000 individuals; similar data can be derived for Kaman-Kalehöyük based on calculations made by Fairbairn and Omura (2005: 20–21). Using the same criteria, the supply potential of Hattusa's storage facilities was sufficient to feed up to 23,000 individuals. Such quantities clearly exceed the yearly nutritional needs of the populations that lived in these cities. Hattusa could hardly have been home to more than 15,000 inhabitants; similarly, the populations of Sarissa and Kaman Kalehöyük appear to have been much smaller than the supply potential of their granaries.[30] The stored grain was not, however, used to feed the population through the disbursement of regular rations, nor was it used to feed the army. Underground granaries could only be opened once, since any change in their inner atmosphere could cause the deterioration of the stored seeds. This means that it was not possible to access the contents of the granaries for daily or occasional consumption. They were instead built to secure seeds over a longer period, as reserves of food or future seed corn capital (Seeher 2000; Diffey, Neef, and Bogard 2017; Castellano and d'Alfonso 2017; Castellano 2018).

There were also other means of storage in widespread use in the Hittite domain, most notably large storage jars of variable capacities up to 2,000 liters. These were generally sunk into the floors of dedicated rooms in Hittite temples and public buildings (Schoop 2011: 254–56). Unlike silos, these storage jars were meant to store staples intended for regular consumption, on a yearly or even a more frequent basis. Significantly, storage jars are at the center of seasonal cultic celebrations that involved filling the jar in the harvesting season (i.e. Fall), and, conversely, emptying the jar in the sowing season.[31]

Staple Accumulation and Writing

The archaeological evidence for the centralized management of agricultural production and the textual evidence of procedures of extraction and redistribution, particularly for the non-private sector, point indisputably to the existence of a complex organization for the extraction of agricultural produce. This system was the foundation of the political economy of the empire. Yet the very limited evidence of the use of writing for the registration of goods entering and leaving public storage facilities is surprising when compared to other early great powers, and particularly those of Mesopotamia. This difference cannot simply be the product of chance or attributed to gaps in the archaeological record.

The technology of Hittite silos and underground granaries may well be derived from local types attested earlier in the Anatolian Bronze Ages (Düring 2010: 266–69; Bachhuber 2015: 52ff.), but their sheer size is without parallel in previous periods. The most remarkable evidence for the development of a centralized economic system in Anatolia before the Hittites is from the Late Chalcolithic levels of Arslantepe (ca. 3300–3000 BCE) on the Upper Euphrates. There, the modes of extraction, storage, and redistribution of staple commodities differ greatly from those described above for the Hittite empire, as they are instead connected with communal feasting and the regular redistribution of meals (e.g., Pollock 2012; Frangipane 2012 and 2016). Moreover, neither the kinds of storage facilities used in the Hittite world nor evidence of urbanization or extensive territorial control are attested at Arslantepe in this period. Arslantepe does, however, provide an excellent model for a highly complex system of accounting that records the circulation of goods without the use of writing, relying instead on controlled distribution through space and sealing deposits (Frangipane 2007).

Similar traditions for the administration of complex systems of accumulation based on sealing practices and without writing became more widespread in Anatolia as part of the urbanization of the Early and Middle Bronze Ages. Sporadic finds (<10) of seals and seal impressions associated with the centralized storage of staple commodities feature in various EBA I–II contexts from Cilicia to Central and West Anatolia, while more substantial clusters begin to appear in the EBA III in spaces associated with storage structures (Bachhuber 2015: 130–36, with literature). Excavations on the main mound at Kültepe have reported the discovery of over a thousand sealed *bullae* in an EBA III palace complex that was equipped with large scale granaries and storage facilities.[32]

Non-literate record keeping through seals continued in Middle Bronze Age Central Anatolia. This time it was associated with a more complex centralized economy that comprised not only staple finance, but also the management of wealth accumulated through long-distance trade. This is best documented by the archive of about 1,300 *bullae* recovered from Room 6 of the Sarıkaya palace of Acemhöyük (Aksaray). In addition to a few impressions of inscribed cylinder seals of Mesopotamian and Syrian origin, these *bullae* included several local sealings used for storage jars and warehouse doors (Özguç 1980; 2015). Similarly, numerous sealed *bullae* found at Karahöyük-Konya were used on various containers, including several storage jars, before being discarded into the large pit where they were eventually found (Alp 1968). Most known Middle Bronze Age sealings from Kültepe/ Kaneš come from the lower town (*kārum*) and supplement the thousands of cuneiform tablets discovered there to document the activities of the Assyrian merchants. The so-called palace of Warsama on the main mound suffered extensive damage at the hands of the earliest excavators, but there are strong indications that it probably had storage rooms and *bullae* archives not dissimilar to those found at Acemhöyük (Özguç and Tunca 2001).

Given their persistence from the fourth to the early second millennium BCE, methods of recordkeeping by means of seals and *bullae* may have been such an integral part of the administrative *modus operandi* in Anatolia that writing was simply deemed unnecessary even after the Hittite court definitively adopted cuneiform beginning in the Old Hittite Kingdom. Normative texts only refer to written documents for property deeds, not for the registration of taxes. Inventory texts concerned with valuable raw materials and luxury goods might be a later innovation of the Empire period, spurred by the superimposition over the system of staple finance of a system of wealth finance based on the extraction of tribute and international exchanges of royal gifts.[33] Scribal recording of staple finance transactions on perishable materials, namely wooden tablets, cannot be ruled out (Marazzi 2000; Herbordt 2005: 36–37; van den Hout 2012). But it is also possible that non-literate recordkeeping traditions did survive in this sector of Hittite administration. In fact, this is suggested by the very name "house of the seal" (É [NA4]KIŠIB) that, as we have seen, was employed in Hittite texts to indicate the main administrative institution in Hittite Anatolia.

Beyond the Norms: The Scope of Taxation

As we have seen, the extant written record concerning taxation does not refer to the entire population subject to the Hittite crown, but only to those people with a direct bond with or obligation to the royal court or administrative and religious institutions. The Hittite law collection in particular reveals nothing or very little about the role of the village in taxation processes.[34] The very logic of §40 shows that people subject to ^{GIŠ}TUKUL, *ILKU*, *saḫḫan*, or *luzzi*- residing in a village were legally distinct from the village community (LÚ.MEŠ URU-*LIM*). Villagers were obliged to take care of fields left vacant by both ^{GIŠ}TUKUL- and *ILKU*-men until permanent replacements were found for them, but they could not themselves take possession of the fields.[35] The village plays a secondary role in this paragraph, merely filling a temporary vacuum in the organization of land plots owned by the crown or by other Hittite institutions bound to the crown. Neither here nor elsewhere in the law collection are there references to the taxes levied from village communities.[36] The only situation in the law collection in which village communities play a central role concerns their assumption of responsibility—and the implied costs—for wrongdoings such as homicide and theft when a culprit cannot be identified (d'Alfonso 2005: 160). While an extractive mechanism is implied, it should not be understood as a form of taxation.

The same legal discrimination between the village community and palace dependents is reflected in the normative *Instruction to the Supervisors* (CTH 266). Upon returning home after a period of leave, the Supervisors are required to interview the ^{GIŠ}TUKUL-men and the elders of the town about any wrongdoings that occurred during their absence:

CTH 266, Rev.

(16'-17') Should you at some point re[turn] to the city, then you shall call out the ^{GIŠ}TUKUL-men (and) the elders (^{LÚ.MEŠ}ŠU.GI),(18') [and] you shall speak to them as follows: (19') "Are the guards of the gates corrupt? Are the men of my household corrupt? (21') Do they take wine for [thems]elves? (22'-24') Do they [pou]r water [for you]? Do the gardeners take the [. . . a]nd the container (25') [and] give them to the ^{GIŠ}TUKUL-men?"[37]

(Adapted from Miller 2013: 268–69)

This text confirms that the elders of the town/village and the ^{GIŠ}TUKUL-men were two distinct legal bodies, whose jurisdictions did not necessarily overlap. The taxes reported in Hittite texts were not imposed on the former group.

Eva von Dassow has recently suggested that the population of any ancient polity would consist of citizens—individuals and households with an affirmative, constitutive role in the existence of the polity itself (von Dassow 2012a and 2012b). Following her line of reasoning, the payment of taxes is a constitutive act of citizenship in any polity at any time. Building on this assumption, each sedentary non-enslaved member of an ancient western Asian polity would pay taxes to the central authority. This cannot be ruled out in the case of the Hittite empire, but there is no evidence to support it. Due to the low productivity of land in Anatolia (see below), it is questionable whether small private or communal plots could sustain the burden of regular tithes.[38]

A different picture of the role of village/town communities emerges from the sources that shed light on the organization of cultic festivals. These communities play a prominent role in the accumulation and redistribution of food in the context of religious events. We know of town communities participating in the redistribution of rations (*MELQĒTU*) connected with the "state cult" festivals, namely those religious celebrations that were dedicated to the main gods of the Hittite pantheon and in which the king took part personally.[39] The following passage from the KI.LAM-festival (CTH 627), for example, reports the allotment of well-defined quantities and types of food that the AGRIG was required to provide to the town communities for consumption in a banquet during the religious festival:

KBo 10.30+, III 2'–15'

2' [1 sheep, 20] ḫališ-[bre]ad loaves of 20 (shekels each), 2 *wagešš[ar]*-bread loaves of 15 (shekels each),

3' 2 containers of *marnuwan*-beer (and) 15 *šarama*-bread loaves

4' the AGRIG of the town of Wattaruwa

5' gives to **the men of the town** of Angulla.

6' They take their seat, they eat and drink.

7' 1 sheep, 20 ḫališ-[bre]ad loaves of 20 (shekels each), 2 *wageššar*-bread loaves of 15 (shekels each),

8' 2 containers of *marnuwan*-beer (and) 15 *šarama*-bread loaves

9' the AGRIG of the town of Zikkurka gives to **the men of the town** of Angull[a.]

10' They take their seat, they eat and drink.

III 22'–31'

22' The *zinḫuri*-men take [1 k]id (and) 1 large ordinary bread

23' [i]n the temple of the god Inar.

24' [20']*ḫališ*-[bread loaves] of 20 (shekels each), 2 *wageššar*-bread loaves of 15 (shekels each),

25' [2' containers of *m*]*arnuwan*-beer the AGRIG of the town of Alisa

26' gives [to the] *zinḫuri*-[m]en

27' [1 sheep 20 *ḫa*]*liš*-[bread loaves] of 20 (shekels each), 2 *wageššar*-bread loaves of 15 (shekels each)

28' [2 containers of *marnuwa*]*n*-beer (and) 15 *šarama*-bread loaves

29' [the AGRIG of the town of K]arahna

30' [gives to the *z*]*inḫuri*-[men]

31' [They take their seat, they e]at and drink.

(Translation based on Singer 1984a: 106–7)

Other functionaries also contributed to the distribution of rations, albeit less frequently than the AGRIGs. These functionaries included the herdsmen ([LÚ.MEŠ]SIPAD) responsible for delivering livestock and the wine-suppliers ([LÚ.MEŠ]ZABAR.DIB).

The *MELQĒTU*-lists were not embedded in the related festival descriptions but set apart on tablets that omit references to the ceremonial proceedings in which the rations were distributed. This suggests that the rations were not intended as cult offerings but served as viatica for teams of priests, performers, and cultic participants during the weeks-long celebration of the festivals. Town communities are frequently responsible for supplying food offerings for the so-called local cults, namely festivals celebrated in honor of local deities without the direct participation of the kings. The agropastoral products delivered by town communities were meant to be used in the rites as offerings to the gods or as provisions (*assanuwar*) for the ritual banquets, in parallel to the *MELQĒTU* of the main festivals. Significantly, some of the grain was poured into a storage jar during the Fall festival, corresponding to the harvest season; it was then extracted during the following Spring festival, both for sowing and for communal consumption during the rites.[40] Although framed as part of the religious system, these practices of storage, consumption, and re-distribution were a basic part of the Hittite economy, particularly at the local level. This would by itself explain the high level of investment by the Hittite administration in recording festivals and rites. Indeed, texts regulating rituals, festivals, and their economic and logistical background together represent almost 80% of all Hittite textual sources. As Marazzi (2006: 113) correctly observed, cultic offerings allowed processes of accumulation to be embedded in the cultic calendar, which was tied to agricultural seasonality and thus provided an appropriate cyclical schedule for the collection of necessary resources. In addition, they monitored the activity of the administrative personnel involved in taxation by obliging them to interact with multiple functionaries and social groups. In the emic perspective, such practices of accumulation and redistribution were deeply entangled with a set of shared beliefs that bound together different agents, thereby fostering a sense of communal belonging.

Parallel to the forms of taxation described in the law collection and other legal texts, religious texts reveal the existence of processes of collection and redistribution of revenue in the form of food and beverages. These were integrated in a broader set of communal cultic practices transposed and incorporated into the official religious agenda. They likely involved larger portions of the population than those covered by normative regulations. From a top-down perspective, this both reinforced ties among different social groups and provided a formidable "soft-power" resource for the extractive system that could make it work without much need for coercion.

Concluding Remarks

The present overview of the evidence for the Hittite staple revenue system offers useful points of comparison with other complex societies. Both the textual and the archaeological evidence correlate with a centralized system based less on distribution than on accumulation in the form of large-scale reserves of primary resources. The low agricultural productivity of the Hittite heartland made state-fueled mass consumption of revenues as attested in Mesopotamia impossible. It also encouraged positive policies that favored the allotment of land use rights in exchange for maintaining institutional human resources. Although the actual mechanisms of the Hittite economy downplay distributive practices, these acquire a special symbolic value through their implementation in the official cult, either as proper ration deliveries to cultic personnel or as part of ritual performance.

The lack of administrative records from the Hittite archives prevents us from understanding what portion of the people living within the territory of the Hittite empire was subject to taxation. Even so, two different modalities of accumulation of revenues emerge with clarity from the available textual evidence.

The Hittite royal court designed legal obligations that regulated and enforced tax payment on the part of specific groups of people; obligations were also associated with plots of land owned by the Hittite royal court and sometimes assigned to institutions or powerful officials. The precise character of these obligations, named *sahhan*, *luzzi-*, *ILKU* and ᴳᴵˢ*TUKUL*, escapes us. Evidence of these obligations from Ugarit and Emar during the period of Hittite hegemony in northern Syria suggests that *ILKU* and ᴳᴵˢ*TUKUL* represented an extraction of physical activity (corvée: see d'Alfonso 2010 with literature therein). Whether *sahhan* and *luzzi-* corresponded to taxation in kind, corvée, or a form of rent is not clear; efforts to make sense of these obligations are hindered by the fact that the terms seem to have lost their original meaning by the time they began to be used in the Early Hittite empire. It is likely, however, that extractive practices based on people and lands under legal obligation were part of a system of income and expenditure that involved centralized control and planning, including informed calculations of expected revenue flows. A significant share of the taxation in kind extracted from plots under royal obligation was reserved for sowing in the next productive cycle. The central administration invested great effort in ensuring that the productivity of these plots remained high and stable. The Hittite administration continually reassigned vacant fields to new men under obligation, to deportees, to institutions, and to officials who would be able to secure high productivity and fulfill the obligations associated with tenancy of the fields.

In parallel, the entire population of towns and villages (URU) participated in the delivery and redistribution of food and beverages in the context of major religious festivals sponsored and presided over by the Great King, as well as at local festivals. It is unclear how much of the raw agropastoral produce delivered for festivals was consumed during the festivals themselves and how much of it was accumulated. That some of the food and beverage revenues—at least in the case of grain—were stored for redistribution at the time of sowing, very likely in autumn, is hinted at in the texts. It is possible that some of these revenues were removed from the local community and invested elsewhere in the political economy of the empire, but there is no clear indication of this in the texts. It is equally unclear how many of the resources required for major festivals were supplied by local communities and how many from the revenues collected by the administration of the royal court. In any case, extraction in the context of festivals was instrumental to maintaining positive relationships with the divine world by securing the regular performance of rituals and connected offerings. In return, the gods provided for the wellbeing of the Hittite Great King, and the Great King for the wellbeing of society as a whole.

These aspects of the Hittite political economy can be reconstructed through a variety of sources, but the evidence does not include a large corpus of administrative texts. This is surprising when compared with Mesopotamia and has often been explained with reference to gaps in the archaeological record or to the possibility that economic and administrative transactions were recorded on perishable materials. Comparison with earlier Anatolian complex societies and indications in the Hittite evidence itself suggest that at least some of the economic administration was conducted without the use of writing. Accumulation and redistribution in the context of local cultic festivals might have operated according to traditional Anatolian practices that are known from pre-urban communities of the Late Chalcolithic period. This would entail administrative procedures based on the use of sealings, which are well-attested in that time. Conversely, the system of obligations visible in the normative texts would represent a development specific to the formation of the new Hittite polity. Embedding the imperial structure within the major and minor local festivals integrated the new political system with the religious practices of the different communities of the empire. The result was the extraction not only of resources, but of social cohesion.

NOTES

1 This contribution was conceived and written by the two authors as a joint effort. That said, d'Alfonso is chiefly responsible for the sections "Sources," "The Norms of Taxation," and "The Infrastructure of Taxation and Accumulation," and Matessi for the section "Beyond the Norms: The Scope of Taxation." Both authors share the credit for the introduction, conclusions, and the section "Staple Accumulation and Writing." Tayfun Bilgin's book *Officials and Administration in the Hittite World* (Berlin: De Gruyter, 2018) appeared after the manuscript was first submitted to the editors. We were therefore unable to include this contribution in our chapter, but invite interested readers to consult this valuable monograph dealing with some of the issues discussed here.

2 In this chapter we adopt the middle chronology, on which see Manning et al. 2016 with further references.

3 For what follows in this paragraph, see Liverani 1988: 28–61 and 504–40 and Schachner 2011a. For the environment and staple economy of Hittite Anatolia, see Klengel 2006 and 2007; Dörfler et al. 2011, and, most recently, Roberts 2017. For an overview of Hittite history and society, see Bryce 2005 and, especially, Klengel 1999, with a fundamental essay by Imparati devoted to the organization of the Hittite state.

4 On this subject see in general Siegelová 1986 and more specifically Liverani 2001, especially pp. 141ff.; Mora 2006; Giorgieri and Mora 2012; van den Hout 2012.

5 Emre and Çınaroğlu 1993; and Hawkins 1993. For *Hattusa*, see also Kozal and Novák 2007.

6 For conscription see in general Beal 1992; see also CTH 272, most recently edited in Miller 2013: 73–77.

7 See also Vigo 2019.

8 See Cammarosano 2018: 139–61. This new economic sensibility for Hittite religious texts inspired many of the papers presented in 2018 at a conference organized on the topic by Hutter and Hutter-Braunsar (now Hutter and Hutter-Braunsar 2019).

9 On these sources and their relevance to Hittite economic history, see Klengel 2005: 3–6.

10 The abbreviation CTH refers to texts numbered according to the *Catalogue des Textes Hittites*, first compiled by Laroche in 1956 but now updated through the online platform *Hethitologie Portal Mainz* (*HPM*: http://www.hethport.uni-wuerzburg.de). KUB and KBo mark individual cuneiform tablets or fragments published under the series *Keilschrifturkunden aus Boghazköi* (Berlin 1921–1990) and *Keilschrifttexte aus Boghazköi* (Leipzig/Berlin 1916–), respectively.

11 Reference editions of the text are Imparati 1964 and Hoffner 1997. A major debate concerns the dating of manuscript A to Hattusili I (17th century BCE: see Archi 2008, with previous literature) or to a reign no earlier than that of Telipinu (16th–15th century BC: see van den Hout 2009). We conform here to the usual custom of referring to paragraphs from the PT by Roman numerals and to paragraphs from the other versions by Arabic numbers.

12 See the different perspectives on this issue expressed by d'Alfonso 2008 and Archi 2008.

13 Cf. §§ 50–51, regarding exemptions for the households of priests and craftsmen in the well-known holy cities of Arinna, Nerik, and Zippalanda, and the statement at the end of the section on the prices of goods (§184): "This is the tariff, as [it has been made?] for the City (i.e. Hattusa)" (Hoffner 1997: 146–47 and 222–23).

14 Cf. §§5, 19a–21, 23 and 54. §5 deals with cases concerning the murder of Luwian or Palaian merchants, with the obvious understanding that the murderer resides in Hatti. Note that burial of the victim is stipulated only if the murder is committed in Hatti: it was evidently impossible to do likewise in *Luwiya*, indicating that this

land was not within the jurisdiction of the enforcing authority. In §23, the flight of a slave to the land of *Luwiya* has legal implications for his owner, who shall pay a reward to whomever "brings him back (i.e. to Hatti)" (*appa weda-*). More ambiguous is the formulation of §19a in manuscript A, where the abduction of a Hittite citizen to *Luwiya* by a Luwian citizen is punished with the forfeiture of the abductor's house. Such a penalty might in fact imply that the jurisdiction of the law extended also to *Luwiya*, where the estate of the abductor is supposed to be (per Yakubovich 2009: 242). However, as per Hawkins (2013a: 34), the penalty imposed may just be a desideratum of the legislator without regard for its actual enforceability. On the other hand, the replacement of *Luwiya* with *Arzawa* in the later version of this paragraph (manuscript B) is a meaningful revision that reflects the geopolitical situation of the Empire period, when *Arzawa* represented the "other" in respect to Hatti in the same way that *Luwiya* appears to have done during the Old Kingdom. On the status of *Luwiya*, see Yakubovich 2009: 239–47, along with the critical reception of his interpretation by Hawkins (2013a–b). See also Matessi 2016: 137–39. In the other cases of abduction involving *Luwiya* (19b–21), Hatti is either the final destination or the abductor is Hittite (see Hoffner 1997: 180, Table 1.1). The remaining paragraph involving lands likely situated beyond Hatti's jurisdiction is §54 (exemptions for the troops of *Sala, Tamalki, Hatra, Zalpa, Tashiniya*, and *Hemuwa*), for which see the comments of Beal: "one should remember that the troops of these places were serving the Hittite king and were thus not necessarily stationed near home" (1992: 74). On Hatti proper as opposed to the whole territory under the rule of the Hittite Great King, see Gerçek 2017 and d'Alfonso, forthcoming.

15 *ki-i* ᴳᴵˢTUKUL-*li-me-et ki-i-ma ša-aḫ-ḫa-me-et.*

16 Cfr. Goetze 1924: 97, 101; Korošec 1945: 209; Imparati 1982; *ead.* 1988; Beal 1988; and, with a somewhat anachronistic interpretation, Haase 1996. See most recently d'Alfonso 2010: 72–78, with further references.

17 While many such texts remain unpublished, most of them, including those cited here, are edited by Souček (1959a–b and 1963). For the interpretation of the structure and function of the *Feldertexte*, we follow here Marazzi 2008: 65–67.

18 There are very few attestations of the term *muškēnu* (log. ᴸᵁMAŠ.EN.KAK) in the Hittite corpus, mostly concentrated in festival or ritual descriptions where they participate as cultic personnel (Souçek 1963: 371–82). A lower ranking position in the army is suggested by the oath of "the men of Hattusa" to Hattusili III, sworn by the princes, the infantry troops, the chariotry, some other categories lost in a lacuna, and then the *muškēnū* (KBo 21.46, i 4. See Miller 2013: 274–75).

19 See Wilhelm 2005, and Rüster and Wilhelm 2012, with further references.

20 Cfr. CTH 224 (Hattusili III to Ura-Tarhunta); CTH 225 (Tuthaliya IV to the heirs of Sahurunuwa). In a similar vein, cfr. CTH 88 (Hattusili III's to the ᴺᴬ⁴*hekurPirwa*) and CTH 85 (Hattusili III to the cult of Ištar). See Imparati 1974, 1977 and 1988; Mora and Balza 2010.

21 For more detailed surveys on pastoralism and its relevance in the Hittite economy, see Beckman 1988 and, most recently, Gerçek 2017.

22 Singer 1984b.

23 Archi 1973; Imparati *apud* Klengel 1999: 343–44; Siegelová 2001.

24 The existence of an É ᴺᴬ⁴KIŠIB at Tapikka/Maşat Höyük can be inferred from an administrative text found there (HKM 100, on which see del Monte 1995: 98–99) and from the fact that the city is attested as the residence of an AGRIG (Singer 1984b: 113–17). On the relations between Tapikka and the É.GALs, see Imparati 1997 and Siegelová 2001: 196–97.

25 For an opposing view, see Pecchioli Daddi 1988. Telipinu's reform of the administrative system is reported in his famous "Edict" (CTH 19), for which see Hoffmann 1984 and van den Hout 2003 (English translation only).

26 For this text see Rüster and Wilhelm 2012: no. 46.

27 The copy of the tablet is published in Alp 1991: 108. For a transliteration, (Italian) translation, and comments, see Del Monte 1995: 122–31. The text is further discussed by Hoffner 2001: 204ff. and Marazzi 2008: 76–79.

28 Among the other texts published by del Monte (1995), HKM 110 seems to have a structure similar to that of HKM 109, but it is unfortunately very fragmentary.

29 Liverani 1988, 116; Jursa 2010: 49.

30 See the discussion in Mielke 2011: 183–84, with further references.

31 Cammarosano 2018: 119–21.

32 Kulakoğlu et al. 2013; and http://antiquity.ac.uk/projgall/kulakoglu343, last accessed Nov. 14, 2019.

33 For the concepts staple and wealth finance and their application to the study of the Hittite economy, see Vigo 2019, with literature.

34 In Hittite texts, as in the other cuneiform traditions, both village and city are indicated by the logogram URU. By village we mean a rural community of free peasants working private or communal land.

35 d'Alfonso 2010: 71–75.

36 d'Alfonso (2010: 74) further discusses §46, dealing with the application of the *luzzi-* in village communities. As d'Alfonso notes, manuscript A reads *tak-ku* URU-*ri* A.ŠÀᴴᴵ.ᴬ-*an i-wa-a-ru ku-iš-ki ḫar-zi*, thus bearing on the whole village community ("if someone in the village holds fields as inheritance share"). d'Alfonso also observes, however, that both later manuscripts (B and C) and the PT clearly indicate that the norm did not apply to any member of the village community other than those holding fields and subject to *saḫḫan*-service:

    B) [*tak-ku* URU-*r*]*i* A.Š[Àᴴᴵ.ᴬ-*an ša-a*]*ḫ-ḫa-an-na i-wa-a-ru ku-iš-ki ḫar-zi*
    C) *tak-ku* URU-*ri ša-aḫ-ḫa-na-aš* A.ŠÀᴴᴵ.ᴬ-*an i-wa-a-*[*ru ku-iš-ki ḫar-zi*]
    PT) *tak-ku* URU-*ri* A.ŠÀᴴᴵ.ᴬ-*an ša-aḫ-ḫa-an-na i-wa-a-ru ku-iš-ki ḫar-zi*

37 After line 25', the ᴳᴵˢTUKUL-men are mentioned twice in fragmentary contexts (26'–28'), at least once in connection with the gardeners, and then the text is broken. We can only speculate whether the missing part indeed concerned the elders in parallel situations.

38 E.g. Archi 1973.

39 Archi 1973: 217–20; Singer 1983: 141–70; Singer 1984a: 106–11; Marazzi 2006: 109–13. For the distinction between "state" and "non-state" or "local" cults (see also below), we follow here Cammarosano 2018: 13–19.

40 On the economy of local cults, see now Cammarosano 2018: 139–58.

WORKS CITED

Alp, Sedat. 1968. *Zylinder- und Stempelsiegel aus Karahöyük bei Konya*. Ankara: Turk Tarih Kurumu.

Alp, Sedat. 1991. *Maşat-Höyük'te Bulunan Çivi Yazılı Hitit Tabletleri / Hethitische Keilschrifttafeln aus Maşat-Höyük*. Ankara: Türk Tarih Kurumu.

Archi, Alfonso. 1973. "L'organizzazione amministrativa ittita e il regime delle offerte cultuali." *Oriens Antiquus* 12: 209–26.

Archi, Alfonso. 2008. "Le 'leggi ittite' e il diritto processuale." In M. Liverani and C. Mora (eds.), *I diritti del mondo cuneiforme (Mesopotamia e regioni adiacenti, ca. 2500–500 a.C.)* (Pavia: IUSS Press), 273–92.

Bachuber, Christoph. 2015. *Citadel and Cemetery in Early Bronze Age Anatolia*. London: Equinox.

Beal, Richard. 1988. "The ^{GIŠ}TUKUL-Institution in Second Millennium Hatti." *Altorientalische Forschungen* 15: 269–305.

Beal, Richard. 1992. *The Organisation of the Hittite Military*. Heidelberg: Winter.

Beckman, Gary M. 1988. "Herding and Herdsmen in Hittite Culture." In E. Neu and C. Rüster (eds.), *Documentum Asiae Minoris Antiquae. Festschrift für Heinrich Otten zum 75. Geburtstag* (Wiesbaden: Harrassowitz), 33–44.

Bryce, Trevor. 2005. *The Kingdom of the Hittites*. Oxford: Oxford University Press.

Cammarosano, Michele. 2018. *Hittite Local Cults*. Atlanta: SBL Press.

Castellano, Lorenzo. 2018. "Staple economies and storage in Post-Hittite Anatolia. Considerations in light of new data from Niğde-Kınık Höyük (Southern Cappadocia)." *Journal of Eastern Mediterranean Archaeology and Heritage Studies* 6: 259–84.

Castellano, Lorenzo and Lorenzo d'Alfonso. 2017. "Kınık Höyük'teki yeni bulgular ışığında: Hitit Çağı'ndan Post-Hititlere geçişte ekonomi ve tarımsal üretim / Economia e produzione agricola nel passaggio tra età ittita e post-ittita: nuove evidenze da Kınık Höyük." *Arkeoloji ve Sanat* 155: 71–82.

d'Alfonso, Lorenzo. 2005. *Le procedure giudizioarie ittite in Siria (XIII sec. a.C.)*. Pavia: Italian University Press.

d'Alfonso, Lorenzo. 2008. "Le fonti normative del secondo millennio a.C. Confronto tra le culture della Mesopotamia e l'Anatolia ittita." In M. Liverani and C. Mora (eds.), *I diritti del mondo cuneiforme (Mesopotamia e regioni adiacenti, ca. 2500–500 a.C.)* (Pavia: IUSS Press), 325–60.

d'Alfonso, Lorenzo. 2010. "'Servant of the King, Son of Ugarit, and Servant of the Servant of the King': RS 17.238 and the Hittites." In Y. Cohen, A. Gilan, and J. L. Miller (eds.), *Pax Hethitica: Studies on the Hittites and their Neighbours in Honour of Itamar Singer* (Wiesbaden: Harrassowitz), 67–86.

d'Alfonso, Lorenzo. Forthcoming. "Borders in the archaeology of the Hittite empire." In *Borders in Archaeology: Changing Landscapes in Anatolia and the South Caucasus ca 3500–500 BCE*, ANES Suppl. Series (Leuven: Peeters).

Del Monte, Giuseppe F. 1995. "I testi amministrativi da Maşat Höyük/Tapika." *Orientis Antiqui Miscellanea* 2: 89–138.

Diffey, Charlotte, Reinder Neef and Amy Bogard. 2017. "The archaeobotany of large-scale hermetic cereal storage at the Hittite capital of Hattusha." In A. Schachner (ed.), *Innovation versus Baharrung: Was macht den Unterschied des hethitischen Reichs im Anatolien des 2. Jahrtausends v. Chr.? Internationaler Workshop zu Ehren von Jürgen Seeher Istanbul, 23–24. Mai 2014* (Istanbul: Ege Yayınları), 185–200.

Dörfler, Walter, Christa Herking, Reinder Neef, Rainer Pasternak and Angela von den Driesch. 2011. "Environment and Economy in Hittite Anatolia." In H. Genz and D. P. Mielke (eds.), *Insights into Hittite History and Archaeology* (Leuven: Peeters), 99–124.

Düring, Bleda S. 2010. *The Prehistory of Asia Minor: From Complex Hunter-Gatherers to Early Urban Societies*. Cambridge: Cambridge University Press.

Emre, Kutlu and Aykut Çinaroğlu. 1993. "A Group of Metal Vessels from Kinik-Kastamonu." In M. J. Mellink, E. Porada and T. Özgüç (eds.), *Aspects of Art and Iconography. Anatolia and its Neighbors. Studies in Honor of Nimet Özgüç* (Ankara: Türk Tarih Kurumu Basımevi), 675–713.

Fairbairn, Andrew and Sachihiro Omura. 2005. "Archaeological Identification and Significance of ÉSAG (Agricultural Storage Pits) at Kaman-Kalehöyük, Central Anatolia." *Anatolian Studies* 55: 15–23.

Frangipane, Marcella (ed.). 2007. *Arslantepe Cretulae. An Early Centralised Administrative System Before Writing*. Rome: Università di Roma "La Sapienza".

Frangipane, Marcella. 2012. "Fourth Millennium Arslantepe: The Development of a Centralised Society without Urbanization." *Origini* 34: 19–40.

Frangipane, Marcella. 2016. "The Development of Centralised Societies in Greater Mesopotamia and the Foundation of Economic Inequality." In H. Meller et al. (eds.), *Rich and Poor: Competing for Resources in Prehistoric Societies, 14/II,* (Halle: Tagungen des Landes Museums für Vorgeschichte), 469–89.

Friedrich, Johannes. 1959. *Die hethitischen Gesetze: Transkription, Ubersetzung, sprachliche Erlauterungen und vollstandiges Worterverzeichnis*. Leiden: Brill.

Gerçek, N. İlgi. 2017. "'A Goatherd Shall Not Enter!': Observations on Pastoralism and Mobility in Hittite Anatolia." In E. Kozal et al. (eds.), *Questions, Approaches, and Dialogues in Eastern Mediterranean Archaeology. Studies in Honor of Marie-Henriette and Charles Gates* (Münster: Ugarit-Verlag), 257–78.

Giorgieri, Mauro and Clelia Mora. 2012. "Luxusgüter als Symbole der Macht: Zur Verwaltung der Luxusgüter im Hethiter-Reich." In G. Wilhelm (ed.), *Organization, Representation, and Symbols of Power in the Ancient Near East*. CRRAI 54 (Winona Lake: Eisenbrauns), 647–65.

Goetze, Albrecht. 1924. *Kleinasien zur Hethiterzeit: Eine Geographische Untersuchung*. Heidelberg: Winter.

Haase, Richard. 1996. "Anmerkungen zum sogenannten Lehensrecht der Hethiter." *Zeitschrift für Altorientalische und Biblische Rechtsgeschichte* 2: 135–39.

Hawkins J. David 1993. "A Bowl Epigraph of the Official Taprammi." In M. J. Mellink, E. Porada and T. Özgüç (eds.), *Aspects of Art and Iconography. Anatolia and its Neighbors. Studies in Honor of Nimet Özgüç* (Ankara: Türk Tarih Kurumu Basımevi), 715–17.

Hawkins, J. David. 2013a. "Luwians versus Hittites." In A. Mouton and I. Rutherford (eds.), *Luwian Identities: Culture, Language and Religion between Anatolia and the Aegean* (Leiden: Brill), 25–40.

Hawkins, J. David. 2013b. "A New Look at the Luwian Language." *Kadmos* 52: 1–18.

Herbordt, Susan. 2005. *Die Prinzen- und Beamtensiegel der hethitischen Grossreichszeit auf Tonbullen aus dem Nişantepe-Archiv in Hattusa.* Mainz: Philip von Zabern.

Hoffman, Inge. 1984. *Der Erlass Telipinus.* Heidelberg: Winter.

Hoffner, Harry A. 1997. *The Laws of the Hittites. A Critical Edition.* Leiden: Brill.

Hoffner, Harry A. 2001. "*Alimenta* Revisited." In G. Wilhelm (ed.), *Akten des IV. Internationalen Kongresses für Hethitologie, Würzburg, 4.–8. Oktober 1999* (Wiesbaden: Harrassowitz), 199–212.

Hutter, Manfred and Sylvia Hutter-Braunsaur (eds.). 2019. *Economy of Religions in Anatolia: From the Early Second to the Middle of the First Millennium BCE. Proceedings of an International Conference in Bonn (23rd to 25th May 2018).* Münster: Ugarit Verlag.

Imparati, Fiorella. 1964. *Le leggi ittite.* Roma: Edizione dell'Ateneo.

Imparati, Fiorella. 1974. "Una concessione di terre da parte di Tudhaliya IV." *Revue Hittite et Asianique* 32: 1–211.

Imparati, Fiorella. 1977. "Le istituzioni cultuali dei ^{NA4}*ḫékur* e il potere centrale ittita." *Studi Micenei ed Egeo-Anatolici* 18: 19–63.

Imparati, Fiorella. 1982. "Aspects de l'organisation de l'état hittite dans les documents juridiques et administratifs." *Journal of the Economic and Social History of the Orient* 25: 225–67.

Imparati, Fiorella. 1988. "Interventi di politica economica dei sovrani ittiti e stabilità del potere." In *Stato, Economia, Lavoro nel Vicino Oriente antico. Istituto Gramsci Toscano. Scritti del Seminario di Orientalistica antica* (Milan: Francoangeli), 225–39.

Imparati, Fiorella. 1997. "Observations on a Letter from Maşat-Höyük." *Archivum Anatolicum* 3: 199–214.

Jursa, Michael. 2010. *Aspects of the Economic History of Babylonia in the First Millennium BC: Economic Geography, Economic Mentalities, Agriculture, the Use of Money and the Problem of Economic Growth.* Münster: Ugarit-Verlag.

Klengel, Horst. 1999. *Geschichte des hethitischen Reiches.* Leiden: Brill.

Klengel, Horst. 2005. "Studien zur hethitischen Wirtschaft: Einleitende Bemerkungen." *Altorientalische Forschungen* 32: 3–22.

Klengel, Horst. 2006. "Studien zur hethitischen Wirtschaft, 2: Feld- und Gartenbau." *Altorientalische Forschungen* 33: 3–21.

Klengel, Horst. 2007. "Studien zur hethitischen Wirtschaft, 3: Tierwirtschaft und Jagd." *Altorientalische Forschungen* 34: 154–73.

Korošek, Victor. 1945. "Einige juristische Bemerkungen zur Šaḫurunuva-Urkunde (KUB XXVI 43 = Bo 2048)." In M. San Nicolò and A. Steinwenter (eds.), *Festschrift für Leopold Wegner, Vol. 2*. Münchener Beiträge zur Papyrusforschung und antiken Rechtsgeschichte 35 (Munich: Beck), 191–222.

Kozal, Ekin and Mirko Novák. 2007. "Geschenke, Tribute und Handelswaren im Hethiterreich: Eine archäologische Bestandaufnahme am Fallbeispiel Hattuša." In H. Klinkott, S. Kubisch and R. Müller-Wollermann (eds.), *Geschenke und Steuern, Zölle und Tribute: antike Abgabenformen in Anspruch und Wirklichkeit* (Leiden: Brill), 323–46.

Kulakoğlu, Fikri, Kutlu Emre, Riyochi Kontani, Sebahettin Ezer and Güzel Öztürk. 2013. "Kultepe-Kaniš, Turkey: Preliminary Report on the 2012 Excavations." *Bulletin of the Okayama Orient Museum* 27: 43–50.

Liverani, Mario. 1988. *Antico Oriente: storia, società, economia*. Roma.

Liverani, Mario. 2001. *International Relations in the Ancient Near East, 1600–1100 BC*. New York: Palgrave.

Lorenz, Jürgen. 2017. "Sahhan und luzzi." In R. de Boer and J. G. Dercksen (eds.), *Private and State in the Ancient Near East. Proceedings of the 58th Rencontre Assyriologique Internationale at Leiden 16–20 July 2012* (Winona Lake: Eisenbrauns), 193–202.

Mann, Michael. 1986. *The Sources of Social Power. Volume I: A History of Power from the Beginning to AD 1760*. Cambridge: Cambridge University Press.

Manning, Sturt W., Carol B. Griggs, Brita Lorentzen, Gojko Barjamovic, Christopher Bronk Ramsey, Bernd Kromer, and Eva Maria Wild. 2016. "Integrated Tree-Ring-Radiocarbon High-Resolution Timeframe to Resolve Second Millennium BCE Mesopotamian Chronology." *PLoS ONE* 11(7): e0157144. DOI: 10.1371/journal. pone.0157144.

Marazzi, Massimiliano. 2000. "Sigilli e tavolette di legno: le fonti letterarie e le testimonianze sfragistiche nell'Anatolia hittita." In M. Perna (ed.), *Administrative Documents in the Aegean and their Near Eastern Counterparts, Proceedings of the International Colloquium, Naples, February 29–March 2, 1996* (Torino: Italian Ministry of Culture), 79–102.

Marazzi, Massimiliano. 2006. "Il cosiddetto 'regime delle offerte cultuali': mondo hittita e mondo miceneo a confronto." In M. Perna (ed.), *Fiscality in Mycenaean and Near Eastern Archives: Proceedings of the Conference held at Soprintendenza Archivistica per la Campania, Naples, 21–23 October 2004* (Paris: De Boccard), 109–21.

Marazzi, Massimiliano. 2008. "Messa a coltura e procedure di gestione e controllo dei campi nell'Anatolia hittita: caratteristiche della documentazione e stato della ricerca." In M. Perna and F. Pomponio (eds.), *The Management of Agricultural Land*

and the Production of Textiles in the Mycenaean and Near Eastern Economies (Paris: De Boccard), 63–88.

Matessi, Alvise. 2016. "The Making of Hittite Imperial Landscapes: Territoriality and Balance of Power in South-Central Anatolia during the Late Bronze Age." *Journal of Ancient Near Eastern History* 3: 117–62.

Mielke, Dirk Paul. 2011. "Hittite Cities: Looking for a Concept." In H. Genz and D. P. Mielke (eds.), *Insights into Hittite History and Archaeology* (Leuven: Peeters), 153–94.

Miller, Jared. 2013. *Royal Hittite Instructions and Related Administrative Texts*. Atlanta: SBL.

Mora, Clelia. 2006. "Riscossione dei tributi e accumulo dei beni nell'impero ittita." In M. Perna (ed.), *Fiscality in Mycenaean and Near Eastern Archives: Proceedings of the Conference held at Soprintendenza Archivistica per la Campania, Naples, 21–23 October 2004* (Paris: De Boccard). 133–46.

Mora, Clelia. 2008. "'La parola del re.' Testi ittiti a carattere politico-giuridico e politico-amministrativo: editti e istruzioni." In M. Liverani and C. Mora (eds.), *I diritti del mondo cuneiforme (Mesopotamia e regioni adiacenti, ca. 2500–500 a.C.)* (Pavia: IUSS Press), 293–324.

Mora, Clelia and Mariaelena Balza. 2010. "Importanza politica ed economica di alcune istituzioni religiose e funerarie nell'impero ittita (Attualità degli studi di Fiorella Imparati)." *Studi Micenei ed Egeo Anatolici* 52: 253–64.

Müller-Karpe, Andreas. 2001. "Untersuchungen in Kuşaklı 2000." *Mitteilungen der Deutschen Orient-Gesellschaft zu Berlin* 133: 225–50.

Özguç, Nimet. 1980. "Seal Impressions from the palaces at Acemhöyük Translated from Turkish" [Trans. by M. J. Mellink]. In E. Porada (ed.), *Ancient Art in Seals* (Princeton: Princeton University Press), 61–99.

Özguç, Nimet. 2015. *Acemhöyük-Burušhaddum I. Cylinder Seals and Bullae with Cylinder Seal Impressions*. Ankara: Turk Tarih Kurumu.

Özguç, Nimet and Önhan Tunca. 2001. *Kültepe-Kaniš: Mühürlü ve Yazıtlı Kil Bullalar/ Sealed and Inscribed Clay Bullae*. Ankara: Turk Tarih Kurumu.

Pecchioli Daddi, Franca. 1988. "La condizione sociale del pastore (^{lú}SIPAD) e dell'amministratore (^{lú}AGRIG): esempi di 'diversità' presso gli Ittiti." In *Stato, Economia, Lavoronel Vicino Oriente antico. Istituto Gramsci Toscano. Scritti del Seminario di Orientalistica antica* (Milano: Francoangeli), 240–48.

Pollock, Susan (ed.). 2012. *Between Feasts and Daily Meals: Toward an Archaeology of Commensal Spaces. eTopoi, Journal for Ancient Studies*. Special Issue 2.

Roberts, Neil. 2017. "The Land of the Hittites: Land, Water and Places." In M. Weeden and L. Z. Ullmann, *Hittite Landscape and Geography* (Leiden: Brill), 17–27.

Rüster, Christel and Gernot Wilhelm. 2012. *Landschenkungsurkunden hethitischer Könige*. Wiesbaden: Harrassowitz.

Schachner, Andreas. 2009. "Das 16. Jahrhundert v.Chr.: Eine Zeitenwende im hethitischen Zentralanatolien." *Istanbuler Mitteilungen* 59: 9–34.

Schachner, Andreas. 2011a. *Hattuscha: Auf der Suche nach dem sagenhaften Großreich der Hethiter*. Munchen: C. H. Beck.

Schachner, Andreas. 2011b. "Von einer anatolischen Stadt zur Hauptstadt eines Großreichs: Entstehung, Entwicklung und Wandel Hattušas in hethitischer Zeit." *Mesopotamia* 46: 79–101.

Schoop, Ulf-Dietrich. 2011. "Hittite Pottery: A Summary." In H. Genz and D. P. Mielke (eds.), *Insights into Hittite History and Archaeology* (Leuven: Peeters), 241–73.

Seeher, Jürgen. 2000. "Getreidelagerung in unterirdischen Großspeichern: Zur Methode und ihrer Anwendung im 2. Jahrtausend v. Chr. am Beispiel der Befunde in Hattuša." *Studi Micenei ed Egeo Anatolici* 42: 261–301.

Siegelová, Jana. 1986. *Hethitische Verwaltungspraxis im Lichte der Wirtschafts- und Inventardokumente*. Prague: Národní muzeum v Praze.

Siegelová, Jana. 2001. "Der Regionalpalast in der Verwaltung des hethitischen Staates." *Altorientalische Forschungen* 28: 193–208.

Singer, Itamar. 1983. *The Hittite KI.LAM Festival. Part One*. Wiesbaden: Harrassowitz.

Singer, Itamar. 1984a. *The Hittite KI.LAM Festival. Part Two*. Wiesbaden: Harrassowitz.

Singer, Itamar. 1984b. "The AGRIG in the Hittite Texts." *Anatolian Studies* 34: 97–127.

Souček, Vladimír. 1959a. "Die hethitischen Feldertexte." *Archiv Orientální* 27: 5–53.

Souček, Vladimír. 1959b. "Die hethitischen Feldertexte." *Archiv Orientální* 27: 379–95.

Souček, Vladimír. 1963. "Randnotizen zu den hethitischen Feldertexten." *Mitteilungen des Instituts für Orientforschung* 8: 368–82.

Van den Hout, Theo. 2003. "The Proclamation of Telipinu." In W. H. Hallo and K. L. Younger (eds.), *The Context of Scripture. Volume I: Canonical Compositions from the Biblical World* (Leiden: Brill), 194–98.

Van den Hout, Theo. 2009. "A Century of Hittite Text Dating and the Origins of the Hittite Cuneiform Script." *Incontri linguistici* 32: 1000–25.

Van den Hout, Theo. 2012. "Administration and Writing in Hittite Society." In M. Balza, C. Mora and M. Giorgieri (eds.), *Archivi, depositi, magazzini presso gli ittiti. Nuovi materiali e nuove ricerche / Archives, Depots and Storehouses in the Hittite World. New Evidence and New Research. Proceedings of the Workshop held at Pavia, June 18, 2009* (Genova: Italian University Press), 41–58.

Vigo, Matteo. 2019. "Staple and Wealth Finance and the Administration of the Hittite Economy." In M. Hutter and S. Hutter-Braunsaur (eds.), *Economy of Religions in Anatolia: From the Early Second to the Middle of the First Millennium BCE. Proceedings of an International Conference in Bonn (23rd to 25th May 2018)* (Münster: Ugarit Verlag), 141–51.

von Dassow, Eva. 2012a. "Workshop: The Public and the State. Foreword." In G. Wilhelm (ed.), *Organization, representation, and symbols of power in the ancient Near East. Proceedings of the 54th rencontre assyriologique internationale at Würzburg 20–25 July 2008* (Winona Lake: Eisenbrauns), 167–69.

von Dassow, Eva. 2012b. "The Public and the State in the Ancient Near East." In G. Wilhelm (ed.), *Organization, representation, and symbols of power in the ancient Near*

East. Proceedings of the 54th *rencontre assyriologique internationale at Würzburg 20–25 July 2008* (Winona Lake: Eisenbrauns), 171–190.

Wilhelm, Gernot. 2005. "Zur Datierung der älteren hethitischen Landschenkungsurkunden." *Altorientalische Forschungen* 32: 272–79.

Yakubovich, Ilya. 2009. *Sociolinguistics of the Luvian Language.* Leiden: Brill.

6

Taxation in Anglo-Saxon England, Fifth–Ninth Centuries CE

PAM J. CRABTREE

Introduction

My primary theoretical interest as an archaeologist is the rebirth of urbanism and the beginnings of state formation in Middle Saxon (ca. 650–850 CE) and Late Saxon (ca. 850–1066) England. The archaeological data I have focused on in my own research are changes in settlement patterns and their relationship to changes in rural economy, including animal husbandry and agriculture. The archaeological study of the so-called "urban revolution" has a long history going back to the work of V. Gordon Childe in the 1920s and 1930s. Childe's comparative studies of Mesopotamia, ancient Egypt, and the ancient Indus highlighted the social surplus as one of the key features in the origins and development of early urban society (1936, see also Childe 1950). Childe noted that farming, including agriculture and animal husbandry, formed the economic basis for the development of complex, urban societies. Yet it was not enough for early farmers to produce a surplus. The agricultural surplus needed to be mobilized so that it could be used to support public architecture, craft specialization, and long-distance trade. Taxation is one important way in which this surplus agricultural production can be mobilized.

In this chapter, I will argue that the methods of resource extraction that developed during the Middle Anglo-Saxon period—notably food rents and tolls (taxes on trade)—helped to provide the economic basis for the development of urbanism and state formation in Late Saxon England. I will focus on the context of Middle Saxon taxation and I will try to explore the methods of extraction as well. To set the stage for this argument, I will briefly discuss the end of Roman Britain in the early fifth century and the economic and political nature of the Early Saxon Period in eastern England (early fifth century to ca. 650 CE). Because historical sources for the early post-Roman period are very limited prior to the late seventh and early eighth century, I will rely primarily on archaeological data.

Other than a few brief mentions of Britain in continental historical sources, the one contemporary text that survives from the Early Anglo-Saxon Period is Gildas's *De Excidio et Conquestu Britanniae* (*On the Ruin and Conquest of Britain*). Written in Latin in the sixth century, Gildas described the Anglo-Saxon conquest of Britain in the form of a three-part sermon.[1] Gildas was a Christian cleric living in what today would be Wales and he describes the conquest of Britain as a part of a broad condemnation of some of the kings and clerics of his age. The next account of English history is Bede's *Ecclesiastical History of the English People* (*Historia Ecclesiastica Gentis Angelorum*) which was not completed until about 731 CE. The first charters appear in the late seventh century, and law codes associated with the kings of Kent and Wessex were initially written in the seventh century, although they survive only in later copies. The late seventh-century Laws of Ine of Wessex survived because they were appended to the late ninth-century laws of Alfred the Great. The Anglo-Saxon Chronicle was written in the late ninth century, although it includes entries for earlier dates. While the Laws of Ine do provide some evidence for taxation in the late seventh century, most of these other historical sources focus on political and ecclesiastical history.

The early Anglo-Saxon period, and the fifth and sixth centuries in particular, are effectively prehistoric. As Hills notes:

> The historical sources tell us reliably only two things. First, that during the fifth century AD Britain ceased to be part of the Roman Empire and was subject to attack from a variety of peoples, including Saxons. Secondly, that the rulers of the peoples living in eastern and southern Britain by the eighth century, and perhaps before that, believed they could trace their ancestry back to heroic Germanic leaders from the continent. (2003: 110)

As a result, archaeology is our main source of evidence of the Early Saxon period and for the earlier parts of the Middle Saxon period as well.

Late Roman Background

Britain was a part of the Roman Empire from the mid-first century CE to about 410 CE. Incorporation into the Roman Empire changed Britain in many significant ways. While some of the largest of the British Iron Age *oppida* might qualify as towns in terms of size, it was the Romans who really established urbanism in Britain. The Romans built a network of towns in Britain, ranging from cities such as London (Londinium) and York (Eboracum), through cantonal capitals such as Winchester (Venta Belgarum), to smaller Roman towns such as Icklingham in Suffolk. Roman Britain was well populated, with most estimates ranging from about 2 to about 5 million people (see, for example, Alcock 2011: 260). Agriculture was intensified to support this large population that included troops along the Roman wall as well as urban dwellers. Many areas of heavy soils were brought under cultivation during the Roman period using a heavy plow, and larger cattle that would have supplied more meat and would also have been useful for traction and transport were first introduced into Britain during the Roman period (see Rizetto et al. 2017).

Roman towns played a variety of roles including ports, markets, administrative centers, and centers for a variety of religious cults. One of the main roles of these towns, however, was the collection of taxes in money and in kind (Esmonde Cleary 1989: 9). In the early centuries of Roman rule, taxes were collected primarily in the *civitas* capitals, but small towns may have played a greater role in tax collection in the late Roman period (Millett 1990: 125, 149).

All this changed in the early fifth century. In 407 CE, the Roman legions were removed from Britain, and there is no evidence that they ever returned. The sixth-century historian Zozimus tells us that in 410 the Emperor Honorius wrote to the citizens of Britain, telling them to see to their own defenses. Todd (1999: 208–9) sees this as an acknowledgement that the ties between Britain and the Roman Empire had been broken. While there is some scholarly debate over whether this letter actually refers to Britain (see, for example, Bartholomew 1982), it is clear that there was never an attempt by the Romans to re-conquer Britain after the legions were withdrawn in 407.

The archaeological record shows that the end of Roman administration had significant effects on many aspects of society and economy in

Britain. Esmonde Cleary (2011) sees fifth-century Britain as a failed state and argues that:

> By the later fifth century the economic, social, and cultural complexity of the populations seems to have undergone massive simplification, with much reduced mobilization of resources, a severe flattening of the social hierarchy and of social specialization and complexity, with concomitant huge reductions in the range of markers for cultural variability and expression. (Esmonde Cleary 2011: 14).

Archaeological evidence shows that the last small-denomination coins that are widespread in Britain are coins of the House of Theodosius (395–402 CE). Unlike prior periods when the coin supply to Britain was limited, there is very limited evidence for counterfeit coinage in the early fifth century. This indicates that coinage played a much less important role in early fifth-century Britain than it did during the Roman period. Most of the towns and cities in Roman Britain seem to have lost their urban character in the first half of the fifth century. The one possible exception is Wroxeter, which may have survived as the center of a small British polity into the late sixth or early seventh century (White and Barker 1998). Based on a reanalysis of the stratigraphy, however, Lane (2014) has recently argued against the continuity of urban settlement at Wroxeter into the sixth or seventh centuries CE.

Early Anglo-Saxon England

The Early Anglo-Saxon period is probably the most poorly understood period in all of English history. Britain experienced migration and settlement from the northwest European continent, but the nature, extent, and dating of this migration is a subject of intense scholarly debate. Estimates of the numbers of Anglo-Saxon migrants vary from fewer than 10,000 to more than 200,000 (Thomas et al. 2006: 2651). The mid-twentieth century view was that large numbers of Anglo-Saxon migrants simply overwhelmed the native Romano-British population (Stenton 1947), a view that prevailed until the last two or three decades of the twentieth century. In the later part of the twentieth century, this migrationist model was replaced by an élite dominance model in which smaller numbers of Anglo-Saxon migrants "achieved military, political and social ascendency" (Thomas et al. 2006: 2651; see also Higham 1992). Some 21st-century scholars have de-emphasized the role of Germanic migration in changing fifth- and sixth-century post-Roman Britain. For example, Oosthuizen (2019: 42) argues that "those who arrived [in Britain] spoke different languages and came to England in small numbers over at least two centuries." She attributes the social and political changes that took place in Britain between the fifth and seventh centuries largely to innovation and adaptation by the native Romano-British population.

There are also substantial changes in settlement patterns, subsistence practices, and material culture in fifth-century eastern and southern Britain that have traditionally been attributed to the Anglo-Saxons. In terms of settlement patterns, most of the fifth- and sixth-century settlements are small and composed of a number of rectangular earth-fast houses surrounded by *grubenhäuser* or sunken-featured buildings, some of which may have served as sheds and outbuildings (see Hoggett 2015 for an up-to-date review). There is little evidence for differentiation in housing before the seventh century. In terms of farming technology, Banham and Faith (2014) have described the early Saxon period as an era of abatement. While there is relatively little evidence for forest regeneration, pasturage seems to have expanded at the expense of arable. Agriculture was concentrated on the lighter soils that could be tilled with an ard or light plow, unlike the heavy plow that was used in Roman Britain. Studies of the faunal remains show that sheep, cattle, and pigs were raised primarily for local consumption. Large cattle disappear from Britain at the end of the Roman period (Rizzetto et al. 2017), probably because they were no longer needed to feed large urban areas and to supply Roman troops along the wall. The zooarchaeological and paleobotanical data from early Anglo-Saxon suggest that agriculture and animal husbandry were focused on local self-sufficiency, rather than on surplus production (see, for example, Crabtree 1990a).

Most of what we know about early Anglo-Saxon society comes from burials and cremations. Burial practices included both inhumation and cremation, and a number of mixed rite cemeteries have also been excavated. Between 30,000 and 40,000 cremation burials are known, and many come from large cremation cemeteries in eastern England, such as

Spong Hill in Norfolk (see, for example, Hills et al. 1994). Both the cremations and the inhumations show variations in grave goods, pointing to variations in identity, status, power, and wealth. At a very basic level, we can argue that Early Anglo-Saxon England was not an egalitarian society. But, as Esmonde Cleary (2011: 14) notes, it was a far less hierarchical society that the Romano-British society that preceded it.

In political terms, early Saxon England was probably made up of a series of small polities. Wroxeter was probably the center of one of these small polities near the Welsh border, while small polities in areas such as the Fenlands are recorded in the Middle Saxon (probably late seventh century) document known as the Tribal Hidage, which appears to be a tribute list for the emerging powerful kingdom of Mercia (See Yorke 1990: Fig. 1). From a social perspective, individuals of different ranks were probably linked by ties of patronage and clientship, and the responsibilities of a client may have included military service and payments of rent. We can say very little about taxation in the fifth and sixth century, except to suggest that taxes must have been paid in kind or in the form of labor service, since coinage went out of regular use in the fifth century. The burden of any taxation must have been light, since there is little evidence for the production of an agricultural surplus. The richer archaeological and historical evidence from the seventh century onward allows us to say more about the subject of taxation.

Seventh-Century Changes

The seventh century was a period of major social, political, economic, and religious changes in Anglo-Saxon England that set the stage for the emergence of more complex societies in the Middle Anglo-Saxon (traditionally dated to between 650 and 850 CE) and Late Saxon (ca. 850–1066) periods. Burials and changes in subsistence practices and settlement patterns point to substantial social changes in seventh-century England. In the seventh century we see the appearance of a number of very wealthy burials, the best known of which is the famous ship burial at Sutton Hoo (Bruce-Mitford 1975; Carver 2005). The rich burial mounds at Sutton Hoo replaced an earlier folk cemetery located about 500 m to the north at Tranmer House (Fern 2015). Other rich seventh-century burials include the so-called "Prittlewell Prince" in Essex (Blair et al. 2004; Blackmore et al. 2019). That burial was placed in a timber-lined chamber that was probably originally covered by a mound, and the grave was accompanied by weapons, feasting equipment, two gold foil crosses, and a lyre. These data suggest that increasing social differentiation was taking place in Anglo-Saxon England by the mid-seventh century CE.

As Childe argued many years ago, the social surplus was a critical factor in the urban revolution. While taxes and tolls could be used to extract the surplus, intensive agricultural systems were needed to produce the surplus in the first place. Archaeobotanical (McKerracher 2016, 2018) and zooarchaeological data (Crabtree 2010, 2012) point to substantial specialization in animal husbandry and intensification in agriculture beginning in the Middle Saxon period, and possibly as early as the late sixth or seventh century, leading to increased agropastoral production.

Animal bone assemblages from the Early Saxon sites such as West Stow (Crabtree 1990b), West Stow West (Crabtree and Campana 2014a), and Kilham in Yorkshire (Archer 2003) indicate that Early Saxon cattle were raised for a combination of meat, milk and traction. Ageing and sexing data suggest that Early Saxon sheep were kept for a combination of purposes including meat and wool. The Early Saxon zooarchaeological record provides no clear evidence for economic specialization. Livestock production was supplemented by a limited amount of hunting, fishing, and fowling. In short, the pattern was one of autarky or economic self-sufficiency.

By the Middle Saxon period, there is evidence for increasing specialization in primary and secondary animal products such as wool and pork. For example, ageing and sexing data for the sheep from Brandon, a high-status Middle Saxon site in Suffolk, suggest that these animals were raised primarily for their wool (Crabtree and Campana 2014b). The Middle Saxon site of Wicken Bonhunt in Essex seems to have specialized in pork production, and this specialization may have developed as early as the end of the Early Saxon Period (Crabtree 2012). Other zooarchaeological data (Sykes 2010) suggest that beginning in the Middle Saxon period, deer hunting was transformed from a subsistence activity to a prestige activity that was controlled by the social and political élites.

McKerracher (2016, 2018) identifies increasing intensification in cereal agriculture during the Middle Saxon Period based on archaeobotanical data recovered from recently excavated Anglo-Saxon sites. He argues that Early Anglo-Saxon farmers grew wheat and barley, and their choices of crops depended primarily on local environmental conditions. Agricultural intensification is seen in the addition of two other cereal crops, oats and rye, in the Middle Saxon Period. In addition, the recovery of a part of a heavy plow from a seventh-century context at Lyminge in Kent (Thomas 2013) suggests that early Middle Saxon farmers were exploiting the heavy soils that had not been widely used for cereal agriculture since the Roman period. The increased use of the heavy clay soils in the Middle Anglo-Saxon Period is another form of agricultural intensification, since the cultivation of these soils requires changing agricultural technology in the form of the use of the heavy plow with an iron share and coulter.

Settlement patterns also change at this time. In addition to the typical small hall and *grubenhaüs* settlement seen at sites such as West Stow (West 1985), we see a number of wealthier settlements that include much larger and more elaborate halls and other structures. These include the recently-discovered hall at Rendlesham, located about 4 miles from Sutton Hoo (Scull et al. 2016), as well as a wealthy seventh-century settlement at Lyminge in Kent (Thomas 2013), and a series of elaborately constructed timber halls at Cowdery's Down in Hampshire (Millet and James 1983). Lyminge is likely to have served as a royal vill in the seventh century, and the royal vills represent some of the earliest known evidence for taxation in Anglo-Saxon England.

The Emporia in Middle Saxon England

Much of our evidence for both regional and long-distance trade during the Middle Saxon period comes from a number of sites known as emporia or *wics*. These sites are arguably the first towns in post-Roman Britain, and they served as centers for craft production and regional and overseas trade (Hill and Cowie 2001). Substantial archaeological research has been carried out at the emporia of Hamwic (Saxon Southampton), Lundenwic (Saxon London), Eorforwic (Saxon York), and Gippeswic (Saxon Ipswich) in Suffolk. These sites flourished in the eighth and early ninth centuries CE, but most seem to have seventh-century foundations.[2] Archaeological research that has been conducted in advance of urban redevelopment in Ipswich, Southampton, London, and York has shed light on the development and layout of the *wic* sites, as well as evidence for trade and craft production within the emporia.

The Origins of Ipswich Project (1974–1990) was designed to study the development of Anglo-Saxon and Early Medieval Ipswich. Thirty-five sites were excavated during the course of the project, including 25 within the Anglo-Saxon and medieval defenses and nine in the suburbs. Unfortunately, the results of the project have never been fully published, but interim reports (Wade 1988, 1993; see also Wade 2001) allow us to reconstruct the archaeological history of the town. The earliest phases of settlement in Ipswich date to the seventh century. In addition to the sunken-featured buildings and pits that are associated with hand-made pottery, the seventh-century Buttermarket Cemetery (Scull 2009) served a small, non-urban community that probably numbered in the low hundreds (Scull 2009: 314). The presence of imported pottery and small-scale craft activity suggests that this community was designed to "channel and control exchange with the continent and the benefits—in revenue, prestige and authority—accruing from this" (Scull 2009: 316).

The seventh-century Ipswich community was small (somewhere between 6 and 30 ha), and its internal structure is unclear. Archaeological data from numerous sites within the town indicate that the site expanded rapidly in the early eighth century to an area of about 50 ha. While a number of small-scale crafts such as bone-working were carried out within Ipswich, the primary craft activity was the production of Ipswich Ware pottery which was established in the early eighth century (Blinkhorn 2012). Unlike earlier Anglo-Saxon pottery which was hand-built and fired in bonfires, Ipswich Ware was finished on a slow wheel and kiln-fired. A number of kilns that were used in the production of Ipswich Ware were identified within the Middle Saxon town. Ipswich ware was widespread throughout the kingdom of East Anglia where it appears to have been used as everyday pottery, since it forms the bulk of the Middle Saxon ceramic assemblages. It was also traded to other areas of Anglo-Saxon England where it may also have been used as containers for other less-visible trade items such as salt (Blinkhorn 2012: 99).

Hamwic, Middle Anglo-Saxon Southampton, was located on the west bank of the Itchen River, to the northeast of the later medieval town. Southampton is a major modern port, and bomb damage during World War II, as well as subsequent urban redevelopment, has allowed for extensive open area excavation within the Anglo-Saxon town. In many ways, the development of Hamwic parallels the development of Ipswich in the seventh to ninth centuries. Excavations carried out in advance of construction of St. Mary's football stadium revealed a wealthy seventh-century cemetery (Birbeck et al. 2005; Stoodley 2011). The cemetery includes several burials with complex weapon assemblages that include items such as swords, shields, and spears. Stoodley (2011: 51) argues that "a good case can be made for [the cemetery's] association with a high-status settlement, such as a royal estate that was involved in controlling trade in the lower Itchen." Historic sources include references to both Hamwic (the emporium) and Hamtun, which may refer to the presence of a royal vill, since the term *tun* seems to imply an administrative role (Stoodley 2002: 317). Unfortunately, we do not yet have any archaeological evidence for the presence of this vill.

Excavations at the Melbourne Street (Holdsworth 1980) and Six Dials (Andrews 1997) sites have provided evidence for the layout of the Middle Saxon Hamwic and for the trade and craft activities that were carried out at the emporium. Many of the craft activities carried out at Hamwic were based on primary or secondary animal products, including bone- and antler-working, butchery, and textile production. Other crafts include iron-, copper-, and gold metalworking. Imported pottery and coins document trade with Carolingian Francia, the Rhineland, the Low Countries, Frisia, and Denmark (Andrews 1997: 254).

The Six Dials excavations also revealed the layout of the emporium. A boundary ditch surrounding the town was dug around 700 CE, but this ditch was not defensive in nature. The major north-south streets were laid out first, and then east-west streets were added to form a grid pattern. The streets were paved with standard sized gravel (Brisbane 1994: 31), and it is likely that the town plan was conceived as a unified entity from the beginning (Bourdillon 1988: 179).

Lundenwic, Middle Saxon London, appears to have been the largest of the four *wic* sites, covering approximately 60 ha with an estimated population of 6,000–7,000 inhabitants (Cowie et al. 2012: xxiii). Excavations at the Royal Opera House (Malcolm *et al.* 2003) and elsewhere in London (Cowie et al. 2012; Fowler and Taylor 2013) have provided a wealth of information on craft activity and trade in this important Anglo-Saxon emporium. It is important to note that all this work has been carried out since 1984, when the location of Middle Saxon London was initially identified by Martin Biddle (1984) and Allan Vince (1984). Lundenwic is located upriver from the Roman and medieval town of London, near the modern Strand area.

The Lundenwic excavations have produced substantial evidence for craft production, including, metal-working, bone- and antler-working, glass-working, and textile manufacture, among others (Cowie et al. 2012: Chapter 7). Evidence from the Opera House excavations shows that the location of the trades was based on a model of "cooperative diversity" where related trades were located close to one another (Malcolm et al. 2003: xv). Cowie et al. (2012: 204) compare Lundenwic to Hamwic and Ipswich and to contemporary continental sites such as Dorestad in the Netherlands and Quentovic in northern France. They note that:

> *Wics* and emporia are, however, generally accepted as a unique phenomenon of their time, their *raison d'être* being the levying of tolls on the exchange, marketing and onward distribution of goods within a network of similar centers and against a backdrop of a variety of smaller sites, involving both coastal and inland suppliers and consumers
>
> (Cowie et al. 2012: 204).

Anglian York or Eorforwic is smaller than the other three Anglo-Saxon emporia. Hamerow (2007: 223) estimates that it may have been home to between 1,000 and 1,500 people. It is also located farther from the coast, at the confluence of the Ouse and the Fosse Rivers. Excavations at the Fishergate site in York were carried out in the 1980s and revealed evidence for a variety of craft activities including metal-working, glass-working, the production of bone and antler combs, fur preparation, textile production, and glass-working (Kemp 1991: 221; Spall and Toop 2008: 13; Palliser 2014: 37). Evidence for trade includes coins, lava querns from the Rhineland, and pottery from France and the Low Countries (Kemp 1991: 213–16).

Coinage, Taxation, and Trade in Middle Saxon England

One innovation that may have facilitated this trade was the development of silver pennies known as *sceattas*. By the late seventh and early eighth centuries coins were being minted in East Anglia (Williams 2013: 136) and elsewhere. By the mid-eighth century, the emporium of Ipswich was linked to the surrounding countryside by markets and a substantial monetary exchange (Scull 2013: 237). Naismith (2013) has argued the Middle Saxon economy was partially monetized, and coinage facilitated marketing by reducing transaction costs.

Early research on the emporia suggested that they were established by the Anglo-Saxon kings to control trade with the continent, especially trade in valuable items (Hodges 1982). In *Dark Age Economics* Hodges (1982) presented what is known as a "prestige goods model" (Frankenstein and Rowlands 1978), suggesting that early Anglo-Saxon kings enhanced their prestige and power by controlling the trade and exchange in rare and expensive goods, and that the emporia played a critical role in this trade. Hodges' model was important because it linked the foundation of the emporia to the beginnings of state formation in Anglo-Saxon England. When the first edition of *Dark Age Economics* was published, the exact location of Lundenwic had not yet been identified, and most of the published archaeological data came from the excavations at Melbourne Street in Hamwic (Holdsworth 1980). Since the archaeological record for the English wics was limited at that time, most of the analysis was based on the study of coins and pottery from Hamwic.

Archaeological work that has been carried out in the nearly 40 years since the original publication of *Dark Age Economics* has emphasized the important roles that the emporia played in regional trade (see, for example, Moreland 2001). Rather than simply controlling trade in prestige items, recent research suggests that the foundation of the emporia allowed the Middle Saxon kings to concentrate and most importantly to tax trade. Reeves were the kings' representatives at these emporia and were responsible for collecting taxes and tolls. The kings could also exert their power to waive taxes on certain items. For example, charter evidence indicates that King Aethelbald of Mercia (d. 757 CE) was able to confer toll exemptions in London on several religious houses in southern England (Russo 1998: 149). Taxation of trade represented another important source of revenue for the powerful Middle Saxon royal houses.

Tribute payments, food rents, and taxes on trade would have provided substantial revenue for the emerging royal houses of Middle Anglo-Saxon England. Finds such as the Staffordshire Hoard (Leahy and Bland 2009) point to the wealth that was acquired by these kings, in the case of the hoard possibly as a result of victory in warfare. The rich agricultural base that was initially established in the seventh century clearly contributed to this wealth, which was one of the things that attracted Vikings to England from the late eighth century onward (see below).

Conclusions and Implications for Late Saxon England

Agricultural intensification and specialization, beginning as early as the later parts of the Early Anglo-Saxon period, provided the agricultural surplus that could be extracted through food rents, tribute, taxes, and tolls by the Middle Saxon kings. The ability to extract this surplus played a critical role in the rapid social and economic changes that took place in England between the mid-fifth and the mid-ninth centuries CE.

The late ninth and tenth centuries presented military challenges to the Anglo-Saxon kingdoms. The first documented Viking raid took place at Lindisfarne Island in northeast England in 793, and the Great Heathen Army invaded eastern England in 865. After a period of protracted warfare, Wessex King Alfred's defeat of the Viking Army at the Battle of Eddington in 878 established Danish control over much of northern and eastern England, but left Wessex in Anglo-Saxon hands.

Defense of the kingdom of Wessex was critical, and Alfred and his successors developed a system of burhs or fortified places designed so that no one in Wessex was more than about 15 miles from a burh. Some of these fortified places made use of old Roman town walls, while others were newly constructed fortifications (Biddle and Hill 1971). The Burghal Hidage is a Late Anglo-Saxon document that provides a list of these places and the taxes that were required for their maintenance, listed in terms of hides. These labor taxes included bridge work, work on fortifications, and military service. The Laws of Ine indicate that these labor taxes have their roots in seventh-century England, at least in terms of military service. These fortified places also provided protected markets, and many, but not all, developed into Late Saxon and medieval towns (see Biddle and Hill 1971). The process is best documented from the Winchester excavations (Biddle 1990), although these important excavations are still incompletely published.

The burghal system was designed for the defense of what eventually became the Kingdom of England, and it clearly played a role in Late Saxon state formation. By providing protected markets, the burghal system also played a role in the establishment and growth of Late Saxon towns in Wessex. What this paper has tried to demonstrate is that urbanism and state formation in the Late Anglo-Saxon period are outgrowths of the systems of taxation and tribute that have their roots in the seventh century and the Middle Saxon period.

Acknowledgments

Some of the research for this paper was carried out while I was a Visiting Research Scholar at the Institute of the Study of the Ancient World in the fall of 2015. My previous research on Anglo-Saxon England was supported by grants from the National Science Foundation, the Wenner-Gren Foundation, and the National Endowment for the Humanities, as well as a Fulbright Full Grant and Renewal (1977–79) to the University of Southampton. I am grateful for the reviewers' comments on earlier drafts of this paper. The mistakes, of course, are all mine.

NOTES

1 Some authors would date this work as early as the late fifth century (see, for example, Higham 1994: 41), but it was undoubtedly written sometime between the end of the fifth century and 550 CE.

2 See Crabtree (2018) and the references therein for a more extensive discussion of the archaeology of the emporia.

WORKS CITED

Alcock, Joan D. 2011. *A Brief History of Roman Britain*. Boston: Little, Brown.

Andrews, P. 1997. *Excavations at Hamwic, Volume 2: Excavations at Six Dials*. Council for British Archaeology Research Report No. 109. London: Council for British Archaeology Research.

Archer, S. 2003. "The Zooarchaeology of an Anglo-Saxon Village: The Faunal Assemblage from Kilham, East Yorkshire." Unpublished MA thesis, University of York.

Banham, Debby and Rosamond Faith. 2014. *Anglo-Saxon Farms and Farming*. Oxford: Oxford University Press.

Bartholomew, Philip. 1982. "Fifth-Century Facts." *Britannia* 13: 261–70.

Biddle, Martin. 1984. "London on the Strand." *Popular Archaeology* 6: 23–27.

Biddle, Martin. 1990. Albert Ricket Archaeological Trust Lecture. "The study of Winchester: Archaeology and history in a British town, 1961–1983." In E. G. Stanley (ed.), *British Academy Papers on Anglo-Saxon England* (Oxford: Oxford University Press), 299–341.

Biddle, Martin and David Hill. 1971. "Late Saxon Planned Towns." *Antiquaries Journal* 71: 70–85.

Birbeck, Vaughn, with Roland J. C. Smith, Phol Andrews, and Nick Stoodley. 2005. *The Origins of Mid-Saxon Southampton: Excavations at the Friends Provident St. Mary's Stadium, 1998–2000*. Salisbury: Wessex Archaeology.

Blackmore, Lynn, Ian Blair, Sue Hirst, and Christopher Scull. 2019. *The Prittlewell Princely Burial: Excavations at Priory Crescent, Southend-on-Sea, Essex, 2003*. London: Museum of London Archaeology.

Blair, Ian, Elizabeth Barham, and Lyn Blackmore. 2004. "My Lord Essex." *British Archaeology* 76: 10–17.

Blinkhorn, Paul. 2012. *The Ipswich Ware Project: Ceramics, Trade, and Society in Middle Saxon England*. Medieval Pottery Research Group Occasional Paper No. 7. [London]: Medieval Pottery Research Group.

Bourdillon, Jennifer. 1988. "Countryside and town: the animal resources of Saxon Southampton." In D. Hooke (ed.), *Anglo-Saxon Settlements* (Oxford: Blackwell), 177–95.

Brisbane, M. A. 1994. "Hamwic (Saxon Southampton): The origin and development of an eighth century port and production centre." *Actes des congrès de la Société d'archéologie médiévale* 4: 27–34.

Bruce-Mitford, Rupert. 1975. *The Sutton Hoo Ship Burial, Volume 1*. London: British Museum.

Carver, Martin Oswald Hugh, 2005. *Sutton Hoo: A Seventh-Century Princely Burial Ground and Its Context*. London: British Museum.

Childe, V. Gordon. 1936. *Man Makes Himself*. London: Watts and Co.

Childe, V. Gordon. 1950. "The Urban Revolution." *Town Planning Review* 21: 3–17.

Cowie, Robert and Lyn Blackmore, with Anne Davis, Jackie Keily, and Kevin Rielly. 2012. *Lundenwic: Excavations in Middle Saxon London, 1987–2000*. Museum of London Archaeology Monograph 63. London: Museum of London.

Crabtree, Pam J. 1990a. "Sheep, Horses, Kine, and Swine: A Zooarchaeological approach to the Anglo-Saxon Settlement of England." *Journal of Field Archaeology* 16: 205–13.

Crabtree, Pam J. 1990b. *West Stow: Early Anglo-Saxon Animal Husbandry*. East Anglian Archaeology 47. Ipswich: Suffolk County Planning Department.

Crabtree, Pam J. 2010. "Agricultural innovation and socio-economic change in Early Medieval Europe: Evidence from Britain and France." *World Archaeology* 42: 122–36.

Crabtree, Pam J. 2012. *Middle Saxon Animal Husbandry in East Anglia*. East Anglian Archaeology 143. Bury St. Edmunds: Suffolk County Council Archaeological Service.

Crabtree, Pam J. 2018. *Early Medieval Britain: The Re-birth of Towns in the Post-Roman West*. Cambridge: Cambridge University Press.

Crabtree, Pam J. and Douglas V. Campana. 2014a. "Wool production, wealth, and trade in Middle Saxon England." In B. S. Arbuckle and S. A. McCarty (eds.), *Animals and Inequality in the Ancient World* (Boulder, CO: University Press of Colorado), 335–52.

Crabtree, Pam J. and Douglas V. Campana. 2014b. "Animal Bone (BRD071)." In A. Tester et al. (eds.), *Brandon, Staunch Meadow, Suffolk: A High-Status Middle Saxon Settlement on the Fen Edge*. East Anglian Archaeology 151 (Bury St. Edmunds: Suffolk County Council Archaeological Service), 350–53.

Esmonde Cleary, A. Simon. 1989. *The Ending of Roman Britain*. Routledge: London.

Esmonde Cleary, A. Simon. 2011. "The Ending(s) of Roman Britain." In H. Hamerow, D. A. Hinton, and S. Crawford (eds.), *The Oxford Handbook of Anglo-Saxon Archaeology*, (Oxford: Oxford University Press), 13–29.

Fern, C. J. R. 2015. *Before Sutton Hoo: The Prehistoric Remains and Early Anglo-Saxon Cemetery at Tranmer House, Bromeswell, Suffolk*. East Anglian Archaeology 155. Bury St. Edmunds: Suffolk County Council Archaeological Service.

Fowler, Louise and Ruth Taylor. 2013. *At the Limits of Lundenwic: Excavations in the North-west of Middle Saxon London at St. Martin's Courtyard, 2006–9*. MOLA Archaeology Studies Series 27. London: Museum of London.

Frankenstein, S. and M. Rowlands. 1978. "The internal structures and regional context of early Iron Age society in south-western Germany." *Bulletin of the Institute for Archaeology* 15: 73–112.

Hamerow, Helena. 2007. "Agrarian production and the emporia of mid Saxon England, ca. 650–850." In J. Henning (ed.), *Post-Roman Towns, Trade and Settlement in Europe and Byzantium, Vol. 1: The Heirs of the Roman West* (Berlin; de Gruyter), 219–32.

Higham, Nicholas J. 1992. *Rome, Britain and the Anglo-Saxons*. London: Seaby.

Higham, Nicholas J. 1994. *The English Conquest: Gildas and Britain in the Fifth Century*. Manchester: Manchester University Press.

Hill, David and Robert Cowie (eds.). 2001. *Wics: Early Medieval Tracing Centres of Northern Europe*. Sheffield: Sheffield Academic Press.

Hills, Catherine M. 2003. *Origins of the English*. London: Duckworth.

Hills, Catherine M., Kenneth Penn, and Robert Rickett. 1994. *The Anglo-Saxon Cemetery at Spong Hill, North Elmham, Part V: Catalogue of Cremations*. East Anglian Archaeology 67. Dereham, Norfolk, UK: Scole Archaeological Committee.

Hodges, Richard. 1982. *Dark Age Economics: Origins of Towns and Trade, AD 600–1000*. London: Duckworth.

Hoggett, Richard. 2015. "From hollow to house: 50 years of discovery at West Stow." *British Archaeology* (September/October 2015): 44–49.

Holdsworth, Philip. 1980. *Excavations at Melbourne Street, Southampton, 1971–76.* British Archaeology Research Report No. 33. London: Council for British Archaeology.

Kemp, R. L., 1991. "The Archaeology of 46–54 Fishergate." In T. P. O'Connor (ed.), *Bones from 46–54 Fishergate.* The Archaeology of York 15/4 (London: Council for British Archaeology), 211–20.

Lane, Alan. 2014. "Wroxeter and the End of Roman Britain." *Antiquity* 88: 501–15.

Leahy, Kevin and Roger Bland. 2009. *The Staffordshire Hoard.* London: British Museum Press.

Malcolm, Gordon and David Bowsher, with Robert Cowie. 2003. *Middle Saxon London: Excavations at the Royal Opera House, 1989–99.* MoLAS Monograph 15. London: Museum of London Archaeology Service.

McKerracher, Mark. 2016. "Bread and surpluses: the Anglo-Saxon 'bread wheat thesis' reconsidered." *Environmental Archaeology* 21: 88–102.

McKerracher, Mark. 2018. *Farming Transformed in Anglo-Saxon England: Agriculture in the Long Eighth Century.* Oxford: Windgather.

Millett, Martin. 1990. *The Romanization of Britain: An Essay in Archaeological Interpretation.* Cambridge: Cambridge University Press.

Millet, Martin and Simon James. 1983. "Excavations at Cowdery's Down Basingstoke, Hampshire, 1979–81." *Antiquaries Journal* 140: 151–279.

Moreland, John. 2001. "Emporia." In P. J. Crabtree (ed.), *Medieval Archaeology: An Encyclopedia* (New York: Garland), 92–97.

Naismith, Rory. 2013. *Money and Power in Anglo-Saxon England: The Southern English Kingdoms, 757–865.* Cambridge: Cambridge University Press.

Oosthuizen, Susan. 2019. *The Emergence of the English.* Leeds: ARC Humanities Press.

Palliser, D. M. 2014. *Medieval York, 600–1540.* Oxford: Oxford University Press.

Rizzetto, Mauro, Pam J. Crabtree, and Umberto Albarella. 2017. "Livestock Changes at the Beginning and End of the Roman Period in Britain: Issues of Acculturation, Adaptation, and 'Improvement'." *European Journal of Archaeology* 20: 535–56.

Russo, Daniel G. 1998. *Town Origins and Early Development in England, c. 400–950 AD.* Westport, CT: Greenwood Publishing Group.

Scull, Christopher. 2009. *Early Medieval (Late 5th–Early 8th Centuries AD) Cemeteries at Boss Hall and Buttermarket, Ipswich, Suffolk.* Society for Medieval Archaeology Monograph 27. Leeds: The Society for Medieval Archaeology.

Scull, Christopher. 2013. "Ipswich: Contexts of Funerary Evidence from an Urban Precursor of the Seventh Century AD." In D. Bates and R. Liddiard (eds.), *East Anglia and Its North Sea World in the Middle Ages* (Woodbridge: Boydell), 218–29.

Scull, Christopher, Faye Minter, and Judith Plouviez. 2016. "Social and Economic Complexity in Early Medieval England: A Central Place Complex of the East Anglian Kingdom at Rendlesham, Suffolk." *Antiquity* 90: 1594–612.

Spall, C. A. and N. J. Toop. 2008. "Before Eorforwic: New light on York in the 6th–7th centuries." *Medieval Archaeology* 52: 1–25.

Stenton, Frank M. 1947. *Anglo-Saxon England.* The Oxford History of England, Vol. 2. Oxford: Clarendon Press.

Stoodley, Nick. 2002. "The origins of Hamwic and its central role in the 7th century as revealed by recent archaeological discoveries." In B. Hårdh and L. Larsson (eds.), *Central Places in the Migration and Merovingian Periods*. Acta Archaeologica Lundensia 8 (Lund: Department of Archaeology and Ancient History, Lund University), 317–31.

Stoodley, Nick. 2011. "Burial practice in seventh-century Hampshire: St. Mary's Stadium in context." In J. Buckberry and A. K. Cherryson (eds.), *Burial in Later Anglo-Saxon England, 650–1100 AD* (Oxford: Oxbow), 38–53.

Sykes, Naomi. 2010. "Deer, land, knives and halls: social change in early medieval England." *Antiquaries Journal* 90: 175–93.

Thomas, Gabor. 2013. "Life before the minster: the social dynamics of monastic foundation at Anglo-Saxon Lyminge, Kent." *Antiquaries Journal* 93: 109–45.

Thomas, Mark G., Michael P. H. Stumpf, and Heinrich Härke. 2006. "Evidence for an apartheid-like social structure in Early Anglo-Saxon England." *Proceedings of the Royal Society B* 273: 2651–57.

Todd, Malcolm. 1999. *Roman Britain*. 3rd ed. Oxford: Blackwell.

Vince, Alan. 1984. "The Aldwych: Mid-Saxon London Discovered." *Current Archaeology* 8: 310–12.

Wade, Keith. 1988. "Ipswich." In B. Hobley and R. Hodges (eds.), *The Rebirth of Towns in the West, A.D. 700–1050/* British Archaeology Research Report no. 68 (London: Council for British Archaeology), 93–100.

Wade, Keith. 1993. "The urbanization of East Anglia: the Ipswich Perspective." In J. Gardiner (ed.), *Flatlands and Wetlands: Current Themes in East Anglian Archaeology*. East Anglian Archaeology Report 50 (Ipswich: Suffolk County Planning Department), 144–51.

Wade, Keith. 2001. "Ipswich." In P. J. Crabtree (ed.), *Medieval Archaeology: An Encyclopedia* (New York: Garland), 173–75.

West, Stanley. 1985. *West Stow: The Anglo-Saxon Village*. East Anglian Archaeology 24. Bury St. Edmunds: Suffolk County Planning Department.

White, Roger and Philip Barker. 1998. *Wroxeter: Life & Death of a Roman City*. Stroud, UK: Tempus.

Williams, Gareth. 2013. "The Circulation, Minting, and Use of Coins in East Anglia, c. AD 580–675." In D. Bates and R. Liddiard (eds.), *East Anglia and Its North Sea World in the Middle Ages* (Woodbridge: Boydell), 120–36.

Yorke, Barbara. 1990. *Kings and Kingdoms in Early Anglo-Saxon England*. London: Routledge.

7

Taxation, Aristocratic Autonomy, and Theories of Reciprocity in the Iranian Empire

RICHARD E. PAYNE

Shortly after acceding to the throne in 531 CE, the king of kings Husraw I initiated a restructuring of the fiscal system. The Iranian court presented the reform as a restoration of Zoroastrian cosmological order, according to which three—or sometimes four—social groups were locked into a multi-millennial interdependency: agricultural laborers, priests, and warriors were each to contribute their particular work to the project of empire, for the success of which the collaboration of these strictly segregated groups was essential. The foundation of political order was located in the distribution of resources from one group to another. In the reported words of Husraw I, "rulership is predicated on the military, the military on financial resources; financial resources are predicated on the land tax (*kharāj*), and the land tax is predicated on the cultivation of land."[1] Or, more metaphorically: "the people of the land and the taxpayers are the hands of the men at arms, whereas the military, its forces, and the fighting men are similarly the hands of the taxpayers and their strength."[2] It was therefore incumbent on Husraw I to nurture the laboring population, to ensure its welfare and enhance its productivity, for the sake of the military. What sounds like an utterly banal description of ancient fiscality—or, more sympathetically, a precocious version of Charles Tilly's "War Making and State Making"—was part of an explicit theorizing of imperial taxation designed to explain its ends to the élite and to elicit compliance within a fiscal regime that depended on the voluntary participation of patrimonial landholders.[3] For the martial forces in question were none other than the great aristocratic houses, often with origins in the post-Hellenistic Parthian order, who commanded and manned the Iranian cavalry-based military.[4] The aim of the present chapter is to recover the politics of persuasion through which aristocrats, protective of their autonomy, participated in the development of a fiscal apparatus that was arguably the most successful at trans-territorial extraction in the ancient Near East, only to be surpassed by its Abbasid successor.[5] Such an approach makes a virtue of a necessity: the richness of the literary evidence for theories of, and debates on, the nature and scope of fiscal power partly compensates for the comparative dearth of documentary texts for the everyday administration, written on perishable parchment.[6]

The study of Iranian taxation has been preoccupied almost exclusively with Husraw I's so-called "reform." The historiographical debate—on its nature, scope, and comparative success—reveals two fundamentally opposed accounts of the Iranian political economy. While all scholars agree the king of kings sought to establish a far more efficient and pervasive fiscal administration as the foundation of a late Sasanian imperial apparatus more centralized than its early and middle Sasanian predecessors, they disagree on the outcome. One chorus argues that the late Sasanian court failed to install more effective mechanisms of extraction, in the face of strident and successful aristocratic opposition.[7] Another argues not only that they did so, but also that the greatest aristocratic houses were disempowered in the process, upsetting traditional social hierarchies as well as the political-economic order.[8] Neither of these accounts remains compelling in either evidentiary or theoretical terms. Underlying both is the presupposition that landed aristocrats, protective of their privileges, would never comply with the fiscal demands of the court, a presupposition that ignores possible political, economic, and even ideological incentives to do so. This chapter will place the late Sasanian reforms and their rhetorical framing within a multi-secular account of Iranian resource extraction and the negotiation, sometimes dialogic, sometimes violent, between the court and the aristocratic houses over the measure of their respective shares of the rents of empire. What neither court nor aristocracy ever imagined was that one could rule without the other, or that imperial surplus should not be shared between them.[9]

It is a truism to say that little can be known of early Sasanian taxation.[10] However limited, the evidence nevertheless suggests the operation of a fiscal system resembling, in its broadest outlines, the better documented Achaemenid and Seleucid regimes: the direct collection of a land tax, at fixed or flexible rates, on royal lands, especially in Mesopotamia; the indirect collection of land taxes through local élites granted a high degree of autonomy; and the collection of a poll tax.[11] The continuous development of irrigation in Mesopotamia and Khuzestan suggests the efforts of the kings of kings to augment their tax base. So, too, the construction of royal cities as centers of rule, proto-industrial production, and markets in precisely those regions. It is unlikely, however, that the early Sasanians placed fiscal burdens on the northern, central, and eastern regions of the empire equivalent to those encountered in the western, economic core. Here great Parthian aristocratic houses possessed massive landed estates that often encompassed, symbolically if not literally, entire regions. The Parthian predecessors of the Sasanians are said to have ruled a decentralized realm, a misleading designation that is perhaps not without accuracy with respect to the fiscal system: regional kings likely possessed fiscal autonomy and transferred little wealth to the court of the Parthian kings of kings, dependent primarily on Mesopotamia's resources.[12] The elimination of such regional kings in the early Sasanian period implies a comparative loss of fiscal autonomy, but third- and fourth-century Sasanians were unlikely to have placed onerous demands on aristocratic houses they were eager to coopt. The sixth-century Armenian historian Ełišē reports that the houses of the Caucasus traditionally submitted a tribute to Seleucia-Ctesiphon modest in comparison to the impositions the middle Sasanian rulers would begin to make.[13]

But the early Sasanians were not without novel sources of revenue. The continuous growth of trans-Eurasian trade in high-value commodities, especially silk garments and silver vessels, from the first century CE through the early seventh was a major source of income.[14] It is hardly accidental that the Sasanians emerged in Fars just as mercantile routes from the East and South Asia to Rome were shifting away from the Red Sea toward the Persian Gulf, or that they quickly asserted control over Central Asian, Indian Ocean, and Mesopotamian emporia, often destroying rival mercantile centers.[15] Rome's supply of silk and other eastern luxuries would remain entirely dependent on merchants passing through Iranian territory until the middle of the sixth century, while Central and East Asian élites began to consume not only Iranian silver, but also Iranian silk garments. Comparative evidence from the Roman world—where the 25% *tetarte* tax was imposed—suggests revenues from taxes on trade could amount to nearly 200 million silver drachms per year (5–10% of the Roman budget), a far more significant sum in an Iran with a vastly smaller population.[16] The early Sasanians also enlisted their religious specialists in the levying of taxes, a role unknown in the Parthian period.

Throughout the four centuries of Iranian rule, Zoroastrian *mowbed* appear in a range of fiscal roles, from housing the archives of the fiscal and military administration of—at least part of—Azerbaijan at the great fire temple of Adur Gushnasp to supervising the central treasury and the imperial tax rolls at Seleucia-Ctesiphon.[17] In the course of the re-form of Husraw I, *mowbed* served as the primary supervisors of the fis-cal system on behalf of the court in the provinces. Such positions likely go back to the third-century origin of the empire, a fundamental aspect of which was the elevation of the priestly élite to positions of political power. In the early 360s, facing the first simultaneous military conflicts on its eastern and western frontiers, Shapur II turned to another class of religious specialists, Christian bishops, to supervise the taxation of the cities of Mesopotamia and Khuzestan, which were largely populated by Roman deportees.[18] The demand that the bishops collect an additional, double poll tax in the context of a military crisis suggests both the de-pendence of the court on religious specialists and urban populations and the *ad hoc*, irregular nature of exactions. Shocked at the arbitrary imposition, at least some bishops refused to collect the additional tax and were executed as a consequence. Most importantly, the episode sug-gests the exhausting, catastrophic wars of the late fourth and fifth cen-turies stimulated the court to innovate ways of extracting more revenue from its population. In an overwhelmingly agrarian economy, in which the great bulk of productive land was in aristocratic hands, such moves invariably forced the court to renegotiate its economic relationship with the landed élite.

In the middle of the fifth century, the Iranian court began to assert di-rect control in at least some regions where aristocratic houses had hith-erto enjoyed fiscal autonomy. The cause was military: the invasions of the Huns in the latter half of the fourth century on the northern and north-eastern frontiers required the court, for the first time in its history, to organize continual rather than seasonal military campaigns, stationing tens of thousands of cavalrymen and infantry in frontier zones to prevent the overrunning of the Iranian heartland.[19] The restructuring of the military and fiscal administration that ensued included the first assessment of aristocratic territories, an event that has gone unacknowledged and undiscussed in previous studies of Iranian taxation. The evidence for such a direct fiscal intervention comes from the only body of literature produced by and for the highest-ranking aristocratic houses: Armenian historiography.[20] Ełišē reported that early in the reign of Yazdgird II (r. 438–457) the court dispatched an official, Dēnšāpuhr, to Armenia to conduct an assessment, *ashkharhagir* in Armenian, literally "a writing of the land."[21] The census resulted, predictably, in an increase in the tax burden levied on the entire region of Armenia—specifically a doubling of the land tax, and the imposition of taxes on ecclesiastical lands, at least according to the narrator hostile to the Iranian court. Importantly, the pretext given for the assessment was the "lightening of the burden of the cavalry," that is, a change in the nature of military service.[22] Dēnšāpuhr's title, *hambarakapet* in Armenian deriving from the Middle Persian term for storehouse (*hambār*), implies involvement in military provisioning.[23] Underpinning aristocratic claims to fiscal autonomy was their commitment to provide the king of kings with military service, to outfit and to supply their own cavalrymen.[24] Such an arrangement was adequate for the seasonal campaigning against the Romans the court undertook in the third and fourth centuries, but the defense against the Huns simultaneously demanded and legitimated a more centralized system of military command and provisioning. The increase in the land tax corresponded, Ełišē suggested, with a reduction in the contributions aristocratic houses were expected to make in terms of equipment and supplies, if not in manpower. The assessment and augmented tax burden enabled the military administration directly to provision and, most importantly, to pay its cavalry, rather than rely on the aristocrats to supply themselves.

Yazdgird II sought to bargain a new contract with the aristocracy, metaphorically speaking, on the grounds of the empire's need of protection from the Huns. The archaeology of fifth-century infrastructural development, from precisely the 440s onward, attests to a high degree of success. Massive fortifications between the Caucasus Mountains and the Caspian and between the Caspian and the Kophet Dag represent some of the largest, most capital-intensive defensive structures known from the ancient world.[25] More relevant to the topic of fiscality, however, are the centrally planned and constructed networks of irrigation that transformed their hinterlands into densely populated, highly productive plains. Such an expansion of the arable in Azerbaijan and Gorgan—as well as in other, as yet unsurveyed regions—shows the court developing Mesopotamian-style zones of agricultural intensification in hitherto fiscally autonomous regions. These large-scale interventions in the northern and northeastern regions of the empire lead to two salient conclusions: firstly, the mid-fifth-century court possessed the capacity to insert itself directly into aristocratic territories, whether through the making of assessments of the kind described for Armenia or through the construction of canals, walls, fortifications, and settlements; secondly, the court was extracting enough silver not only to maintain an army numbering at least 100,000 continuously on its frontiers, but to fund large-scale infrastructural projects.[26] The apparent fiscal robustness of the middle Sasanian court suggest that the assessment of Armenia was part of a larger extension of the fiscal purview of the court that included other regions and that the court successfully persuaded or coerced its aristocracy to comply with novel demands. The Armenians, admittedly, embarked on a major rebellion in 450 to resist the fiscal and military reforms, but, by 484, had acquiesced to participate in the revised structures of rule, as long as an Armenian aristocratic house, the Mamikoneans, could superintend the regional administration.[27] Here we arrive at a key incentive to compliance in a new fiscal system that gave the court far more control over resources: the opportunities for enrichment that new military and fiscal offices provided the aristocracy, not to mention major grants of newly arable land.

If scholars have assumed the only way the court could enhance its mechanisms of extraction was by weakening the aristocracy, precisely the opposite is the case. To return to the sixth-century reform of Husraw I that continued the process of restructuring begun in the preceding century, seals and sealings on *bullae* published a decade ago document the identities of the officials superintending the fiscal and military administrations. Some *spāhbed*, the four military commanders at the head of a quadripartite system, designated their membership in great Parthian houses—Sēdōš of the house of Mihrān, spāhbed of the North, a jurisdiction encompassing the Caucasus and Azerbaijan, a region the Mihrānids had long dominated.[28] Others included unmistakable markers of their Parthian lineage, as Parvaneh Pourshariati has shown in the case of the *spāhbed* of the East, Dād-Burz-Mihr, a representative of the house of Kārēn dominant in Khurasan.[29] The identities of the fiscal administrators, *āmārgar*, active throughout the empire in the late Sasanian period remain unknown, but their activities seem primarily to have taken place under the aegis of the regional military commanders, the *marzbān* or *spāhbed*.[30] In other words, the fifth through sixth-century reforms did not aim to displace the great houses from their traditional territorial centers, but rather to enlist their regional authorities and powers—the basic mechanism of extraction remained the aristocratic capacity to demand rents from the laboring population on patrimonial lands, which we now know from the Qom documents to have been tightly, centrally administered.[31] What changed circa 440–540 was that a greater share—and the evidence does not allow for precision—of the surplus was transferred to imperial treasuries, whether at Seleucia-Ctesiphon or in the hands of regional military commanders serving the court. Importantly, exactions were now denominated, if not always levied, in coin, in precise, inflexible amounts.[32]

The key component of Husraw's reform was the assessment of fixed sums on regional circumscriptions, based on an evaluation and enumeration of its lands.[33] If the measures did not liberate the Sasanians from their dependency on the aristocracy, they did enable the court to determine, in advance, the amount of tax imposed on particular regions, essential for monitoring the functioning of the system and for long-term planning. According to the historiographical tradition, Husraw I replaced a tax assessment based on the shifting scale of agricultural production, known in Arabic texts as *muqāṣama*, with a tax assessment based on a fixed measurement of land and its productive capacities, Arabic *misāḥa*.[34] The shift embodies the renegotiation of control over the mechanisms of extraction between the aristocracy and the court: *muqāṣama* allows large landowners to determine the share of surplus granted to the court, in the absence of a pervasive administration measuring yields everywhere, every season, an institutional arrangement unimaginable in antiquity (or even today); *misāḥa* better served the interests of courts seeking to augment their revenues within the logical limitations of the premodern state, requiring a single measurement of lands and assessment of tax that could serve as the basis for a fiscal regime over the course of decades, if not centuries.[35] Literary accounts of the dramatic installation of a *misāḥa* in conjunction with an empire-wide census during the reign of Husraw I should be regarded as the culmination of a process beginning in the middle of the fifth century, rather than evidence for a fiscal revolution, as historians have often styled Husraw's reform. They represent the ideal form of the fiscal system in the minds of the late Sasanian court élite, which produced the *Xwadāy-nāmag* (Book of Kings) on which they were based. The sixth century witnessed not a radical upending of the social and political-economic order, but rather a gradual recalibration—ongoing from the middle of the fifth century—of the share of surplus the court received from the aristocracy and the efficiency of the system of extraction and redistribution. The *misāḥa* nevertheless significantly enhanced the power of a court that gained the capacity to predict its revenues and to demand fixed assessments from entire regions. The precise list of taxes levied on late Sasanian Tabaristan—300,000 drachms together with bales of silk and other high-value commodities—preserved in the early thirteenth century *Tārīkh-e Ṭabaristān* seems accurately to record the delivery of a fixed assessment to the court by perhaps the most refractory of regional aristocracies.[36]

The upshot of the long restructuring was a court that extracted and redistributed ever greater sums of silver, at least until late in the reign of Husraw II (590–628). Early Islamic historiographers and geographers with access to Sasanian administrative records reported a 25% increase in revenues over the course of the sixth century, from roughly 360 million drachms during the reign of Kawad to 420 million drachms early in the reign of Husraw II.[37] The numismatic evidence supports these accounts: the number of mints steadily expanded, while the quantity of silver coins minted and put into circulation grew throughout the late Sasanian period, culminating with the reign of Husraw II.[38] The coins also attest, unsurprisingly, to a connection between minting and military activity. Mints in the northeastern frontier zones produced far more coinage when campaigns were being conducted within them, and an enormous outburst of omissions corresponded with the beginning of Husraw II's campaign to conquer the Eastern Roman Empire in the first years of the seventh century.[39] The claim of the Armenian historian Ełiše that the court increased taxation in order to provision and pay its cavalrymen was undeniably accurate. And if some aristocrats joined Ełiše in scorning the proposed taxes-for-salaries bargain, others found in the reform system a means to enrichment, a share in the dizzying revenues that resulted from the ongoing expansion of arable land and the comparatively efficient levying of taxes on its laborers.

Making compliance in the fiscal regime compelling was an ideological framework that re-articulated aristocratic power in reciprocal terms. Across the various literary texts the late Sasanian court produced, representations of the harmonious interdependence of four social classes—warriors, priests, agricultural laborers, and merchants/artisans—consistently emerge. If the early Sasanian inscriptions had announced the inception of a hierarchical social order with patrimonial aristocrats dominating the mass of commoners, sixth-century accounts vaunted the mutually beneficial relations of aristocrats and their inferiors, with warriors providing protection in exchange for a share of the fruits of agricultural labor. Kingship appears as a prerequisite for such social reciprocity, policing the behavior of agents as well as the boundaries between the four classes. Such theories of royally-reinforced reciprocity have long been interpreted against the backdrop of the so-called Mazdakite rebellion around the time of Husraw I's accession in 531.[40] According to the traditions of the late Sasanian court, the rebellion aimed to upend the aristocratic social hierarchy through the large-scale redistribution, even collectivization, of arable land, in what Patricia Crone famously called a form of Zoroastrian communism.[41] However, despite the proliferation of scholarship on the rebellion, neither its extent nor even its social and political impacts can be discerned in the current state of the evidence. Equally ominous threats to aristocratic domination, by contrast, are well documented early in the reign of Husraw I, when the first urban-based rebellion against the Iranian court took place in Khuzestan. The merchants and artisans of its cities attempted to replace Husraw I with his son, claiming the right of rebellion previously restricted to the aristocracy for the urban élite.[42] It was quickly suppressed. But reports of such challenges to aristocratic supremacy within a political-economic order that included increasingly moneyed, frequently non-Zoroastrian urban élites capable of rallying the laboring populations of their hinterlands triggered anxieties among what sixth-century texts designated the warrior and priestly classes. In disseminating its elaborate, exaggerated, dramatic accounts of urban élites and even peasants rebelling against their aristocratic masters, the court of Husraw I sought precisely to introduce and to heighten such anxieties.

Theories of reciprocity provided a means of re-consolidating a political order the selfsame texts represented as in danger of being undone. Iranian élites were urged, in the first instance, to direct their attention to the "poor," a novel grouping within the social imaginary. The laboring population, almost wholly invisible in earlier texts, became a primary concern of courtly literature in the middle of the sixth century. Husraw I undertook the reform to lighten the burdens of the poor and to liberate them from unjust, unpredictable, and punitive exactions. The Arabic term *faqīr* in these translated texts corresponded with Middle Persian *driyōš*, a term that in Zoroastrian discourse elicited a paternalistic, ethical concern not dissimilar to the English term "poor," inflected with Christian meanings.[43] The late Sasanian court introduced the Zoroastrian category of the dignified poor to form an empire-wide collective of agricultural laborers dependent not only on their patrimonial landowners, but also on the king of kings, charged to intervene on their behalf in vaguely defined cases of "injustice." Husraw I proclaimed a desire to visit each village, to consult with each inhabitant, while lamenting the impracticality of a venture that would impose even greater demands on the laboring population to supply his entourage.[44] In outlining a vision of society in which the king of kings personally monitored the activities of individual agricultural producers, the late Sasanian court cut through the layers of mediation between rulers, aristocrats great and small, and their laboring dependents, to grant the sovereign unmediated access to the poor—and, implicitly, to its surplus. Such a vision was not a matter of abstract theorizing. The *Thousand Judgments*, an early seventh-century juridical compendium, reported that the court of Husraw I required religious authorities, *mowbed*, to inscribe their seals with the title, *driyōšān jādag-gōw*, "advocate of the poor," recasting the provincial officials most closely linked with the Sasanian house as representatives for the laboring population.[45] Seals of such advocates of the poor have survived from across the empire, attesting to the dissemination of the novel ideology of the poor in countless acts of quotidian administrative praxis.[46]

In exchange for the extension of royal authority implied in evocations of the poor, the court promised its élite salaries. The warrior class was to obtain a share of the surplus of agricultural laborers as compensation for protection, in an idealized vision of a society bound through reciprocal relations.[47] Crucial for the argument was therefore another, equally important promise: that, in opposition to the Mazdakite rebels (whether real or imagined), the court would police boundaries between classes and ensure that just as aristocratic warriors were not reduced in status, so laborers, or merchants, did not gain in theirs. If a major theme of the sixth century was aristocratic anxiety about the loss of power, the court extended salaries in silver as a mark of distinction for the warrior class. The fiscal reform of Husraw I was enacted in conjunction with a restructuring of the military that included the division of the empire into four centralized commanderies and the payment of fixed "salaries" (*rochik* in Armenian) on an annual basis to aristocratic cavalrymen registered at court.[48] Military salaries were hardly in novelty, as the evidence discussed for the fifth century makes plain. What Husraw's court seems to have accomplished was to have regularized payments that previously were made on an *ad hoc* basis, for instance, during campaigns. The fixed rate imposed on productive lands enabled the court to foresee its revenues and, therefore, to commit to annual salaries in the future. To collect such payments, according to an Armenian account, aristocratic cavalrymen had to present themselves at court, be inscribed in its rolls, and subject themselves to centralized command, often entailing deployment far from one's native land: the Armenians in question were installed at Isfahan.[49] The enhanced fiscal system thus facilitated the court's exercise of greater control over its military manpower. Such capacities underpinned imperial expansion in Central Asia, the Caucasus, and Arabia, as well as its victories over Rome, culminating in the early seventh-century conquest of the Roman Near East. The output of silver coinage in the fifth and sixth centuries maps patterns of military activity, and the absence of coinage that archaeologists have noted at military sites reflects the care with which warriors handled and hoarded their salaries rather than a non-monetized military. If silver coinage was a major factor in the very origins of Iranian military power, its significance only increased with the newfound capacities of the late Sasanian court.

Husraw I's court, however, framed its revamping of the military in terms of the solidarity, even extreme egalitarianism, of aristocratic cavalrymen on campaign. In one of the accounts of the reign most frequently recurring in surviving versions of the *Book of Kings*, the king of kings who had acquired the most autocratic power was presented as the first among equals, or, rather, the first among aristocratic equals. Husraw encharged Babak, an aristocrat at court, with reforming the military, in particular, its system of provisioning and payment within what al-Ṭabarī called the *dīwān al-muqātila*, "the *dīwān* of the warriors."[50] The appearance of the term *dīwān* in Middle Persian in late Sasanian seals suggests that al-Ṭabarī did not deploy the term anachronistically and that the early Islamic institution derived from an Iranian precedent, as did other key early Islamic fiscal institutions, such as *kharāj*.[51] Babak held a dramatic assembly of the empire's cavalry forces at the court in Seleucia-Ctesiphon to mark the reform.[52] On inspection of individual warriors and their equipment, he would then distribute salaries. When he noticed that one particularly important warrior was absent, however, he returned the cavalrymen to their residences. The absent warrior was none other than the king of kings, and Babak required Husraw to appear alongside the other cavalrymen for inspection, as a prerequisite for proceeding with the distribution of salaries. The ruler donned the very same equipment his aristocratic counterparts wore—precisely enumerated down to "the two plaited cords, which the rider let hang down his back from his helmet"—and joined them on the parade grounds, equal in his function as a warrior.[53] The king of kings was paid 4,001 silver drachms, only a single coin more than the highest-earning aristocratic cavalrymen.

Diametrically opposed to the contemporaneous image of Husraw as the autocratic advocate of the poor, the image of the king of kings as the first among aristocratic equals assembled for campaign assured the élite that accepting salaries, review, and centralized command would augment rather than undermine its status and authority. It evoked a long Sasanian tradition of conceiving imperial power as a partnership between aristocracy and autocracy, in which the former was to act in the interests of the latter. If the fiscal and military reforms gave the king of kings unprecedented despotic power, the ultimate aim of imperial order, the narrative of Babak suggested, remained the growth of aristocratic wealth and power, with regular military salaries a novel source of enrichment to complement existing patrimonial portfolios. The ideological productions of the court persuaded its élite of the material advantages of a "restoration" of an idealized form of beneficent, Zoroastrian order that made the king of kings the linchpin of the reciprocal relationship between the laboring and warrior classes.

Acceptance of the taxes-for-salaries bargain embodied in the discourse of reciprocity hardly resolved the structural antagonism inherent in aristocratic empire, nor should we allow the court's schematic, aspirational representations of a universally applied, regularly and efficiently administered fiscal "system" obscure the massive gaps in the reach of a regime over a highly fractured continental empire. Even Husraw I admitted to an inability to discipline, let alone tax, the inhabitants of the Alborz Mountains.[54] An account in the Armenian history of Pseudo-Sebeos captures the operation of the "reformed" late Sasanian fiscal regime. To pay salaries to its aristocrats on the northwestern, Anatolian frontier, the court dispatched an *āmārgar*—literally "accountant," a fiscal administrator—from Seleucia-Ctesiphon to the province with a sum of silver. A group of six Armenian great aristocrats together with 2,000 cavalrymen robbed the accountant en route, with the aim of using the treasure to purchase Hun mercenaries in a rebellion. Their bid to take advantage of the fragile position of a fiscal administrator in the provinces rapidly resulted in in-fighting among the rebels, with three of them returning contrite to the court.[55] Soon thereafter these same three aristocrats—Mamak Mamikonean, Step'anos Siwni, and Kotit lord of the Amatunik'—were back in Seleucia-Ctesiphon (re-) inscribing themselves in the roles of salaried cavalrymen.[56] Such a moment of breakdown in the fiscal and military administration, memorable enough to merit inclusion in an Armenian history written from an aristocratic perspective, reveals the limits as well as the success of the fiscal regime that emerged in the course of the fifth and sixth centuries. On the one hand, the court continued to depend on the voluntary participation of its aristocrats. Their withdrawal from the system resulted in its immediate breakdown, and even a direct fiscal emissary from the court was prone to be plundered by its own élite. On the other hand, the regular disbursement of salaries made the court hard to abandon, as the one-time profits to be derived from disruption paled in comparison to the long-term profits to be gained from imperial service, whether from direct payments or from control over monetary transfers and exchanges that provided ample opportunities for formalized, institutionalized "corruption."[57] Even the dropouts could quickly return to participate in the system.

What such effective bargaining with provincial aristocratic houses enabled was the enlisting of their institutional structures across far-flung territories in the service of the court. It is remarkable that the best evidence for Iranian fiscality in practice comes from its most ungovernable terrain, unimaginably distant from Seleucia-Ctesiphon, where the temptation to depart from Iranian service in favor of alternatives, or to escape state power altogether, was strongest: the highland valleys of the Hindu Kush, or the barren highlands of Eastern Anatolia along the Roman frontier. The theories of reciprocity and of a fixed, hierarchical, class-based social order that the late Sasanian court propagated anchored a negotiation of competing material interests—what share of tribute a patrimonial landowner could keep, what share should be given to the imperial treasury—in a normative framework that guaranteed the privileges and prosperity of the two parties, aristocratic and autocratic respectively. The discourse defined a set of shared norms concerning political-economic obligations that translated *ad hoc* arrangements into enduring institutions. It is tempting to say that the ideology legitimated the fiscal regime of the state, and such a characterization is not without accuracy. But compliance and the ascription of legitimacy are two very different things. The Armenians who hijacked an *āmārgar* and then returned to the court to seek salaries could act compliant without ascribing legitimacy. More productive than the Weberian language of legitimacy would be to speak more straightforwardly of shared representations and norms that could be invoked to frame political action in ways mutually advantageous to aristocrats and autocrats alike. Through the discourse of reciprocity, patrimonial élites could reinforce their own political-economic positions in the very act of granting greater power to the court. The "reform" of the fiscal regime ultimately served to enrich and empower the entire ruling class, by and for whom empire had been created in the third century. They could also renegotiate their bargain with a court whose demands for military service and taxes exceeded their expectations, as they did following Husraw II's spectacularly costly wars against the Romans.[58] His successor, Kawad II (r. 628), repealed taxes for the entire empire for three years as recompense.[59] Such regular renegotiations of the relative contribution of the aristocracy to the court defined the Iranian imperial project in late antiquity. The political compact endured until the Arab Muslims upended the foundations of aristocratic and autocratic power alike, before combining Iranian institutions with innovations of their own to erect a still more pervasive fiscal regime, far more disruptive socially, politically, and economically in its effects.

NOTES

1 Al-Masʿūdī, *Murūj al-dhahab*, v. II (Barbier de Meynard and Pavet de Courteille 1861–1917: 210).

2 *Sīrat Ānūširwān* (Imāmi 1987: 195; trans. Grignaschi 1966: 21).

3 Tilly 1985.

4 Nikonorov 2005: 146–47; Pourshariati 2008; Wiesehöfer 2010: 137–39.

5 For the conflict, competition, and negotiation between rulers and their ruling classes over their respective shares in the in the tributes of their rule—whether in the form of rents or taxes—and over the extent of their respective spheres of autonomy as the defining feature of preindustrial politics, see Haldon 1993.

6 The only documentary texts for the Iranian administration that have survived derive either from the short-lived occupation of Egypt 619–628 CE or from the so-called Bactrian archive, which includes parchments from a highland valley in southern Bactria from the third through early eighth centuries. Both corpora document the comparative efficacy and intensity of the Iranian fiscal regime in some of its most peripheral regions. For overviews, see Sims-Williams 2008 and Weber 2013.

7 Pourshariati 2008; Rubin 1995, 2000.

8 Wiesehöfer 2010; Howard-Johnston 1995, 2008.

9 On the co-constituted nature of autocracy and aristocracy in the Iranian order, see Payne 2017.

10 Morony 1984: 105–7; Gyselen 1999. The exception is the study of Goodblatt (1979), which demonstrates the ubiquity of the collection of a poll tax from the fourth century onward—at least in Mesopotamia—on the basis of Talmudic evidence.

11 Aperghis 2004, provides a synthetic overview of the sources of Seleucid state revenue that usefully emphasizes long-term continuities, self-conscious royal strategies for maximizing revenue, and the stimulating effects of exacting taxes in coin, all of which are useful starting points for a study of Iranian taxation. Monson 2015, by contrast, stresses the variability of the fiscal strategies of Hellenistic

rulers, with more coercive demands and higher tax rates characteristic of less stable regimes prioritizing immediate revenue over future revenues.

12 Hauser 2016, argues for the stability and integrity of the Parthian Empire on the basis of a regime of regional sub-kings generally cooperative with the kings of kings and gradually replaced with members of the Arsacid house. The Parthians were able to out-mint their Hellenistic predecessors, in conjunction with military campaigns, suggesting that their extractive capacity should not be underestimated: Sinisi 2012: 284–85

13 Ełišē, *Vasn Vardananc' ew Hayoc' Paterazmin* (Ter-Minasean 1957: 23; trans. Thomson 1982: 77).

14 Payne 2018.

15 Morony 2004a: 184–88; Seland 2011; Banaji 2015.

16 Scheidel 2015: 160–61; Wilson 2015: 23–24. For the slim evidence for Sasanian commercial taxes, see Morony 1984: 117–18.

17 Firdawsī, *Šāhnāme* (Khaleghi-Motlagh 1987–2000, v. 7 [1997]: 95); Macuch 1987: 177; Shaked 1990; Rubin 1995: 255–56, 272–74. The administrative roles of the priestly élite are amply documented in the sigillographic record, even if their precise functions and the contours of their authorities often remain unclear: Gyselen 2002a: 57–69; Gyselen 2007: 44–45.

18 Pigulevskaya 1963: 169–75; Morony 2004b; Mosig-Walburg 2005; Payne 2015: 38–44; Smith 2016: 111–15.

19 Howard-Johnston 2010: 41–46; Payne 2014: 295–96; Payne 2017: 195–97.

20 On the Armenian historiographical tradition and its aristocratic perspectives, see Greenwood 2002 and Thomson 2004.

21 Ełišē, *Vasn Vardananc' ew Hayoc' Paterazmin* (Ter-Minasean 1957: 22; trans. Thomson 1982: 75).

22 Ełišē, *Vasn Vardananc' ew Hayoc' Paterazmin* (Ter-Minasean 1957: 22; trans. Thomson 1982: 75).

23 Ełišē, *Vasn Vardananc' ew Hayoc' Paterazmin* (Ter-Minasean 1957: 143; trans. Thomson 1982: 194).

24 Armenian historiographical sources emphasize the autonomy of aristocratic commanders over their own forces, their *carayut'iwn*: Preiser-Kapeller 2015: 189–90.

25 Gadjiev 2008; Aliev et al. 2006; Sauer et al. 2013; Alizadeh 2014. See Howard-Johnston 2012 and Payne 2017, for analyses of their functions.

26 Howard-Johnston 2012; Howard-Johnston 2014.

27 Garsoïan 2009.

28 Gyselen 2002b; Gyselen 2007: 47–53.

29 Gyselen 2007: 252; Pourshariati 2008: 114–16.

30 Khurshudian 2003: 162–63; Gyselen 2002a: 110–13; Gyselen 2007: 42–43. One of the few narrative descriptions of the fiscal administration, the case of the mid-fifth century *marzbān* Vasak controlling the Armenian treasury, implies the *āmārgar* operated under his command: Łazar Pa'rpec'i, *Patmut'iwn Hayoc'* (Ter-Mkrtchean and Malxasean 1904: 83; trans. Thomson 1991: 129).

31 Weber 2008.

32 Wickham 2005: 74–76, emphasizes that taxes were more often collected in kind than in coin, even in the highly monetized late Roman fiscal regime.

33 Firdawsī, *Šāhnāme* (Khaleghi-Motlagh 1987–2000, v. 7 [1997]: 93–95); Al-Ṭabarī, *Ta'rīkh al-rusul wa al-mulūk* (de Goeje 1964–1965: 960–61; trans. Bosworth 1999: 256); Pigulevskaya 1937; Morony 1984: 51–52, 115–16. Reference to an imperial cadastral survey, *ashkharhagir*, available to the Turk conquerors of Albania in the early seventh century confirms the reference to a pan-imperial assessment and applies that the associated documentation was available in regional fiscal offices, not only at court: Movses Daskhurants'i, *Patmut'iwn Ałuanits'* (Arakelyan 1983: 167; trans. Dowsett 1961: 104).

34 Rubin 1995: 267, 291–92; Campopiano 2013: 18–19; Gariboldi 2015: 58. Morony (1984: 99–105) emphasizes that the change was not uniformly imposed, with *muqāsama* continuing to be practiced in some areas of Mesopotamia well into the early Islamic era.

35 Campopiano 2011: 243–50.

36 Sárközy 2014: 703–79.

37 Al-Ṭabarī, *Ta'rīkh al-rusul wa al-mulūk* (de Goeje 1964–1965: 1042; trans. Bosworth 1999: 377); Banaji 2006: 275.

38 Kolesnikov 1998.

39 Schindel 2006; Howard-Johnston 2014: 163–71. The Caucasian numismatic material awaits synthetic analysis, but see Khurshudian 2003: 176–99, for middle and late Sasanian mints and finds in the region.

40 Crone 1991: 23–27.

41 Crone 1994. Macuch 2015, demonstrates how Mazdakite cosmology—at least as represented in the Zoroastrian sources—substituted the patrilineal Iranian social hierarchy with a matrilineal model.

42 Pigulevskaya 1963: 221–28; Payne 2015: 125–26. See also the rebellion of Nisibis later in the sixth century: Pigulevskaya 1946: 111–12.

43 Sundermann 1976; Colditz 2000: 204–5. For the political potency of the category of the poor, innovated in terms of Christian ideology, in supporting the autocratic rule of the contemporary late Roman emperors, see Brown 2002.

44 *Sīrat Ānūširwān* (Imāmi 1987: 195; trans. Grignaschi 1966: 21).

45 *Hazār Dādestān (MHD)*, ed. and trans. Macuch 1993: 593 and 596; Garsoïan 1981.

46 Gyselen 2007: 44–45.

47 *Sīrat Ānūširwān* (Imāmi 1987: 201; trans. Grignaschi 1966: 26). See also the reassertion of class boundaries in *Letter of Tansar* (Minovi 1932: 12–13; trans. Boyce 1968: 37–39).

48 *Patmut'iwn Sebeosi* (Abgaryan 1979: 94; trans. Thomson 1999: 41).

49 *Patmut'iwn Sebeosi* (Abgaryan 1979: 94; trans. Thomson 1999: 41).

50 Al-Ṭabarī, *Ta'rīkh al-rusul wa al-mulūk* (de Goeje 1964–1965: 963; trans. Bosworth 1999: 262); al-Dīnawārī, *Al-akhbār al-ṭiwāl* (Guirgass 1888: 74–75); Firdawsī, *Šāhnāme* (Khaleghi-Motlagh 1987–2000, v. 7 [1997]: 101–5); Bal'ami,

Tārīkhnāmah-yi Ṭabarī (Bahār 1963: 1040–53; trans. Zotenberg 1867–1874: 227–32).

51 Gyselen 2003; Sinisi 2008. For the Iranian origin of *ḥarāj*, see Khan 2007 and Khan 2013: 23–26.

52 Al-Ṭabarī, *Taʾrīkh al-rusul wa al-mulūk* (de Goeje 1964–1965: 964–65; trans. Bosworth 1999: 262–63).

53 Al-Ṭabarī, *Taʾrīkh al-rusul wa al-mulūk* (de Goeje 1964–1965: 964; trans. Bosworth 1999: 263).

54 *Sīrat Ānūširwān* (Imāmi 1987: 190; trans. Grignaschi 1966: 21).

55 *Patmutʿiwn Sebeosi* (Abgaryan 1979: 87–89; trans. Thomson 1999: 32–34).

56 *Patmutʿiwn Sebeosi* (Abgaryan 1979: 94; trans. Thomson 1999: 41).

57 For the profits to be gained from control of the fiscal system at the local level in the Roman world, for instance through *adaeratio*, see Banaji 2001.

58 Movses Daskhurantsʿi, *Patmutʿiwn Aluanitsʿ* (Arakelyan 1983: 144–45; trans. Dowsett 1961: 89–90).

59 Movses Daskhurantsʿi, *Patmutʿiwn Aluanitsʿ* (Arakelyan 1983: 149; trans. Dowsett 1961: 92).

WORKS CITED

Abgaryan, G. A. 1979. *Patmutʿiwn Sebeosi*. Yerevan: Izdatelstvo Akademii Nauk Armyanskoi SSR.

Aliev, Askar A. et al. 2006. "The Ghilghilchay Defensive Long Wall: New Investigations." *Ancient West & East* 5: 143–77.

Alizadeh, Karim. 2014. "Borderland Projects of Sasanian Empire: Intersection of Domestic and Foreign Policies." *Journal of Ancient History* 2: 93–115.

Aperghis, G. G. 2004. *The Seleukid Royal Economy: The Finances and Financial Administration of the Seleukid Empire*. Cambridge: Cambridge University Press.

Arakelyan, V. 1983. *Patmutʿiwn Aluanitsʿ Ashkharhi*. Yerevan: Izdatelstvo Akademii Nauk Armyanskoi SSR.

Bahār, Muḥammad Taqī Malik al-Shuʿarāʾ. 1963. *Balʿamī: Tarjumah-ye Tārīkh-e Ṭabarī*. Tehran: Idārah-ye Kull-e Nigārish-e Vizārat-e Farhang.

Banaji, Jairus. 2001. *Agrarian Change in Late Antiquity: Gold, Labor, and Aristocratic Dominance*. Oxford: Oxford University Press.

Banaji, Jairus. 2006. "Precious Metal Coinages and Monetary Expansion in Late Antiquity." In F. de Romanis and S. Sorda (eds.), *Dal Denarius al Dinar: L'Orient e la Moneta Romana* (Rome: Istituto Italiano di Numismatica), 265–303.

Banaji, Jairus. 2015. "'Regions that Look Seaward': Changing Fortunes, Submerged Histories, and the Slow Capitalism of the Sea." In F. De Romanis and M. Maiuro (eds.), *Across the Ocean: Nine Essays on Indo-Mediterranean Trade* (Leiden: Brill), 114–26.

Barbier de Meynard, Charles and Abel Pavet de Courteille (eds.). 1861–1917. Al-Masʿūdī: *Murūj al-dhahab wa maʿādin al-jawha*. In idem, *Les prairies d'or*, v.I–IX (Paris: Imprimerie Impériale).

Bosworth, C. E. 1999. *The History of al-Ṭabarī. Vol. V: The Sāsānids, the Byzantines, the Lakhmids, and Yemen.* Albany: State University of New York Press.

Boyce, Mary. 1968. *The Letter of Tansar.* Rome: Instituto Italiano per il Media ed Estremo Oriente.

Brown, Peter. 2002. *Poverty and Leadership in the Later Roman Empire.* Hanover: University Press of New England.

Campopiano, Michele. 2011. "Land Tax *ʿalā l-misāḥa* and *muqāsama*: Legal Theory and the Balance of Social Forces in Early Medieval Iraq (6th–8th Centuries CE)." *Journal of the Economic and Social History of the Orient* 54: 239–69.

Campopiano, Michele. 2013. "L'administration des impôts en Irak et Iran de la fin de l'époque Sassanide à la crise du califat Abbaside (iv–x siècles)." In X. Ballestín and E. Pastor (eds.), *Lo que vino de Oriente: Horizontes, praxis y dimensión material de los sistemas de dominación fiscal en Al-Andalus (ss. VII–IX)* (Oxford: Archaeopress), 17–27.

Colditz, Iris. 2000. *Zur Sozialterminologie der iranischen Manichäer: Eine semantische Analyse im Vergleich zu den nichtmanichäischen iranischen Quellen.* Wiesbaden: Harrassowitz.

Crone, Patricia. 1991. "Kavad's Heresy and Mazdak's Revolt." *Iran* 29: 21–42.

Crone, Patricia. 1994. "Zoroastrian Communism." *Comparative Studies in Society and History* 36: 447–62.

De Goeje, M. 1964–1965. *Annales, quos scripsit Abu Djafar Mohammed ibn Djarir at-Tabari.* Leiden: Brill.

Dowsett, C. J. F. 1961. *The History of the Caucasian Albanians.* London: Oxford University Press.

Gadjiev, Murtazali. 2008. "On the Construction Date of the Derbend Fortification Complex." *Iran and the Caucasus* 12: 1–16.

Gariboldi, Andrea. 2015. "The Great 'Restoration' of Husraw I." In C. Jullien (ed.), *Husraw Ier reconstructions d'un règne: sources et documents* (Paris: Association pour l'Avancement des Etudes Iraniennes), 47–84.

Garsoïan, Nina. 1981. "Sur le titre *Protecteur des pauvres.*" *Revue des études arméniennes* 15: 21–32.

Garsoïan, Nina. 2009. "La politique arménienne des Sassanides." In Ph. Gignoux, C. Jullien, and F. Jullien (eds.), *Trésors d'Orient: Mélanges offerts à Rika Gyselen* (Paris: Association pour l'Avancement des Etudes Iraniennes), 67–79.

Greenwood, Timothy. 2002. "Sasanian Echoes and Apocalyptic Expectations: A Reevaluation of the Armenian History Attributed to Sebeos." *Le Muséon* 115: 323–97.

Grignaschi, Mario. 1966. "Quelques spécimens de la literature sassanide conserves dans les bibliothèques d'Istanbul." *Journal Asiatique* 254: 1–142.

Goodblatt, David M. 1979. "The Poll Tax in Sasanian Babylonia: The Talmudic Evidence." *Journal of the Economic and Social History of the Orient* 22: 233–95.

Guirgass, V. 1888. *Kitāb al-akhbār al-ṭiwāl.* Leiden: Brill.

Gyselen, Rika. 1999. "Fiscal System, II: Sasanian." *Encyclopaedia Iranica, vol. IX* (London: Routledge): 639–46.

Gyselen, Rika. 2002a. *Nouveax matériaux pour la géographie historique de l'empire sassanide: sceaux administratifs de la collection Ahmad Saeedi*. Paris: Association pour l'Avancement des Etudes Iraniennes.

Gyselen, Rika. 2002b. "Lorsque l'archéologie rencontre la tradition littéraire: les titres militaires des *spāhbed* de l'empire sassanide." *Comptes rendus de l'Académie des Inscriptions et Belle Lettres* 145.1: 447–58.

Gyselen, Rika. 2003. "Dīwān et 'trésorie' sassanides: première attestations sigillographiques." *Studia Iranica* 32: 123–26.

Gyselen, Rika. 2007. *Sasanian Seals and Sealings in the A. Saeedi Collection*. Louvain: Peeters.

Haldon, John. 1993. *The State and the Tributary Mode of Production*. London: Verso.

Hauser, Stefan. 2016. "Münzen, Medien und der Aufbau des Arsakidenreiches." In H. Börm and A. Luther (eds.), *Diwan: Studies in the History and Culture of the Ancient Near East and the Eastern Mediterranean* (Duisburg: Wellem), 433–92.

Howard-Johnston, James. 1995. "The Two Great Powers in Late Antiquity: A Comparison." In A. Cameron (ed.), *The Byzantine and Early Islamic Near East, Volume III: States, Resources, and Armies* (Princeton: Darwin Press): 157–226.

Howard-Johnston, James. 2008. "State and Society in Late Antique Iran." In V. S. Curtis and S. Stewart (eds.), *The Sasanian Era: The Idea of Iran, Volume III* (London: I.B. Tauris), 118–29.

Howard-Johnston, James. 2010. "The Sasanians' Strategic Dilemma." In H. Börm and J. Wiesehöfer (eds.), *Commutatio et contentio: Studies in the Late Roman, Sasanian, and Early Islamic Near East* (Düsseldorf: Wellem Verlag): 37–70.

Howard-Johnston, James. 2012. "The Late Sasanian Army." In T. Bernheimer and A. Silverstein (ed.), *Late Antiquity: Eastern Perspectives* (Oxford: Gibb Memorial Trust): 87–127.

Howard-Johnston, James. 2014. "The Sasanian State: The Evidence of Coinage and Military Construction." *Journal of Ancient History* 2: 144–81.

Imāmi, Abū al-Qāsim (ed.). 1987. *Sīrat Ānūširwān*. In *Tajārib al-umam* (Tehran: Dār Surūsh): 188–209.

Khaleghi-Motlagh, Jalal (ed.). 1987–2000. *Abū al-Qāsim Firdawsī: Šāhnāme*. 8 vols. New York: Bibliotheca Persica.

Khan, Geoffrey. 2007. "Newly Discovered Arabic Documents from Early Abbasid Khurasan." In P. M. Sijpesteijn et al. (eds.), *From Al-Andalus to Khurasan: Documents from the Medieval Muslim World* (Leiden: Brill): 201–15.

Khan, Geoffrey. 2013. *Arabic Documents from Early Islamic Khurasan*. Berlin: Freie Universität Berlin.

Khurshudian, Eduard. 2003. *Armeniya i Sasanidskii Iran: Istoriko-Kulturologicheskoe Issledovanie*. Almaty: Ministry of Foreign Affairs of the Republic of Armenia.

Kolesnikov, Ali I. 1998. *Denezhnoe Xozyaistvo v Irane v VII Veke*. Moscow: Vostochnaya Literatura.

Macuch, Maria. 1987. "Sasanidische Institutionen in frühislamischer Zeit." In Ph. Gignoux (ed.), *Transition Periods in Iranian History: Actes du symposium de Fribourg-*

en-Brisgau (22–24 Mai 1985) (Louvain: Association pour l'Avancement des Études Iraniennes), 177–79.

Macuch, Maria. 1993. *Rechtskasuistik und Gerichtspraxis zu Beginn des siebenten Jahrhunderts in Iran: Die Rechtsammlung des Farroḥmard I Wahrāmān.* Wiesbaden: Harrassowitz.

Macuch, Maria. 2015. "Legal Implications of Mazdakite Teaching According to the Dēnkard," In C. Jullien (ed.), *Husraw Ier reconstructions d'un règne: sources et documents* (Paris: Association pour l'Avancement des Etudes Iraniennes), 155–74.

Minovi, Mojtaba. 1932. *Nāmah-e Tansar bih Jushnasf.* Tehran: Matbaʿah-e Majlis.

Monson, Andrew. 2015. "Hellenistic Empires." In A. Monson and W. Scheidel (eds.), *Fiscal Regimes and the Political Economy of Premodern States* (Cambridge: Cambridge University Press), 169–207.

Morony, Michael G. 1984. *Iraq after the Muslim Conquest.* Princeton: Princeton University Press.

Morony, Michael G. 2004a. "Economic Boundaries? Late Antiquity and Early Islam." *Journal of the Economic and Social History of the Orient* 47: 166–94.

Morony, Michael G. 2004b. "Population Transfers between Sasanian Iran and the Byzantine Empire." In A. Carileet al. (eds.), *La Persia e Bisanzio* (Rome: Accademia Nazionale dei Lincei), 161–79.

Mosig-Walburg, Karin. 2005. "Christenverfolgung und Römerkrieg: Zu Ursachen, Ausmaß und Zielrichtung der Christenverfolgung unter Šāpūr II." *Iranistik* 7: 5–84.

Nikonorov, Valery P. 2005. "K Voprosu o Parfyanskom Nasledii v Sasanidskom Irane: Voennoe Delo." In idem (ed.), *Tsentralnaya Aziya ot Akhemenidov do Timuridov: Arkheologiya, Istoriya, Etnologiya, Kultura* (St. Petersburg: Institut Istorii Materialnoi Kulturi): 141–79.

Payne, Richard E. 2014. "The Reinvention of Iran: The Sasanian Empire and the Huns." In M. Maas (ed.), *The Cambridge Companion to the Age of Attila* (Cambridge: Cambridge University Press): 282–99.

Payne, Richard E. 2015. *A State of Mixture: Christians, Zoroastrians, and Iranian Political Culture in Late Antiquity.* Berkeley: University of California Press.

Payne, Richard E. 2017. "Territorializing Iran in Late Antiquity: Autocracy, Aristocracy, and the Infrastructure of Empire." In C. Ando and S. Richardson (eds.), *Ancient States and Infrastructural Power: Europe, Asia, and America* (Philadelphia: University of Pennsylvania Press): 179–217.

Payne, Richard E. 2018. "The Silk Road and the Iranian Political Economy in Late Antiquity." *Bulletin of the School of Oriental and African Studies* 81: 227–50.

Pigulevskaya, Nina. 1937. "K Voprosu o Podatnoi Reforme Khosroya Anushervana." *Vestnik Drevnei Istorii* 1: 143–54.

Pigulevskaya, Nina. 1946. *Vizantiya i Iran na Rubezhe VI i VII Vekov.* Moscow: Izdatelstvo Akademii Nauk SSSR.

Pigulevskaya, Nina. 1963. *Les villes de l'état iranien aux époques parthe et sassanide: Contribution à l'histoire sociale de la Basse Antiquité.* Paris: Mouton & Co.

Preiser-Kapeller, Johannes. 2015. "Vom Bosporus zum Ararat: Aspekte der Wirkung und Wahrnehmung des byzantinischen Reiches in Armenien vom 4. bis 10. Jahrhundert." In C. Gastgeber and F. Daim (eds.), *Byzantium as Bridge between West and East* (Vienna: Verlag der Österreichischen Akademie der Wissenschaften): 179–215.

Pourshariati, Parvaneh. 2008. *Decline and Fall of the Sasanian Empire: The Sasanian-Parthian Confederacy and the Arab Conquest of Iran.* London: I. B. Tauris.

Rubin, Zeev. 1995. "The Reforms of Khusro Anushirvan." In A. Cameron (ed.), *The Byzantine and Early Islamic Near East, Volume III: States, Resources, and Armies* (Princeton: Darwin Press), 227–97.

Rubin, Zeev. 2000. "The Sassanid Monarchy." In A. Cameron et al. (eds.), *Cambridge Ancient History, vol. 14: Late Antiquity: Empire and Successors, a.d. 425–600* (Cambridge: Cambridge University Press), 638–61.

Sárközy, Miklós. 2014. "A Sasanian Taxation List or an Early Islamic Booty? A Medieval Persian Source and the Sasanian Taxation System." In Z. Csabai (ed.), *Studies in Economic and Social History of the Ancient Near East in Memory of Péter Vargyas* (Budapest: L'Harmattan), 701–14.

Sauer, Eberhard et al. 2013. *Persia's Imperial Power in Late Antiquity: The Great Wall of Gorgān and Frontier Landscapes of Sasanian Iran.* Oxford: Oxbow Books.

Scheidel, Walter. 2015. "State Revenue and Expenditure in the Han and Roman Empires." In W. Scheidel (ed.), *State Power in Ancient China and Rome* (Oxford: Oxford University Press): 150–80.

Schindel, Nikolaus. 2006. "The Sasanian Eastern Wars in the Fifth Century: The Numismatic Evidence." In A. Panaino and A. Piras (eds.), *Proceedings of the Fifth Conference of the Societas Iranologica Europaea* (Milan: Mimesis): 675–90.

Shaked, Shaul. 1990. "Administrative Functions of Priests in the Sasanian Period." In G. Gnoli and A. Panaino (eds.), *Proceedings of the First European Conference of Iranian Studies: Part I, Old and Middle Iranian Studies* (Rome: Istituto Italiano per il Medio ed Estremo Oriente), 261–73.

Seland, Eivind Heldaas 2011. "The Persian Gulf or the Red Sea? Two Axes in Ancient Indian Ocean Trade, Where to Go and Why." *World Archaeology* 43: 398–49.

Sims-Williams, Nicholas. 2008. "The Sasanians in the East: A Bactrian Archive from Northern Afghanistan." In V. S. Curtis and S. Stewart (eds.), *The Sasanian Era: The Idea of Iran, III* (London: British Museum), 88–102.

Sinisi, Fabrizio. 2008. "Another Seal of a Sasanian Dīwān." *East and West* 58: 377–83.

Sinisi, Fabrizio. 2012. "The Coinage of the Parthians." In W. E. Metcalf (ed.), *The Oxford Handbook of Greek and Roman Coinage* (Oxford: Oxford University Press): 275–94.

Smith, Kyle. 2016. *Constantine and the Captive Christians of Persia: Martyrdom and Religious Identity in Late Antiquity.* Oakland: University of California Press.

Sundermann, Werner. 1976. "*Commendatio pauperum*: Eine Angabe der sassanidischen politisch-didaktischen Literatur zur gesellschaftlichen Struktur Irans," *Altorientalische Forschungen* 4: 167–94.

Ter-Minasean, E. (ed.). 1957. *Ełiše: Vasn Vardanay ev hayots' paterazmin.* Yerevan: Izdatelstvo Akademii Nauk Armyanskoi SSR.

Ter-Mkrtchean, G. and S. Malxasean (eds.). 1904. *Łazar of P'arp: Patmut'iwn Hayoc.* Tbilisi: Tparan Ōr.N. Aghaneani. (Repr. Delmar [New York] 1985).

Thomson, Robert W. 1982. *History of Vardan and the Armenian War.* Cambridge: Harvard University Press.

Thomson, Robert W. 1991. *The History of Łazar P'arpec'i.* Atlanta: Scholars Press.

Thomson, Robert W. 1999. *The Armenian History attributed to Sebeos.* Liverpool: Liverpool University Press.

Thomson, Robert W. 2004. "Armenian Ideology and the Persians." In Antonio Carile et al. (eds.), *La Persia e Bisanzio* (Rome: Accademia Nazionale dei Lincei), 161–79.

Tilly, Charles. 1985. "War Making and State Making as Organized Crime." In P. Evans, D. Rueschemeyer, and T. Skocpol (eds.), *Bringing the State Back In* (Cambridge: Cambridge University Press), 169–91.

Weber, Dieter. 2008. *Berliner Pahlavi-Dokumente: Zeugnisse spätsassanidischer Brief- und Rechtskultur aus frühislamischer Zeit.* Wiesbaden: Harrassowitz.

Weber, Dieter. 2013. "Die persische Besetzung Ägyptens 619–629 n. Chr." In F. Feder and A. Lohwasser (eds.), *Ägypten und sein Umfeld in der Spätantike vom Regierungsantritt Diokletians 284/285 bis zur arabischen Eroberung des Vorderen Orients um 635–646* (Wiesbaden: Harrassowitz), 221–46.

Wickham, Chris. 2005, *Framing the Early Middle Ages: Europe and the Mediterranean, 400–800.* Oxford: Oxford University Press.

Josef Wiesehöfer. 2010. "The Late Sasanian Near East." In C. Robinson (ed.), *The New Cambridge History of Islam, v. I: The Formation of the Islamic World, Sixth to Eleventh Centuries* (Cambridge: Cambridge University Press), 98–152.

Wilson, Andrew 2015. "Red Sea Trade and the State." In F. De Romanis and M. Maiuro (eds.), *Across the Ocean: Nine Essays on Indo-Mediterranean Trade* (Leiden: Brill), 13–32.

Zotenberg, M. Hermann. 1867–1874. *Chronique de About-Djafar-Mo'hammed-ben-Djarir-ben-Yezid Tabari.* Paris: Imprimerie Imperiale.

TAX TRANSITIONS

8

Fiscal Transformation during the Formative Period of Ancient Chinese Empire (Late Fourth to First Century BCE)

MAXIM KOROLKOV

The early Chinese empires of Qin and Han (221 BCE–220 CE) were the product of a series of conquest campaigns by the state of Qin during the second half of the fourth century and the third century BCE.[1] These campaigns eventually resulted in the unification of the Sinitic world in 221 and the empowerment of the Qin ruler, known as the August Thearch (*huangdi* 皇帝), a title conventionally rendered as "emperor" in English. More than a century of almost ceaseless Qin expansion in the middle and late Warring States period (453–221) was made possible by an extraction system that, insofar as our sources enable us to reconstruct, took shape in the fourth century, especially during the reforms associated with the Qin statesman Shang Yang 商鞅 (also known as Gongsun Yang 公孙鞅, Wei Yang 衛鞅, and Lord Shang 商君, d. 338). Initially driven by the military imperative to resist its economically advanced eastern neighbors, the Qin fiscal regime emphasized a number of features: direct state command of conscripted manpower and unfree labor; direct in-kind taxation of a relatively circumscribed fiscal base; intensive monitoring of fiscal agents; and high volatility of state expenditure, itself a function of frequent warfare that necessitated irregular levies, changing taxation rates, and other forms of periodic fiscal intensification. The Qin also maintained an extensive state economy of agricultural farms, artisanal workshops, mines, lumber mills, and so on.

Designed primarily to finance warfare and the concomitant centralization of power in the bureaucratic government, this system suffered chronically from high monitoring costs, a limited ability to transfer revenues over long distances, and a resultant reliance on forced labor. Moreover, its distributive effects pitted the principal (the Qin state) against its agents (those entrusted with tax-collection) and ruled out the possibility of fiscal compromise between the central authorities, local officials, and provincial élites, effectively defeating the government's efforts to incorporate vast territories conquered during the final decade of the Warring States era. The fiscal institutions of the Warring States Qin already started to erode under the short-lived Qin Empire (221–207). Their thorough reformation during the first century of the Western Han era (206 BCE—9 CE) led to the formation of a new tax regime that enabled a fiscal settlement between the state and local élites. This "imperial consensus" was central to the longevity of empire as a social, political, and economic mode of organization in continental East Asia.

This essay analyzes the evolution of fiscal institutions during the formative period of ancient Chinese empire. In the first section I consider policies of extraction that took shape during the Qin reforms of the fourth century BCE and supported the conquests that led to imperial "unification." The second section analyzes the distributive effects of the fiscal model of the Warring States Qin and argues that it imposed severe limitations on the empire's ability to secure the loyalty of its own local agents, let alone to coopt the élites and populations of conquered territories. The third section explores how the fiscal transition under the Western Han contributed to the emergence of a new tax regime that responded to the challenges faced by the Qin while simultaneously giving rise to new challenges for the imperial state. Changes in taxation practices took place over long periods of time and largely consisted of *ad hoc*, sometimes local adjustments and innovations. Nevertheless, the crucial differences between state-organized resource and labor extraction in the late Warring States Qin and in the imperial Han justify their characterization as two distinct fiscal models, each of which took shape in response to specific challenges of state- and empire-building. Historically connected, these two taxation models represent a repertoire of extractive instruments that were, in different combinations, utilized by the subsequent imperial and regional regimes in China.

1. The Qin Fiscal Model: Financing Conquest (Late Fourth—Third Centuries BCE)

1.1. Background of the Fiscal Reforms in the State of Qin

After the Zhou royal court fled its old base in the Wei River basin for the new capital of Luoyang in 770 BCE, the economic and political centers of the Sinitic world shifted eastwards.[2] The Great Plain and the Shandong peninsula in North China became arenas of accelerated state formation, fostering the development of new economic practices and forms of administrative organization.[3] The old Zhou heartland of Guanzhong, or the Wei River basin, was gradually taken over by the Qin polity that originated in the highlands to the west of Guanzhong and began its eastward expansion along the upper reaches of the Wei River in the late eighth century.[4] Although it was able to consolidate control over the upper and middle Wei River basin and launch episodic campaigns to the east of the Yellow River, Qin remained relatively marginal on the political map of the Spring and Autumn period (770–453).[5] In particular, Qin struggled to keep pace with the fiscal developments in the eastern regions of the Zhou world. The earliest evidence of systematic land taxation in Qin is from as late as 408, some two centuries after such measures are recorded for the eastern states of Qi and Lu (in the present-day Shandong Province), the leaders in fiscal innovation.[6] Another major economic novelty of the late Spring and Autumn period, coined money, was introduced in Qin in 336, almost three centuries after the first issues of coinage on the Great Plain (Shiji: 15.727).[7]

There is no single compelling explanation for the Qin's slow adoption of these new fiscal strategies. Archaeologists have paid attention to the conservative cultural habits of the Qin élite manifest in the mortuary evidence from the Spring and Autumn period (Shelach and Pines 2006: 210–12). Was this part of a broader socio-economic conservatism that a powerful aristocracy was able to impose on Qin policies? Military competition presented a powerful incentive for administrative and fiscal reforms in the Zhou world. Qin's withdrawal from interstate politics in the late Spring and Autumn and early Warring States periods, partly caused by internal troubles and a crisis of princely power, may also explain the lack of impetus for reforms.[8]

To understand the features of the pre-reform as well as post-reform organization of surplus extraction in the state of Qin, one should also consider the topographic features of its Guanzhong heartland. This was a relatively narrow river valley encompassing an area of about 12,300 square kilometers surrounded by scarcely inhabited mountains in the south and the loess plateau to the north. The archaeological record suggests that the loess plateau was not the site of agricultural settlement before the Warring States period (Falkenhausen 2006: 284). Thereafter, Qin agricultural expansion in this region was triggered by mounting population pressure in the Wei River valley and probably facilitated by the broader availability of iron tools (Shelach 2015: 291–93). The relatively circumscribed topography of Guanzhong encouraged the direct management of manpower by the ruler's household.[9] From very early in Qin history, its rulers presided over enormous tomb-building projects that far surpassed their eastern peers in terms of scale and labor cost, a phenomenon that some scholars have characterized as "gigantomania" (Falkenhausen and Shelach 2014: 37–51).

The relatively compact territorial configuration of Qin lands in Guanzhong also reduced incentives for improving the state's capacity to transfer resources over long distances. By contrast, at the beginning of the Warring States period the polities on the Great Plain, notably the states of Wei, Han, and Zhao, presided over dispersed landholdings that called for greater efficiency in revenue collection and distribution.[10] With their dense network of flourishing urban centers in which groups of merchants and artisans enjoyed a long tradition of considerable autonomy from princely power, these polities were more akin to leagues of city-states than to centralized states built around the figure of the ruler.[11] In the late fifth and early fourth century, their dynamic economies and administrative innovations gave them a military edge, such that Wei was for some time the most powerful state (Yang 2003: 291–92).

The traditions of state economy—in particular, the mobilization and management of labor—provided Qin rulers with the independent resources required to implement initially unpopular reforms over the resistance of aristocratic élites, an effort that proved fatal for radical reformers in some other Warring States.[12] The mid-Warring States Qin enjoyed a number of "advantages of backwardness" that translated into a specific assortment of fiscal principles and policies. As in many other historical contexts, the immediate impulse for change was provided by the military setbacks that Qin experienced in the late fifth and early fourth centuries BCE, when the most powerful state of the day, Wei, succeeded in establishing a bridgehead on the western bank of the Yellow River that threatened the Qin homeland.[13] The taxation reforms in Qin were from the beginning designed to finance the war effort. The resulting system imitated many of the administrative achievements of Qin's eastern neighbors but also bore visible imprints of Qin's own tradition of surplus extraction.

1.2. Taxes and Levies in the Warring States and Imperial Qin

Our main source for the chronology of fiscal innovation in the state of Qin is the *Shiji* chapter titled the "Basic annals of Qin" (*Qin ben ji* 秦本紀), which is based on the fragments of the official Qin chronicle still extant in the middle of the Western Han era (Fujita 2008: 221–69). According to these records, regular land taxation was implemented in Qin from 408 BCE (Shiji: 15.708). Official markets were established in 378, and market taxes were probably introduced around this time (Shiji: 6.289). The first population census was conducted in 375, though the introduction of household registration and the grouping of households into units of five is credited to Shang Yang some two decades later (Shiji: 6.289, 68.2230).

The pace of fiscal change accelerated under Duke Xiao 孝公 (362–338) and his chief advisor Shang Yang. A new land surveying scheme was applied from 350 (Shiji: 5.203, 15.723). Two years later, a new type of tax, the *fu* 賦, was recorded for the first time. This is often identified with capitation tax, *koufu* 口賦, which is well-attested for the Han Empire but is never mentioned in the Qin sources (Shiji: 5.203, 15.724).[14] More likely, the term represented a variety of levies, some of which are recorded in the excavated documents. The household levy, *hufu* 戶賦, was among the most important *fu* taxes (Shuihudi Qin mu zhujian zhengli xiaozu 1990: 132, slip 165; Chen, Songchang 2015: 107, slips 118–120). Labor conscription was among the key mechanisms of surplus extraction. The forced labor system in the state of Qin was by no means limited to temporary mobilizations of statute labor. The vast state sector of the Qin economy utilized the labor of convicts, debtors, as well as private slaves purchased by the government. These people were made to work as agricultural laborers, to toil as artisans in state-managed factories, to labor in construction projects, and to perform a broad range of other tasks.

In this section, I will address these elements of the Qin fiscal system in order to identify its functional principles and distributional consequences.

1.2.1. LAND TAXATION

Throughout the Warring States and early imperial eras, land taxation was the foundation of state finance, though its share in the total value of tax revenues declined over time. The land tax was originally collected in kind as a share of the harvest. Apart from the grain tax, hay and straw were also collected per unit of land. These were used as fodder for horses and livestock at the government-managed farms, for construction purposes, and as the matting material for storage, office, and residential facilities.[15]

Maximizing agricultural production was the top priority of state-strengthening reforms in Qin.[16] Each commoner household was in principle entitled to one *qing* (ca. 4.6 hectares) of arable land. Households with more than one adult male were required to split into separate units so that agricultural labor was fully utilized; this also increased the number of military recruits, as these were levied per household.[17] A legal document dated September 27, 309, was discovered during the 1979–1980 excavation of a Warring States Qin cemetery at Haojiaping in northern Sichuan Province.[18] It outlines the land surveying scheme for the demarcation of uniform lots for subsequent distribution among households (Sichuan sheng bowuguan et al. 1982: 1–21; Hulsewé 1985: 211–15). This regulation was likely a revision of the surveying norms in the Qin "Statutes on fields" (*tian lü* 田律) (Barbieri-Low and Yates 2015, vol. 2: 710–11 n47).

Land surveying in Haojiaping was carried out in an almost ideal environment for the imposition of a new field system and tenure regime. Qin had recently conquered the region and established farming colonies composed of settlers arriving from its Guanzhong heartland.[19] The same did not apply to the old agricultural lands in the Wei River basin, where official surveyors had to deal with existing patterns of landholding. The ideologists of Qin reforms advocated for a large-

scale resettlement program in Guanzhong that was intended to attract migrants from overpopulated regions in the lower reaches of the
Yellow River. The original Qin population (*gu Qin min* 故秦民) was
to devote itself exclusively to military service (Jiang 1986: 4.92; Pines,
forthcoming).[20]

Although the feasibility of such a wholesale replacement of the agricultural population is doubtful, the foundation of thirty-one new counties in Guanzhong during the Shang Yang reforms (Shiji: 68.2232) likely
involved the opening up of large swaths of land for agricultural use,
which was then distributed in a government-managed scheme. Topographical data collected by modern scholars confirms that much of the
agricultural land in Guanzhong was at some point reorganized according to the Qin surveying model, which attests to an unprecedented, and
unrepeated, government effort to rebuild the agricultural landscape of
the entire region (Leeming 1980: 153–204). Mortuary evidence from the
late Warring States period also indicates that there was immigration
from the eastern parts of the Zhou world (Falkenhausen 2006: 319).
The factors instrumental to the Qin program of centralized land distribution were state-organized migrations, government control over the
production and dissemination of iron agricultural tools, and the state-
sponsored hydraulic projects that opened up large tracts of wasteland
for cultivation.[21]

The key advantage of land distribution was that it rendered agricultural produce measurable for extraction purposes and spared state officials the effort of time-consuming inquiry into local land tenure. The
geography of Qin colonization can be explained by the logistical needs
of the army. During the late Warring States period, ceaseless campaigns
were taking Qin armies far from their supply bases. This rendered grain
transportation from Guanzhong prohibitively expensive precisely when
campaigns of attrition became a new reality of warfare (Lewis 1999:
620–32).

Archaeological and textual evidence allows the identification of three
major zones of colonization. The settlement of Qin colonists was likely
accompanied by the surveying and distribution of land, as recorded in
the Haojiaping text (see Figure 8.1). One of these zones was located in
the lower Fen River basin and in the Sanmenxia area where the Yellow River enters the Great Plain. Control over these territories secured

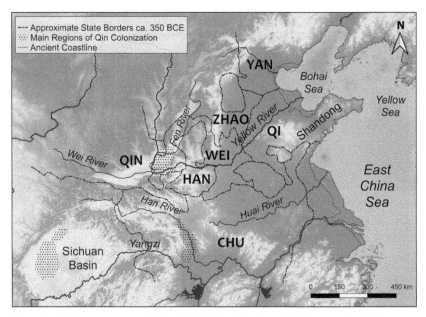

Figure 8.1. Qin conquests and Qin colonization, fourth and third centuries BCE. Map by author.

access to the Great Plain, an arena of lengthy and bloody campaigns throughout the mid- and late Warring States period. Another zone included parts of Chengdu plain in Sichuan and transportation corridors connecting it to Guanzhong. This region provided logistical support in the major campaign against the state of Chu along the Yangzi valley in 279–278 (Shiji: 5.213, 70.2290).[22] Finally, Qin settlement was carried out on the conquered Chu lands in the Han River valley and to the north of Middle Yangzi. This region was Qin's vital military stronghold in the south and, eventually, the bridgehead for southward expansion at the end of the Warring States period.[23]

From the fiscal viewpoint, the colony model presented several logistical and administrative advantages for the Qin central government. First, by shifting the supply base closer to the theaters of war and reducing transportation costs, it improved the state's capacity to directly manage military supplies and reduced the need to rely on private merchants. Qin was familiar with markets, and the *Book of Lord Shang* mentions "army markets" (*jun shi* 軍市) that were probably used for military procurement. But the *Book of Lord Shang* also states that merchants should not be allowed to privately transport grain to such markets and emphasizes that "the suppliers of grain will have no private [benefits]" (Jiang 1986: 1.15–16; Pines 2017: 129). Here, the traders (*shang* 商) figure more as state agents charged with distributing the grain collected and delivered by the central administration than as private entrepreneurs profiting from their participation in military procurement, as became typical in later periods. Even these markets were of limited value in the official supply system. Excavated legal and administrative texts attest to the overwhelming dominance of staple finance in the Warring States and imperial Qin so far as official rations and emoluments were concerned.[24] In the official archive of Qianling County at the southern frontier of the Qin Empire, only one document appears to refer to a ration (*lin* 廩) issued in money (Chen, W. 2012a: 292, tablet 8–1214), as opposed to more than 150 records of rations in kind.

Second, land surveying enabled the relatively accurate assessment of the taxation base, since the area of arable land was measured and its distribution among taxpaying households recorded.[25] Effectively, this exploitation-ready taxation base could be created within a very short period of time, which was particularly important when resources needed to be deployed to provision armies on campaign. All major zones of Qin colonization were located along the important routes of riverine transportation by which grain was shipped to the theaters of war. In this regard, a note is due on the provisioning of armies in the field during the Warring States period. Living off of the storehouses of the enemy was a common practice and is advocated in some influential texts, including the *Book of Lord Shang* (Jiang, ed. 1986: 4.92).[26] However, the protracted campaigns of attrition that characterized contemporary warfare made supply lines between the armies in the field and the agricultural base in the rear vital for military success. This is vividly illustrated by the Changping 長平 campaign (262–260), when the Zhao army was forced to surrender after its supply lines were severed by Qin troops (Shiji: 73.2333–2335). The strategists of the age took it for granted that an army embarking on a major campaign should be provisioned from a supply base in the rear, preferably by water (Shiji: 70.2290–2291).

Third, the dependence of settlers on the state reduced incentives for tax resistance and favored compliance. Settlers depended on the state for land grants, seed grain, assistance in case of crop failure, irrigation schemes such as Dujiangyan 都江堰 on the Chengdu Plain in Sichuan, and protection against the often hostile local population.[27] This facilitated administration of the newly conquered territories and created conditions for intensive extraction.

Another key feature of Qin land taxation was the fluctuating tax rate. Until recently, it was believed that both Qin and Han levied tax as a fixed percentage of a notional average harvest, the only difference being that the former collected a higher percentage than the latter, a tithe as opposed to 1/15 and then 1/30 under the Han.[28] The recent discovery of excavated legal fragments, administrative records, and official mathematical manuals attest to a very different collection regime. Instead of fixing the tax rate as a portion of a notional average harvest, Qin officials were annually reassessing extraction levels on the basis of actual crop conditions. Information was collected by monitoring the impacts of weather conditions and natural disasters, changes in soil quality, the agricultural equipment employed by farmers, and so on. Local officials were required to provide regular updates to the central government, which decided on tax quotas. The quotas were then issued to county authorities, who split them among subordinate districts, farming communities, and ultimately, the taxpaying households.[29]

The system was designed to enable the extraction of a greater portion of agricultural surplus at the cost of high monitoring expenses. This favored exploitation of a spatially circumscribed fiscal base of which central authorities had detailed knowledge.[30] While very little is known about land taxation in other Warring States polities, some scholars argue that on the Great Plain and in Shandong the tax system was likely similar to that which prevailed in the Han Empire, namely fixed tax rates based on the notional average harvest.[31]

Implementation of the flexible rate system depended on the efficiency and integrity of state agents responsible for processing information. Excavated legal fragments record abuses that the lawgivers sought to prevent and penalize (Zhongguo wenwu yanjiusuo et al. 2001; Yang 2008: 333; Yang 2009b: 173–85). To monitor the behavior of officials, Qin instituted a complex accounting system that generated multiple independent records submitted by local government offices. These records were susceptible to cross-checking, and there were strict deadlines for submitting accounts. The law severely penalized state functionaries who failed to meet reporting requirements.[32] The central government also sought to employ the heads of farming communities and even common farmers as a check on local officials. To this end, taxpayers were notified of annual tax rates, required to be present during the assignment of individual tax quotas, and probably issued special documents to certify that their fiscal obligations had been fulfilled (Zhongguo wenwu yanjiusuo et al. 2001: 122–24, slip 150; Yang 2009a: 179–80).[33]

The scale of long-distance transfers of tax grain in the Qin period remains unclear. An itinerary from the Peking University collection suggests that grain was shipped over long distances to the imperial storage facilities, among them the Aocang 敖倉 Granary to the north-east of Luoyang (Xin 2013a: 17–27; Xin 2013b: 177–279). Considerable imports were also necessary to maintain military garrisons at the frontier. Qianling County, for example, produced only a fraction of the grain reserves needed to feed conscripts, convicts, and officials stationed there.[34] Documents excavated in local government archives and from officials' tombs reveal the minute legal regulation of grain shipment corvée and detailed travel itineraries. Both point to the state's intensive involvement in large-scale, long-distance transfers of bulk goods, particularly grain.[35]

1.2.2. LABOR SERVICES AND UNFREE LABOR

In their hostile critique of their dynastic predecessor, Han intellectuals were particularly vehement in attacking Qin immoderation in exploiting their subjects' labor. One of the most influential critics, Dong Zhongshu 董仲舒 (179–104), accused Qin of increasing labor duty thirtyfold compared to idealized antiquity (Hanshu: 24A.1137). The First Emperor of Qin was notorious for initiating enormous construction projects, including the Great Wall, the Apang palace, and his own burial complex, at some point mustering no less than seven hundred thousand individuals for the latter two projects alone (Shiji: 6.256). High levels of labor mobilization have recently been reconstructed from the archaeological evidence, although such calculations involve a broad margin of error.[36] As argued previously, Qin's emphasis on labor services as a major component of its fiscal system was probably a function of Guanzhong's geography, which favored direct control over people, and of

Qin's lagging economic development, and particularly the late monetization of its economy.

During the mid- and late Warring States period, subjects were mobilized for two purposes: military and labor service. The latter consisted primarily of construction and transportation, including the shipment of grain. In practice, the two were never strictly segregated. The majority of untrained farmers levied for military service ended up performing auxiliary work for the trained soldiers: collecting wood and fodder, building walls, transporting tax grain and other goods.

The foundation of the labor system was an annual month-long term of service (*yao* 徭). This was obligatory for all adult males as well as for minors of serviceable age; only holders of social ranks above the fourth level were exempt (Chen, Songchang 2015: 152, slip 253). The *yao* could be levied either directly by the central government or by the commandery and local authorities, though these were obligated to request permission before doing so. Such requests from local authorities involved minute budgeting of labor expenditure that specified the amount of work that needed to be done and measured the resulting labor needs on the basis of legally stipulated productivity norms. Only with approval from the central government could local authorities then proceed to mobilize subjects within their territorial jurisdictions (Shuihudi Qin mu zhujian zhengli xiaozu 1990: 47, slips 122–124; Chen, Songchang 2015: 119–20, slips 156–59).

Concern about the impact of labor mobilizations on its subjects incentivized the Qin government to pay closer attention to the economic conditions of taxpayers. The government assessed household wealth to estimate each household's capacity to resist external shocks in the form of the state's demand for the labor of its members and livestock.[37] While property taxes do not appear to have played an important role in the Qin fiscal system, the development of bureaucratic tools to keep track of the distribution of material resources proved important in attempts to introduce systematic property taxes during the mid-Western Han period.[38] These regulations were dictated by the concern that excessive mobilizations would lead to the disruption of the agricultural economy and to social unrest.[39] The conflict inherent in the pursuit of the state's two principal purposes—the maintenance of agricultural production and social order on the one hand, and, on the other, the temporary removal of laborers from their farms to achieve the state's labor-intensive goals, both in the context of waging war and in the engineering of social and economic landscapes—was exacerbated by Qin territorial expansion, which necessitated long-distance transfers of manpower and longer terms of service.

Like many other Qin fiscal institutions, *yao* labor services emphasized centralized control over resources. This prioritized the needs of the center over those of local authorities. Local needs were partly satisfied by other forms of labor mobilization, particularly the "services in shifts of duty" (*geng* 更). Workers mobilized in this context served in monthly shifts and performed a variety of tasks within their home counties (see, for example, Chen, W. 2012a: 191–92, tablet 8–651). Many junior administrative functionaries and their staff were recruited to work in precisely this way, serving their monthly shifts of duty; this is also true of employees at state-managed husbandry farms and artisanal workshops (Shuihudi Qin mu zhujian zhengli xiaozu 1990: 22–23, slips 13–14; Chen, Songchang 2015: 116, slips 145–46; 192–93, slips 295–96; 204, slip 329; Peng et al. 2007: 295–305, slips 474–87). As in the case of *yao* conscripts, however, *geng* personnel could be mobilized for the purposes of the central government, such as guarding the frontiers, and were then unavailable for local use. This situation is reflected in a recently published excavated document from the Qin county of Qianling, which reflects a severely understaffed local government: only 51 of 103 officials on the roster were actually present. Thirty-five others were mobilized to perform *yao* labor services, probably outside of the county (Chen, W. 2018: 167–68, tablet 9–633). The county archival records also illustrate the solution to the central government's systematic claims on local labor resources: convicts and other unfree laborers were routinely employed as assistant administrative personnel, couriers, and as the government's commercial agents (Korolkov 2015: 132–56).

Penal labor was one of the most frequently applied punishments in the Qin and early Western Han legal systems. A number of recent studies suggest that penal labor sentences were life-long under the Qin (You 2009: 1–52; Miyake 2016: 64–81), though convicts were periodically amnestied, especially when they were settled as colonists in the newly conquered regions. Far from being uniform, convict society was composed of a range of legal statuses. The family members and property of criminals sentenced to the severest terms of hard labor were seized, so that these convicts effectively became completely dependent on the state for their subsistence. Other forms of penal labor, particularly that of "bond-servants and bondwomen" (*lichenqie* 隸臣妾), presupposed some degree of autonomy for the convicts. They were allowed to have families and could make their living through various economic activities, including craftsmanship, commerce, and work as hired labor at those times when they were not obliged to work for the state. This arrangement reduced the cost to the state of administering the penal labor system.

By imperial Qin times, the state-managed system of unfree labor was integrated with the private markets for dependent laborers. Local governments leased out or sold their surplus labor and purchased private slaves for incorporation into convict labor gangs (Chen, W. 2012a: 93–94, tablet 8–154; 197, tablet 8–664 + 8–1053 + 8–2167; Chen, W. 2018: 300–1, tablet 9–1406; Peng et al. 2007: 359–63, slips 99–123). Debates concerning the ambivalent legal status of major convict groups, notably the "bondservants," remain inconclusive. Some scholars argue that they should be properly defined as state slaves rather than convicts (for differing opinions on this subject, see, for example, Lim 2006: 90–103; Li 2007: 681–82; Barbieri-Low and Yates 2015, vol. 1: 196). Although "bondservants and bondwomen" clearly figure in many legal texts as criminals serving a sentence of penal labor, other records are equally clear that they could be leased out or even sold to private parties.

I would argue that the ambiguity concerning the legal and social position of state-dependent unfree laborers, generally referred to as *tuli* 徒隸, is related to the state's claim to a degree of control over all unfree individuals regardless of who possessed the right to their labor. Legal records from the late Warring States and imperial Qin periods indicate that although individuals seized for the crimes of their relatives could be sold to private owners, the state retained the right to buy them back if the criminal sentence was revised (Peng et al. 2007: 359–63, slips 99–123). Slave owners could, in turn, request that the state purchase their slaves when they were unable to manage them, subject to their acceptance of the "fair market price" offered by officials (Shuihudi Qin mu zhujian zhengli xiaozu 1990: 154–55, slips 37–41).

Transmitted records also convey the Qin state's claim to the role of sole distributor of labor resources in the economy.[40] Extant accounts of Shang Yang's reforms suggest that dependent laborers and agricultural land were allocated in accordance with social rank (*jue* 爵). The chapter "Within the Borders" (*Jing nei* 境內) of the *Book of Lord Shang*, tentatively dated 350–300 BCE, prescribes the appointment of one "retainer" (*shuzi* 庶子) and the grant of one *qing* (ca. 4.6 hectares) of arable land and nine *mu* (ca. 0.4 hectares) of residential land for each additional level of rank (Jiang 1986: 5.119; for the dating of this chapter, see Pines 2017: 52–53). The *Shiji* biography of Shang Yang specifies that these retainers were bond-persons (*chenqie* 臣妾) (Shiji: 68.2230). The latter title is reminiscent of, though not identical to, that of bondservant and bondswomen convicts in the excavated documents.

While the legal and administrative documents excavated to date do not regulate the redistribution of dependent labor as they do agricultural land, very large arable parcels assigned to individuals of higher social ranks imply the allocation of laborers in line with the accounts of the *Book of Lord Shang* and the *Shiji* (see Peng et al. 2007: 216–18, slips 310–13). The conditional transfer of rights to labor, rather than full-fledged private ownership, could explain the observed legal ambiguity of convict and slave statuses manifest in the routine transfers of convicts to private parties and of slaves to the state-managed convict labor force.

The pool of unfree laborers available to the state was supplemented by debtors.[41] Individuals who took loans in grain or cash from the state, or leased cattle or agricultural tools, could be required to work off their debts if they failed to repay their loans in time. The same applied to fines and redemption fees owed to the state. By means of a bureaucratic procedure, debts could be transferred between local authorities, so that the labor of debtors could be redeemed at places other than the counties that had originally issued loans or imposed fines.

Records of the Qin frontier administration excavated at Liye, Hunan Province, demonstrate that conscripted servicemen and officials were often required to serve additional terms at the imperial frontier in order to work off their debts. In effect, this helped the state secure access to manpower where it was most needed but difficult to secure locally. Qin's experiment in the interregional transfer of debts highlights the role of frontier management as a catalyst for financial innovation in the emerging empire. Insofar as it involved setting up quantifiable standards of labor value expressed in monetary terms, the state's effort to rationalize its access to labor opened up a venue for monetizing labor services and developing a market for labor substitutes. This became an important factor in the overall monetization of taxation under the Western Han.[42]

Unfree laborers were an indispensable resource for the functioning of the state economy and administrative apparatus. As was the case with regular labor obligations, decisions concerning the deployment of convict labor were highly centralized. The use of labor across the empire was informed by the priorities of the central government rather than by local demand. This can be observed in the sharp fluctuations in the number of convicts in Qianling County, which appear to align with the dynamics of imperial politics in the South.[43] The concentration of about seven hundred thousand convicts in two major construction projects in the vicinity of the Qin capital Xianyang—specifically to build the Apang Palace and the mausoleum complex of the First Emperor—was likewise achieved by severely taxing the quantity of labor available to local authorities across the empire.

1.2.3. FU 賦 LEVIES AND THE MONETIZATION OF TAXES

The extractive practices of the Warring States Qin were based on labor levies and in-kind land tax, but they also included a number of additional levies called *fu* 賦. Later historians often identified these with the capitation tax of the Han Empire, the *suanfu* 算賦, which was levied on the adult population. The official annals of the Han founding emperor Gao (202–195 BCE), however, unambiguously state that this tax was first introduced in 203 (Hanshu: 1A.46). No mention of a capitation tax has, moreover, been found in excavated Qin documents or in the transmitted record of Qin fiscal organization.

A legal case record from the collection of Qin documents acquired by the Yuelu Academy sheds some light on the origins of *fu*. The term was used to indicate communal contributions toward extraordinary expenses such as funeral expenses for the destitute (Zhu and Chen 2013: 153–65, slips 108–36, esp. 155, slip 114; Lau and Staack 2016: 188–210, esp. 197–98). In a similar fashion, *fu* taxes may have originally been emergency levies, raised in particular to cover military needs

(Shiji: 5.204).[44] By the late Warring States period, however, some *fu* were already collected on regular basis. The *fu* also appear to have been the first levies to undergo at least partial monetization, which may suggest the increasing monetization of military finance.

One of the most important *fu* taxes mentioned in contemporary documents was household tax, the *hufu* 戶賦 (Shuihudi Qin mu zhujian zhengli xiaozu 1990: 132, slip 165; Hulsewé 1985: 177). One item in the Qin "Statute on finance" (*jinbu lü* 金布律) makes clear that the *hufu* was collected every year in two installments, first in the tenth month (when the Qin calendrical year began) as one *shi* and fifteen *jin* of hay (ca. 33.5kg), and then in the fifth month in the amount of 16 monetary units (Chen, Songchang 2015: 107, slips 118–20). This levy may have originated as an extension of the land-tax in hay and straw imposed on households that were not engaged in agricultural production. The parallel regulation in the early Western Han statute further specifies that the in-kind part of this tax could be payable in money "after the county's needs (for hay) were satisfied" (Peng et al. 2007: 193, slip 255; Barbieri-Low and Yates 2015, vol. 2: 700–1).

The household tax was not the only *fu* claimed by the Qin authorities. Liye documents mention at least three other *fu*, namely "regular tax" (*hengfu* 恒賦), "righteous tax" (*yifu* 義賦) presumably paid by non-*huaxia* ("barbarian") tribes in recognition of Qin authority, and "feather tax" (*yufu* 羽賦). These *fu* are supplemented by a number of isolated uses of the graph *fu* ("levy").[45] Insofar as only one of these levies is said to be "regular" (*heng* 恒), it is possible to infer that the others were collected on a more *ad hoc* basis. This could substantiate the later condemnations of Qin emperors for claiming as much as two-thirds of their subjects' income in various *fu* at the peak of Qin's military spending and in the extravaganza of monumental construction (Shiji: 118.3090).

While the in-kind part of some *fu* taxes was retained by counties and probably used to replenish local stockpiles, cash had to be remitted (lit. "transported," *shu* 輸) in full to the commandery authorities. In the Qin administrative system, it was these authorities that were primarily responsible for military spending, including the manufacture of weapons and armor and the levying of troops. The same centralization of the monetary income of the local authorities applied to its other cash revenues.

1.2.4. MARKET TAXES

Along with the monetized part of the household tax, taxes on commercial transactions were the major fiscal sources of monetized income. Qin law required that trade be conducted at official markets (*shi* 市) by registered traders enrolled in the groups of five for mutual responsibility (Shuihudi Qin mu zhujian zhengli xiaozu 1990: 36–37, slip 68; Hulsewé 1985: 53).[46] In at least some counties in the late Warring States Qin, a specialized Bureau of the Market (*shi cao* 市曹) was established to oversee market activities (Zhu and Chen 2013: 129–30, slips 64–65; Lau and Staack 2016: 152–53). By imperial Qin times some categories of merchandise like ceramics could be traded outside of official markets, but traders were required to self-report for taxation purposes. Itinerant trading was permitted on a short-term basis for periods less than ten days. For longer periods, traders were required to register at the official markets or risk a fine and the confiscation of their merchandise and earnings (Chen, Songchang 2015: 109, slips 124–26).

Legal statutes and administrative documents from the Qin and early Western Han periods mention two monetary taxes levied on those engaged in commercial activity: the market tax (*shizu* 市租) and the authorization fee (*zhi* 質) levied on high-ticket sales such as slaves, horses, or cattle.[47] As in the previously discussed case of household taxation, local governments were not authorized to dispose of income from the majority of commercial taxes. Early Western Han law required that the money collected as market taxes (*zu*) and authorization fees (*zhi*) be reported to the central government along with the income from the household tax and revenues from imperial parks (for which see the next section).

Local authorities were expressly prohibited from using these funds without authorization (Peng et al. 2007: 254, slips 429–30). This suggests that they were included among the "forbidden moneys" (*jin qian* 禁錢), the term used in the Qin and Han empires to refer to monetary taxes earmarked for the imperial court or central government spending but stored in county treasuries (Hanshu: 19A.732, comm. 1, 64B.2834; Hou Hanshu: 26.3600). Local authorities were only allowed to apply for permission to use these reserves after they had exhausted their own stocks of cash (Chen, Songchang 2015: 197–98, slips 308–11).

Much less clear from the surviving documents are the sources of monetary revenue for the local governments. The imperial Qin "Statute on finance" from the Yuelu Academy collection mentions "other minor income in coin" (*ta shaoru qian* 它稍入錢) without specifying their origin (Chen, Songchang 2015: 108, slips 121–23). Yet it is clear that this income was used to cover local expenses. A Qin document states that "minor income" was insufficient to cover the expenses incurred by Qianling County in 211 (Chen, W. 2012a: 146–47, tablet 8–427). In the Western Han Empire, documents excavated from the fortifications on the north-western frontier cite a shortage in "minor income" as a cause of the local government's inability to fulfill its obligations (Gansu sheng wenwu kaogu yanjiusuo et al. 1990: 510, E.P.F. 22–487; 511, E.P.F. 22–522). By the mid-Western Han period, "minor income" was an important part of local finances, and it was probably already becoming increasingly important in the Qin Empire (Wu 2013: 226–27).

The collection of market taxes involved comprehensive verification and control. Taxpayers were required to personally ensure that their money was deposited in the collection jar and then received one of three identical receipts, or tallies (*quan* 券). The market official in charge of collecting the tax retained another one of these receipts, and the third was submitted to the county court at the end of the month along with the jar itself (Chen, Songchang 2015: 108, slips 122–23). In this way, Qin legislators tried to involve taxpayers in monitoring the behavior of tax-collecting officials.

1.2.5. INCOME FROM THE STATE ECONOMY

It is difficult to clearly define the vast state sector of the Qin economy and to draw a line separating it from the "private" sector. In terms of fiscal policy, the state sector of the economy was subject to management by officials, and the government disposed of all its income. By contrast, the state could only claim part of the produce of the "private" economy through taxation. In practice, however, the state and private sectors intertwined so much as to render this distinction problematic.[48]

For most of the Warring States period, there is no evidence for the domain economy as something distinct from the state economy. Even after the establishment of the specialized office (sometimes called ministry) of the Privy Purse (or Lesser Treasury, *shao fu* 少府) toward the end of the period, there is little to suggest that its funds were exclusively used to cover the imperial household's expenditure as opposed to state spending more generally.[49] Conversely, the labor resources of the state economy were routinely deployed in what we would now characterize as household projects, e.g., construction of palaces and tombs for the emperor and imperial clansmen and the maintenance of imperial parks. In the following discussion, therefore, the domain economy is not distinguished from the state economy: all income from economic assets directly controlled and managed by government officials was available for disposal by centralized institutions as they saw fit.

The state economy relied on the vast pools of unfree labor. Penal labor appears to have been the most frequently applied punishment in Qin criminal justice. It provided the state with a labor force that could be deployed throughout the year for an unlimited time. Another important labor pool was created through the mechanism of state lending to private individuals who were allowed to work off their loans. Convicts were employed for a variety of tasks, including those that could also be performed by labor levies. There were also specific areas of the state economy that depended on convict labor, agriculture foremost among them. The Qin state operated agricultural farms managed by a special department of county government, the Office of Fields (*tian guan* 田官, also called the Division of Fields, *tian bu* 田部) under the Supervisor of Fields (*tian sefu* 田嗇夫).

Another branch of the county government, the Office of Husbandry (*chu guan* 畜官), was in charge of animal farms. Documents from the Qin tomb at Longgang indicate that in the Qin Empire "forbidden parks" (*jin yuan* 禁苑) provided grazing land for "horses, cattle, and sheep belonging to the county offices" (*xian guan ma niu yang* 縣官馬牛羊) (Zhongguo wenwu yanjiusuo 2001: 106, slip 100). "Forbidden parks" were part of the larger system of facilities operated across the empire but subordinate directly to the central government rather than to local authorities. These facilities and their staff were called "metropolitan offices" (*du guan* 都官) and included miscellaneous assets such as iron foundries (*tie guan* 鐵官, lit. "office of iron"), horse stalls (ma guan 馬官, lit. "office of horses"), and various artisanal workshops (*gong guan* 工官, lit. "office of artisans"; *zhi guan* 織官, lit. "office of weavers"). Although "metropolitan offices" depended on local authorities for manpower and food supplies, they were accountable directly to the central government, which also disposed of their resources and income (Chen, Songchang

2018: 138–77). The exclusion of these important productive assets from the purview of local governments promoted greater centralization of revenues and further reduced the economic power of local authorities.

When it was not overseen directly by the central government, craft production constituted an important source of both materials and monetary income for local authorities. Convict and debt laborers worked side by side with conscripted professional artisans in local workshops. Especially valuable convict craftsmen and craftswomen were obliged to continue working for the government even if they were amnestied. Female weavers appear to have been particularly highly prized; they were mobilized to produce textiles at state workshops, which were then sold or distributed to government personnel, servicemen, and unfree laborers, and could also serve as currency (Kakinuma 2011: 249–307). Iron tools produced at state-managed facilities were leased out to farmers (Shuihudi Qin mu zhujian zhengli xiaozu 1990: 23–24, slip 15; 50, slips 128–29; Zheng Shubin et al. 2013: 116, tablet 10–673; 117, tablet 10–1170). Any attempt to leave workshops without prior authorization qualified as absconding—a crime that was penalized on the basis of the value lost to the state, estimated at 60 coins per day of absence (Chen, Songchang 2015: 41, slips 7–9; Chen, Songchang 2017: 70, slip 92). Although some of the output of these workshops was consumed by the court or distributed among government officials, military servicemen, and dependent laborers, some of it was earmarked for sale at the market (Shuihudi Qin mu zhujian zhengli xiaozu 1990: 42–43, slip 97; Peng et al. 2007: 254, slip 429). The importance of this monetary income to local governments is implied by a document circulated by Dongting Commandery that urged subordinate counties to make use of the convicts in their custody to engage in market-oriented production (*wei zuo wu chan qian* 為作務產錢), the proceeds of which could be used to cover the needs of various county offices (*zi gei* 自給). This instruction is cited by the Office of Fields for the Qianling County court in its efforts to secure convict laborers for precisely this purpose (Chen, W. 2018: 185–86, tablet 9–710). The Office of Fields did not specialize in manufacturing, yet its officials felt it necessary to produce for the markets in order to get access to much-needed cash.

Not only artisans were expected to engage with the market by selling their products, but the same also applied to other branches of the state economy. One of the common tasks assigned to convicts, for example, was gathering firewood. In fact, this task lent its name to one of the groups of convict laborers, "the gatherers of firewood for shrines" (*gui xin* 鬼薪). An imperial Qin ordinance encouraged county governments to sell this firewood along with reeds (*wei* 葦), most likely collected by convicts, to replenish the county's reserves of cash (*ru qian xian guan* 入錢縣官) (Chen, Songchang 2017: 198, slip 302). County governments annually assessed their officials' achievements in marketing the output of the state sector, and these assessments were important in decisions regarding officials' promotion or demotion (Shuihudi Qin mu zhujian zhengli xiaozu 1990: 35, slip 63; Chen, W. 2012a: 343–44, tablet 8–1516). Significantly, the law did not require that this monetary income be reported or transferred to either the commandery or the central authorities, which suggests that the proceeds of such market transactions were an important source of money for the local governments. Towards the end of the Warring States era and during the imperial Qin period, the state economy increasingly combined its old role of providing subsistence for state-employed personnel with its new role of maximizing monetary income.

2. The Distributive Effects of the Qin Fiscal Model and Its Limitations as an Imperial Taxation Regime

The Qin state approached the end of the Warring States period with a developed system of resource extraction. In this system, the state exerted direct control over the labor force to maximize agricultural and craft production. It managed the labor force through resettlement, the distribution of land to farming households, and the systematic mobilization of manpower. State control focused on the strategically important areas along the rivers and other transportation routes, on administrative centers, and on areas in the proximity of theaters of war. Insofar as taxation was primarily conducted in kind, transportation costs were the state's major concern, as it attempted to operate supply chains directly rather than outsourcing this task to private merchants. In institutional terms, this organizational model was likely an outgrowth of the economy that took shape in the Qin heartland in the Wei River basin during the centuries preceding its outward expansion, where a tradition of centralized organization of large-scale labor projects prevailed. This heritage is also manifest in the functional ambivalence of the state's financial agencies. The Office of Fields, for instance, was simultaneously both a ministry of agriculture overseeing the distribution of land and the collection of land tax and a direct operator of state-owned agricultural farms worked by convicts (Yamada 1993: 44–45).

The main goal of taxation was to finance wars. In view of high transportation costs and the low level of monetization of the fiscal system, the Qin administration sought to create supply bases close to the loci of state consumption. Measuring the taxation base and assessing revenues were paramount for military budgeting. Intensive exploitation of advantageously located but circumscribed enclaves proved to be a more efficient strategy than less aggressive control of what may have been a far larger taxation base in the eastern regions of the Zhou world. This strategy also had important ramifications for the relationships between the principal and agents within the fiscal system.

The limited geographical scale of revenue transfers did not correlate with a high degree of control over fiscal income by the local authorities.[50] The Qin government monitored its local functionaries intensely in order to centralize state finances. The state's "scribal capacity" was radically upgraded beginning in the mid-fourth century BCE. Scores of specialized, hereditary scribes were trained in official schools specifically for employment in the state administration (Shuihudi Qin mu zhujian zhengli xiaozu 1990: 63, slip 191). This considerably reduced the cost of producing and circulating the written documents that were instrumental to centralized supervision. Monitoring techniques included the independent submission of accounts by offices involved in administrative transactions; archival storage of copies of documents to facilitate cross-checking; strict deadlines for submission of periodic accounts; and an elaborate system of penalties for functionaries failing to meet these requirements. Moreover, the central government sought to use the heads of farming communities and even common taxpayers as a check on the behavior of its agents. While the effectiveness of these measures is difficult to evaluate, the attempt to employ an independent body of controllers external and possibly hostile to the bureaucratic organization attests to the state's commitment to monitoring local officials—even at the risk of alienating them.

Far from being a privileged and exclusive social stratum, local functionaries largely consisted of temporarily mobilized personnel receiving in kind subsistence rations for their services.[51] In a society where a person's social rank rather than his official position served as the main marker of status and claim to material wealth and legal privilege, official service was at best a form of social security providing minimal subsistence, and at worst an onerous burden often imposed on people as a penalty.[52] The limited incentivization of state agents combined with monitoring pressure contributed to an environment in which low-ranking local functionaries were potentially subversive toward the state. From the outset of the anti-Qin revolt in 209 BCE, low-ranking local officials, along with the remains of the old aristocracy, provided leadership for the rebel forces.

The central government's program of monitoring local expenditure to maximize the utility of its spatially circumscribed fiscal base faced two structural challenges. First, most income came from direct taxation (land tax, household and other *fu* taxes), labor mobilization, or the dispersed state economy (agricultural farms, artisanal workshops), all of which were managed at the local level. Local authorities were best positioned to make use of this income by legal (retaining their official portion of fiscal income) or illegal means (concealing revenue). The specific configuration of the Qin fiscal regime (relatively small size of the state; circumscribed, intensively exploited fiscal base; strong incentive for the central authorities to maximize extraction to finance wars) facilitated the monitoring of local agents and tilted the distribution of revenue in favor of the center (see Table 8.1). But this could not be sustained in the long run, especially after the rapid and vast territorial expansion at the end of the Warring States era.

Second, the Qin conquest of the monetized economies to the east and south-east of Guanzhong and the growing monetization of the Qin economy itself increased the importance of monetary revenues. Local authorities, in particular, were now required to procure materials through markets instead of relying on centralized distribution. At the same time, almost all monetary revenues were claimed by the central authorities, leaving county governments with "minor income" that was so haphazard that historians are still struggling to identify its exact sources. Among the more important sources for this income are the monetized

TABLE 8.1. Collection and Distribution of Fiscal Revenues in the State of Qin

Tax		Medium of Collection	Use of Revenue	Distribution of Revenue
Land tax		Grain	Military provisioning Court provisioning	Transfer to the loci of military consumption or grain storage
			Provisioning of administrative personnel and laborers levied by local government	Local use, accountable to the central government
		Hay and straw, commutable to cash (in imperial period)	Provisioning of horses and cattle; matting and construction material	Local use
Labor services		Labor	Construction, transportation, policing, variety of economic tasks at local level	Use by the central government. Use by the local government on authorization
Household tax		Hay and straw, commutable to coin	Military finance: same as land tax in hay and straw	Local Use
		Coin, commutable to cloth	Market purchases, monetary rewards	Remitted to the central government
Other fu taxes		Unclear, probably partly in coin	Military finance	Remitted to the central government (?)
Commercial taxes	*Market tax*	Coin	Market purchases, monetary rewards	Remitted to the central government
	Authorization fees			
	"Minor incomes"			Local use
Income from the state economy		In kind	Consumption by government personnel	Transfer to distant loci of consumption; local use
		Coin	Market purchases, monetary rewards	Local use

residues of household tax and, at least in some places during the imperial period, the land tax in hay and straw, as well as whatever local authorities were able to sell from the output of the state economy under their management. It should be remembered that some of the most profitable enterprises like minting coins, producing iron tools, and the exploitation of timber, wildlife, and other natural resources in "forbidden parks" were operated directly by the central government.

What all these sources of income have in common is their marginality relative to the mainstream, in-kind extraction regime practiced by Qin. Hay and straw levies could be commuted to cash payments only to the extent that the state's need for these materials—a need generated by livestock farms, transportation infrastructure, and storage facilities—was satisfied. Effectively, it was contraction in these areas of state consumption that had the potential to ameliorate local shortages of cash revenue. In other words, other things being equal, we would expect local governments in the Qin Empire to have been interested in the decline of some branches of the state economy and the concomitant reduction of state consumption (which, during the Warring States period, was primarily of a military nature, including rewards and material bonuses for meritorious servicemen). This would make more in-kind revenues available for monetization. We would also expect that if left to its own devices, the local state economy would rebalance itself toward more market-oriented activities to meet the local authorities' demand for monetary liquidity. After the Qin state economy collapsed together with the Qin Empire, the distributional effects of its fiscal regime became an important factor in preventing the rulers of the subsequent Han Empire, who otherwise inherited the administrative and fiscal institutions of its predecessor, from rebuilding Qin's command economy.

The final feature of the Qin fiscal model to be emphasized here is the very limited scope it provided for satisfying various groups of powerful local actors through the redistribution of tax revenues. This was already apparent in the case of state officials. Another vivid example is provided by the archaeologically attested expulsion of the Chu aristocratic lineages from the region surrounding their capital on the Middle Yangzi, conquered by the Qin in 279–278 BCE. The antagonization of local élites is further exemplified by the resettlement of the "powerful and wealthy" (*hao fu* 豪富) of conquered states after the completion of conquests in 221 (Shiji: 6.239). However, intense control over the tax base and the amount of revenue collected and spent, accompanied by attempts to alienate all private parties from benefiting from the process of resource extraction, meant that the spatial scope of the Qin fiscal model could not be easily scaled up without a revolution in communication technology. The alternative was the revision of the extractive institutions themselves, which was what the Qin imperial government ultimately attempted and which was accomplished by its Han successors.

Between 230 and 221, the Qin armies progressively annihilated all other "warring states" and formally unified the entirety of the Zhou world. This decade of conquest resulted in the incorporation of vast territories with monetized markets, powerful landholding and mercantile groups, and land tenure systems different from those of Qin. Some adjustments to the Qin fiscal system were already being made prior to "unification," but much more thorough revision became necessary to make the new empire financially tenable.[53] The major problems the imperial government experienced concerned the rising transaction costs in the operation of taxation, the circumscribed taxation base, the monetization of state expenditure, and the growing role of markets, which challenged the "physiocratic" model of revenue extraction and redistribution. The attempted solutions are better understood not as a comprehensive reform program but rather as *ad hoc* responses to specific challenges.

Fostering the expansion of the agricultural tax base in the newly conquered territories was among the top priorities for the imperial government. The time-honored colonization strategy was still applied, but it hardly presented a viable alternative to taxing local populations and existing landholdings. In 216 the government requested its subjects to self-declare landed possessions. Scholars consider this measure to be a tacit recognition of existing land tenure systems by the imperial government, predicated on the payment of taxes (Yang 2009a: 126–63). The state effectively acknowledged the limitations of its claim to act as arbiter in the distribution of arable land in return for an increase in revenue. That many Qin subjects indeed answered this call is attested by private petitions to the Qianling County government to record private landholdings in "permanent registers" (*heng ji* 恆籍) (Chen, W. 2018: 477–78, tablet 9–2344).

Recognition of local land tenure some five years after "unification" suggests that the central government was already struggling with surging monitoring costs in the wake of recent and dramatic territorial expansion. The Qin system of resource extraction relied on intensive monitoring of both the fiscal base and agent behavior. During much of the Warring States period, the relatively limited scale of the fiscal base and high levels of extraction justified this approach.

Some bureaucratic mechanisms of supervision and cross-control deployed by the Qin government have already been discussed above. To improve the efficiency of control over agencies, Qin local administration was divided into two parallel systems of offices (*guan* 官) and bureaus (*cao* 曹). The former was in charge of operating various economic facilities, such as storehouses, granaries, and so on. While offices could be located in the countryside, near the sites of production or storage that they managed, the magistrate's scribes (*lingshi* 令史) who conducted the work of the bureaus were based at the county court, probably next to each other in the same office. Their job was to look through the accounts and evaluations delivered by the offices, collate them with other records that reflected the dynamics of government-owned assets, and authorize the documents for subsequent submission to the central government.[54] The system was probably designed to facilitate the monitoring of the state economy by county governments that were themselves accountable to the center. That this system was discontinued by the Han government may attest to its high operating costs.

Increasing monetization of the Qin imperial economy presented market-based solutions for reducing the management and monitoring costs in the state economy. By the time the Qin conquests were completed, the state storage agencies were actively participating in market transactions. An article of the statute "On the Controller of Works" requires offices to purchase with money the grease and glue they needed for their everyday functioning, instead of waiting for these materials to be allocated by the central government (Shuihudi Qin mu zhujian zhengli xiaozu 1990: 50, slips 128–29). Local government agencies also purchased slaves, horses, feathers (presumably for the manufacture of arrows), and clothes for their personnel while at the same time selling surplus commodities in their storehouses (Chen, W. 2012a: 20, tablet 6–7; 93, tablet 8–154; 197, tablet 8–664+8–1053 + 8–2167; 367, tablet 8–1604; 374, tablet 8–1662; 387, tablet 8–1755 Chen, W. 2018: 163, tablet 9–609; 185, tablet 9–709 + 9–873; 239, tablet 9–992). A group of documents excavated at Liye records the commercial deeds of the Qianling county granary, which was selling surplus from official sacrificial activities to private individuals (Peng 2009; Sanft 2014). Other texts routinely refer to the sale of grain, ale, salt, and other comestibles from county supplies, as well as to the sale of other tradable commodities such as the hides and horns of livestock and clothes produced at state-managed workshops (Chen, W. 2012a: 62, tablet 8–102; 168, tablet 8–490 + 8–501; 223, tablet 8–771; 246, tablet 8–907 + 8–923 + 8–1422; 286, tablet 1162; Chen, W. 2018: 57, tablet 9–56 + 9–1209 + 9–1245 + 9–1928 + 9–1973; 161, tablet 9–597; 267, tablet 9–1138; Shuihudi Qin mu zhujian zhengli xiaozu 1990: 24, slips 16–20; Liye Qin jiandu bowuguan et al. 2016: 56, tablet 10–1170). These records indicate that the Qin state was eager to make a profit as it adjusted the volume of stockpiles to meet its actual needs.

An ordinance from the Yuelu Academy collection, which is dated to the imperial Qin period, sheds light on the changes taking place in military finance (Chen, Songchang 2017: 116–17, slips 146–48). The regulation deals with the purchase of food, beverages, clothing, and other supplies by army officers:

●令曰：吏從軍治粟將漕長輓者，自敦長以上到二千石吏，居軍治粟漕長輓所，得賣（買）所飲食衣服物及所以飲食居處及給事器兵，買此物而弗飲食衣服用給事者，皆爲私利。毋重車者，得買以給事，舍，毋過□□□人。

The ordinance stipulates: When army officers in charge of grain [supplies] are responsible for transportation of supplies by water or by land (lit.: using two-wheeled carts), from the rank of corporal[55] and up to [the level of high-ranked] officials with the salary grade of 2,000 piculs who hold the position in the army responsible for grain provisioning by water or by land, they are allowed to purchase beverages, food, clothes, as well as kitchenware, domestic utensils, and implements and weapons that they need to perform their duties. If they purchase these goods but do not use them as food and clothes or to perform their duties, this is considered private profiteering. If there are no heavy carts [for transportation], they are allowed to buy these to perform their duties. For the accommodation lodges, [the number of people] (staying there?) should not surpass … individuals.

The ordinance appears to be addressing a situation in which the centralized system of army provisioning was failing, so that the logistics officers had to procure food, clothing, transportation, and other supplies on the private market. It is unclear whether these were the specially established "army markets" mentioned in the Book of Lord Shang or ordinary markets along the army's marching route. Detailed legal regulation suggests not only that this mode of military procurement had already become a common practice by imperial Qin times, but also that it fostered the merging of official function and commercial activity.

The monetization of the state economy had important distributional consequences. My analysis suggests that income from the sale of surplus stocks constituted an important source of monetary liquidity for the otherwise cash-thirsty local governments. While most of the other monetary income had to be remitted to the central authorities, a large part of the monetized residual produce of the state economy was probably initially considered a "minor" or marginal income to be retained for local needs. This incentivized local authorities to replenish their cash reserves by engaging in market transactions and prioritizing those sectors of the state economy that were best suited to generating monetary income, such as the production of textiles and lacquerware. Consequently, the entire state economy gradually drifted away from its traditional role as subsistence provider for state-employed personnel and laborers and toward the market-driven role of profit maximizer.

This transformation, however, was by no means determined by the intrinsic development of Qin economic institutions. The drift toward engagement with markets during the Qin imperial period was balanced by an equally pronounced surge in the scale of state-managed labor projects exemplified by the construction of long walls along the northern frontier, the highway network that connected the empire's capital to distant provinces, and the First Emperor's mausoleum, to mention but the best-recorded projects. A thorough revision of the Qin taxation regime became possible only in the wake of the violent demise of the empire at the end of the third century BCE.

3. The Han Fiscal Transition: Toward an Imperial Consensus (Second to First Century BCE)

The fall of the Qin Empire led to a temporary disintegration of centralized political order in the East Asian oecumene. One of the successor states, Han, eventually consolidated control over the Qin homeland of Guanzhong, and then, through some ingenious alliance-building, nominally reunified most of the Qin imperial possessions. Nevertheless, more than half of the new empire was divided between autonomous polities, a situation that endured for the first half-century of Han rule. Fiscal decentralization accompanied administrative decentralization. Regional princedoms enjoyed considerable autonomy in raising and spending their revenues.[56] During the same period, the core elements of the Qin fiscal model were progressively abandoned, and a fixed-rate, low-tax regime took shape. This regime produced more predictable income flows for the central government, reduced monitoring expenses, and laid the foundation for coopting provincial élites through distributed access to resources and fiscal revenues. These goals were achieved at the cost of a reduced state capacity to mobilize resources in times of emergency and increased the central government's dependence on the cooperation of élites in fiscal matters.

Changes in the fiscal system were conditioned by ongoing economic developments: the expansion of the money supply and the monetary economy. The collapse of the Qin state dramatically decreased the central government's productive capacity, including its ability to issue coin. Private coinage filled the gap. Private currency was legal for most of the first seventy years of Han rule, resulting in the continuous devaluation of *banliang* 半兩 coinage despite the government's many attempts to stabilize the weight of bronze money (Hanshu: 24B.1152–1157). The result was a considerable expansion of the volume of coins in circulation, which increasingly enabled the state to monetize labor levies and taxes in kind. The progress of the monetary economy and the labor market reduced the state's need to mobilize manpower directly. The convict labor force shrank dramatically in the wake of legal reforms by the first Han rulers. Equally, the institutions of regular labor service and universal military conscription gradually declined during the Western Han period and were abandoned under the Eastern Han Empire (25–220 CE).[57]

The fiscal organization of the Han Empire has been studied much more extensively than that of the Qin.[58] On the following pages, I focus on the dynamics of the imperial fiscal transition and its distributional implications for the central government, bureaucrats, and provincial élites, as well as on its impact on the long-term pattern of imperial China's fiscal history.

3.1. Monetization of Labor and in-Kind Levies

As is true of many elements of the Han fiscal transition, the monetization of labor levies was rooted in the practices of the Qin command economy of the Warring States era. The official imposition of fixed monetary and commodity values for labor implied legal recognition of its fungibility. Late Warring States Qin statutes allowed individuals to substitute their labor obligation to the state with labor of identical value provided by a different person or even an animal (Shuihudi Qin mu zhujian zhengli xiaozu 1990: 51, slips 137, 140; Hulsewé 1985: 68–69; Korolkov, forthcoming). By the beginning of the Western Han period, labor substitutes were broadly available for hire, and their wage could vary by a large margin depending on market conditions (Cang 2012: 157).

The institution of labor substitutes originally developed as an unofficial arrangement between private parties, but was soon recognized by the state as it explored ways to increase the flexibility of its labor supply.[59] By the mid-second century BCE, labor levies and capitation taxes collected at the local level were routinely merged under the term "levies and taxes," reflecting "convertibility between the service and the tax" (Hsing 2014: 173). Even though the precise mechanisms of collecting the combined "levies and taxes" remain unclear, it may be assumed that local authorities were making decisions on the basis of the actual need for labor; once this need was met, surplus labor levies were commuted to cash payments. This fiscal measure was part of a broader policy pursued by the first Han emperors to reduce the size of the unfree labor force supplied from the state coffers. Later in the Western Han period, the monetization of labor services culminated in the emergence of a new tax, *gengfu* 更賦, or "tax [in substitution of] a term [of statute labor]," which was designed to supersede private market arrangements for corvée substitutes.[60] The proceeds of this tax were used to hire laborers when and where the government needed them, especially in the frontier regions where large amounts of cash were transferred from the empire's hinterland (Wang 2007: 67–68).

Commutation of in-kind taxes to cash payments already began under the Qin Empire. Statutes permitted the payment of coin in lieu of the household tax, and, at least in some areas, also in lieu of the land tax in hay and straw (Chen, W. 2018: 152–53, tablet 9–543 + 9–570 + 9–835). The early Western Han "Statute on fields" recognized cash payment of the land tax in hay and straw as an empire-wide practice. Local officials were instructed to collect this tax in coin once local needs for the raw materials were satisfied (Peng et al. 2007: 187–88, slips 240–41; 193, slip 255; Barbieri-Low and Yates 2015, vol. 2: 606–97, 700–1). The government's reduced need for in-kind income was probably affected, among other factors, by the destruction of many of the state-managed livestock farms after the collapse of Qin. The first Han emperors were unable and probably unwilling to restore this important branch of the state economy, and thus did not need the vast quantities of hay and straw required to sustain it.[61]

3.2. Decline of the Forced Labor System

In his recent comparative study of slavery and forced labor in Early China and the Roman World, the economic historian Walter Scheidel identifies the role of the state as critical to explaining the difference between the unfree labor regimes in the Mediterranean and East Asian empires. While private slavery was typical for the former, the latter developed "an extensive gulag-like system of penal servitude" controlled and operated by the state (Scheidel 2017b: 146). However, the state-organized system of unfree labor was not an intrinsic feature of the economy of early Chinese empires. It was an outcome of a specific configuration of economic conditions and fiscal and administrative practices in the late Warring States Qin. It took shape in the process of territorial expansion and was part of Qin's "physiocratic" extraction model, which presupposed direct state mobilization of labor and in-kind resources. This system was already under severe stress by the end of the Warring States era. New policies and practices developed to reduce the running costs of the unfree labor economy. Private markets played an important role in this process, which accelerated after the fall of the Qin Empire.

In traditional historiography, Emperor Wen's (180–157) momentous legal reforms (Hanshu: 23.1099)—namely the abolition of laws of impoundment and the mutilation of prisoners, as well as the introduction of fixed-term labor sentences—were celebrated as an exemplar of humane rule. Modern scholars also recognize these reforms as one of the milestones in the legal and social history of early Chinese empires, but they point out that the emperor and his advisors were building upon long-term trends in the development of penal labor institutions that can be traced back to the Qin period. Fixed-term labor sentences, in particular, originated in the practice of debt labor, which was limited by the time needed to work off the sums owed to the government; it was also rooted in the supplementary sentences imposed on individuals who committed crimes after having already been reduced to convict status (You 2009: 42–44). Scholars further emphasize the linkage between the legal reforms, the abatement of the government's demand for unfree labor, and efforts to reduce the cost of the state economy, the largest part of which was likely the standing army of convicts (Miyake 2016: 147–51; You 2009: 43; Sun 2015b: 96).

Along with regular amnesties, the reform of the penal labor regime was a radical solution to the problem of its maintenance costs with which the Qin government had already grappled. Among other measures, Qin instituted convict statuses whose bearers were afforded the means to support themselves when not employed by the state. Emperor Wen's reforms rendered these measures redundant, and the "bondservant" status gradually disappeared in their wake (Sun 2015b: 95). The strong Han-era criticism of the excessive use of forced labor and the enormous numbers of convicts in the Qin state conveys the impression that by mid-Han times the size of the unfree labor force had been reduced significantly from its Qin heights.

The decline in demand for unfree labor had many sources. These included the retrenchment of production and distribution systems operated by the state, the dramatic contraction of territories administered by the imperial government, the temporary cessation of frontier expansion, and the transition to fiscal policies that relied less on direct control over human resources. One of the major employers of large convict gangs, the county-level Offices of Fields, already began declining under the Qin Empire and were stripped of all but purely ritual functions in the course of the Western Han period (Yamada 1993: 58).

Centralized administration contracted dramatically when almost two thirds of the imperial territory—including almost all lands to the south of the Yangzi River—were surrendered to the supporters and relatives of the Han founder. For the next fifty years, they were governed as semi-autonomous principalities. The demand for administrative assistants and runners, who were often recruited from among the convicts, reduced accordingly. Equally important, the transition to a fixed-rate harvest tax regime, recognition of private land tenure, and the gradual contraction of the state-managed land-distribution schemes contributed to the expansion of the taxation base, even though it was exploited less intensively than under the Warring States Qin fiscal regime. This effectively reduced the central government's dependence on direct command of labor to develop enclaves of intensified agricultural production.

3.3. Regularization of State Income and Expenditure

The Qin fiscal system developed in order to finance military campaigns and was therefore designed to face extraordinary surges in state expenditure. This was achieved through the concentration of state extraction in strategically important and logistically advantageous areas, the centralization of decision-making concerning state spending, and the close monitoring of resources and local fiscal agents so as to forestall attempts to retain or privatize revenues earmarked for use by the central government. This system survived into the early years of Western Han, when its founder Emperor Gao (202–195) campaigned against his dissident generals and allies-turned-regional princes. The military threat posed by enfeoffed regional rulers declined toward the end of the 180s, when a political *modus vivendi* was established between the central government and autonomous princedoms in the eastern half of the realm. The reigns of Emperors Wen (180–157) and Jing (157–141) were celebrated in traditional historiography as a period of peace and prosperity (Shiji: 10.437–438; Hanshu: 4.134–136, 5.153).[62]

It is during these decades that the principles of land taxation were radically revised. The first attempts to introduce a land tax based on a fixed assumption concerning output were made under Emperor Gao and his successor Emperor Hui (195–188). Experiments continued through the reign of Emperor Wen, until the tax was finally fixed as 1/30 of the nominal average harvest in 156 (Hanshu: 24A.1135). The transition to the fixed-rate system, which was likely applied in the eastern part of the Warring States world prior to the Qin conquest, was probably necessitated by the gradual expansion of the central government's control over these economically advanced regions during the first half-century of Han rule, and became possible with the reduction of military spending after the completion of Emperor Gao's campaigns. Along with other factors considered below, the reduction in military spending stabilized overall state expenditure and created conditions for a low-tax regime.[63]

Capitation tax also underwent regularization during the early years of the Western Han. As discussed previously, in the Qin fiscal system, a number of *fu* taxes were levied on households and individuals. According to transmitted sources, many of these taxes had military origins and were probably initiated as irregular levies, but by the late third century BCE at least some of them were collected on a regular basis. At the very beginning of the Han era, a new monetary capitation tax was introduced, the *suanfu* 算賦, in what may be interpreted as yet another effort to simplify and regularize the overly complex legal and fiscal regimes of the Qin Empire.[64] The annual amount of this tax, however, was not fixed. It depended on the needs of the local governments that used these tax proceeds to cover expenses, including the increasingly monetized payment of salaries to their officials. A cache of documents excavated from an official's tomb at Fenghuangshan, Hubei Province, and dated from the beginning of Emperor Jing's reign, contains a tax collection record for a group of local villages (Hubei sheng wenwu kaogu yanjiu suo 2012: 97–101; Qiu 1974: 49–63; Hsing 2014: 165–66). Tax was collected over the course of a year in a number of installments. The collected amounts differed for each installment. Scholars have argued that the schedule of tax collection was aligned with county government spending. The latter varied from year to year, which accounts for the lack of a fixed annual tax amount (Gao 1983).

As in the case of land taxation, we need to look into the relationship between the patterns of tax collection and state spending in order to understand the rationale for fiscal change. At the beginning of the Western Han, local authorities retained a large portion of the proceeds of the capitation tax in order to pay their functionaries. This constituted a radical departure from the Qin practice of remunerating officials with grain rations rather than monetary payments. In fact, much of the local administrative personnel in the Qin state and empire were recruited in fulfillment of their labor service obligations and did not constitute a professional, full-time bureaucracy (Miyake 2013). Only a small portion of functionaries belonged to the salaried officialdom (*youzhi* 有秩) that received fixed monthly disbursements in grain. Government spending on its personnel could therefore vary widely, depending on the number of functionaries employed in a particular time at a particular location.

This situation changed under the Western Han when full-time, salaried officialdom expanded to incorporate lower-level functionaries who had previously served on a part-time basis and performed their tasks in shifts of duty (Miyake 2013: 160–61). While it is unclear whether this was the result of the growing collective bargaining power of local officialdom vis-à-vis the central government, a conscious and deliberate government policy, or both, the transition to regular salaried bureaucracy increased the predictability of state spending. At some point during the Western Han period, the capitation tax for adults was fixed at 120 coins per year, the figure conveyed in transmitted records of Han institutions.[65] By the end of the Western Han, annual expenditure on the maintenance of the bureaucratic apparatus was stable enough for the relevant figures to be widely known and discussed by contemporary authors.[66]

The professionalization of bureaucratic and military service during the Western Han period and the abatement of war-related expenses (with the exception of Emperor Wu's Xiongnu campaigns, discussed below) were key factors in the regularization of state expenditure, which facilitated the transition to a fixed-rate fiscal regime. Effectively, the central government was able to define the share of surplus production necessary for its functioning under normal circumstances and to translate this into extraction rates that were acceptable to its subjects, particularly to the provincial élites and local officials. Cooperation by these two groups was indispensable for obtaining data about local conditions, such as population numbers and the area of land under cultivation. This settlement was an essential outcome of the imperial fiscal transition. It contributed immensely to the longevity of Han fiscal institutions, but also delimited state power in imperial China.

3.4. From Revenue Maximization to Satisfying an Élite Coalition

The Qin fiscal regime had two aims: first, to maximize the central government's revenue from a relatively circumscribed tax base; and, second, to command labor and in-kind resources and direct them toward the locations of state projects, be they military bridgeheads, transportation routes, fortified seats of local government, frontier outposts, or sites of monumental construction. This model left little room for fiscal negotiation between the state and the élites who enjoyed little or no share in the surplus production extracted by the state. As a result, official service was constructed as an obligation rather than a privilege. One major problem with the Qin fiscal model, then, was that it incurred enormous costs in monitoring agent behavior. These expenses become less surmountable as territorial expansion progressed. By the beginning of the Western Han period, and probably as early as the Qin Empire, the central government adopted the principle of local appointment for all but senior provincial and local functionaries, which became the norm for the rest of China's imperial history (Yan 1961: 345–83; Liao 2000: 82–89). The results were predictable. A provincial social network reconstructed on the basis of the private archive of a clerk who served in one of the empire's eastern commanderies during the closing years of Western Han reveals close and informal ties between provincial officeholders and landowning élites. Such connections are also well-attested in transmitted sources (Korolkov 2012: 311–25).

The collapse of the Qin Empire accelerated processes that were already under way. Because the state's capacity to directly command and transfer manpower and resources deteriorated after the fall of Qin, the central government became more dependent on the cooperation of provincial society for the collection of increasingly monetized taxes. This provided a strong incentive for the empire's new rulers to develop a fiscal consensus with the provincial and local élites. It is probably not a coincidence that this development took place at the same time that a large number of non-Qin associates of the Han founder from the eastern regions of the Warring States world advanced to the top ranks in the imperial establishment.

The low-tax, fixed-rate fiscal regime gradually introduced during the first half of the second century BCE had two major benefits. First, it left a sufficient share of resources unclaimed by the state, which was therefore available for private extraction through rent and money-lending. Second, it created a predictable stream of income for the state while allowing its tax-collecting agents to benefit from economic growth. Increases in the taxable population often remained un- or underreported to the central authorities. As long as the received net revenue was sufficient to satisfy its needs, the imperial government tended to turn a blind eye to the misreporting of tax-related data, even though some top-ranking dignitaries including, on one occasion, the emperor himself lamented the prevalence of such behavior.[67]

In one recorded example, commandery officials reported extraordinarily high numbers of elderly people who enjoyed tax exemptions for themselves and household members, such that a considerable portion of the actual revenue was concealed from central authorities (Gao 1998: 110; Hsing 2014: 182–84). In addition to downright misappropriation of collected revenues, provincial officials benefited from the new balance of revenue distribution between the central and local governments, in which most income from direct taxes was retained and spent locally, primarily to pay the salaries of officials (Lianyungang shi bowuguan et al. 1997: 77–78; Scheidel 2015: 178–80). Instead of competing for revenues with its agents, the central government came to rely heavily on the income from empire-wide monopolies on the production and sale of iron and salt, which owed their profitability to the expansion of commerce within the empire (Glahn 2016: 113–20).

The imperial fiscal consensus solved the twofold problem of reducing monitoring expenses for the central government and satisfying an élite coalition that, as Qin experience suggested, was capable of dismantling an imperial order of which it was not a beneficiary. However, it also reduced the central government's capacity to mobilize resources for emergency spending, thus creating a potential source of tension between the state and its élite constituencies.

3.5. Solutions for Emergency Spending: Taxing Property and Commerce

Regularizing state spending and income was essential for the creation of a long-standing fiscal compromise between the state and the élites, but it severely curtailed the central government's capacity to react to fiscal challenges such as surges in military expenditure. The first seven decades of the Western Han were marked by sustained peace, only interrupted by a brief episode of revolt in 154 BCE. However, starting in the late 130s, Emperor Wu of Han (141–87) launched a series of campaigns against the nomadic Xiongnu in the north.[68] These campaigns lasted for about three decades until the beginning of the first century BCE and entailed enormous expenditure. Huge armies were deployed and supplied over distances of hundreds of kilometers of scarcely populated, harsh terrain. Military garrisons stretched along the northwestern frontier to connect the empire with its dependencies and allies in Central Asia.[69] The fiscal side of this story is well known, since it became a major point of reference in the political-economic debates that unfolded after Emperor Wu's death.[70] What is of interest here is how the state aligned available taxation tools in a new "emergency arsenal" when earlier, Qin-style solutions for fiscal intensification were no longer available.

The registration of property for fiscal purposes and the taxation of commerce were already known in Qin, but their role was relatively marginal. Property was registered primarily to allow a more equitable levying of labor services: wealthier households were required to contribute labor before less prosperous ones. Under Emperor Wu, the Han government attempted to levy a six percent property tax systematically on those engaged in commercial enterprises and a three percent tax on artisans. Additional assessments were made on boats and carts (Hanshu: 24B.1166–1167). The law was effectively directed against landowners who invested in commerce and moneylending. Its enforcement resulted in mass repression of the wealthy groups in the provinces and in the partial disruption of local economic structures.[71]

Another fiscal measure rooted in the Qin economic experience was the introduction of a state monopoly on the production of salt and iron. As previously noted, Qin operated an extensive network of iron workshops, the products of which were routinely leased to farmers, although it remains unclear whether or not private production of iron tools was outlawed in the Qin as it came to be under Emperor Wu's monopoly. The salt monopoly was based on a different principle. Producers were obliged to lease their tools from the state and sell salt to the government at a fixed price, so that the state operated distribution rather than production (Hanshu: 24B.1165–1166; Nishijima 1986: 603). Effectively, the salt monopoly was associated with another fiscal policy, the "equitable delivery" (*junshu* 均輸), under which the government "used public funds . . . to smooth out price fluctuations by buying goods when prices were low and selling them when prices were high," thereby reducing private speculation in essential goods like grain and salt (Hanshu: 24B.1167–1168; Glahn 2016: 116). Formerly believed to have been Emperor Wu's innovation, this policy can be traced back to the beginning of the Western Han and probably to the Qin Empire.[72]

Emperor Wu's fiscal policies represented a marked deviation from the original principles of the military-physiocratic state. According to Richard von Glahn, they signified the emergence of a mercantilist fiscal state that relied on the mobilization of economic resources rather than military manpower and shifted revenue extraction toward indirect taxes paid in money (Glahn 2016: 118). These policies continued the general trend toward the monetization of state revenues that can be traced back to the imperial Qin. They utilized fiscal and economic-managerial techniques developed under the Qin system, such as the registration of household wealth and the state administration of the salt and iron industries. From the government's point of view, the newly developed set of fiscal measures constituted a response to the challenge of emergency military spending. Although Emperor Wu's policies were widely criticized not only during the court debates of the first century BCE but also in traditional historiography, they became an indispensable part of the empire's fiscal toolkit.

4. Concluding Remarks

The dominant mode of taxation in China's early empires is duly characterized as a low-rate fiscal regime that extracted surplus production from a small peasantry (Lewis 2015: 282). In spite of some interruptions, particularly during the Northern Song period (960–1127 CE), this regime survived into the late imperial period (Ming and Qing empires, 1368–1911 CE). It was therefore the financial foundation of the Chinese imperial state through most of its history.[73] As argued here, one reason for the longevity of this fiscal regime was the fact that it reflected an economic and political settlement between the centralized state, on the one hand, and the élites, whose members staffed the imperial bureaucracy and served as the government's fiscal agents in the provinces, on the other. This mode of organization was determined primarily by the territorial scope of the empire, which made it prohibitively expensive to monitor the behavior of officials and collect information about the fiscal base. The central government had no choice but to offer its agents strong incentives for participation in state institutions.

The core elements of the "imperial fiscal consensus" crystallized after two centuries of fiscal experiments accompanied by bargaining and violent clashes between the state and the élites. The most notable episode was the demise of the Qin Empire leading to what I have here called "the imperial fiscal transition." This was already presaged by the administrative and fiscal developments under the short-lived Qin Empire: the principle of local appointment of officials gained currency, in-kind taxes were gradually monetized, the market for labor substitutes expanded, and the public sector increasingly engaged with private markets. It nevertheless took the violent destruction of much of the state economy and the ascent of a new generation of central officials of non-Qin origin to revise fundamental fiscal principles such as the direct command over manpower and resources and the intensive monitoring of a relatively circumscribed taxation base.

The failure of the Qin fiscal model was not, however, coterminous with the abandonment of its mechanisms under following dynasties. The imperial fiscal settlement was conditioned upon a developed monetary economy and relatively low and stable levels of state spending. Whenever one of these conditions did not apply, the state faced the prospect of a fiscal crisis, prompting the implementation of emergency policies to manage it. As the Han Emperor Wu and many rulers of the latter periods learned, such policies always targeted the wealth of the rich and consequently encountered strong opposition from the landowning and commercial élites, which had, by the end of the Western Han era, already coalesced with local officialdom. As a rule, the imperial authorities could not afford to alienate these powerful groups for a long period of time, so the emergency fiscal policies had to be rescinded as soon as the immediate threat of the government's insolvency abated—and often before.

Even such "mercantilist" solutions were, however, unavailable when the state had to increase spending—typically for military purposes—at the same time that monetary exchange was declining or interrupted. When these two conditions coincided, élites tended to turn from disgruntled critics into mortal enemies of the regimes that, in turn, embarked on radical programs of social and economic leveling, usually through attempts to establish direct ties with peasant society.[74] By doing so, the rulers of the state were essentially resorting to the key principles and policies of the Warring States Qin model: state-sponsored social engineering, which involved various economic redistribution schemes, particularly for land; intense monitoring of the taxation base and local state agents; and the mass mobilization of unpaid, including penal, labor, which was employed in the vast state sector of the economy.[75] While the imperial fiscal settlement remained normative for most of China's imperial history, periodic oscillations between the command and market-oriented economic-managerial policies attest to the lasting ideological and practical attractiveness of Qin-style economic organization for empire-builders in China, particularly during periods of acute economic crises and tensions in state-élite relations.

NOTES

1 All subsequent dates are BCE unless otherwise indicated.

2 For a study of the political events that accompanied the fall of the Western Zhou and the eastward relocation of the Zhou capital, see Li 2006: 193–278.

3 For a recent overview of the political and socio-economic changes during the Spring and Autumn (771–453) and Warring States periods, see Glahn 2016: 44–83. For an archaeological perspective, see Falkenhausen 2006.

4 The early history of Qin before and immediately after the relocation of its political centers to the Guanzhong region is conveniently summarized in Zhao 2014: 53–70 and Teng 2014.

5 Having said this, we must bear in mind that the most important written sources for the history of the Spring and Autumn period—the chronicle of the state of Lu 魯 that gave its name to the period and the *Zuozhuan* ("Zuo Tradition," or "Zuo Commentary to the Spring and Autumn Annals") that eventually came to be viewed as a commentary tradition for the Lu chronicle—both originated in the eastern regions of the Zhou world and may have underemphasized the role of the far-western Qin state in the political affairs of the period (Pines 2005–2006: 10–34). Still, Qin's sluggishness in introducing the new fiscal institutions developed by its eastern neighbors suggests that the historiographical tradition of Qin backwardness is not completely groundless.

6 The earliest recorded attempt to establish statewide centralized taxation was undertaken by the state of Lu in 594 (Zuozhuan: 11.614). For the introduction of land taxation in Qin, see Shiji: 15.708.

7 Note, however, that there is more than one interpretation of this evidentiary record. While most scholars regard 336 BCE as the birthdate of Qin coinage, Kakinuma Yōhei 柿沼陽平 argues that the *Shiji* implies official recognition of the Qin round coin, *banliang* 半兩, as sole legal tender within the borders of the state (Kakinuma 2015: 52). This suggests that the coin circulated before this date.

8 For internal troubles in Qin in the fifth century, see Shiji: 5.198–200 and Pines 2017: 9. I refer to the regional lords of the Spring and Autumn and early Warring States periods as "princes"—though their actual titles could have differed—to differentiate them from the King of Zhou, who remained the nominal overlord of the Zhou world. In the course of the fourth century, the rulers of the major "warring states" proclaimed themselves kings (*wang* 王). By that time, the rulers of the powerful southern state of Chu had assumed this title for centuries.

9 Traditions of such management were firmly established by Qin's political predecessor in the Wei River basin, the Western Zhou state (1045–771, but its control over Guanzhong began long before the earlier of these dates), and many of its practices and much of its personnel were probably taken over by the Qin as the center of their polity moved into Guanzhong in the eighth century. In his study of the Western Zhou administrative regime, Li Feng observes that the state-managed landed properties "constituted the main source of revenue of the Western Zhou state and were used to cover the expenses of the central government (and partly probably also of the royal house) and to support the Zhou military" (Li 2008: 158–59).

10 Han, Wei, and Zhao emerged following the collapse of Jin, the most powerful state in northern China and one of the prominent actors in the Spring and Autumn political arena. The power of its ruling house declined during the sixth century, ushering in a civil war between ministerial lineages that had divided the state into three independent polities by the mid-fifth century.

11 For the applicability of the city-state model to the analysis of political organization in pre-imperial China, see Yates 1997: 71–90. For the two distinctive patterns of socioeconomic and political development in the Warring States era—one characterized by private entrepreneurship and the considerable autonomy of the merchant and artisan classes, and another by centralized autocratic power and bureaucratic control over economic resources—see Glahn 2016: 82–83.

12 The story of the Chu statesman Wu Qi 吳起 (d. 381), one of the leading reformers of the early Warring States period, epitomizes the fate of an itinerant advisor whose position of power rested entirely on the favor of rulers and whose reform attempts were frustrated by the locally embedded aristocratic and court élites (Shiji: 65.2165–2169).

13 For the impact of war expenditure on the consolidation of fiscal power in the early modern European states, see, for example Tilly 1990: 67–95.

14 For identification of this tax with the capitation tax known from the Han-era sources, see, for example, Sun 2004: 354.

15 For the central role of land tax in the Qin and Han fiscal systems, see, for example, Lewis 2015: 285–86.

16 As is consistently reiterated in the early chapters of the *Book of Lord Shang*. See, for example, Chapter 2 "Order to cultivate wastelands" (*ken ling* 墾令) (Jiang 1986: 1.6–19). For the early date of this chapter, which was probably composed during Shang Yang's lifetime, see Pines 2016: 19. For a discussion of Qin policies to encourage agricultural production, see Cai 2009: 17–20.

17 For the size of land plots allocated to commoners and to holders of higher meritorious ranks, see Peng et al. 2007: 216–18, slips 310–13. This norm derives from the early Western Han collection of statutes, but the principle of ranked land allotments was most likely borrowed from Qin law, even though we cannot be sure that the Qin applied the same quotas as Han. For the legally prescribed division of large households, see Shiji: 68.2230. Recently excavated Qin administrative docu-

ments cast some doubt on the degree to which this requirement was observed in practice, at least in some places (Li 2009: 5–23).

18 This text is usually characterized as a "statute" (*lü* 律), but I suggest it should be understood as an ordinance (*ling* 令) that amended the "Statute on Fields." This is the avowed purpose of the text itself: "to [make] changes and revisions to the [legal article] on the layout of agricultural fields" 更脩為田律. It should be noted that the term *lü* could apply equally to the statutes and to their individual articles.

19 The Qin conquest of this region coincides chronologically with the appearance of large numbers of non-local burials, including those with typical features of Qin funeral customs such as flexed burial, east-west tomb orientation, and "catacomb" burials. These tombs are associated with the Qin settlers whose arrival is independently attested by transmitted historical records. For a discussion of the geography of Qin burials outside of Guanzhong during the Warring States period, see Zhao 2001: 619–30.

20 The chapter that advocates this program, "Attracting the people" ("Lai min" 徠民), is one of the latest in the *Book of Lord Shang* and probably dates to around 250. This suggests that it may contain reflections on Qin colonization policies that had already been in place for some seventy years by the time the text was composed. For the date of the chapter, see Pines 2016: 17–18.

21 The best known state-managed irrigation scheme carried out in Guanzhong in the mid-third century was the construction of the Zheng Guo Canal 鄭國渠, but it was probably preceded by similar projects on a smaller scale (Lander 2015).

22 For the Qin conquest and colonization of Sichuan, see also Sage 1992: 119–56.

23 For summaries of archaeological evidence of Qin colonization, see Teng 2003: 126–33 and Zhao 2001: 619–30. For the strategic importance of control over the Han River valley and territories to the north of the Middle Yangzi, see Sun 2015a.

24 For military grain rations, see Shuihudi Qin mu zhujian zhengli xiaozu: 82–83, slips 11–15, and Hulsewé 1985: 108–9. For the rations issued to local officials, see, for example, Chen, W. 2012a: 265, tablet 8–1031; 268, tablet 8–1046; 271–72, tablet 8–1063; 297, tablet 8–1238; 313, tablet 8–1345 + 8–2245; 356, tablet 8–1550. In contrast to the Western Han period, there is no record of Qin officials receiving monetized salaries.

25 Excavations in Liye have discovered a Qin ordinance demanding that the distribution of newly opened up land among the farmer households be reported, as well as an actual record of the distribution of such land. See Hunan sheng wenwu kaogu yanjiusuo 2017: 7, tablet 9–40, and Chen, W. 2012a: 345–47, tablet 8–1519.

26 The *Book of Lord Shang* refers to *Yi Zhou shu* 逸周書 (*The Extant Documents of the Zhou*), a collection of texts purportedly dated to the Western Zhou period, many of which were composed much later. See Huang et al. 2007: 2.122.

27 For the construction of Dujiangyan Dam and its impact on agricultural production on the Chengdu Plain, see Sage 1992: 148–50 and Huang et al. 2007: 62.

28 For changes in the taxation rate during the Western Han period, see Hanshu: 24A.1127–1135. For a recent English-language discussion of Qin and Han land taxation, see Lewis 2015: 285–86.

29 For a study of the Qin land taxation system on the basis of excavated textual evidence, see Yamada 1993: 32–59; Yang 2008: 331–42; Yang 2009b: 164–86; Yang 2015a: 119–41; Nan 2001: 236–40.

30 A record of land tax collection in Qianling County excavated at Liye suggests that a mechanism was developed within the Qin land taxation system to make sure that extraction rates did not exceed a certain level, most likely ten percent of estimated crop yields. The actual amounts of tax grain collected from a unit of land differed from district (*xiang* 鄉) to district, so the taxation rate varied between 9.18% of produce in the district immediately surrounding the county town and 7.15% in the remotest of the three districts, with a county average of 8.61%. See Chen, W. 2012a: 345–47, tablet 8–1519.

31 For an attempt to reconstruct the land taxation systems in the "eastern states" on the basis of evidence in the Warring States treatises on policy, political philosophy, and economy like *Guanzi* 管子, *Guoyu* 国語, and *Mengzi* 孟子, see Yang 2008: 338–42.

32 For scribal training in the early empires, see the "Statutes on scribes" (*shi lü* 史律) in the early Western Han collection of statutes, Peng et al. 2007: 295–305, slips 474–87; Barbieri-Low and Yates 2015, vol. 2: 1084–1111. For accounting requirements and deadlines, see, for example, Guo 2011: 86–95.

33 For receipts issued to individual taxpayers, see Chen, Songchang 2015: 149, slips 244–246. This legal article refers to labor service obligations, but tax tallies (*quan* 券) are also frequently mentioned in conjunction with the collection of land and other taxes. I suggest that these tallies served to keep track of the collection of different sorts of taxes in the Qin fiscal system.

34 For large-scale grain imports into Qianling County from other more productive areas of Dongting Commandery, see, for example, Chen, W. 2012a: 369, tablet 8–1618; Chen, W. 2018: 58, tablet 9–63.

35 For the legal regulation of labor services associated with the transportation of tax grain at the beginning of the Western Han period, see Peng et al. 2007: 247–50, slips 408–15; Barbieri-Low and Yates 2015: 900–3.

36 For a very high estimate of two million people mobilized in various imperial projects under the First Emperor and his successor, see Shelach 2014: 131.

37 For the legal regulation prescribing the mobilization of manpower and the resources of wealthier households, see Chen, Songchang 2015: 117, slips 148–150. For the similar early Western Han regulation, see Peng et al. 2007: 248–50, slips 411–15; Barbieri-Low and Yates 2015: 902–3. For the link between the property census and labor mobilization, see Shi 2015: 1–32; Guo 2011: 154–55.

38 The single mention of property tax (*zi shui* 貲稅) in a legal case from the Yuelu Academy collection of Qin documents refers to a market trader who failed to declare her property to the government (Zhu and Chen 2013: 153–65; Lau and Staack 2016: 188–210).

39 See, for example, a circular issued by the governor of Dongting Commandery in 219 BCE that cites an imperial ordinance instructing subordinate officials to refrain from labor mobilizations during the agricultural season (Hunan sheng wenwu kaogu yanjiusuo 2006: 192).

40 Cf. Walter Scheidel's conclusion that in early imperial China the state played a key role in maintaining and operating the system of forced labor (Scheidel 2017b: 133–50).

41 For labor punishments and the system of penal labor in the Qin and Han empires, see Miyake 2016: 60–158. The importance of convict labor is highlighted by numerous excavated documents from the Qin county center at Liye concerning the management of convicts (Gao 2013: 132–43; Korolkov 2015: 132–56).

42 For a study of debtor labor in the Qin Empire, see Korolkov, forthcoming.

43 The extraordinary concentration of convicts, conscripted laborers, and soldiers in Qianling in 216 BCE and the precipitous decline in their numbers in the following years, is revealed by two independent types of documents from Liye that are available in relatively large numbers: (i) the records of rations issued to convicts and servicemen; and (ii) the registers of convict laborers. This concentration can be explained by the empire's preparation for the new round of southward expansion in 215–214, such that manpower was first amassed along the southern frontier before being moved further south.

44 This comment by Qiao Zhou 譙周 (201–270 CE) is quoted in the Tang-era *Suoyin* 索隱 commentary to the *Shiji*. On the relationship between the origins of *fu* and military spending, see Ma 2001: 27–37.

45 For the *hengfu*, see Chen, W. 2012a: 147–48, tablet 8–433. For the *yifu*, see Chen, W. 2012a: 290, tablet 8–1199. This may or may not be the same tax that was paid by tribesmen at the Nan Commandery in the beginning of the Western Han period in lieu of labor service obligations: see Peng et al. 2007: 332, slips 2–3; Barbieri-Low and Yates 2015, vol. 2: 1174–75. For the *yufu*, see Chen, W. 2012a: 384, tablet 8–1735. The You 酉 River basin where Qianling County was located was an important producer of bird feathers used to manufacture arrows; see, for example, Chen, W. 2012a: 82–83, tablet 8–142; 84–89, tablet 8–145; 196–97, tablet 8–663. For the use of feathers in arrow production, see Chen, W. 2012a: 332, tablet 8–1457 + 8–1458. For a discussion of the "feather tax," see Shen 2013: 6–10. For other records of the *fu* levy in Liye documents, see, for example, Chen, W. 2012a: 63, tablet 8–104; 441, tablet 8–2179; 478, tablet 8–2544 (in this later case, the word may be used in its verbal function, "to pay [tribute], to provide [services]").

46 For the spatial organization and administration of the official markets in the Qin and Han empires, see Barbieri-Low 2007: 118–31.

47 While many scholars have argued that *shizu* was an annual market stall rent rather than a tax on the value of sold goods, the opposite opinion has gained currency as more excavated legal documents are becoming available. See Hiranaka 1952: 18–34; Yamada 1993: 408–9; Yang 2015b: 273–88. On the *zhi* authorization fee, see Chen 2012b: 69–79, esp. 72.

48 For an English-language account of the public sector of the Qin economy, see Hulsewé 1987.

49 While very little is known about the organization of the Qin office of the Lesser Treasury, examples from the Western Han period may be illustrative. The introduction to the *Hanshu* "Table of officials and dignitaries" (*bai guan gong qing biao* 百官公卿表), which remains the most detailed outline of the organization of the central government in the Western Han and, by extension, the Qin Empire, mentions many subordinate offices that changed their organizational affiliation from the Privy Purse to the imperial Ministry of Finance (*zhisu neishi* 治粟內史 under the Qin and at the beginning of Han, subsequently renamed to *danongling* 大農令 and then *dasinong* 大司農), the paramount central government office in charge of managing the state economy, as well as between the Privy Purse and other offices of the empire's central government. Consider the example of the *sihu* 寺互 office, which was most likely in charge of weapon or armor manufacturing. It was initially (that is, likely, under the Qin or at the beginning of Western Han) subordinate to the Privy Purse but was eventually resubordinated to the central government's office of the Commander of the Middle (*zhong wei* 中尉), charged with the security of the capital region, for which see Hanshu: 19A.732–733. While such changes in subordination most likely served the goal of coordinating military production under the officer responsible for the defense of the capital, it also seems likely that the *sihu* workshops supplied imperial troops even when they were still part of the Privy Purse establishment. The same is probably true of the numerous other workshops under the Privy Purse that contributed to the armament and maintenance of the empire's troops, costs that in principle had to be paid from state coffers rather than from those of the imperial household. There are other such examples.

50 As suggested by Lewis, who draws no distinction between the Qin and Han fiscal regimes (Lewis 2015: 282–307). For high transportation costs in the early Chinese empire compared to the Mediterranean world as a factor in the less aggressive transfer of revenue in the Han than in the Roman Empire, see Scheidel 2015: 178–80. While having a sea to connect its far-flung territorial possessions was certainly an enormous logistical advantage for any premodern empire, the "spatial circumscription" (to use Lewis's term) of early Chinese empires appears to be overstated in light of the recently excavated itineraries and other documents attesting to long-distance riverine transportation of bulky cargo, including grain shipments between the Yangzi and Yellow River basins.

51 Ration receipts from Liye demonstrate that low-ranking functionaries received the same amounts of grain as convicts and conscripted laborers and soldiers, for which see Huang 2015.

52 For a general discussion of the transition from a rank-based social hierarchy to one based on official position, see Yan 2009.

53 Yamada, for example, believes that a number of (still poorly understood) administrative reforms were implemented in the state of Qin around 227 when it was

already halfway through the process of eliminating other Warring States. Yamada also argues convincingly that the expansion of the Qin state into the regions of rice agriculture was accompanied by the introduction of a new legal form, "ordinances on agriculture" (or fields, *tian ling* 田令), as opposed to the statutes on agriculture (or fields, *tian lü*) designed for Guanzhong with its crops of millet and wheat. These ordinances addressed the specific environmental and social conditions of the newly conquered lands in the Yangzi basin (Yamada 1993: 46–52).

54 For some recent studies of the organization of county government and its division into offices and bureaus, see, for example, Tsuchiguchi 2015: 1–38; Zou 2016: 132–46; Li and Tang 2016: 131–58; Sun 2018: 71–120.

55 I adopt the translation of the Qin military rank *dun (tun) zhang* 敦（屯）長 proposed in Hulsewé 1985: 108.

56 The statute on officials' salaries in the early Western Han legal collection is limited to the regions under the direct control of the central government, implying that officials in regional princedoms were remunerated by their respective sovereigns rather than by the emperor (Chen 2004: 33–35). For the text of the statute, see Peng et al. 2007: 257–95, slips 440–73; Barbieri-Low and Yates 2015, vol. 2: 951–1083. The salaries of officials were one of the major items of government expenditure (Scheidel 2015). For attempts by local lords to attract immigrants by reducing the fiscal burden, see, for example, Shiji: 106.2822.

57 For the legal reforms during the reigns of Empress Lü (195–180) and Emperor Wen (180–157) that were intended to reduce the numbers of convict laborers and economize on their maintenance, see Miyake 2016: 140–58. For the abolition of universal military service, see Lewis 2000.

58 For some recent contributions, see Watanabe 2010; Guo 2011; Cang 2012; Lewis 2015; Glahn 2016: 100–20.

59 Local administrations in the Qin Empire were permitted to lease convicts in their custody to private individuals to economize on their provisioning. Conversely, when additional labor was needed, it could be acquired in the market through the purchase of slaves (Shuihudi Qin mu zhujian zhengli xiaozu 1990: 32, slip 48; Chen, W. 2012a: 306–7, tablet 8–1287; 367, tablet 8–1604).

60 Many important details of *gengfu* are still debated, such as the amount of tax that had to be paid and the definition of the social groups that were obliged to pay it. See, for example, Gao 1982: 77.

61 Note the difference in the legal treatment of trespassing on other people's land while grazing one's cattle. While the Qin statute stipulated confiscation of livestock, an identical Han regulation required the payment of a monetary fine, suggesting that the state was no longer interested in increasing the size of its herds (Zhongguo wenwu yanjiusuo 2001: 107, slip 102; Peng et al. 2007: 192–93, slips 253–54).

62 For the political history of the early Western Han period, see Loewe 1986: 110–52.

63 For the application of a fixed-rate land tax in the eastern part of the Warring States world, see Yang 2008.

64 For Emperor Gao's avowed commitment to the simplification of Qin's legal system, see, for example, Hanshu: 23.1096.

65 See, for example, Ru Chun's 如淳 (third century CE) commentary to the *Hanshu* record about the introduction of *suanfu* tax in the Han Empire, in Hanshu: 1A.46.

66 For an overview, see Nishijima 1986: 593.

67 In his decree dated to 49, Emperor Xuan complained that provincial officials submitted falsified accounts (Hanshu: 8.273). The emperor had no effective way of dealing with this problem. Neither did his successors.

68 During the "revolt of seven feudatories," most of the fighting took place between rebellious and loyal regional lords with limited involvement of the central government's forces (Loewe 1986: 141–42).

69 For a detailed account of Emperor Wu's campaigns in the north and his expeditions to Central Asia, and for an estimate of their costs, see Chang 2007.

70 The most detailed account of these debates is the "Discourse on Salt and Iron" (*Yantielun* 鹽鐵論) by Huan Kuan 桓寬, which records the dispute between the advocates and critics of Emperor Wu's fiscal policies. The dispute took place at the court of Emperor Zhao 昭帝 (87–74) in 81 (Wang 2011).

71 A group of bureaucrats dispatched to commanderies to enforce the new laws became known as "cruel officials" (*kuli* 酷吏), reflecting the regional élite's attitude toward Emperor Wu's fiscal policies (Shiji: 122.3135–3154).

72 The early Western Han collection of legal statutes excavated at Zhangjiashan include a statute on equitable delivery (*junshu lü* 均輸律) (Peng et al. 2007: 180–82, slips 225–27; Barbieri-Low and Yates 2015, vol. 2: 667–77). The term also appears in the recently published Qin documents from Liye, where it refers to the distribution of convict laborers inside the Dongting Commandery. See Hunan sheng wenwu kaogu yanjiusuo 2017: 6, tablet 9–23. The term is also mentioned in the Qin "Statute on absconding" from the Yuelu Academy collection, see Chen, Songchang 2015: 42, slip 10. The titles of some Qin officials contain possible references to responsibilities associated with "equitable delivery" (Zhang 2012; Barbieri-Low and Yates 2015, vol. 2: 670, n. 6).

73 For the revival of mercantilist fiscal policies and taxation of commerce under the Northern Song, see Glahn 2016: 226–35. For taxation in the late empires, see Deng 2015.

74 For a recent analysis that identifies violence and particularly mass warfare as the major driver of wealth equalization, see Scheidel 2017a. In China's case, more specifically, scholars observed that mass peasant warfare at the end of the "dynastic cycles" "contributed to the improvement of the commoners' lot," for which see Pines 2012: 161.

75 The early Ming Empire presents one of the most vivid examples of the reproduction of fiscal institutions developed during the first fiscal transition (Huang 1998; Glahn 2016: 285–88). Another and more recent incarnation of the

Qin-style command economy occurred in the course of the communist reconstruction of the Chinese economy and society in the 1950s, which was accompanied by strong ideological references to the Qin reformer Shang Yang and the First Emperor of Qin (Teiwes 1987; Pines 2017: 109–10).

WORKS CITED

Barbieri-Low, Anthony. 2007. *Artisans in Early Imperial China*. Seattle and London: University of Washington Press.

Barbieri-Low, Anthony, and Robin D. S. Yates. 2015. *Law, State, and Society in Early Imperial China: A Study with Critical Edition and Translation of the Legal Texts from Zhangjiashan Tomb no. 247*. Leiden: Brill.

Cai, Wanjin 蔡萬進. 2009. *Qin guo liangshi jingji yanjiu* 秦國糧食經濟研究 [*Studies in the grain economy of the Qin state*]. Zhengzhou: Daxiang.

Cang, Zhifei 臧知非. 2012. *Qin Han fuyi yu shehui kongzhi* 秦漢賦役與社會控制 [Taxation and social control under Qin and Han empires]. Xi'an: Sanqin.

Chang, Chun-shu. 2007. *The Rise of the Chinese Empire*. Vol. 2: *Frontier, Immigration, and Empire in Han China, 130 B.C.—A.D. 157*. Ann Arbor: University of Michigan Press.

Chen, Songchang 陳松長. 2015. *Yuelu shuyuan cang Qin jian* 岳麓書院藏秦簡 [*Qin bamboo slips from the Yuelu Academy collection*]. Vol. 4. Shanghai: Shanghai cishu.

Chen, Songchang 陳松長. 2017. *Yuelu shuyuan cang Qin jian*. Vol. 5. Shanghai: Shanghai cishu.

Chen, Suzhen 陳蘇鎮. 2004. "Hanchu wangguo zhidu kaoshu" 漢初王國制度考述 [A study of the princedom system of the Early Han]. *Zhongguo shi yanjiu* 中國史研究 3: 27–40.

Chen, Wei 2012a. *Liye Qin jiandu jiaoshi* 里耶秦簡牘校釋 [*Annotated edition of the Qin documents on wooden slips from Liye*]. Vol. 1. Wuhan: Wuhan daxue.

Chen, Wei. 2012b. "Guanyu Qin yu Han chu "ru qian xiang zhong" lü de jige wenti" 關於秦與漢初"入錢缿中"律的幾個問題 [On some problems related to the Qin and early Han legal article on "the money that has to be entered into the cash jar"]. *Kaogu* 考古 8: 69–79.

Chen, Wei. 2018. *Liye Qin jiandu jiaoshi* 里耶秦簡牘校釋 [Annotated edition of the Qin documents on wooden slips from Liye]. Vol. 2. Wuhan: Wuhan daxue.

Deng, Kent Gang. 2015. "Imperial China under the Song and late Qing." In A. Monson and W. Scheidel (eds.), *Fiscal Regimes and the Political Economy of Premodern States* (Cambridge: Cambridge University Press), 308–41.

Falkenhausen, Lothar von. 2006. *Chinese Society in the Age of Confucius (1000–250 BC): The Archaeological Evidence*. Los Angeles: Cotsen Institute of Archaeology, University of California.

Falkenhausen, Lothar von, and Gideon Shelach. 2014. "Introduction: Archaeological Perspectives on the Qin 'Unification' of China." In Y. Pines et al. (eds.), *Birth of an Empire: The State of Qin Revisited*. Berkeley (Los Angeles: University of California Press), 37–51.

Fujita, Katsuhisa. 2008. Shiji *Zhanguo shiliao yanjiu*《史記》戰國史料研究 [*A study of the Warring States materials in the* Shiji]. Shanghai: Shanghai guji.

Gansu sheng wenwu kaogu yanjiusuo 甘肅省文物考古研究所, Gansu sheng bowuguan 甘肅省博物館, Wenhuabu guwenxian yanjiushi 文化部古文獻研究室 and Zhongguo shehui kexueyuan lishi yanjiusuo 中國社會科學院歷史研究所, eds. 1990. *Juyan xinjian* 居延新簡 [*New documents on wooden slips from Juyan*]. Beijing: Wenwu.

Gao, Dalun 高大倫. 1998. "Yinwan Han mu mudu "jibu" zhong hukou tongji ziliao yanjiu" 尹灣漢墓木牘"集簿"中戶口統計資料研究 [A study of household data in the "Collected registers" on a wooden tablet from the Han tomb at Yinwan]. *Lishi yanjiu* 歷史研究 5: 110–23.

Gao, Min 高敏. 1982. *Qin Han shi lunji* 秦漢史論集 [*Collected studies in Qin and Han history*]. Zhengzhou: Zhongzhou shuhuashe.

Gao, Min. 1983. "Cong Jiangling Fenghuangshan shihao Han mu chutu jiandu kan Handai de kouqian, suanfu zhidu" 從江陵鳳凰山十號漢墓出土簡牘看漢代的口錢、算賦制度 [Capitation tax system of the Han era as reflected in the documents excavated from the Han tomb no. 10 at Fenghuangshan, Jiangling Municipality]. *Wenshi* 文史 20: 25–39.

Gao, Zhenhuan 高震寰. 2013. "Cong *Liye Qin jian (yi)* "zuotu bu" guankui Qin dai xingtu zhidu" 從《里耶秦簡（壹）》管窺秦代刑徒制度 [Viewing the convict labor regime during the Qin period from the "registers of convict laborers" in the *Liye Qin jian*, vol. 1]. *Chutu wenxian yanjiu* 出土文獻研究 14: 132–43.

Glahn, Richard von. 2016. *The Economic History of China: From Antiquity to the Nineteenth Century*. Cambridge: Cambridge University Press.

Guo, Hao 郭浩. 2011. *Handai difang caizheng yanjiu* 漢代地方財政研究 [*A study of local finances during the Han Dynasty*]. Jinan: Shandong daxue.

Hanshu 漢書 [*The Records of Han*]. 12 vols. Beijing: Zhonghua, 1962.

Hiranaka, Reiji 平中苓次. 1952. "Kandai no eigyō to "senzo" ni tsuite" 漢代の営業と「占租」について [On commerce and "self-reporting for taxation purpose" during the Han period]. *Ritsumeikan bungaku* 立命館文学 86: 18–34.

Hou Hanshu 後漢書 [*The Records of Latter Han*]. 12 vols. Beijing: Zhonghua, 1965.

Hsing, I-tien. 2014. "Qin-Han Census and Tax and corvée Administration: Notes on Newly Discovered Materials." In Y. Pines et al. (eds.), *Birth of an Empire: The State of Qin Revisited*. Berkeley (Los Angeles: University of California Press), 155–86.

Huang, Huaixin, et al. 2007. *Yizhoushu huijiao jizhu* 逸周書彙校集注 [*Collected editions and annotations of the* Yizhoushu]. Shanghai: Shanghai guji.

Huang, Ray. 1998. "The Ming fiscal administration." In D. Twitchett and F. Mote (eds.), *The Cambridge History of China*. Vol. 8: *The Ming Dynasty, 1368–1644. Part 2* (Cambridge: Cambridge University Press), 106–71.

Huang, Haobo 黃浩波. 2015. *Liye Qin jian (yi)* suojian linshi jilu 《里耶秦簡（一）》所見稟食記錄 [Records of grain rations in *Liye Qin jian*, vol. 1]. *Jianbo* 11: 117–39.

Hubei sheng wenwu kaogu yanjiu suo 湖北省文物考古研究所. 2012. *Jiangling Fenghuangshan Xi Han jiandu* 江陵鳳凰山西漢簡牘 [*Western Han documents on bamboo and wood from Fenghuangshan, Jiangling*]. Beijing: Zhonghua.

Hulsewé, Anthony. 1985. *Remnants of Ch'in Law: An Annotated Translation of the Ch'in Legal and Administrative Rules of the 3ʳᵈ Century B.C. Discovered in Yün-meng Prefecture, Hu-pei Province, in 1975*. Leiden: Brill.

Hulsewé, Anthony. 1987. "The Influence of the 'Legalist' Government of Qin on the Economy as Reflected in the Texts Discovered in Yunmeng County." In S. R. Schram (ed.), *Foundations and Limits of State Power in China* (Hong Kong: Chinese University Press)., 211–35.

Hunan sheng wenwu kaogu yanjiusuo 湖南省文物考古研究所. 2006. *Liye fajue baogao* 里耶發掘報告 [*Excavation report on Liye*]. Changsha: Yuelu shuyuan.

Hunan sheng wenwu kaogu yanjiusuo 2017. *Liye Qin jian (er)* 里耶秦簡 (貳) [*Qin documents from Liye, vol. 2*]. Beijing: Wenwu.

Jiang, Lihong 蔣禮鴻 1986. *Shangjun shu zhuizhi* 商君書錐指 [*The Book of Lord Shang, edited and annotated*]. Beijing: Zhonghua.

Kakinuma, Yōhei 柿沼陽平. 2011. *Chūgoku kodai kahei keizaishi kenkyū* 中国古代貨幣経済史研究 [*A study of the history of monetary economy in ancient China*]. Tokyo: Kyūko Shoten.

Kakinuma, Yōhei. 2015. *Chūgoku kodai no kahei* 中国古代の貨幣 [*Currency in ancient China*]. Tokyo: Yoshikawa Hironikan.

Korolkov, Maxim. 2012. "Greeting Tablets" in Early China: Some Traits of the Communicative Etiquette of Officialdom in Light of Newly Excavated Inscriptions." *T'oung Pao* 98: 295–348.

Korolkov, Maxim. 2015. "Convict Labor in the Qin Empire: A Preliminary Study of the "Register of Convict Laborers" from Liye." In Fudan daxue lishixue xi 復旦大學歷史學系 and Fudan daxue chutu wenxian yu guwenzi yanjiu zhongxin 復旦大學出土文獻與古文字研究中心, (eds.), *Jianbo wenxian yu gudaishi: di er jie chutu wenxian qingnian xuezhe guoji luntan lunwenji* 簡帛文獻與古代史：第二屆出土文獻青年學者國際論壇論文集 [*Manuscripts on Bamboo and Silk and Ancient History: The Proceedings of the Second Young Scholars International Conference on Excavated Manuscripts*] (Shanghai: Zhongxi), 132–56.

Korolkov, Maxim. Forthcoming. "Between Command and Market: Credit, Labor and Accounting in the Qin Empire (221–207 B.C.E.)." In E. Sabattini and C. Schwermann (eds.), *Between Command and Market: Economic Thought and Practice in Early China* (Leiden and Boston: Brill).

Lander, Brian. 2015. "Environmental Change and the Rise of the Qin Empire: A Political Ecology on Ancient North China." Ph.D. dissertation, Columbia University.

Lau, Ulrich, and Thies Staack. 2016. *Legal Practice in the Formative Stages of the Chinese Empire: An Annotated Translation of the Exemplary Qin Criminal Cases from the Yuelu Academy Collection*. Leiden and Boston: Brill.

Leeming, Frank. 1980. "Official Landscapes in Traditional China." *Journal of the Economic and Social History of the Orient* 23, no. 1/2: 153–204.

Lewis, Mark. 1999. "Warring States Political History." In M. Loewe and E. Shaughnessy (eds.), *The Cambridge History of Ancient China: From the Origins of Civilization to 221 B.C.* (Cambridge: Cambridge University Press), 587–650.

Lewis, Mark. 2000. "The Han Abolition of Universal Military Service." In H. van de Ven (ed.), *Warfare in Chinese History* (Leiden: Brill), 35–76.

Lewis, Mark. 2015. "Early Imperial China, from the Qin and Han through Tang." In A. Monson and W. Scheidel (eds.), *Fiscal Regimes and the Political Economy of Premodern States* (Cambridge: Cambridge University Press), 282–307.

Li, Feng. 2006. *Landscape and Power in Early China: The Crisis and Fall of the Western Zhou, 1045–771 BC*. Cambridge: Cambridge University Press.

Li, Feng. 2008. *Bureaucracy and the State in Early China: Governing the Western Zhou*. Cambridge: Cambridge University Press.

Li, Li 李力. 2007. *"Lichenqie" shenfen zaiyanjiu* "隸臣妾"身份再研究 [*The "lichenqie" status revisited*]. Beijing: Zhongguo fazhi.

Li, Mingzhao 黎明釗. 2009. "Liye Qin jian: huji dang'an de tantao" 里耶秦簡：戶籍檔案的探討 [Qin documents from Liye: A study of an archive of household registers]. *Zhongguo shi yanjiu* 2: 5–23.

Li, Mingzhao, and Tang Junfeng 唐俊峰 (Chun Fung Tong). 2016. "Liye Qin jian suojian Qin dai xian guan, cao zuzhi de zhineng fenye yu xingzheng hudong—yi ji, ke wei zhongxin" 里耶秦簡所見秦代縣官、曹組織的職能分野與行政互動——以計、課為中心 [Functional differentiation and administrative interaction between the office and bureau organizations in the Qin counties as reflected by the Qin documents from Liye, with the focus on the account and evaluation documents]. *Wuhan daxue jianbo yanjiu zhongxin* 武漢大學簡帛研究中心, *Jianbo* 13: 131–58.

Lianyungang shi bowuguan 連雲港市博物館, Donghai xian bowuguan 東海縣博物館, Zhongguo shehui kexueyuan jianbo yanjiu zhongxin 中國社會科學院簡帛研究中心 and Zhongguo wenwu yanjiusuo 中國文物研究所. 1997. *Yinwan Han mu jiandu* 尹灣漢墓簡牘 [*Manuscripts on bamboo and wood from the Han tomb at Yinwan*]. Beijing: Zhonghua.

Liao, Boyuan 廖伯源. 2000. *Jiandu yu zhidu* 簡牘與制度 [*Documents on bamboo and wood and the political regime*]. Guilin: Guangxi shifan daxue.

Lim, Byeong-Deog 林炳德. 2006. "Qin Han de guan nubi he Han Wen-di xingzhi gaige" 秦漢的官奴婢和漢文帝刑制改革 [State-owned slaves during the Qin and Han periods and Han Emperor Wen's reform of penal regime]. In Bu Xianqun 卜憲群 and Yang Zhenhong 楊振紅 (eds.), 簡帛研究 [*Studies in the bamboo and silk manuscripts*] (Guilin: Guangxi shifan daxue), 90–103.

Liye Qin jiandu bowuguan 里耶秦簡牘博物館, Zhongguo renmin daxue guoxueyuan 中國人民大學國學院 and Zhongguo renmin daxue lishi xueyuan 中國人民大學歷史學院 (eds.). 2016. *Liye Qin jiandu bowuguan cang Qin jian* 里耶秦簡牘博物館藏秦簡 [*Qin documents stored at the Liye museum of Qin documents*]. Shanghai: Zhongxi.

Loewe, Michael. 1986. "The Former Han Dynasty." In D. Twitchett M. Loewe (eds.), *The Cambridge History of China*. Vol. 1: *The Ch'in and Han Empires, 221 B.C.—A.D. 220* (Cambridge: Cambridge University Press), 103–222.

Ma, Yi 馬怡. 2001. "Handai de zhufu yu junfei" 漢代的諸賦與軍費 [*Fu* levies and military spending during the Han era]. *Zhongguo shi yanjiu* 3: 27–37.

Miyake, Kiyoshi 宮宅潔. 2013. "Handai guanliao zuzhi de zuixia ceng—'guan' yu 'min' zhijian" 漢代官僚組織的最下層—"官"與"民"之間 [The Lowest Tier of the Han Bureaucratic Organization—Between 'Officials' and 'People']. *Zhongguo gudai falü wenxian yanjiu* 中國古代法律文獻研究 7: 127–61.

Miyake, Kiyoshi. 2016. "Laoyixing tixi de jiegou yu bianqian" 勞役刑體系的結構與變遷 [Structure and evolution of the system of penal labor]. In K. Miyake (ed.), *Zhongguo gudai xingzhi shi yanjiu* 中國古代刑制史研究 [*Studies in the penal system in ancient China*]. Transl. Yang Zhenhong et al. (Guilin: Guangxi shifan daxue), 60–158.

Nan, Yuquan 南玉泉. 2001. "Longgang Qin jian suo jian chengtian zhidu jiqi xiangguan wenti" 龍崗秦簡所見程田制度及其相關問題 [Regime of "norms for the fields" reflected in the Qin documents from Longgang and related questions]. In X. Li李學勤 and X. Guihua 謝桂華 (eds.), *Jianbo yanjiu* 2001 (Guilin: Guangxi shifan daxue), 236–40.

Nishijima, Sadao. 1986. "The Economic and Social History of Former Han." In D. Twitchett M. Loewe (eds.), *The Cambridge History of China*. Vol. 1: *The Ch'in and Han Empires, 221 B.C.—A.D. 220* (Cambridge: Cambridge University Press), 545–607.

Peng, Hao 彭浩, Chen Wei 陳偉 and Kudō Motoo 工藤元男, 2007. *Ernian lüling yu Zouyanshu: Zhangjiashan ersiqihao Han mu chutu falü wenxian shidu* 二年律令與奏讞書：張家山二四七號漢墓出土法律文獻釋讀 [*The Statutes and Ordinances of the Second Year and The Collected Cases Submitted for Revision: Annotated Legal Manuscripts Excavated from the Han Tomb No. 247 at Zhangjiashan*]. Shanghai: Shanghai guji.

Peng, Hao. 2009. "Du Liye Qin jian "jiaoquan" buji 讀里耶秦簡"校券"補記 [Notes on the "control tallies" among the Qin documents from Liye]. In Zhongguo shehui kexueyuan kaogu yanjiusuo 中國社會科學院考古研究所, Zhongguo shehui kexueyuan lishi yanjiusuo 中國社會科學院歷史研究所 and Hunan sheng wenwu kaogu yanjiusuo (eds.), *Liye gucheng, Qin jian yu Qin wenhua yanjiu: Zhongguo Liye gucheng, Qin jian yu Qin wenhua guoji xueshu yantaohui lunwenji* 里耶古城、秦簡與秦文化研究：中國里耶古城、秦簡與秦文化國際學術研討會論文集 [*Studies on the ancient town of Liye, Qin documents and Qin culture: Proceedings of the international conference on China's ancient town of Liye, Qin documents and Qin culture*] (Beijing: Kexue), 196–200.

Pines, Yuri. 2005–2006. "Biases and Their Sources: Qin History in the *Shiji*." *Oriens Extremus* 45: 10–34.

Pines, Yuri. 2012. *The Everlasting Empire: The Political Culture of Ancient China and its Imperial Legacy*. Princeton: Princeton University Press.

Pines, Yuri. 2016. "Dating a Pre-Imperial Text: The Case Study of the *Book of Lord Shang*." *Early China* 39: 1–40.

Pines, Yuri. 2017. *The Book of Lord Shang: Apologetics of State Power in Early China*. New York: Columbia University Press.

Pines, Yuri. Forthcoming. "Waging a Demographic War: Chapter 15 ("Attracting the People") of the *Book of Lord Shang* Revisited"

Qiu, Xigui 裘錫圭. 1974. "Hubei Jiangling Fenghuangshan shihao Han mu chutu jiandu kaoshi" 湖北江陵鳳凰山十號漢墓出土簡牘考釋 [A study of documents excavated

from tomb no. 10 at Fenghuangshan, Jiangling Municipality, Hubei Province].
Wenwu 7: 49–63.

Sage, Steven. 1992. *Ancient Sichuan and the Unification of China*. Albany: State University of New York Press.

Sanft, Charles. 2014. "Paleographic Evidence of Qin Religious Practice from Liye and Zhoujiatai." *Early China* 37: 327–58.

Scheidel, Walter. 2015. "State Revenue and Expenditure in the Han and Roman Empires." In W. Scheidel (ed.), *State Power in Ancient China and Rome* (Oxford: Oxford University Press), 150–80.

Scheidel, Walter. 2017a. *The Great Leveler: Violence and History of Inequality from the Stone Age to the Twenty-First Century*. Princeton: Princeton University Press.

Scheidel, Walter. 2017b. "Slavery and Forced Labor in Early China and the Roman World." In H. J. Kim, F. Vervaet, and S. F. Adali (eds.), *Eurasian Empires in Antiquity and the Early Middle Ages: Contact and Exchange between the Graeco-Roman World, Inner Asia and China* (Cambridge: Cambridge University Press), 133–50.

Shelach, Gideon. 2014. "Collapse or transformation? Anthropological and archaeological perspectives on the fall of Qin." In Y. Pines et al. (eds.), *Birth of an Empire: The State of Qin Revisited*. Berkeley (Los Angeles: University of California Press), 113–38.

Shelach, Gideon. 2015. *The Archaeology of Early China: From Prehistory to the Han Dynasty*. Cambridge: Cambridge University Press.

Shelach, Gideon, and Yuri Pines. 2006. "Secondary State Formation and the Development of Local Identity: Change and Continuity in the State of Qin (770–221 B.C.)." In M. Stark (ed.), *Archaeology in Asia* (Malden: Blackwell), 202–30.

Shen, Gang 沈剛. 2013 "Gong", "fu" zhijian—shilun *Liye Qin jian (yi)* zhong de "qiu yu" jian "貢""賦"之間——試論《里耶秦簡》【壹】中的"求羽"簡 [Between "tribute" and "tax": A preliminary discussion of the documents concerning the "procurement of feathers" in the first volume of the *Qin documents from Liye*]. *Zhongguo shehui jingji shi yanjiu* 中國社會經濟史研究 4: 6–10.

Shi, Yang 石洋. 2015. "Qin Han caichan diaocha zhidu chutan" 秦漢財產調查研究初探 [A preliminary study of the property census regime under Qin and Han]. *Hanxue yanjiu* 漢學研究 33.1: 1–32.

Shiji 史記 [*Records of the Grand Historian*]. 10 vols. Beijing: Zhonghua, 1959.

Shuihudi Qin mu zhujian zhengli xiaozu 睡虎地秦墓竹簡整理小組 (ed.). 1990. *Shuihudi Qin mu zhujian* 睡虎地秦墓竹簡 [*Bamboo Slips from the Qin Tomb at Shuihudi*]. Beijing: Wenwu.

Sichuan sheng bowuguan 四川省博物館 and Qingchuan xian wenhuaguan 青川縣文化館. 1982. "Qingchuan xian chutu Qin gengxiu tianlü mudu" 青川縣出土秦更修田律木牘 [A wooden tablet with the Qin statute on the change in the field system excavated at Qingchuan County]. *Wenwu* 1: 1–21.

Sun, Kai 孫楷. 2004. *Qin Huiyao* 秦會要 [*Essentials of the Qin*]. Shanghai: Shanghai guji.

Sun, Wenbo. 2015a. "Qin ju Hanshui yu Nan-jun zhi zhi—yi junshi jiaotong yu zaoqi junzhi wei shijiao de kaocha" 秦據漢水與南郡之置－以軍事交通與早期郡制為視角的

考察 [Qin control over the Han River basin and the establishment of Nan Commandery: A study of the military transportation and early stages of commandery administrative regime]. In L. Zeng 曾磊, S. Wenbo, X. Chang 徐暢, and L. Lanfang 李蘭芳 (eds.), *Feiling guanglu: Zhongguo gudai jiaotong shi lunji* 飛軨廣路：中國古代交通史論集 [*Flying bells and wide road: Collected studies in the ancient history of transportation in China*] (Beijing: Zhongguo shehui kexueyuan), 42–66.

Sun, Wenbo. 2015b. "Qin ji Han chu de sikou yu tuli" 秦及漢初的司寇與徒隸 [*Sikou* and convicts during the Qin period and in the beginning of Han]. *Zhongguo shi yanjiu* 3: 73–96.

Sun, Wenbo. 2018. "Bureaus and Offices in Qin County-Level Administration in Light of an Excerpt from the Lost *Hongfan wuxing zhuan (Great Plan Five Phases Commentary)*", C. Wei and E. Shaughnessy (eds.), *Bamboo and Silk* 1: 71–120.

Teiwes, Frederick. 1987. "Establishment and Consolidation of the New Regime." In R. MacFarquhar and J. Fairbank (eds.), *The Cambridge History of China*. Vol. 14: *The People's Republic*. Part I: *The Emergence of Revolutionary China 1949–1965* (Cambridge: Cambridge University Press), 51–143.

Teng, Mingyu 滕銘予. 2003. *Qin wenhua: cong fengguo dao diguo de kaoguxue guancha* 秦文化：從封國到帝國的考古學觀察 [*The Qin Culture: An Archaeological Study of the Transition from a Vassal State to the Empire*]. Beijing: Xueyuan.

Teng, Mingyu. 2014. "From Vassal State to Empire: An Archaeological Examination of Qin Culture." In Y. Pines et al. (eds.), *Birth of an Empire: The State of Qin Revisited*. Berkeley (Los Angeles: University of California Press), 71–112.

Tilly, Charles. 1990. *Coercion, Capital, and European States, AD 990–1990*. Cambridge, MA: Basil Blackwell.

Tsuchiguchi, Fuminori 土口史記. 2015. "Riye Shin kan ni miru Shin dai kenshita no kansei kōzō" 里耶秦簡にみる秦代県下の官制構造 [Sub-county administrative organization under the Qin Dynasty as reflected in the Liye Qin documents]. *Tōyō shi kenkyū* 東洋史研究 73.4: 1–38.

Wang, Helen. 2007. "Official Salaries and Local Wages at Juyan, North-West China, First Century BCE to First Century CE." In L. Lucassen (ed.), *Wages and Currency: Global Comparisons from Antiquity to the Twentieth Century* (Bern and Berlin: Peter Lang), 59–76.

Wang, Liqi 王利器. 2011. *Yantielun* 鹽鐵論 [*Dispute on Salt and Iron*]. Beijing: Zhonghua.

Watanabe, Shinichiro. 2010. *Chūgoku kodai no zaisei to kokka* 中国古代の財政と国家 [*Finance and state in ancient China*]. Tokyo: Kyoko shoin.

Wu Wenling 鄔文玲. 2013. "Liye Qin jian suojian "hufu" ji xiangguan wenti suoyi" 里耶秦簡所見"戶賦"及相關問題瑣議 [A preliminary study of the questions related to the "household levy" in the Qin documents from Liye]. *Jianbo* 8: 215–28.

Xin, Deyong 辛德勇. 2013a. "Beijing daxue cang Qin shuilu licheng jiance de xingzhi he niming wenti" 北京大學藏秦水陸里程簡冊的性質和擬名問題 [To the questions of nature and title of the records of distances along the water and overland routes in the Peking University collection of Qin documents]. *Jianbo* 8: 17–27.

Xin, Deyong. 2013b. "Beijing daxue cang Qin shuilu licheng jiance chubu yanjiu" 北京大學藏秦水陸里程簡策初步研究 [A preliminary study of the Qin mileage chart on bamboo slips from the Peking University collection]. *Chutu wenxian* 4: 177–279.

Yamada, Katsuyoshi 山田勝芳. 1993. *Shin Kan zaisei shūnyū no kenkyū* 秦漢財政収入の研究 [*Studies in financial income and expenditure in the Qin and Han empires*]. Tokyo: Kyūko shoin.

Yan, Buke 閻步克. 2009. *Cong jue ben wei dao guan ben wei: Qin Han guanliao pinwei jiegou yanjiu* 從爵本位到官本位：秦漢官僚品位結構研究 [*From the rank-defined social status to office-defined social status: A study of the structure of bureaucratic status in the Qin and Han periods*]. Beijing: Sanlian.

Yan, Gengwang 嚴耕望. 1961. *Zhongguo difang xingzheng zhidu shi* 中國地方行政制度史 [*A history of local administrative regime in China*]. Vol. 1: *Qin Han difang xingzheng zhidu* 秦漢地方行政制度 [*Local administrative regime in the Qin and Han empires*]. Taipei: Zhongyang yanjiuyuan lishi yuyan yanjiusuo.

Yang, Kuan 楊寬. 2003. *Zhanguo shi* 戰國史 [*History of the Warring States*]. Shanghai: Shanghai renmin.

Yang, Zhenhong 楊振紅. 2008. "Cong xinchu jiandu kan Qin Han shiqi de tianzu zhengshou" 從新出簡牘看秦漢時期的田租徵收 [Land tax collection during the Qin and Han periods as reflected in newly excavated documents on bamboo and wood]. *Jianbo* 3: 331–42.

Yang, Zhenhong. 2009a. "*Ernian lüling* yu Qin Han "ming tian zhai zhi"《二年律令》與秦漢"名田宅制" ["Statutes and ordinances of the second year" and land allocation regime under the Qin and Han empires]. In Z. Yang (ed.e), *Chutu jiandu yu Qin Han shehui* 出土簡牘與秦漢社會 [*Excavated documents and the Qin-Han society*] (Guilin: Guangxi shifan daxue), 126–63.

Yang, Zhenhong. 2009b. "Longgang Qin jian zhu "tian", "zu" jian shiyi buzheng" 龍崗秦簡諸"田"、"租"簡釋義補正 [New interpretation of the Longgang fragments with graphs "tian" and "zu"]. In Z. Yang (eds.), *Chutu jiandu yu Qin Han shehui* 出土簡牘與秦漢社會 [*Excavated documents and the Qin-Han society*] (Guilin: Guangxi shifan daxue), 164–86.

Yang, Zhenhong. 2015a. "Qin Han shiqi de tianzu zhengshou" 秦漢時期的田租徵收 [Collection of the land tax in the Qin and Han periods]. In Z. Yang (ed.), *Chutu jiandu yu Qin Han shehui (xubian)* 出土簡牘與秦漢社會（續編）[*Excavated documents and the Qin-Han society (part two)*] (Guilin: Guangxi shifan daxue), 119–41.

Yang, Zhenhong. 2015b. "Qin Han shiqi de shi zu" 秦漢時期的市租 [Market tax during the Qin and Han periods]. In Z. Yang (ed.), *Chutu jiandu yu Qin Han shehui (xubian)* 出土简牍与秦汉社会. 续编 (Guilin: Guangxi shi fan da xue chu ban she), 273–88.

Yates, Robin D. S. 1997. "The City-State in Ancient China." In D. Nichols and T. Charlton (eds.), *The Archaeology of City-States: Cross-Cultural Approaches* (Washington, DC: Smithsonian Institution Press), 71–90.

You, Yifei 游逸飛. 2009. "Shuo "ji chengdan chong"—Qin Han xingqi zhidu xinlun" 說"繫城旦舂"——秦漢刑期制度新論 [On the 'detained among the wall-builders and grain-pounders'—A new analysis of the duration of penal labor sentences under the Qin and Han]. *Xin shixue* 新史學 20.3: 1–52.

Zhang, Chunlong 張春龍. 2012. "Liye Qin jian dijiu ceng xuandu" 里耶秦簡第九層選讀 [Selected readings from the ninth layer of Qin documents from Liye]. Paper presented at the International Workshop on the Study of Chinese Manuscripts Written on Bamboo Slips and Silk 2012: Studies on Qin Manuscripts Written on Bamboo Slips and Silk 中國簡帛學國際論壇2012：秦簡牘研究. Wuhan University, China.

Zhao, Huacheng 趙化成. 2001. "Qin tongyi qianhou Qin wenhua yu lieguo wenhua de pengzhuang ji ronghe" 秦統一前後秦文化與列國文化的碰撞及融合 [Conflict and fusion of Qin and other states' cultures before and after the Qin unification]. In Su Bai 蘇白 (ed.), *Su Bingqi yu dangdai Zhongguo kaoguxue* 蘇秉琦與當代中國考古學 [*Su Bingqi and contemporary Chinese archaeology*] (Beijing: Kexue), 619–30.

Zhao, Huacheng. 2014. "New Explorations of Early Qin Culture." In Y. Pines et al. (eds.), *Birth of an Empire: The State of Qin Revisited*. Berkeley (Los Angeles: University of California Press), 53–70.

Zheng, Shubin 鄭曙斌, Zhang Chunlong 張春龍, Song Shaohua 宋少華 and Huang Puhua 黃樸華. 2013. *Hunan chutu jiandu xuanbian* 湖南出土簡牘選編 [*Selected excavated documents from Hunan*]. Changsha: Yuelu shuyuan.

Zhongguo wenwu yanjiusuo 中國文物研究所 and Hubei sheng wenwu kaogu yanjiusuo 湖北省文物考古研究所. 2001. *Longgang Qin jian* 龍崗秦簡 [*Qin documents from Longgang*]. Beijing: Zhonghua.

Zhu, Hanmin 朱漢民, and Chen Songchang. 2013. *Yuelu shuyuan cang Qin jian*. Vol. 3. Shanghai: Shanghai cishu.

Zou, Shuijie 鄒水杰. 2016. "Jiandu suojian Qin dai xianting lingshi yu zhucao guanxi kao" 簡牘所見秦代縣廷令史與諸曹關係考 [A study of the relationship between the scribes at the county court and the bureaus under the Qin Empire as reflected in the documents on bamboo and wood]. In Y. Zhenhong and W. Wenling 鄔文玲 (eds.), *Jianbo yanjiu 2016. Chun xia juan* [*Spring-Summer Issue*]: 132–46.

Zuozhuan (Chunqiu jingzhuan jijie) 左傳（春秋經傳集解）[*The Zuo Commentary (Collected annotations to the classic of "Spring and Autumn" and its commentary)*]. Shanghai: Shanghai guji, 2007.

9

The Fiscality of Foreign Relations in the Roman Republic (241–146 BCE)

JAMES TAN

Although the Roman Republic took over two hundred years to conquer "The Middle Sea," the real transition from Italian hegemon to Mediterranean empire occurred in the critical century from the end of the First Punic War (241 BCE) to the destruction of Carthage and Corinth (146 BCE). It was in those years that generations of statesmen had to decide what kind of overseas empire they would rule. How was it to be managed? Who would do the day-to-day governing? Who would be the winners and who would be the losers? In particular, the need to establish extractive systems would be shaped by the regime's response to two questions: Was there a desire for direct and active governing of the peripheries; and was there any impetus to maximize public revenues? The answer to each of those was increasingly "no."

There was no mastermind who examined the burgeoning empire and drew up a white paper to guide tax policy in the various provinces.[1] Nor were there deep, path-dependent institutions demanding replication in province after province. Instead, there was an *ad hoc* element to the peculiar system of each new territory.[2] Yet this does not mean that the outcomes were random; there is an identifiable trend towards administrative devolution. Despite the adoption of a relatively intensive extractive system in the first province (Sicily), subsequent Roman decision-makers preferred to detach themselves from tax collection and to delegate the task to local communities, even if that came at the price of lower revenues.[3] That was never an explicit plan. Instead, over years of governors and local élites working out how hegemony would work in a place like Spain, it turned out that Roman enthusiasm for administration was tepid compared to local enthusiasm to retain control of affairs. The latter progressively confirmed its control of things like tax collection, and leaders found that they preferred this to the more intensive Sicilian system.

Such a preference reflects, I will argue, the regime's increasingly entrenched response to the two negative answers provided above. The Roman aristocracy's refusal to empower any of its members with control over the state treasury meant that there were few incentives to maximize public revenue, since no individual or faction was sufficiently powerful to enjoy the fruits of that wealth. At the same time, the aristocracy's disinterest in directly governing Rome's provinces left space for—even necessitated—a prominent role for provincial élites.[4] These two (dis)incentives combined in a peculiar way. Since the regime needed to co-opt local rulers in lieu of direct Roman administration, and since they were relatively uninterested in the scale of revenues, Roman élites were free to use light and unobtrusive taxation as a means of enticing provincial cooperation. They could even use fiscal concessions as a reward to encourage loyalty. In what follows, I will examine how the demands of domestic politics and foreign policy shaped provincial extraction.

However, to understand how these forms of exploitation developed—to understand how the imperial fiscal system came to be—it is necessary to start with a characterization of Roman aristocratic politics. It was around this domestic political environment that the extractive systems of the provinces were shaped.

Roman Rule at Home

Some time around 500 BCE (conventionally 509), the last king of Rome lost his seat of power and over time a new regime arose from those families best placed to take the reins.[5] This regime tweaked its rules and reformed its ways over the next three centuries, until it was the very portrait of a competitive aristocracy defensively preserving the basic equality of its leading members.[6] One overriding fear defined the boundaries for all political activity at Rome: the fear that the aristocracy might be subjected to the (possibly tyrannical) power of an individual man. To that end, the structures and practices of public life were forced to conform to four principles.

1. *Tenure of power was to be brief.* Each year's magistrates were to be limited to annual terms and no one—unless in the most desperate military circumstances—was to hold office in successive years. Over time, the frequency with which individuals could hold office became more and more limited, until regulations banned holding the consulship twice within a ten-year period.

2. *No leader was to hold office without a colleague.* The classic illustration of this principle is in the consulship, the highest office at Rome and always part of an annual pair. To be consul alone was to be an oxymoron.

3. *Control of public resources was always to be in the hands of the aristocratic collective.* Although Polybius states that consuls could access treasury funds as needed, it is clear that in practice the senate (the collection of former office holders) voted on all dispensations of public money.[7] It was all but impossible for a consul to spend from the fisc without approval from his peers.

4. *The demands of office had to be sufficiently low and sufficiently generic that any reasonable aristocrat could be expected to have mastered them, if elected.* The aristocratic ideal of office-holding was expressed in Scipio Aemilianus's formulation of political qualifications: "out of integrity comes respect, out of respect comes elective office, out of elective office comes the right to command, and out of the right to command comes freedom."[8] This was no technocratic ruling class. Instead, it was understood that the moral excellence of aristocracy prepared one to lead an army, write a law, judge a case or govern a province. There thus had to be no specialist knowledge required of office beyond the military and legal training expected of any blue-blooded youth.

This system of power sharing was remarkably defensive. The Roman aristocracy came to a collective decision that it was better to limit the autonomy and opportunities of each individual in office than to risk any member abusing power to gain control over the state and the rest of the aristocracy. What they feared was apparent whenever crises overturned the usual pattern of office-holding. During the direst wars—those against the Samnites, Hannibal and the Cimbri, for example—the demand for competence rose, and a relatively small number of unusually competent individuals held office repeatedly and in successive years.[9] These few came to outshine and outrank their peers in galling ways. In the absence of an emergency, therefore, the élite preferred to restrain the most competent, to distribute power more broadly, and to place a low ceiling on the extent to which any member might hold it. Each aristocrat relinquished the possibility that he might gain extended control over affairs in order to ensure that no other would either.

The Early Roman Fiscal State

The aristocracy's jealously guarded equality had an important fiscal consequence: Rome's leaders became unusually disinterested in expanding public revenues. A range of structural factors—brief terms of office, collegiality, a lack of autonomy in accessing and spending public money—removed incentives to increase Rome's public wealth. An enterprising office-holder could have established new revenues, but by the time the riches began to pour in, his term of office would have expired and a new crop of leaders would have taken up office to enjoy these new fruits. There was no king or emperor at Rome who would benefit from increasing revenues over the long or even medium term. On the contrary, there was at least one clear advantage to a weak, relatively impoverished state: it made tyranny both less likely and less of a threat. A more richly endowed treasury might tempt an aristocrat to aim at autocratic control, and if successful, that wealth would make him a more menacing prospect.[10] The result was a system in which even the most powerful Romans understood that they would have only fleeting control of public revenues. While the appeals of private wealth were lost on none, therefore, the appeals of public wealth were meager to most leaders.

The Republic's early fiscal history reflects these incentives. Leaving aside the windfalls of booty and plunder, Rome's treasury had traditionally sat atop a tripod of revenues.[11] The first leg of the tripod was raised from indirect taxes, tolls and customs dues. Mistress of the Tiber River—she controlled boat traffic in each direction as well as the land crossing at the Tiber Island—Rome must long have enjoyed some revenue from those passing by.[12] Collection of these dues was presumably in the hands of contractors, though the evidence does not abound.[13] In addition to tolls, there were revenues from a few transactions such as the sale of salt and the manumission of slaves.[14]

The second leg comprised rents and fees imposed on those exploiting public land. Rome had long enjoyed tracts of publicly owned farmland and pasture, and it was understood that those who used it were to pay a fee or rent.[15] This may have originated with the leasing of marginal land for pasturing animals, and Pliny the Elder believed that censorial revenues were known as *pascua* because pasture was the original source of *vectigal*.[16] Some public land contained valuable natural resources, like the Silva Sila's vast reserves of timber.[17] Again, these rents were collected by contractors.

The third leg was a war levy known as *tributum*. A tax on total property, *tributum* was instituted in the late fifth century as a revenue source to sustain military pay during the siege of Veii.[18] It was only levied, however, when military affairs required it; in peaceful years—not that there were many of those—the state did not call for *tributum*, and it could in theory be refunded to payers if the campaign turned out to be profitable.[19] That refundability might suggest that *tributum* was only intended to be necessary in lieu of plunder, but there is little evidence to suggest that it was anything short of ubiquitous, and Rosenstein has shown that booty only rarely matched the costs of campaigns.[20] There are frustratingly few details about how *tributum* was collected. The consensus is that military pay was paid out from the wealthy estates of a group known as the *tribuni aerarii*, who then replenished their funds by collecting *tributum* from less wealthy landowners as a percentage of overall declared wealth.[21] As such, it was a relatively invasive system for the taxpayers, but it placed few if any demands on elected officials. The entire job was outsourced to the *tribuni aerarii*. By 167 BCE, however, *tributum* was no longer collected, as plunder and overseas revenues rendered it unnecessary.

This was a slender fiscal base for world domination. Despite Rome's impressive military success in the third century—it was in this period that she cemented control over Italy, Sicily, Sardinia, Corsica, and parts of Spain, the Adriatic and North Africa—there seems not to have been any notable public profit.[22] The record of public building in the city reveals that, aside from repairs, there is only limited building in the half century between 250–201 BCE: eleven temples were vowed, one stadium was built (the Circus Flaminius) and two roads were paved (Clivus Publicius and Via Flaminia). Contrast this with the years 200–151, when Rome was receiving lucrative (but temporary) indemnities from conquered foes: there is evidence for eleven temples, one paved road (Clivus Capitolinus), two sets of arches, two commercial spaces (the Emporium and the Tabernae Argentariae Novae), three basilicas, one bridge, and nine sets of porticoes.[23] The difference in the lists would grow even starker if regional building (including roads) were included, but the evidence is much thinner.[24] During the Second Punic War (218–201 BCE), moreover, in which Hannibal's invasion of Italy demanded unusually high expenses, public finance failed to keep up with costs.[25] Michael Taylor has persuasively argued that Roman revenues, even during the halcyon days of the Greek conquests, were still far below those of the Hellenistic kingdoms Rome vanquished.[26] There was evidently very little room for deterioration in the budget. Rome had survived down to 200 BCE on a fragile fiscal base that, though evidently adequate for her wars in Italy and Sicily, was not sufficient for remaking infrastructure or transforming the footprint of the state within Roman society.

Despite the relative penury of the Roman treasury, however, few leaders tried to remedy the situation. Why? Rome's fiscal performance of course suffered under ancient economic conditions, but this would not explain why Rome's finances would lag behind those of contemporary Greek states. Even when offered new territories and people to exploit, moreover, Roman leaders showed little appetite for public revenues. As they conquered Italy, for example, they required many of their new subjects to pay tribute not in money, but in troops, and it is clear that the use of non-Roman soldiers was not confined to the peninsula.[27] This antipathy to public revenues was in part because individual policymakers stood to gain little from fattening the treasury, since each leader enjoyed such tenuous and fleeting control over it. Attempts to increase public revenues might even be viewed with suspicion, since they aroused fears of demagoguery—precisely this charge would be levelled at Gaius Gracchus between 123 and 121, when he was killed.[28] The old fiscal base would not, however, sustain a growing empire with fleets and garrisons. The provinces would have to be tapped in some way. This was especially so once Rome's leaders chose to end *tributum* in 167, which meant that tax revenues were overwhelmingly raised abroad and thus became inextricably parts of foreign relations rather than domestic policy. New wars meant new provinces, new administrative challenges, and new expenses, yet, while the precise decision-making structure remains a mystery, it is clear that there was no blueprint for how to extend Rome's existing fiscal mechanisms abroad. Each province would receive its own system.

Direct Taxation in the Provinces: Sicily, Sardinia, the Spains, Macedonia, Africa and Achaea

Although Sicily was annexed in 241 BCE, it took another three decades for the Romans to find a permanent settlement. They originally left the eastern end of the island under the control of their ally, Hiero II of Syracuse, and made an annual trip to collect whatever tax the western cities were obliged to collect and hand over. Importantly, five cities were granted freedom from taxation in recognition of good relations.[29] During the Second Punic War (218–201), however, the island's fiscal state was reorganized under a classic tax farming system known at Rome as the *lex Hieronica*.[30] To collect a tithe of grain, local cities would draw up lists of farmers and sown fields, which would then be perused by potential local contractors. The governor would hold auctions for the various tax farms; the successful bidders would strike a deal with the farmers about how much would be levied at the threshing floor; and then the tithe would be collected at harvest. The system worked well. It was heavily regulated (in favor of the taxpayer), produced a tidy profit for both contractor and state, and survived with few modifications throughout the Republic. Much less is known about the Sardinian situation. There is later evidence that some Sardinian communities paid a kind of tribute (*stipendium*) on top of a tithe, but there is no proof that this constituted the original settlement or that the attested tithes themselves were annual rather than *ad hoc* events.[31] One likely explanation is that those who originally organized the island imposed a tithe when the province was first established, but that communities that later rebelled were burdened with an additional tribute on top.[32] The original plan was to manage Sicily and Sardinia without adding more than one high official (the praetor peregrinus), but this proved inadequate and two new praetorships in the year 227 allowed a permanent administrative presence on each island.[33] Whether this reform was prompted by fiscal concerns is unclear. No evidence attests to it, but it is notable that the Carthaginian indemnity expired in 232 or 231, and Rome was operating a fleet of two hundred ships in 229. It is reasonable to speculate that a decision in 228 to increase the administrative presence in the provinces was due to the fact that, in the absence of the Carthaginian indemnity, existing revenues could not fund Rome's ambitions.[34] Sicily and Sardinia would have to be squeezed for more.

The next phase in Roman fiscal expansion occurred when the Romans expelled the Carthaginians from Iberia in 206 BCE, and split the conquered territory into Nearer (North-Eastern) and Further (Southern) Spain. The first decades of occupation probably witnessed *ad hoc* levies of grain and some form of payment to support the legions stationed in Iberia, but it was not until 179 at the earliest that such arrangements were formalized in treaties with individual communities as fixed tribute, possibly as or with a half tithe of grain.[35] This seems to have required local groups to deliver payments directly to the governor's staff, but problems ensued. Regulations had to be imposed which forbade the use of prefects to intervene in the collection of corn—presumably because they had been taking too much and charging too little—and Cato lambasted a governor of 174 for incorrectly assessing what was owed by the Lusitani.[36] The process was clearly far less intensive than the tax farming system familiar from Sicily, but it did still place a significant burden on the governor and his staff, especially if he chose to be intrusive.

By the middle of the second century BCE, then, the western provinces were delivering large quantities of grain via mechanisms which ranged from the quite bureaucratically demanding tax farms of Sicily to the community-by-community collection of tribute in Spain. Governors in none of these provinces were collecting large quantities of cash.

The trend away from hands-on administration continued elsewhere. The round of wars with Carthage and Macedon either side of the year 200 BCE resulted in the withdrawal of Roman forces and the imposition of indemnities which had to be delivered to Rome each year over a fixed period. Carthage had to pay 10,000 talents over fifty years. The Macedonians, who had made the mistake of supporting Carthage's Hannibal and were soon invaded by the Romans, were left with an annual indemnity of 1,000 talents over ten years. The legions next defeated Sparta for an indemnity of 500 talents over eight years and then extracted the enormous sum of 15,000 talents from the Seleucids over twelve years thanks to the Battle of Magnesia in 190. A victory over the Aetolians rounded out this period for 500 talents over six years.[37]

Rome's first interventions in Africa and Greece were thus characterized by troop withdrawals and fiscal windfalls.[38] After 167 BCE, however, Roman policy-makers tired of the Macedonian and Illyrian monarchies. They overthrew the kingdoms in order to establish four independent republics in the north of Greece, each of which was required to pay to the Romans in perpetuity half of the old tribute that was owed to the kings.[39] Yet these republics were neither administered by a Roman governor nor garrisoned by Roman troops. Instead, each simply delivered its tribute directly to Rome in the fashion of the old indemnities. From the Romans' perspective, the system ran itself.

In the watershed year of 146 BCE, the conquerors would tweak that policy. Wars in North Africa and Southern Greece were ended in that year with the capture and pillage of glorious cities (Carthage and Corinth). To those who had been allies, Roman policy did much as it had done in Macedonia, breaking up larger states and leaving behind independent polities. For former enemies, the results were disastrous. In Africa (roughly modern Tunisia), much of the land was ceded to allies, while two forms of tribute—one a poll tax and another a land tax—were imposed on the rest. The precise method of collection is unknown, but there was some role for contractors.[40] Tracts of territory were also converted into public land, which at least notionally required payment to the state in the form of a lease, though organization of these areas seems to have been dismal.[41] Overall, the fiscal settlement demonstrated a remarkable lack of avarice, and Rome's leaders willingly ceded much of the province to local cities to manage themselves.[42]

In 148 CE Macedonia's four republics lost their independence and were organized into the province of Macedonia. But the earlier fiscal arrangement remained, with tribute collected locally and handed over to the Roman hegemon, though in this case there was now a governor on site to receive it.[43] Areas of Achaea that had opposed the Romans seem, too, to have been obliged to collect and pay tribute, even if there was no governor or formal province of Achaea.[44]

The installation of a governor in Macedonia represented an intensification of Roman rule, but the method of extraction remained the same. Local communities would collect the payments and hand over the total. The pattern seems clear. Sicily was an experiment in relatively intensive extraction, but the Romans did not follow that precedent. Elsewhere, there was an increasing desire to let local communities manage the system and deliver collective payments to the Romans with little intervention. The trend towards increasing reliance on locals would be halted by Gaius Gracchus, who imposed an intrusive and intensive tax farming system on Asia (western Turkey) in 123 BCE. In many ways, however, he was the exception who proved the rule, since he was unusually intent on increasing public profits (and was killed!).[45] The incentives that drove his policies produced a new and more intensive system of extraction, and the course of Roman imperialism and fiscal history changed with it. That shift, however, is beyond the scope of this paper.

Indirect Taxes and Other Revenues

By 200 BCE at the latest Rome had also begun issuing contracts to tax farmers who would collect customs and tolls at ports and cities throughout the Empire.[46] This was apparent early in the contracting for tolls at the landlocked city of Capua and the harbor at Puteoli.[47] The censors of 179 let out more and more contracts for such indirect taxes.[48] Gaius Gracchus then auctioned yet further contracts in 123–122.[49] The collector of tolls and customs had by the end of the Republic become the face of the Empire for so many who passed through it.[50]

An important part of Rome's overall revenues flowed from the exploitation of natural resources. These could involve forests like the Silva Sila discussed above, or new mines in Spain, Macedonia, and elsewhere.[51] There were pasture lands and fisheries to lease out.[52] There is not much direct evidence for how these revenues were collected, and while the scholarly consensus holds that contractors were employed from the beginning, there are nevertheless strong reasons for believing that anyone who wished to operate in the mines could do so, provided that they paid a fee or a percentage to the Roman authorities.[53] It is impossible to quantify the contribution of these revenues, but there is every reason to believe that they were high—the scale of mining is even apparent in atmospheric pollution preserved in glacial ice cores—and they had the advantage of supplying necessary commodities like silver, iron, timber and pitch.[54]

Badian was right when he noted that the proliferation of these indirect taxes allowed the suspension of *tributum* at home.[55] This probably had advantages for landholding Italians, who were no longer taxed on their overall property, and moved the burden onto (both élite and non-élite) commerce.

Explaining the Formation of Roman Provincial Exploitation

There can be no doubt that the Romans were familiar with more intensive, more profitable extraction, because that is precisely what they employed in Sicily. And they knew it. If one requires proof that they recognized that system's value, turn to the extended panegyric (a rarity in descriptions of tax!) in Cicero's third speech against C. Verres. Yet this was not the model for extraction in other provinces. Elsewhere, Roman statesmen preferred less intensive systems. Whereas the *lex Hieronica* in Sicily required the governor to manage tax collection in detail—to guarantee the accuracy of each inventory of land and seed, to oversee the many auctions of tax farms across Sicily, to adjudicate the many disputes between tax farmers and taxpayers— the systems imposed on other provinces tended to let local leaders measure, collect, convey and arbitrate tax payments themselves. Sicily would remain the only province requiring two quaestors to manage its finances.[56] Why?

There are certainly numerous answers to that question. Path dependence presumably played a role: it was easier and more efficient to work with pre-existing local institutions than to rip them up and impose a new system.[57] Sicily was also its own unique place. Other provinces would vary according to the military presence of the Romans, the degree of urbanization, the administrative capacities of locals, etc., so that the Sicilian system could not easily be transplanted elsewhere.[58] Perhaps most importantly, the final Sicilian system was created by a proconsul, M. Valerius Laevinus, who seems to have been particularly interested in public finance at a time when Rome's public finances were particularly dire.[59] That was a historical anomaly.

Fiscal practices are, however, inescapably political practices. It is not enough to explain a mode of extraction in terms of its ability to yield revenues. Instead, it is necessary to embed Rome's provincial extraction within the context of Rome's politics and Rome's relations with provincial communities. Valerius Laevinus notwithstanding, élite Romans tended to have unusually low appetite for public revenues and for direct administration of provinces. Hoping for what Levi might identify as "quasi-voluntary compliance," they were thus willing to sacrifice profits and control in order to entice provincial leaders to manage the systems for them.[60] Rome's aristocratic policy-makers lowered tax yields and delegated administration to local élites because they correctly surmised that provincial leaders would more likely cooperate in Roman rule if they could run the fiscal system themselves. Roman provincial extraction therefore reflected a set of political preferences: the prioritization of local cooperation over the maximization of public profits. Rome's unusually low appetite for revenue allowed greater freedom to lower net taxation and to offer concessions. This in turn attracted the collaboration of provincials, who recognized a good deal when they saw one, and created categories of fiscal privilege that became cornerstones of the Empire's organization.[61] These points will be explored in the remainder of the paper.

Because the average Roman aristocrat could not be expected to manage a complex provincial administration—and because the technologies of rule were quite limited—it was preferable to have local leaders manage the extractive system in their own areas.[62] To ensure peaceful cooperation, the Romans would need to tailor a variety of policies to the interests of wealthy provincials and leave them satisfied with their lot, and there was indeed an overarching Roman practice of favoring the wealthy in conquered areas. In that context, extractive systems were parts of a larger attempt to conciliate cooperative local leaders.[63]

The proliferation of indirect taxes, for example, ensured that the fiscal burden would not fall too harshly on the agriculture of landed families, but instead would be shifted to merchants and other (sometimes élite) entrepreneurs. Indirect taxes alone, however, afforded too narrow a set of revenues. Direct taxation of agriculture would also be required, and here policy-makers tended to grant communities a great deal of autonomy in deciding how to collect them. With the exception of Sicily, where the *lex Hieronica* prevented communities from controlling their own tax collection processes, the provinces saw local leaders collect the payments from each payer and hand the lump sum over to the Romans.[64] This must have been more than welcome among the most powerful households of the provinces. Not only did it allow local leaders to manipulate local tax collection in their own favor—or simply to embezzle revenues—it reinforced their own roles as leaders.[65] Once Rome demanded some payment, somebody on site had to coordinate it, and so long as senators themselves were hesitant to play that role, there was an opportunity for local élites to exercise leadership. This was exactly what their ambitions craved. They might pay it up front and compensate themselves later, they might hire contractors, but they would almost certainly represent the community in handing the money over to the Romans. But at each step their superior status would be demonstrated and reinforced. It avoided lumping all provincials into a basket of "subjects" and facilitated a status distinction between local leaders and led. Creating a more hands-off tax system was a way of objectifying local authorities less as subordinates and more as partners in rule.[66]

A further appeal for the provincial leaders was the overall rate of taxation. There is inadequate evidence to ascertain precisely how intensive Roman taxation in the provinces was, but it does seem to have been relatively low. Spanish leaders were sufficiently enamored with their treaties that they fought to preserve them as the *status quo*.[67] The Macedonians and Illyrians were taxed just half what they had been under the old monarchy. They may have had to pay for expenses previously covered by the crown—especially defence—but there can be no denying that the Romans could have pressed them more severely.[68] In Africa, as noted above, the Romans simply handed over large tracts of land for other polities to control and to tax.[69] There is, moreover, little evidence that taxation provoked rebellions against Roman rule. Without a doubt, most Roman Republican taxes were lower than the one-third of grain and one-half of fruits demanded by the Seleucids at 1 Maccabees 10:30.

The Romans' tolerance of low rates and local corruption was a direct result of their satisfaction with—even insistence upon—relatively low revenues. Though the bestowal of various exemptions and privileges was an established part of Greek diplomacy, the Hellenistic kings were not so free to forego revenues as the thrifty Romans, and the practice exploded.

Moreover, exemptions became especially prevalent in areas more dependent on local cooperation. Of the 68 cities and towns in Sicily, where the fiscal system demanded little cooperation from local élites, only five enjoyed freedom from Roman taxation.[70] In Spain, however, where the participation of locals was more important, immunity had (at least by the mid-first century CE) been granted far more frequently. In the later Roman province of Hispania Citerior, for example, Pliny tells us that 54 out of 189 towns were immune from taxes; in Baetica, an impressive 55 out of 175 were free from taxation.[71] Some Greek cities, like Ambracia, were granted the privilege of collecting their own tolls (*portoria*).[72] Celtiberians were also granted immunity from taxes, though the Romans came to have second thoughts about that.[73] Specific individuals could be granted freedom from taxation, and some were even exempted from having to contribute to the repayment of a home city's debts.[74] Crucially, Rome explicitly reserved the right to renege on the exemption if a city did not live up to its privileges.[75] On the other hand, communities could be punished just as they could be rewarded. Cicero described the tribute paid in Africa and Spain as the "price of war" (*poena belli*) against Rome.[76] Terms could also be rewritten after rebellions for short periods. When the Ilergetes in Spain were defeated, for example, they had that year's tribute doubled and had to contribute six months' supply of corn and clothing.[77] Most deviously, the Romans could punish one city by altering the fiscal arrangements of another: when they made Delos a duty-free port after the Battle of Pydna in 168 BCE, for example, they intentionally undermined Rhodes's position as the leading entrepôt of the Greek world.[78]

All of this represents the embedding of taxation within a hegemonic or imperial system of carrots and sticks. That system relied, however, on the Romans' willingness to forego revenues in favor of political benefits, and that willingness in turn relied on the low priority of public wealth within Roman aristocratic politics. In other words, the interests of the aristocracy—interests at odds with the centralization of resources—granted Roman leaders an unusual degree of flexibility in adopting fiscal means to achieve their ends in the provinces. The result was not merely an extractive system defined by imperial politics, but an empire organized through fiscal categories. If provincial élites made the right decisions—i.e., were unfailingly loyal to Rome—then they tended to be rewarded with superior fiscal arrangements. If, however, cities made the wrong decisions, then harsher taxation could be used as punishment. The result was a web of provincial and allied communities classified and defined not simply by ethnic, legal, or military relationships, but by the presence or absence of fiscal ones.[79] The geographer Strabo, for example, defined a Roman province by the imposition of Roman tax collectors as opposed to other areas that were free or ruled by kings.[80] Servius, a commentator on Vergil's *Aeneid*, also demonstrates the categorization of foreign peoples according to fiscal relationships: "there used to be communities who paid tax to Rome (*stipendiariae*), communities bound to Rome by treaty (*foederatae*, [most of whom supplied troops]), and communities free from obligation (*liberae*)."[81] Rome therefore came to rule not a single, homogenous empire or even a set of provinces, but a multitude of cities and peoples bound to Rome by treaty arrangements defining their privileges and burdens. Cities could be conceived of as belonging to a territory or ethnicity, but also to a set of fiscal categories ranging from untaxed to heavily taxed. The freedom to arrange such a broad spectrum of fiscal privilege and burden was a direct result of the Romans' willingness to sacrifice revenue in return for local cooperation.

Conclusions

For most of the second century, Rome's provincial tax systems, with their moderate profits and mild administrative demands, were a perfect reflection of the political élite's preferences. The ruling class's preoccupation with preventing any individual from controlling public affairs meant firstly that no leader was allowed to benefit from increased state resources; and secondly that the demands of office had to be low enough for a large number of annual magistrates to cope, lest positions of power be the preserve of the few truly competent leaders of each generation. Thus Roman policy insisted that relatively meager public revenues would suffice. Freed from the need to maximize profit, the élite was able to adopt much less intensive styles of provincial administration and exploitation. They thus chose to reduce the demands they placed on themselves, and to rely on local élites to run each province. In order to co-opt these élites, they developed extractive mechanisms that kept revenues relatively low and increasingly devolved control of tax affairs to local communities.

The priorities that shaped this state of affairs grew increasingly salient for decision-makers. With the settlement of Sicily in the Hannibalic War, the Romans adopted the bureaucratically intensive but highly profitable system known as the *Lex Hieronica*, but the administrative price grew more obvious as time went on. That was especially true in unpacified areas. Those leaders familiar with the Sardinian and Spanish situations knew that the administrative demands of the Sicilian system—especially if transposed onto a less urbanized, more explosive province—would be impossible while governors were leading legions against formidable foes, and so it was progressively decided not to impose an intensive system of direct taxation, but to rely on local leaders and indirect taxes, even if that meant lower revenues. This suited the élite well. Keener on war than administration, the average Roman leader was indifferent to the revenue costs of a system that taxed more lightly but freed him to lead his troops. Across generations, this set of preferences kept pushing Roman policy more and more towards less intensive revenue systems. By the mid-second century, Rome's form of fiscal exploitation in the provinces was consequently a light one. This was not, however, the result of magnanimity—élite Romans certainly toiled to increase private profits. Instead, it reflected the élite's desire to minimize its own administrative duties and to maintain a working détente with provincial élites who played critical roles—and saw obvious advantages—in running the tax system. The result was a form of rule characterized in part by the degree to which the masters did or did not grant fiscal reprieve. And the reason the Romans were so free to make such concessions was that there was no stakeholder who saw a personal benefit in higher public revenues.

Over time the incentives for that system would become more complicated. By the late Republic, at least some leaders—and many ordinary citizens, too—came to view the Empire as a cash cow ready to be milked.[82] By the time of the Gracchi brothers (133–121 BCE), some were proposing a more intensive approach to extraction, even if others preferred the *status quo*. Most of the old system in Sicily, Spain, Greece and Africa would, however, persist unchanged, and that remained the case even once the Republic fell and was replaced by autocracy.

NOTES

1 Ñaco del Hoyo 2003a. The term "province" can be anachronistic for this early period and its low level of institutionalisation, but it remains by far the most convenient way to describe foreign territories ruled by the Romans. The classic discussions of this problem include Richardson 1986: 4–9, Kallet-Marx 1995: 18–29, and Crawford 1999: 177; and see now also Díaz Fernández 2015: ch. 1.

2 For a clear and concise overview of the developing provincial system, see Crawford 1999.

3 For a concise overview of Roman expansion in the treatment of conquered peoples, see Hillard and Beness 2013.

4 Crawford 1999: 188–89.

5 A very conventional account can be found at Cornell 1995.

6 For the sociology of this competitive élite, see especially Hölkeskamp 2010 and 2017, and the useful overview at Brennan 2014. For a more formalist account, see Astin 1989 and Lintott 1999.

7 Polyb. 6.12.8, where the claim that consuls could spend public money should probably be limited to time spent on campaign. On the reality of senatorial oversight, Walbank 1957: 677–78.

8 Scipio Aemilianus 32 Malcovati: *ex innocentia nascitur dignitas, ex dignitate honor, ex honore imperium, ex imperio libertas.*

9 Cornell 1995: 360–61 and Hölkeskamp 2010: 28 n11 for examples.

10 For an expanded version of this thesis, see Tan 2017.

11 The clearest treatment remains Frank 1933, but see also Kay 2014 ch. 2–4 for the second century.

12 It is implausible in the extreme that a city dominating the routes both along and across the Tiber did not charge for passage. For sources and discussion, see De Laet 1949. Cf Andreades 1933: 138 (cited by De Laet) where he posits an origin for *portoria* in gifts given to local magnates for safe passage. The total value of these was probably not great. For the Second Punic War, Frank paid them short shrift: "The import and export duties collected at a few harbours were (2½–5%) still insignificant" (Frank 1933: 79).

13 Badian 1972: 23–4.

14 For salt, see Plin. *HN* 32.89 and Giovannini 1985. Livy 2.9.6 believed that a public salt monopoly trade was instituted as early as 508, and Ogilvie 1965: 257 suggests that the invasion of Porsenna and the Latin War may have forced archaic Rome's hand by threatening the supply from Ostia. This may well, however, be myth and conjecture. Livy 29.37.6 details in more convincing ways the reform of M. Livius Salinator in 204, by which contracts were let for the sale of salt at a fixed price in Rome, with higher prices beyond the city. It is explicitly referred to as a *vectigal* (public revenue), and Livy claims that the plebs saw it as a vindictive move against them by the censor. One Roman author, Pliny the elder, found it believable that the kings of India made more money from their control of salt than from pearls

and gold (*Hist. Nat.* 31.77), so the salt revenues were presumably not insignificant. Frank, on the other hand, was unimpressed with the Romans' salt monopoly: "we can hardly assume a profit to the state" (1933: 140). He adds evidence for a salt tax in Sardinia. For the 5% tax on manumissions, see Cic. *Att.* 2.16.1 and historical context at Oakley 1998: 182–83.

15 Roselaar 2010. For a case that *ager publicus* was not originally leased as a source of revenue, see Rathbone 2003. Rathbone's case that the Romans promptly privatized *ager publicus* is, however, difficult to accept. Among various problems, the most serious is that there was still public land within 50 miles of Rome as late as the year 200 BCE, and all of it must have been conquered much earlier (Livy 31.13.2–9, with Roselaar 2010: 127–28). Clearly, the Romans had not been in a hurry to convert that public land into private estates.

16 Plin. *Hist. Nat.* 18.11. It is unclear how the rents for pastoral land were paid before coinage, but the demands of public animal sacrifice meant that payment in kind from shepherds and drovers would have been welcome.

17 Rome controlled half of the forest: Dion. Hal. 20.15.2. It remained both state-owned and a critical source of naval timber for as long as warships were wooden: see, for example, Davis 2006: 62.

18 On the date of *tributum* with further references, see Mersing 2007.

19 For the scarcity of peaceful years, see Harris 1990: 495 and Oakley 2002: 15. For discussion of *tributum*, see Nicolet 1976. See also Nicolet 2000, summarized in English at Nicolet 1980: 161–64. For its scale, see Rosenstein 2016b.

20 Rosenstein 2016a.

21 The role of *tribuni aerarii* is probable but not certain. It was first suggested by Nicolet 1976:46–55, and is followed by, among others, Brunt 1990: 354. For the amount levied, see Crawford 1978 and Rosenstein 2016b.

22 See Monson 2015: 197–200 for a review of Rome's comparatively light taxation. On the short-term unprofitability of Rome's wars, see Rosenstein 2016a.

23 Admittedly, the second period is much better attested in the sources, but this cannot be the whole story. Among other points, the second century censors could build so much because the city had not already been developed in earlier periods. Chronological lists of building can be found in three different works: Platner and Ashby 1929; Richardson 1992; Palombi 2010.

24 For building in wider Italy, see still Gros 1978. For roads, Laurence 1999.

25 Marchetti 1978 and Tan 2017: ch. 5.

26 Taylor 2017: 143–80.

27 See Tan 2020 for an examination of Roman extraction in Italy. For the use of foreign soldiers elsewhere in the Empire, see Prag 2015a.

28 The best account of Gracchus's career remains Stockton 1979.

29 The clearest summary can be found at Prag 2013, who speculates that the tax was paid in coin, with a longer examination of the Sicilian tithe at Erdkamp 2005: 209–18. See also now Day 2017 for the politics. For speculation that a much more immediate organization of Sicily took place, see Serrati 2000 and 2016: 104–6, or

for a middle ground (extension of Hiero's tax system in 227 BCE, when the first praetor arrived), see Pinzone 1999: ch. 1. On the importance of Sicily as the original instance of dividing subject cities according to tax status, see still Badian 1958: 37–42. On the thriving civic culture of Sicilian cities, see Prag 2015a.

30 Ñaco del Hoyo 2011: 384. The system is described at Carcopino 1914; Scramuzza 1937: 237–40; Badian 1972: 79–80; Lintott 1993: 75; Nicolet 2000: 279–80.

31 Ñaco del Hoyo 2003b; Roppa and van Dommelen 2012: 54.

32 Livy 36.2.13, 37.2.12, 41.17.2, 42.31.8. See also: Frank 1933: 140; Lintott 1993: 71–72; Prag 2013: 61; Ñaco del Hoyo 2019: 76–77; and Schulz 1997: 214.

33 For discussion of the additional praetors, see Brennan 2000: 89–93, Díaz Fernández 2015: 110–19 and Day 2017.

34 On the Carthaginian indemnity, Polyb. 1.63.3. On the fleet, Polyb. 2.11.1.

35 Arguing that *stipendium* was probably regularized by Ti. Gracchus during his propraetorship in 180–78 BCE, Richardson 1986: 72, 160–61, and esp. 115–16; Lintott 1993: 72–73; and López Castro 2013: 69. Arguing for a later date, Howgego 1994: 17; Ñaco del Hoyo 2003a: 218–22, cf. 2019: 85–6. App. *Iber.* 44 explicitly claims that tribute was part of the treaties established by Ti. Gracchus around 179, and though some read Appian as attesting to subsequent cancellation (Curchin 1991: 60–61), it seems that exemption was only provided to individual cities like Segeda. Appian (*Iber.* 43) is also explicit that later the Spanish remembered Gracchus' arrangements fondly, and his son was well received because of that memory (Plut. *Ti. Gr.* 5). Cic. 2.*Verr.* 3.16.12 says that the Spanish provinces paid a *vectigal certum* called *stipendarius*, on which see Soraci 2010: 54–56, 65 and Ñaco del Hoyo 2019: 79–80.

36 Livy 43.2.12 and Ps- Asc. 203 (Stangl), with Ñaco del Hoyo 2019: 79–80.

37 The evidence for indemnities and booty in this period is collected at Frank 1933: 127–35. See also Kay 2013: 135–40.

38 Díaz Fernández 2015: 142–44 and Kay 2013, arguing that Romans were more than satisfied with these temporary fiscal gains.

39 Convenient summaries can be found at Derow 1989: 317–18 and Rosenstein 2012: 218–22.

40 The clearest treatments remain Broughton 1929: ch. 1; Haywood 1938: 4–5; and now Gargola 2017: 354–55, who argues for particularly mild and delayed exploitation of Africa. *ILS* 901 records a *publicanus* involved in the collection of African taxes: *Fonteio Q. f. q. mancup. stipend. ex Africa*. See also Lintott 1993: 77 and Gargola 2017: 354. On whether there was even a regular governor of Africa in the second century, see the doubts of Gargola 2017.

41 Quinn 2004: 1601.

42 Cic. 2.*Verr.*3.12 and App. *Pun.* 135, with Broughton 1929: 15–17 and Ñaco del Hoyo 2019: 80–81. On the meaning of *vectigal certum stipendiarium*, see Soraci 2010: 54–56.

43 A clear summary at Larsen 1938: 302–3.

44 The question of tribute in Achaea is a vexed one with insufficient evidence to cut the knot: see Ferrary 1999: 70–71, *contra* Kallet-Marx 1995: 50–60, arguing that Achaea was not taxed until 86 BCE. Much depends on the (subjective) plausibility of a tax-free status across all of Achaea. On the status of the province: Kallet-Marx 1995: 49–51.

45 See the argument at Tan 2017: ch. 6.

46 The standard accounts remain De Laet 1949 and Badian 1972. There may well have been earlier practices surrounding *portoria* in subject or allied cities—e.g. App. *Sic.* 2 for Sicily—but the evidence is not particularly forthcoming.

47 The collection of *portoria* in Capua and Puteoli were leased by the censors of 199 (Livy 32.7.3).

48 Livy 40.51.9: *Portoria quoque et vectigalia . . . multa instituerunt.*

49 Vell. Pat. 2.6: *C. Gracchus nova instituebat portoria.*

50 Purcell 2005. Cicero knew well that this face was loathed by many of the Mediterranean's inhabitants (*Flac.* 19).

51 The standard treatment of Roman mining in Spain is Domergue 1990. For a recent review of early Roman mining in English, see Kay 2014: 43–58.

52 Fisheries: Marzano 2013: 15–16. Pasturage: See for example, Cic. II.*Verr.* II.169, where L. Carpinatius runs the *scriptura* of the entire island *pro magistratu.*

53 So Richardson 1976 contra various scholars, with references at Ñaco del Hoyo 2001: 371–72 and Kay 2014: 49–58. There are various reasons for adopting Richardson's rejection of contracting, but the best to my mind is the evidence at Livy 45.29.11, that the Romans imposed on the iron and copper miners of Macedonia half the rate that the king had previously demanded. A halved rate can only imply a fixed rate, and a fixed rate can only exclude the possibility of auction. If there were no auctions, then contracting is inconceivable. See also Strab. 3.10, where the Roman *demos'* mining revenues from New Carthage are expressed *per diem* (cf. also Livy 34.21.7). This, too, is inconsistent with quinquennial auctions.

54 For references, Kay 2014: 46–47.

55 Badian 1972: 62–63.

56 Prag 2014.

57 For an examination of Rome's adoption of pre-existing "tax laws," see Hillard and Beness 2013: esp. 137–38 and Serrati 2016.

58 On the importance of local Sicilian institutions, see Erdkamp 1998: 109–10. It is likely important that the next experiments in provincial administration after Sicily took place in Sardinia and Spain, entirely different places where the landscape was less urbanized, the subjects more hostile and the local political units dizzyingly complex. For the challenges of administering the Spanish provinces, see Edmondson 1996.

59 Valerius Laevinus was central to the roll out of a new silver currency as consul in 210 BCE, and would go on to create a new type of public land to repay public creditors in 200. Sicily's singularly intensive tax system likely owed a great deal to

this one man's interest in public finance and to the demand for a more profitable type of cereal tribute during the ordeals of Hannibal's invasion. For references, see Broughton 1951: 277–96, with Livy 31.13.7–9 on the repayments in 200. For the importance of grain in these years, see Erdkamp 2007: 106.

60 Levi 1988: 49.

61 Of course, taxes were not the whole story. Brunt 1990: 273, for example, also emphasizes the appeal of Rome's guarantees of the *status quo* for existing provincial élites, while Ando 2000 examines provincial acceptance of Roman rule from an ideological and communicative perspective.

62 Mann 1986: 296–97, 526–27 and Brunt 1990: 62. Ideally, the Romans relied on cities: Reynolds 1988 is an excellent overview. See also Dahlheim 1977: 64–65, as well as Lintott 1993: 129, Ferrary 1999: 71–72 and Migeotte 2014. Also Mitchell 1999: 30–31: "Cities, to a greater or lesser degree, took responsibility for collecting taxes and other dues owed to Rome, provided services in kind, policed their territories, and provided the infrastructure for local economic organisation." He goes on, however, to point out that any similar unit would do, from village to federation, so long as it could meet the administrative tasks expected of it, but that the city was the most common (so also Dmitriev 2005: 310).

63 Roman leaders consistently favored local oligarchies. In Capua, for example, the wealthy were rewarded for remaining loyal to Rome even as the rest of the population flew into opposition (Livy 8.11.16, 14.10). In Thessaly, Ti. Quinctius Flamininus reconstituted councils and courts on the basis of property qualifications (Livy 34.51.6). See also L. Mummius in Achaea (Paus. 7.16.9). For discussion, see Brunt 1990: 270–75, Cornell 1995: 363, Oakley 1998: 558, Derow 2015: 35, 49, 68, Dmitriev 2011: 347–48 and Harris 2016: 30. For the larger, ongoing phenomenon of élite co-optation, see Ando 2000 and Bang 2013: 438–49 with further references.

64 In Sicily there seems to have been some role for the *magistratus Siculus*, for which see Carcopino 1914: 33–34 and Bell 2007: 189–92. Cic. II. *Verr.* 3.26, 29–31, 36–37 leave little doubt that the tax collector and the individual taxpayer worked directly with each other in at least some communities.

65 On élite tax avoidance, see Schulz 1997: 218–20, assuming the use of tenant farmers instead of slaves, while Fröhlich 2006 is a complete and lengthy investigation of corruption in Greek cities. For a sense of how much local leaders might be profiting from the management of local revenues, see Cic. *Att.* 6.2.5 with Badian 1972: 114. In a rhetorical context, Cicero elsewhere assures voters that the falsification of city accounts was extremely easy, and cites one instance of a local magistrate who pocketed the money he had been paid to supply public grain, forcing the city to provide it out of its own revenues (Cic. *Flacc.* 21, 45). Jos. *B.J.* 1.524, 1.625 and *J.A.* 14.163 illustrate the tendency for élites—in this case royal—to profit from Rome's financial demands. Jos. *J.A.* 14.201 has Caesar remit part of Judaea's tribute, and explicitly forbid anyone from paying the old amount, careful to prevent the local élite from continuing to tax the old amount, providing the

Romans with the new amount, and pocketing the difference. For a similar case from Termessus, see Crawford 1999: 197–98.

66 For the agenda of allies and provincials in currying influence with Romans, see Terrenato 1997: 107–8, as well as a long bibliography on eastern cities, including Bernhardt 1985: 169–82, Ferrary 1997, and Merola 2001: ch. 2.

67 App. *Iber.* 43, Polyb. 35.2.15, Plut. *Vit. Ti. Grac.* 5. This affection may of course reflect subsequent abuses as much as earlier generosity. See for discussion Richardson 1986: 112–23.

68 Livy 45.18.7, 26.14.

69 Broughton 1929: ch. 1.

70 Pliny *HN* 3.88, Cic. 2.Verr.3.13.

71 Pliny *HN* 3.7, 3.18.

72 Livy 38.44.4. For later examples with precise language, see Termessus at *Lex. Ant. Term.* 5, 9, and Delos at *CIL* 1².2500. For tax exemption as a status in Greece in this and later periods, see Bernhardt 1980.

73 App. *Iber.* 44.

74 E.g, *ILLRP* 513.

75 App. *Iber.* 44.

76 Cic. 2 *Verr.* 3.12

77 Richardson 1986: 72. That flexibility owed a lot to the improvisational nature of Roman taxation, especially in Spain: see Ñaco del Hoyo 2007. For other instances of tax changes as rewards or punishments, see for example Livy 45.18.7, 45.26.14, Caes. *BG* 7.76, "Caes." *Bell. Hisp.* 42, *Bell. Afr.* 7, 33, and 98.

78 Polyb. 30.31.10, where the Rhodians themselves are made to lament the policy.

79 Santangelo 2007: 57–58: "The clearest sign of [some cities'] lower condition was not political, but economic."

80 Strabo 17.3.24: For Strabo, the Roman world is divided into four parts: 1. Parts ruled by kings; 2. provinces to which prefects and tax collectors are sent (*phorologoi*, not *demosionai*); 3. free cities; 4. parts controlled by some priests, *dynastai* and *phylarchoi*.

81 Serv. *Aen.* 3.20.

82 Noreña 2016 for "an emerging vision of overseas territory as fiscal rather than strategic space." See also France 2001: 362 on the developing notion of provincial revenues as a just aspect of empire.

WORKS CITED

Ando, C. 2000. *Imperial Ideology and Provincial Loyalty in the Roman Empire*. Berkeley: University of California Press.

Andreades, A. M. 1933. *History of Greek Public Finance*. Cambridge MA: Harvard University Press.

Astin, A. E. 1989. "Roman Government and Politics. 200–134 B.C." In A E. Astin et al. (eds.), *Cambridge Ancient History, Vol. 8*. 2nd ed. (Cambridge: Cambridge University Press), 163–96.

Badian, E. 1958. *Foreign Clientelae (264–70 B.C.)*. Oxford: Oxford University Press.

Badian, E. 1972. *Publicans and Sinners: Private Enterprise in the Service of the Roman Republic*. Oxford: Oxford University Press.

Bang, P. 2013. "The Roman Empire II: The Monarchy." In P. Bang and W. Scheidel (eds.), *The Oxford Handbook of the State in the Ancient Near East and Mediterranean* (Oxford: Oxford University Press), 412–72.

Bell, M. 2007. "An Archaeologist's Perspective on the Lex Hieronica." In J. Dubouloz, J. and S. Pittia (eds.), *La Sicile de Cicéron: Lectures des Verrines* (Besançon: Presses universitaires de Franche-Comté), 187–203.

Bernhardt, R. 1980. "Die immunitas der Freistädte." *Historia: Zeitschrift für Alte Geshcichte* 29: 190–207.

Bernhardt, R. 1985. *Polis und römische Herrschaft in der späteren Republik (149–31 v. Chr.)*. Berlin: De Gruyter.

Brennan, T. C. 2000. *The Praetorship in the Roman Republic*. New York: Oxford University Press.

Brennan, T. C. 2014. "Power and Process under the Republican 'Constitution'." In H. I. Flower (ed.), *The Cambridge Companion to the Roman Republic*. 2nd ed. (Cambridge: Cambridge University Press), 19–53.

Broughton, T. R. S. 1929. *The Romanization of Africa Proconsularis*. Baltimore: Johns Hopkins University Press.

Broughton, T. R. S. 1951. *The Magistrates of the Roman Republic vol. 1*. Atlanta: Scholars Press.

Brunt, P. A. 1990. *Roman Imperial Themes*. Oxford: Oxford University Press.

Carcopino, J. 1914. *La Loi de Hieron et les Romains*. Paris: Boccard.

Cornell, T. J. 1995. *Beginnings of Rome: Italy and Rome from the Bronze Age to the Punic Wars (c. 1000–264 BC)*. London: Routledge.

Crawford, M. H. 1978. "Review of C. Nicolet, *Tributum: recherches sur la fiscalité directe sous le république romaine* and A. Chastagnol et al, *Armées et fiscalité dans le monde antique*." *Journal of Roman Studies* 68: 189.

Crawford, M. 1999. "Origini e sviluppi del system provinciale romano." in A. Giardina and A. Schiavone (eds.), *Storia di Roma* (Turin: Einaudi), 177–202.

Curchin, L. A. 1991. *Roman Spain: Conquest and Assimilation*. London: Routledge.

Dahlheim, W. 1977. *Gewalt und Herrschaft: Das provinziale Herrschaftssystem der römischen Republik*. Berlin: De Gruyter.

Davis, J. A. 2006. *Naples and Napoleon: Southern Italy and the European Revolutions 1780–1860*, Oxford: Oxford University Press.

Day, S. 2017. "The People's Role in Allocating Provincial Commands in the Middle Republic." *Journal of Roman Studies* 107: 1–26.

De Laet, S. J. 1949. *Portorium*. Bruges: Latomus.

Derow, P. S. 1989. "Rome, the Fall of Macedon and the Sack of Corinth." In A E. Astin et al. (eds.), *Cambridge Ancient History, Vol. 8*. 2nd ed. (Cambridge: Cambridge University Press), 290–323.

Derow, P. 2015. *Rome, Polybius, and the East*. Oxford: Oxford University Press.

Díaz Fernández, A. 2015. *Provincia et Imperium: El mando provincial en la República Romana (227–44 a.C.)*. Sevilla: Editorial Universidad de Sevilla-Secretariado de Publicaciones.

Dmitriev, S. 2005. *City Government in Hellenistic and Roman Asia Minor*. Oxford: Oxford University Press.

Dmitriev, S. 2011. *The Greek Slogan of Freedom and Early Roman Politics in Greece*. Oxford: Oxford University Press.

Domergue, C. 1990. *Les Mines de la Péninsule Ibérique dans l'Antiquité romaine*. Rome: Collection de l'École Française de Rome.

Edmondson, J. 1996. "Roman Power and Provincial Administration in Lusitania." In E. Hermon (ed.), *Pouvoir et imperium (IIIe s. av. J.-C.—Ier s. ap. J.-C.)* (Naples: Jovene), 163–211.

Erdkamp, P. 1998. *Hunger and the Sword: warfare and food supply in Roman Republican wars (264–30 B.C.)*. Amsterdam: J. C. Gieben.

Erdkamp, P. 2005. *The Grain Market in the Roman Empire: A Social, Political and Economic Study*. Cambridge: Cambridge University Press.

Erdkamp, P. 2007. "War and State Formation." In P. Erdkamp (ed.), *Companion to the Roman Army* (Malden MA: Blackwell), 96–113.

Ferrary, J.-L. 1997. "The Hellenistic World and Roman Political Patronage." In P. Cartledge, P. Garnsey and E. Gruen (eds.), *Hellenistic Constructs: Essays in Culture, History and Historiography* (Berkeley: University of California Press), 105–19.

Ferrary, J.-L. 1999. "La Liberté des cites et ses limites." *Mediterranean Antiquity* 2: 69–84.

France, J. 2001. "Remarques sur les tributa dans les provinces nord-occidentales du Haut-Empire romain." *Latomus* 60: 359–79.

Frank, T. 1933. *Rome and Italy of the Republic. An Economic survey of Ancient Rome, Vol. 1*. Baltimore: Johns Hopkins University Press.

Fröhlich, P. 2006. *Les Cités grecques et le contrôle des magistrats (IVe–Ier siècle avant J.-C.)*. Geneva/Paris: Droz.

Gargola, D. J. 2017. "Was There a Regular *Provincia Africa* in the Second Century?" *Historia* 66: 331–61.

Giovannini, A. 1985. "Le sel et la fortune de Rome." *Athenaeum* 73: 373–87.

Gros, P. 1978. *Architecture et Société à Rome et en Italie centro-méridionale aux deux derniers siècles de le République*. Brussels: Latomus.

Harris, W. V. 1990. "Roman Warfare in the Economic and Social Context of the Fourth Century B.C." In W. Eder (ed.), *Staat und Staatlichkeit in der frühen römischen Republik* (Stuttgart: Franz Steiner Verlag), 494–510.

Harris, W. V. 2016. *Roman Power: A Thousand Years of Empire*. Cambridge: Cambridge University Press.

Haywood, R. M. 1938. "Roman Africa." In T. Frank (ed.), *An Economic Survey of Ancient Rome Vol. 4* (Baltimore: Johns Hopkins University Press), 3–119.

Hillard, T. and L. Beness. 2013. "Choosing Friends, Foes and Fiefdoms in the Second Century BC." In D. Hoyos (ed.), *A Companion to Roman Imperialism* (Leiden: Brill), 127–40.

Hölkeskamp, K.-J. 2010. *Reconstructing the Roman Republic*. Princeton: Princeton University Press.

Hölkeskamp, K.-J. 2017. *Libera Res Publica. Die politische Kultur des antiken Rom— Positionen und Perspektiven*. Stuttgart: Franz Steiner Verlag.

Howgego, C. J. 1994. "Coin circulation and the Integration of the Roman Economy," *Journal of Roman Archaeology* 7: 5–21.

Kallet-Marx, R. 1995. *Hegemony to Empire: The Development of the Roman Imperium in the East from 148 to 62 B.C.* Berkeley: University of California Press.

Kay, P. 2013. "What Did the Attalids Ever Do for Us? The View from the Aerarium." In P. Thonemann, *Attalid Asia Minor: Money, International Relations, and the State* (Oxford: Oxford University Press), 121–48.

Kay, P. 2014. *Rome's Economic Revolution*. Oxford: Oxford University Press.

Larsen, J. A. O. 1938. "Roman Greece." In T. Frank (ed.), *An Economic Survey of Ancient Rome Vol. 4* (Baltimore: Johns Hopkins University Press), 259–498.

Laurence, R. 1999. *The Roads of Roman Italy: Mobility and Cultural Change*. Oxford: Oxford University Press.

Levi, M. 1988. *Of Rule and Revenue*. Berkeley: University of California Press.

Lintott, A. W. 1993. *Imperium Romanum: Politics and Administration*. London: Routledge.

Lintott, A. W. 1999. *The Constitution of the Roman Republic*. Oxford: Oxford University Press.

López Castro, J. J. 2013. "The Spains, 202–72 BC." In D. Hoyos (ed.), *A Companion to Roman Imperialism* (Leiden: Brill), 67–78.

Mann, M. 1986. *The Sources of Social Power: A History of Power from the Beginning to A.D. 1760, Vol. 1*. Cambridge: Cambridge University Press.

Marchetti, P. 1978. *Histoire économique et monétaire de la deuxième guerre punique*. Brussels: Académie royale de Belgique.

Marzano, A. 2013. *Harvesting the Sea: The Exploitation of Marine Resources in the Roman Mediterranean*. Oxford: Oxford University Press.

Merola, G. D. 2001. *Autonomia Locale Governo Imperiale: Fiscalità e amministrazione nelle province asiane*. Bari: Edipuglia.

Mersing, K. M. 2007. "The War-Tax (Tributum) of the Roman Republic: A Reconsideration." *Classica et Mediaevalia* 58: 215–35.

Migeotte, L. 2014. *Les finances des cités grecques: aux périodes classique et hellénistique*. Paris: Les Belles Lettres.

Mitchell, S. 1999. "The Administration of Roman Asia from 133 BC to AD 250." In W. Eck nd E. Müller-Luckner (eds.), *Lokale Autonomie und römische Ordnungsmacht in den kaiserzeitlichen Provinzen vom 1. bis 3. Jahrhundert* (Munich: Oldenbourg), 17–46.

Monson, A. 2015. "Hellenistic Empires." In A. Monson and W. Scheidel (eds.), *Fiscal Regimes and the Political Economy of Premodern States* (Cambridge: Cambridge University Press), 169–207.

Ñaco del Hoyo, T. 2001. "Publicani, Redemptores, y el 'Vectigal Incertum' en Hispania y Occidente (218–123 a.C.)." In L. Hernández Guerra et al. (eds.), *La Península Ibérica hace 2000 años. Actas del I congreso internacional del Historia Antigua* (Valladolid 2001), 366–75.

Ñaco del Hoyo, T. 2003a. *Vectigal Incertum. Economía de guerra y fiscalidad republicana en el Occidente mediterráneo: Su impacto en el territorio (218–133 a.C.).* British Archaeological Reports 1158. Oxford: Archaeopress.

Ñaco del Hoyo, T. 2003b. "Roman Realpolitik in Taxing Sardinian Rebels (177–175 B.C.)," *Athenaeum* 91: 533–40.

Ñaco del Hoyo, T. 2007. "The Late Republican West: Imperial Taxation in the Making?" In O. Hekster, G. de Kleijn, and D. Slootjes (eds.), *Crises in the Roman Empire: Proceedings of the Seventh Workshop of the International Network Impact of Empire (Nijmegen, June 20–24, 2006)* (Leiden: Brill), 219–31.

Ñaco del Hoyo, T. 2011. "Roman Economy, Finance, and Politics in the Second Punic War," In D. Hoyos (ed.), *A Companion to the Punic Wars* (Malden, MA: Blackwell), 376–92.

Ñaco del Hoyo, T. 2019. "Rethinking stipendiarius as tax terminology of the Roman Republic. Political and military dimensions," *Museum Helveticum* 76: 70–87.

Nicolet, C. 1976. *Tributum: Recherches sur la fiscalite directe sous la republique romaine.* Bonn: Habelt.

Nicolet, C. 1980. *The World of the Citizen in Republican Rome.* Berkeley: University of California Press.

Nicolet, C. 2000. *Censeurs et publicains: Économie et fiscalité dans le Rome antique.* Paris: Fayard.

Noreña, C. 2016. "Law's Imperialism: Conceptions of Empire in Republican Statutes." Rethinking Roman Imperialism in the Middle and Late Republic (c. 327—49 BCE) (Session 58, paper 4). 147th Annual Meeting of the Society for Classical Studies. Hilton San Francisco Union Square Hotel, San Francisco, CA. 8 January 2016.

Oakley, S. P. 1998. *A Commentary on Livy, Books VI–X, Vol. 2: Books VII–VIII.* Oxford: Oxford University Press.

Oakley, S. 2002. "The Roman Conquest of Italy." In J. Rich and G. Shipley (eds), *War and Society in the Roman World* (London: Routledge), 9–37.

Ogilvie, R. M. 1965. *A Commentary on Livy Books 1–5.* Oxford: Oxford University Press.

Palombi, D. 2010. "Roma tardo-repubblicana: verso la città ellenistica." In E. La Rocca, C. Parisi Presicce, and A. Lo Monaco (eds.), *I giorni di Roma, l'età della conquista* (Milan: Skira), 65–82.

Platner, S. B. and T. Ashby. 1929. *A Topographical Dictionary of Ancient Rome.* Oxford: Oxford University Press.

Pinzone, A. 1999. *Provincia Sicilia: ricerche di storia della Sicilia romana da Gaio Fla-minio a Gregorio Magno*. Catania: Edizioni del Prisma.

Prag, J. R. W. 2013. "Sicily and Sardinia-Corsica: The First Provinces." In D. Hoyos (ed.), *A Companion to Roman Imperialism* (Leiden: Brill), 53–65.

Prag, J. R. W. 2014. "The Quaestorship in the Third and Second Centuries B.C." In J. Dubouloz, S. Pittia, and G. Sabatini (eds.), *L'imperium Romanum en perspective* (Besançon: Presses Uni Franche Comté), 193–209.

Prag, J. R. W. 2015a. "*Auxilia* and *Clientelae*: Military Service and Foreign *Clientelae* Reconsidered." In M. Jehne and F. Pina Polo (eds.), *Foreign Clientelae in the Roman Empire: A Reconsideration* (Stuttgart: Franz Steiner Verlag), 281–94.

Prag, J. R. W. 2015b. "Cities and Civic Life in Late Hellenistic Roman Sicily," *Cahiers du Centre Gustave Glotz* 25: 165–208.

Purcell, N. 2005. "The Ancient Mediterranean: The View from the Customs-House." In W. V. Harris (ed.), *Rethinking the Mediterranean* (Oxford: Oxford University Press), 200–32.

Quinn, J. C. 2004. "The Role of the Settlement of 146 in the Provincialization of Af-rica," *L'Africa romana* 15: 1593–1601.

Rathbone, D. W. 2003. "The Control and Exploitation of *Ager Publicus* in Italy under the Roman Republic." In J.-J. Aubert (ed.), *Tâches publiques et entreprise privée dans le monde romain* (Geneva: University of Neuchâtel), 135–78.

Reynolds, J. 1988. "Cities." In D. Braund (ed.), *The Administration of the Roman Empire* (Exeter: University of Exeter Press), 15–51.

Richardson, J. S. 1976. "The Spanish Mines and the Development of Provincial Taxa-tion in the Second Century B.C." *Journal of Roman Studies* 66: 139–52.

Richardson, J. S. 1986. *Hispaniae: Spain and the Development of Roman Imperialism*. Cambridge: Cambridge University Press.

Richardson, L. 1992. *A New Topographical Dictionary of Ancient Rome*. Baltimore: Johns Hopkins University Press.

Roppa, A. and P. van Dommelen. 2012. "Rural Settlement and Land-Use in Punic and Roman Republican Sardinia," *Journal of Roman Archaeology* 25: 49–68.

Roselaar, S. T. 2010. *Public Land in the Roman Republic: A Social and Economic History of Ager Publicus in Italy, 396–389 BC*. Oxford: Oxford University Press.

Rosenstein, N. 2012. *Rome and the Mediterranean, 290 to 146 BC: The Imperial Repub-lic*. Edinburgh: University of Edinburgh Press.

Rosenstein, N. 2016a. "*Bellum se ipsum alet*? Financing Mid-Republican Imperialism." In H. Beck, M. Jehne, and J. Serrati (eds.), *Money and Power in the Roman Republic* (Brussels: Latomus), 114–30.

Rosenstein, N. 2016b. "Tributum in the Middle Republic." In J. Armstrong (ed.), *Brill's Companion to War and Society from New Kingdom Egypt to Imperial Rome* (Leiden: Brill), 80–97.

Santangelo, F. 2007. *Sulla, the Elites and the Empire: A Study of Roman Policies in Italy and the Greek East. Impact of Empire 8*. Leiden: Brill.

Schulz, R. 1997. *Herrschaft und Regierung: Roms Regiment in den Provinzen in der Zeit der Republik*. Paderborn: Schöningh.

Scramuzza, V. M. 1937. "Roman Sicily." In T. Frank (ed.). *An Economic Survey of Ancient Rome. Vol. 3* (Baltimore: Johns Hopkins University Press), 225–377.

Serrati J. 2000. "Garrisons and Grain: Sicily between the Punic Wars." In C. Smith and J. Serrati (eds.), *Sicily from Aeneas to Augustus* (Edinburgh: Edinburgh University Press), 115–33.

Serrati, J. 2016. "The Financing of Conquest: Roman Interaction with Hellenistic Tax Laws." In H. Beck, M. Jehne, and J. Serrati (eds.), *Money and Power in the Roman Republic* (Brussels: Latomus), 97–113.

Soraci, C. 2010. "Riflessioni storico-comparative sul termine 'stipendiarius'." In M. R. Cataudella, A. Greco, and G. Mariotta (eds.), *Strumenti e tecniche della riscossione dei tributi nel mondo antico: Atti del convegno nazionale, Firenze, 6–7 dicembre 2007* (Padua: Sargon), 3–80.

Stockton, D. 1979. *The Gracchi*. Oxford: Oxford University Press.

Tan, J. 2017. *Power and Public Finance at Rome (264–249 BCE)*. New York: Oxford University Press.

Tan, J. 2020. "The *Dilectus-Tributum* System and the Settlement of Fourth Century Italy." In J. Armstrong and M. Fronda (eds), *Romans at War: Soldiers, Citizens, and Society in the Roman Republic* (London: Routledge), 52–75.

Taylor, M. "State Finance in the Middle Roman Republic: A Reevaluation," *American Journal of Philology* 138. 2017: 143–80.

Terrenato, N. 1997. "*Tam Firmum Municipium*: The Romanization of Volaterrae and its Cultural Implications," *The Journal of Roman Studies* 88: 94–114.

Walbank, F. W. 1957. *A Historical Commentary to Polybius, Vol. 1*. Oxford: Oxford University Press.

10

Changes and Limits of Royal Taxation in Pharaonic Egypt (2300–2000 BCE)

JUAN CARLOS MORENO GARCÍA

Introduction

The end of the 3rd millennium BCE has usually been considered a period of state and urban collapse across the ancient Near East. The breakdown of the Old Kingdom in Egypt, the fall of the Akkadian empire in Mesopotamia, and the end of the first wave of urbanization in the Levant has led many historians to posit that a vast crisis engulfed the territories extending from Nubia to the Iranian plateau and from Anatolia to the Persian Gulf. A crisis of this magnitude, along with its aftermath, would have exerted a significant influence on the memories of those who lived through it and promoted social and cultural changes on a vast scale.[1] Researchers have often privileged environmental and climatic change as the main cause of this apparent crisis (e.g., Dalfes, Kukla and Weiss 1994; Weiss 2012), but recent research is increasingly uncomfortable with this hypothesis.[2]

In the case of Egypt, some scholars argue that chaos overwhelmed the land and that the old order simply vanished. This view is based on the end of the unified monarchy (which ruled from the end of the 4th millennium to 2160 BCE), the division of Egypt between several regional powers, and the need to rebuild the tax system when the kingdom was again united under a single king around 2050 BCE. Later literary compositions appear to support this dismal reconstruction. They refer to the destruction of archives, the persecution and murder of scribes, the abolition of taxes, and the overturning of the social order, such that respectable Egyptians longed for the restoration of order and authority. Closer analysis of these sources suggests, however, that this view is reductive and simplistic. It is based on an overly literal reading of ancient texts

TABLE 10.1. Chronology of Ancient Egypt

Period	Chronology (years BCE)	Major Political Events
Early unified monarchy	3100–2613	Narmer, from Abydos, becomes the first pharaoh of a unified Egypt.
Early Old Kingdom (dynasties III–V)	2613–2345	Centralization of power in the king's family. Later on, the state gradually expands its power base through the incorporation of "new men" and a more active presence in the provinces.
Late Old Kingdom (dynasties VI–VIII)	2345–2160	Provincial centers flourish in the Delta and in Upper Egypt. Their leaders gain in power and political influence.
First Intermediate Period	2160–2055	Division of the country into two kingdoms: Heracleopolis (Lower and Middle Egypt) and Thebes (Upper Egypt)
Reign of Mentuhotep II and unification of Egypt	2055–2004	Conquest of Heracleopolis and reunification of the country. Capital: Thebes.
Early Middle Kingdom (dynasties XI–XII)	2004–1773	Unified monarchy. Capital: Itjtawy (south of Memphis).

that were intended more to legitimize new rulers than to describe actual events. The crisis of the monarchy and of its tax system was rooted instead in a complex combination of economic, social, and political factors that arose from the disruption of Nile Valley trade networks controlled by the king and from the emergence of local competitors. In this vein, and contrary to many assumptions about the monolithic nature of pharaonic power, it seems that the integration of Egyptian regions into the kingdom was looser than previously thought and that regional interests could occasionally clash with those of the pharaohs. Pharaohs were obliged to mediate between factions within the élite and to accommodate the interests of the provincial nobility. When they could not do so effectively, the monarchy became increasingly irrelevant while a new order emerged from the struggles and arrangements between regional actors.[3]

Given these premises, four preliminary aspects are crucial to any consideration of the changes and limits of royal taxation in the period 2300–2000 BCE: (1) the actual collecting capacity of the crown immediately prior to the crisis of the monarchy around 2150 BCE; (2) the continuity or disruption of the tax system in the last centuries of the 3rd millennium

BCE; (3) the decline of the crown's control over foreign trade; and (4) the emergence of regional centers of power.

Filling Pharaoh's Treasury at the End of the 3rd Millennium BCE

The titles of Egypt's officials and the bombastic declarations of their biographical inscriptions suggest high levels of centralization and state control of the economy. It is easy to be seduced by such claims: official titles and declarations evoke a rigid administrative hierarchy with clearly defined competences, functions, and bureaux, all in the service of an efficient monarchy that could collect, mobilize, and distribute resources on a vast scale without any apparent opposition. The documentary record implies that several major departments were directly involved in collecting taxes, among them the Granary, the Treasury, the House of Gold, and the House of Life. This impression is misleading not only because flexibility prevailed over rigid hierarchies and departmental boundaries (officials intervened in many different areas during their careers despite their official titles, depending on the favour and the will of the king), but also because the limits and competences of such departments frequently overlap. The Treasury and the House of Life, for example, delivered the same precious objects as rewards to officials honoured by the king. Another problem is that we have no concrete notion of the actual function and collecting capacity of these institutions. For example, did the Granary control all grain in Egypt, or only part of it? Was its main function simply to store and distribute grain to meet the needs of the crown, like feeding the court, providing for officials, and sustaining workers engaged by the state? Was the Treasury charged with the control of all sorts of precious objects (from gold and silver to ivory, unguents, and high-quality textiles), or only with control of objects requisitioned for particular purposes?

The earliest royal annals demonstrate that the main tax concern of the monarchy was to control cattle and gold, the primary forms of mobile wealth. Egypt was very likely the major supplier of gold in the Early Bronze Age international economic sphere, connecting the gold-producing areas of Nubia and the Eastern Desert with the Near East through Byblos and possibly Ebla. As for the Granary, there is as yet no evidence for centralized grain collecting or for a countrywide (re)distributive system. Instead, a network of agricultural centers belonging to the crown stockpiled grain and disbursed it to the crown as necessary. This network also included the temples and their assets in land and labor. It is possible that these centers delivered grain to institutions like the (royal) Residence, the temples, the Granary, the palace, and others, thus forming an intricate network of deliveries in which each institution functioned autonomously, delivering grain to the king, to the temples, or to other institutions as needed and/or when requested.[4] The precise relationship between the Granary, the Treasury, the House of Life, and this network of centers of production and processing (*ḥwt, pr-šnʿ, njwt mꜣwt, gs-pr,* etc.) is not at all clear; it is likewise unclear how deliveries of goods and workers from the domains of élite households fit into the picture when these were requested by the king. To further complicate matters, the "palace" comprised several institutions (the Residence, the Great House, the House of the King, the Palace-ʿḥ, etc.), whose specific competences are uncertain. Finally, there is also some evidence that in the middle of the 3rd millennium BCE provinces supplied grain and dates to the teams of workers that performed specific tasks for the monarchy (Tallet 2018). Of course, corruption, underassessment of taxes owed to the central government by local potentates, the very costs of collecting and transporting taxes, and the income retained more or less "legally" by local authorities and intermediaries meant that there could be substantial discrepancies between nominal gross demands and actual net revenue (Monson and Scheidel 2015: 19). This might explain why revenue collection was more intense at very specific points, such as the agricultural domains and productive centers founded and directly controlled by the crown, than it was elsewhere in the tax system (Jursa and Moreno García 2015).

Surviving records do not allow us to produce even an approximate figure of the percentage of grain collected by and circulating through networks ultimately controlled by the king. In the absence of better data, I estimate that this percentage did not represent a high proportion of the total cereal production of Egypt—possibly less than 15–20%, to suggest an order of magnitude.[5] As for precious metals and other goods, passages in the royal decrees of Coptos reveal that around 2400–2150 BCE temples (at least that of the god Min at Coptos) obtained and stored metals that were subsequently taxed by the Overseer of Upper Egypt, the official responsible for general administrative affairs in the region extending from Elephantine, at the southern border of Egypt, to the capital

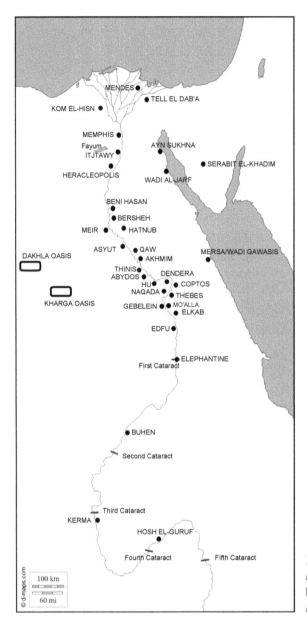

Figure 10.1. Map of ancient Egypt. Base map by D-maps, adapted by author.

Memphis in the north. It was the Overseer of Upper Egypt who kept and updated lists of workers employed on behalf of the crown, and according to the inscription of Iny, he was also involved in controlling valuable products imported from foreign lands. As is the case for cereals, it is impossible to assess the value of the income derived from taxes on trade. We do know, however, that pharaohs appointed officials at the "gateways" of the Nile Valley, not only in Elephantine and at the borders of the Delta, but also at special sites that served as points of departure and arrival for caravans, like Thinis, Aphroditopolis, and Coptos (Moreno García 2013: 134–36; 2017a).

In any case, the final decades of the Old Kingdom monarchy show no trace of disruption to Egypt's administrative organization and tax-system (Moreno García 2013: 146–51; Papazian 2016). A number of royal decrees found at Coptos demonstrate that the king was still founding agricultural domains for the local temple, that his authority was recognized, and that local officials worked on his behalf, obeying instructions concerning the extraction and transportation of blocks of stone. A letter found at Elephantine reveals that corrupt officials were subject to the king's justice, reinforcing the notion of administrative continuity. Such continuity is further apparent in the titles of officials at the time. Ankhi, an official who lived around the 23rd or 22nd century BCE (a period usually characterized as chaotic and prone to political fragmentation and social unrest), bore titles that indicate that he was involved in exercising control over the economic output of the country, as he was "overseer of every repast of the king that heaven gives and earth creates," "overseer of every repast of the king in all his places," and "overseer of the production of every desert," and "overseer of all vegetation" (Altenmüller 2012). Ankhi was far from unique and, in fact, several contemporary officials boasted of similar administrative and fiscal responsibilities, often using metaphorical titles closely related to provisioning the king's table and the Treasury: "overseer of everything that heaven gives and earth creates," "overseer of the abundance of the field of offerings of the king," etc. In other cases, as was also true for Ankhi, these titles explicitly included deserts and marshland, for instance in titles like "overseer of every repast of the king that heaven gives and earth creates (and which comes) out of the production of every desert," "one who reckons up the production of the deserts, marshlands, and heaven," and "overseer of the repast of the king who reckons up the production of the deserts, marshlands, and heaven" (Fischer 1996a: 32–33, 40 pl. 6).[6] Finally, Hetepeni, an official who bore some of these titles, was also a "commander of the king's scribes who reckons the troops (of men and cattle) in the Double Domain"—all of Egypt, in other words.

Two conclusions can be drawn from this evidence. First, control over people, territory, and resources continued to be a primary concern for the central administration, as it had been in previous centuries. Second, this was still a period of stability, in which the central role of the king enjoyed formal recognition. There was continuity in Egypt's administrative organization and in the chain of command, suggesting that the crown's tax system continued to function during the very late Old Kingdom period. It is, however, possible that the increased frequency of expressions stressing control over production and over border areas immediately prior to the collapse of the monarchy points instead to problems underlying the organization of the kingdom, including the capacity of the king to control its resources. Coptos emerges as a pivotal area, because the leaders of this province suddenly accumulated substantial power and wealth, married into the royal family, organized expeditions to the quarries, and were able to transmit their privileged position and authority to their descendants (Goedicke 1967: 172–225; 1994; Mostafa 1984–1985; 1987; and 2005). The documentary evidence from the temple of Min suggests that the same family was in control of this institution for several generations and that it was their main power base. Situated in a strategic geographical setting, Coptos was close to the gold mines of the Eastern Desert, to the route that connected Coptos with Hu and the Western Desert, and to the route that led to the Red Sea, the last being especially important in a period when the port of Mersa/Wadi Gawasis was becoming a key node in trade with the land of Punt in the southern Red Sea area.

A handful of powerful provincial families appear to have controlled trade with foreign lands, or at least to have monitored the arrival of foreign goods in Egypt. As noted above, during the last decades of the Old Kingdom the Overseer of Upper Egypt regularly collected gold, copper, and some kind of jewelry or precious items from the temple of Min at Coptos, along with other goods and taxes, especially in the form of compulsory work (Goedicke 1967: 117–27, 137–47). Temples were supposed to collect and store metals that could subsequently be taxed by the king. In fact, a later text also from Coptos shows that a local chief donated an astonishing quantity of precious items to the local temple. They included forty gold and copper vessels, gold and silver pieces, lapis-lazuli and turquoise, thirty-six collars decorated with lapis-lazuli, and substantial amounts of incense and myrrh (Goedicke 1994). The fact that the monarchy had already collapsed or was about to had no apparent effect on the flow of precious items from abroad. The later inscription in the tomb of Setka at Elephantine reveals that this local potentate imported myrrh from Byblos, gold and copper from Punt (southern Red Sea), incense from Nubia (more precisely, from the land of Yam), and precious items like ebony, ivory, and exotic animals from other locations. Setka then shipped these goods to Heracleopolis in the north. The local chiefs at Coptos and Elephantine obtained foreign goods and exercised control over the flow of precious goods into Egypt, a role that persisted after the collapse of the monarchy. The recent discovery of imported First Intermediate Period Egyptian pottery at the Delta of Gash and at Mahal Teglinos in Eastern Sudan indicates that Egyptian materials could arrive in this area not only via the Nile valley, but also via the Eastern Desert and the Red Sea coast (Manzo 2017: 50–51). Egyptian leaders were able to finance and organize trading activities with foreign areas such as the Levant, the southern Red Sea, and Nubia even when no pharaoh ruled over the whole country. Setka was even able to travel along the Nile and traverse territory under Theban control with no apparent difficulty, despite the fact that Thebes and Heracleopolis were at war.

That Coptos and Elephantine were crucial nodes in Egypt's trade with foreign lands, and that foreign trade was largely in their hands already in the late Old Kingdom period, is further apparent from an analysis of three titles. The title "one who places the fear of Horus [=the king] in foreign lands" was held by eleven officials: two of them were buried at Saqqara and lived around 2400 BCE (Kaiemtjenenet) and 2300 BCE (Ikhi I), but the rest came from Elephantine (Tjetji, Harkhuf, Sabni, Intef-Mekhu and Pepynakht-Heqaib), the area of Coptos (Inikaf and Henti), and the Dakhla oasis (two anonymous dignitaries) and lived from the middle of the Sixth Dynasty to the very end of the 3rd millennium BCE. The title "one who brings back the produce/ornaments of foreign lands (to his lord)" and its variants was held by eleven officials, two from Saqqara (Ikhi I and Iny, probably buried in the Memphite area), five from Elephantine (Tjetji, Harkhuf, Sabni, his son Sabni, and Pepynakht-Heqaib), and two from Coptos (Inikaf and Henti), while two more (Idi and Neferhetepu) are only attested in rock inscriptions in the area of Elephantine and Wadi Hammamat respectively (Kuraszkiewicz 2014; Diego Espinel 2015–2016; Moreno García 2017a). In fact, archaeological evidence is beginning to show that caravan leaders from Elephantine were conducting trade with the Levant on a purely private basis as early as the 23rd century BCE (Forstner-Müller and Raue 2008). The third title concerns control over a "gateway" (r3-'3), and it includes several variants: "overseer of the northern gateway." "overseer of the southern gateway," "overseer of the narrow entrance of the southern land," etc. (Somaglino 2010). Setting aside the cases of Userkafankh, who lived during the 5th dynasty, and Khabaukhnum, who lived at the end of the 6th (both of whom are buried in the area of Memphis), all other attested controllers of "gateways" are from the provinces, namely from Elephantine (Sabni and his son Sabni), Edfu (Qar), Hu (Tjauty), Deir el-Gebrawy (Djau-Shemay and his son Djau), and Heliopolis (Sobeki and Meru). Their distribution reveals that southernmost Egypt and the area of Middle Egypt around Deir el-Gebrawy became important centers in the flow of foreign goods during the 6th dynasty.

This situation changed at the very end of the Old Kingdom or the very beginning of the First Intermediate period. In that time, the leaders of Coptos and Thebes appear to be the main agents in exercising control over trade in foreign goods. Tjauti of Coptos was "one who fills the heart of the king in the gateway of Upper Egypt," while Intef of Thebes similarly claimed to be "one who fills the heart of the king in the southern gateway" (Somaglino 2010). As in the case of Coptos, the sudden importance of localities such as Hu and Deir el-Gebrawy in the late Old Kingdom period seems to be connected to their control of the movement of wealth from neighbouring foreign areas. There may have been conflict between Coptos and Thebes over a route leading to Hu (Darnell 2002: 30–37); but in all events Thebes eventually established control over it. In light of the three categories of titles analyzed above, it is easier to understand why the titles referred to at the beginning of this chapter mention the deserts as a focus of attention for tax officials at the end of the Old Kingdom period. Flows of wealth from Nubia, the Red Sea (through the Coptos/Thebes area), the oases, the Western Desert, and Asia appear to flourish, thereby enhancing the social and political importance of those places that were well positioned to monitor the circulation of goods: Elephantine, Coptos, and Middle Egypt. In localities like Balat in the Dakhla oasis, which was probably founded as a trading post on the route to Nubia and the areas further to the West, the political system survived the collapse of the monarchy and continued to engage in the same activities as before. This is equally true of Coptos, Thebes, and Elephantine. Their role can therefore not be reduced to that of agents of the monarchy.

The examples of Coptos, Elephantine, Deir el-Gebrawy, and Balat are part of a broader phenomenon, namely the rising power of élites in Upper Egyptian provinces. This trend is scarcely attested in previous centuries. The use of terms like "feudalism" to describe this development is misleading. In fact, it might be better understood as a consequence of the intensification of trade flows from and towards Nubia, the Red Sea, and the deserts surrounding the Nile Valley. This intensification was accompanied by the creation of a network of production and storage centers (ḥwt) that covered all of Upper Egypt and supplied caravans and expeditions. One consequence was the elevation of local leaders as indispensable providers of logistical support (food, equipment, cloth, transport, workforce, etc.). Judging from the quality of the tombs of these local leaders, their titles (in many cases related to the court) and the titles of their followers, considerable wealth was expended in the provinces of Upper Egypt and likely directed toward building up political and patronage networks. The abandonment of the Nubian trade center Buhen, the development of the Red Sea port of Mersa/Wadi Gawasis, the foundation of Balat in the oasis of Dakhla, the increasing importance of the area of Middle Egypt between Asyut and Beni Hasan (the endpoint of caravans coming from the oases and from Libya), and, finally, the inscriptions of the caravan leaders of Elephantine demonstrate that new developments in Nubia occasioned a reaction in Egypt. Nubia appears to be more organized politically, to the point that the inscribed figurines known as *execration texts*, with their lists of peoples and lands potentially dangerous to Egypt, show an overwhelming presence of Nubian territories and people. It appears that Egypt attempted to bypass the commercial circuits controlled by Nubian leaders by exploiting the desert trails and the maritime route of the Red Sea. It is also possible that the organization of commercial expeditions into Nubia intensified and became more complex and expensive. Creating, maintaining, and financing a network of stations along the Nile Valley therefore became essential and required the involvement of local leaders in Upper Egypt whose collaboration had to be rewarded in some way.

For these reasons, it is not surprising that the rebellion against the central monarchy began in the area of Coptos/Thebes and Elephantine, or that a new hub of trade with the Mediterranean, centered at Heracleopolis, became a major political power after the collapse of the Old Kingdom. Political crisis did not produce chaos and misery, but rather the contrary: towns thrived (Elephantine, Edfu, Dendera, Asyut, etc.), people of relatively low status displayed more wealth in their tombs, and a chain of trade and exchange clusters dotted the Nile Valley between Nubia and the Mediterranean: Kerma, Elephantine, Coptos/Thebes, Asyut/Beni Hasan, Heracleopolis, and the Western margins of the Nile Delta (Kom el-Hisn, Barnugi). This was a period when Asiatics and Nubians settled in Egypt and began playing an active role as soldiers and traders in the service of the rulers of such clusters. The rivalries and alliances between these centers characterize the last decades of the 3rd millennium BCE. This was, moreover, a period of political and administrative innovation. The old institutions of the monarchy were no longer operative. This is indicated by the rise of cities and "citizens" to a prominent role, the development of consultative bodies close to kings (such as the *sḥ n sr.w* ("chamber of dignitaries")), the creation of new institutions (such as the *'t* and *'ẖnw.ty* ("chamber"), first attested at Heracleopolis), and the emphasis on private accumulation of wealth. Accordingly, when a new pharaoh finally sat on the throne of a reunified Egypt around 2050 BCE, the old institutions had to be restored or, perhaps more precisely, reinvented—including the Treasury.

A final point concerns the goods that were traded and why they prompted all of these changes. The most prominent goods were gold from Nubia and the Eastern Desert, fine textiles from Egypt, exotic precious goods from Africa (ebony, ivory, exotic hides, and plants), aromatic resins from the southern Red Sea, copper from Jordan, and slaves and even leather and grain (the flow of large Egyptian vessels into Nubia, likely full of foodstuffs, increased during the First Intermediate Period: Hafsaas-Tsakos 2010: 390–92). Judging from the administrative tablets in Ebla (Biga 2012; Biga and Roccati 2012) and the recently published inscriptions of Iny (from Saqqara?) and Setka of Elephantine, gold, metals, myrrh, and linen were exported to the Levant, while silver, slaves, lapis lazuli, and tin made the reverse journey to Egypt. If the land of Dugurasu in Eblaite sources should indeed be identified as Egypt, then the volume of these exchanges was extensive. In any case, the last centuries of the 3rd millennium BCE were a period of intense commercial exchange between northeastern Africa, the Aegean, the Levant, Mesopotamia, and Central Asia. Egypt appears to have functioned as a strategic mediator, because goods from the southern Red Sea and Nubia reached the Levant and Mesopotamia through the Nile Valley (Moreno García 2017a and 2017b). Two items stand out and seem to have played a crucial role: gold and myrrh. Heracleopolis, the main political power in northern Egypt, was heavily involved in the traffic of myrrh. It was there that Setka of Elephantine sent shipments of this aromatic plant, whereas the titles of some officials buried at Heracleopolis reveal that a specific administrative office related to myrrh was operative there (*ḥȝw m ʿt-ʿntyw* ("measurer in the chamber of myrrh"), *wr ʿt-ʿntyw* ("chief of the department of myrrh"): Pérez-Die 2005: 242, 248; Willems 2007: 95; Diego Espinel 2011: 200–2 and 246–50; cf. also Diego Espinel 2017). Later, during the very late 3rd and early 2nd millennium BCE, the area of Bersheh replaced Heracleopolis as the main entrepôt for the circulation of myrrh. It was in this period that Asiatics and Nubians frequented the area and intervened in its political affairs. Many rulers mentioned at Bersheh and Hatnub bore the unique epithet *mrry ʿntyw* ("one who loves myrrh," cf. Doxey 1998: 305). Djehutinakht, a dignitary in the service of Ahanaht, the "great chief" of the province of Bersheh during the reign of Mentuhotep II, referred to his superior as "the overseer of priests to whom valuables are brought from foreign lands, (namely) myrrh and galena" (Willems 2007: 33). Iha, another dignitary in the service of Ahanakht, was "a chieftain of the House of [myrrh, who loc]ked away precious oils" (Willems 2007: 67).

There is some evidence that areas that had been under Heracleopolitan control continued to conduct their own trade when they fell under Theban sway. A Nubian graffito from around 1938 BCE reveals that a group of people from the same household, which included two women (one from Kom el-Hisn and the other from Sais, in the Delta), left its traces at Wadi Korosko, an important route leading to gold fields in the Eastern Desert (Davies 2014). The men are described as *ḥnms* "friends"

(Satzinger and Stefanović 2014: 344). In fact, neither the leader of the group nor its individual members bear any title at all, be it military or "civil." The presence of women in the group further reinforces the idea that it was comprised of "civilians," perhaps involved in logistical activities for a royal expedition and/or in trading activities (Žába 1974: 56–57 [28a-m]; cf. also 38 [9]). Another graffito, further south, was inscribed by a certain Khesebed from Bersheh, whose name literally means "lapis lazuli" (Žába 1974: 205–6 [211]). As for Thebes, the titles of many officials of king Mentuhotep II, who reunified the country, reveal that the search for precious items and the control of the routes through which they circulated was one of his major strategic concerns (Moreno García 2017a).

Claims concerning control over the production of the deserts or about bringing back the produce of foreign lands—like those that appear in the inscriptions mentioned above—indicate a sudden concern about desert areas, foreign trade, and the circulation of commodities across the borders of Egypt during the last years of the Old Kingdom. In this context, Coptos and Elephantine played an increasingly crucial and autonomous role. It is not a coincidence that precisely these areas finally escaped the control of the king around the middle of the 22nd century BCE, as the inscription of Ankhtifi of Moʿalla reveals. A crucial question emerges: what was the impact of these events on the tax system of the pharaonic state?

The Infrastructure of Taxation in the Late 3rd Millennium BCE

If, as previously argued, trade through the Nile Valley played an increasingly important role in the last centuries of the 3rd millennium BCE, this was possible because of a network of production and storage centers scattered along the Nile that belonged to the crown. These centers collected taxes and placed them at the service of the crown. At the same time, local potentates were elevated to the position of representatives of the king under the supervision of the Overseer of Upper Egypt.

The main production and storage centers of the crown were the aforementioned ḥwt. Their mission was to produce and store foodstuffs and other goods for distribution to caravans and expeditions. This is stated clearly in a passage from the inscription of Herkhuf, a caravan leader from Elephantine:

Orders have been brought to the governor(s) of the new agricultural domains, the companion(s), and the overseer(s) of priests commanding that supplies be furnished from what is under the charge of each of them from every *ḥwt* belonging to a processing center and from every temple, with no exemption. (Strudwick 2005: 333)

The role played by the *ḥwt*-centers in provisioning the king's agents is also exemplified by the inscriptions of Hatnub, which refer to the equipment delivered by the local *ḥwt* to the teams of workers sent to the quarries, the organisation of the expeditions by an overseer of *ḥwt*, and the close relationship between the *ḥwt* and the agricultural domains of the crown (Moreno García 2007 and 2013). An administrative text from Elephantine, dated to about 2000 BCE, mentions deliveries of cereals, dates, and cattle by a governor of a *ḥwt* to several dignitaries, including a messenger arriving in Elephantine on a mission for the king (von Pilgrim 1996: 285–300). Finally, an administrative document from the early 2nd millennium BCE enumerates various kinds of textiles delivered to an official; he received them from a warehouse, from a work camp (*ḫnrt*), and from a locality or royal center named *ḥwt-ḫty* "the *ḥwt* of (king) Khety" (Simpson 1986: 14, pl. 14).

ḥwt-centers appear as crucial nodes in the geography of the Egyptian tax system of the 3rd millennium BCE. They were established in almost every province and served as agricultural centers with their own fields, cattle, and workers; they also functioned as local warehouses where agricultural and possibly craft production (sandals, cloth, ropes, etc.) was stored and delivered to royal agents. Together with temples, the *ḥwt* formed a network of royal centers which made possible the collection of taxes and the mobilisation of the labor force of the country, placing both at the disposal of the crown along the Nile Valley. Additionally, the *ḥwt*-centers were involved in the production of textiles (Moreno García 2007 and 2013). Judging from the extant evidence, it appears that this network constituted the backbone of the state's extractive system. The fields and workers attached to temples and *ḥwt* provided most of the work and goods demanded by the state, while tax levies from villages and households played a comparatively lesser role. It also appears that the state distributed rations/wages in exchange for the specific services it demanded and never as part of an alleged "redistribution" system that operated at the level of Egypt as a whole (Jursa and Moreno García 2015; Warden 2014: 223–43; Warden 2016).

The increasing importance of Upper Egypt on account of the routes that crossed this region (both by land and along the Nile) led to the creation of the position of overseer of Upper Egypt, a post often held by viziers. The overseer of Upper Egypt supervised and coordinated the activities of the officials of the crown in this area. Among his many duties were the organization of lists of people obliged to perform compulsory work for the king, the organization of transport duties, the collection of precious metals, the organization of new agricultural domains, and the keeping of archives. Weni, an official who lived around 2300 BCE, is perhaps the best-known overseer of Upper Egypt. He described his responsibilities in these terms:

> I acted for him as overseer of Upper Egypt in a satisfactory manner so that no one there did any harm to his fellow, I doing every task, assessing everything due to the (Royal) Residence in this Upper Egypt twice, every regular corvée due to the (Royal) Residence in this Upper Egypt twice; carrying out my official duties so as to make my reputation in this Upper Egypt. (Jursa and Moreno García 2015: 143)

In this text, Weni stresses his efficiency by stating that he doubled the taxes and the compulsory work ordinarily due in Upper Egypt. Temples and *ḥwt* were thus subject to his authority. As leader of an expedition, Weni mentions that governors of *ḥwt* and temples were to provide him with troops. The scope of the activities of the agents of the crown in the provinces involved other activities, depending on local conditions and resources. One of these was the expansion of cattle production, as the inscription of Qar of Edfu reveals (Moreno García 2013: 131). Overseers of Upper Egypt also appear to have monitored foreign trade missions: in his biographical inscription, Iny proclaims that upon the successful completion of a mission he went down to the court together with the overseer of Upper Egypt in order to inspect the produce (*inw*) he had brought from abroad (Marcolin and Espinel 2011: 574).

The local agents of the king imitated the lifestyle typical of the royal court and of the palatial élites. They maintained huge retinues formed by their families, followers, and subordinates. Their decorated tombs and luxurious goods provide abundant information about their wealth, retinues, and links to the court. Minor provincial courts flourished almost everywhere in Upper Egypt at this time, to the point that the development of the fiscal structure of the monarchy in this region must have accommodated the local expenditure of a significant part of the taxes raised. The paradox, then, is that the initial measures implemented to raise the income of the monarchy and to facilitate the circulation of goods between Nubia, the deserts, and the capital involved the reinvestment of a substantial part of the revenue in the provinces. The political consequences are obvious. Potential foci of accumulation of wealth and political power posed a threat to the monarchy in the long term, including the emergence of local political agendas and alliances that did not necessarily align with those of the distant sovereign.

When rebellions finally erupted, part of the tax infrastructure seems to have vanished. Ankhtifi of Mo'alla, an official dispatched to southernmost Egypt to restore order and to oppose rebellious Coptos and Thebes, still obeyed the overseer of Upper Egypt based in Abydos—at least nominally. By contrast, the inscription of a follower of the first documented autonomous Theban ruler, the Great Chief of Upper Egypt Antef, reveals a completely different political environment. This environment was dominated by meetings between potentates of Upper and Lower Egypt (Fischer 1996a: 83–90); the authority of Antef himself extended over Dendera and he was known as Antef the Great. The old political order had collapsed, as had the central tax system. The challenge for local leaders was to rebuild taxation systems in their territories, especially as flows of wealth were now passing through the Western Delta, the Fayum/Heracleopolis, Middle Egypt and the Theban area, and Elephantine. This was a period of rivalries, when fortresses punctuated the landscape and ḥwt-centers still existed (their governors, ḥqȝ ḥwt, are well documented), but their number declined significantly and their resources were now probably in the hands of local leaders. In fact, there are signs that the former network of ḥwt-centers was broken, at least in some areas. Thus, for instance, a literary text known as *The Teaching for Merikare* describes events that supposedly took place during the reign of the Heracleopolitan king Merikare. Whether this composition really dates to Merikare's reign and its contents describe the conditions prevalent in his kingdom is still a matter of debate. In any case, some passages stress the importance of building *ḥwt*-centers in the context of the fiscal reorganization of northern Egypt, as though these centers had disappeared or were no longer in use:

> Look, the [land] which they had destroyed is made into provinces and every great town [is refounded], officials are appointed and provided with labor-services, with knowledge of every tax. Pure priests are provided with taxable fields," "the labor-services of the Delta belong to you," "the region of Djedsut totals ten thousand men, commoners and pure priests who are without labor-service. Officials have been in it since the time of the (royal) Residence; the borders are confirmed, its strongholds are mighty; many northerners irrigate it as far as the Delta, taxed in grain in charge of the pure priests," and "build *ḥwt* (centers) in the Delta! (Parkinson 1997: 223–24)

Similar conditions appear to prevail in Southern Egypt. Neferukayet, the spouse of Antef II, one of the first Theban kings, reorganized the administration of the territories under their authority: "She has reorganized Upper Egypt, the van of men, from Elephantine to the Aphroditopolite province, with women together with governors of *ḥwt* (centers) and dignitaries from the whole land" (Lichtheim 1988: 43). An unfortunately poorly preserved royal inscription of king Antef II mentions events that concluded with the consolidation of the southern frontier of an unknown province, the integration of its authorities (governors and chiefs of the army) and some measures relating to *ḥwt* and fortresses (Schenkel in Arnold 1976: 50–51, pl. 42 and 52). In the context of Antef II's campaigns in the Thinite and Aphroditopolite provinces, it is quite possible that these measures were intended both to consolidate the border of the Theban kingdom there and to reorganize the administration and the production centers of the crown in the area. Another one of Antef II's inscriptions states that he conquered the Thinite province and established his northern frontier in the province of Aphroditopolis after having opened all the fortresses there (Schenkel in Arnold 1976: 52–53, pl. 53). That is why, about a century later, the scribe of the cadaster and overseer of fields Antefiqer, who lived under the reign of Senusret I (1956–1911 BCE), stated: "there had served as scribe of the watered fields of Thinite Abydos my father and the father of my father since the time of Horus Wahankh, the king of Upper and Lower Egypt, the Son of Re Antef (II)" (Lichtheim 1988: 73). All of these measures and the strategic position of the Thinite province on the routes of the oases of the Western Desert are referred to explicitly in the inscription of the overseer of troops Djemi:

> I marched against Abydos, which was under the enemy. I caused him to go down to his realm from the center of the city, there was none who had the power to march against him. I taxed the people of Wawat for every [chief?] who had been in the area. I brought taxes from the Thinite province (and) I was praised for it. (Darnell 2008: 99)

Another inscription mentions an official appointed as overseer of exemptions in the Thinite province (Fischer 1961).

Local leaders in other provinces under Theban control, like Gebelein, play an ambiguous role. They navigated between service to the authorities in Thebes and their own local interests. The Royal seal-bearer Iti, for instance, boasted about his support of Thebes ("I was a great pillar in the Theban nome, a man of standing in the Southland"). Simultaneously, Iti enjoyed sufficient autonomy (he states that he nourished Gebelein while Thebes was hungry) to regard Thebes with a certain ironic detachment ("whether I served a great lord, or served a small lord, no fault of mine occurred"; Lichtheim 1988: 31–32). Merer, an officiant in a sanctuary at Gebelein, states that he made offerings in two temples for the ruler as he had done previously for thirteen rulers (Lichtheim 1973: 87–88). The stela of Hetepi of Elkab relates that it was only during the reign of Antef III that the area between Thebes and Elephantine was definitively integrated in the Theban kingdom (Gabra 1976). Control over resources, especially those from the desert routes, was crucial for these early Theban rulers, and it provides some clues about their strategic priorities and their economic and tax concerns. The inscriptions of the overseer of the seal Tjetji, who served under kings Antef II and Antef III, are exemplary in this respect:

> The treasury was in my hand under my seal, being the choicest of every good thing brought to the majesty of my lord from Upper and Lower Egypt; being everything that gladdens the heart as tribute of this entire

land, through fear of him throughout this land; and what was brought to the majesty of my lord by the chiefs who rule the desert, through fear of him throughout the foreign lands. He gave these things to me, knowing the excellence of my performance. I accounted for them to him without there ever being a fault of mine deserving punishment, because my competence was great. (Lichtheim 1988: 46–48)

Of course, the scope of the managerial activities developed by Tjetji also include the reorganization of the administration and the evaluation of the wealth of the kingdom: "as for any royal department that the majesty of my lord entrusted to me, and for which he made me carry out a commission according to his ka's desire, I did it for him. I improved all their procedures," and "I built a barge for the city and a boat for all service: the accounting with the magnates, and every occasion of escorting or sending." Bringing precious foreign goods to Egypt thus appears to have been a major concern for the nascent Theban kingdom, judging from an inscription probably dating from the reign of Antef II (Mathieu 2008): "it was with beautiful southern goods, which he had brought back from his victories, that he built monuments for Montu and that he satisfied Amun." Such goods included myrrh and a kind of precious unguent called *ḥknw*.

There appears to be a basic difference between the Heracleopolitan and Theban kingdoms. Thebans were trying to reorganize the fiscal configuration of the territories they progressively brought under their control and, in doing so, they seem constrained to build *ex novo*, as if the previous Old Kingdom structures had all but vanished or ceased functioning in southernmost Egypt. As is true in other domains (such as the composition and transmission of new funerary texts, the reintroduction of high-quality monumental art and epigraphy, etc.: Willems 2014: 81–82), Thebes appears to have been forced to import these elements from the north. There, in the areas apparently under Heracleopolitan control, formal "classic" art, epigraphy, and court etiquette survived. When the country was reunified, the influence and, perhaps, the managerial experience of officials from the region of Heracleopolis was substantial in Thebes. However, the political organization of the Heraclepolitan kingdom was more fragile and looser than that of Thebes, and at least some Middle Egyptian potentates enjoyed great autonomy of action, a situation they were able to preserve after reunification. In fact, an inscription from Asyut suggests that the two main sectors of the Heracleopolitan élite were the governors (*ḥȝty-ʿ*) of Upper Egypt and the notables (*bwȝw*) of Heracleopolis (Moreno García 2017a). Beneath the formal veneer of a restored monarchy and the return to a classicism inspired by the artistic canon of the Old Kingdom, the reality was that the Theban kingdom incorporated provincial élites with their own interests and autonomous institutions. This set limits on the reconstruction of the tax system in subsequent centuries.

Reunification of the Country and Reconstruction of the Tax System

The historical circumstances that finally culminated in the reunification of Egypt under the rule of the Theban king Mentuhotep II remain obscure. Judging from the archaeological evidence, it appears that negotiation with the powerful lords of Middle Egypt and the élites of Heracleopolis made it possible for the small Theban kingdom (about 12% of the Egyptian Nile Valley) to secure nominal control over the remaining 88% of the country, which was conquered and incorporated in only a few years. This development hinged on respect for established interests in newly integrated regions, the co-opting of local élites, the harmonization of the interests of the élites of Thebes with those of the rest of the country, and the implementation of a fiscal policy that could once again direct abundant resources to the king. The establishment of a monopoly over the trade networks across the Red Sea and from Northeastern Africa to the Mediterranean appears to have been of primary importance (Moreno García 2017a).

Judging from the administrative titles of several officials of Mentuhotep II, control over precious goods remained crucial. The inscriptions from his reign record campaigns against the peoples living east of Thebes, in the mountainous desert areas between the Nile and the Red Sea, and perhaps also in Libya. Other military interventions sought to secure control over Nubia and the routes of the Western Desert and the oases, to the point that an exceptional inscription found at Jebel Uweinat, in the area of the actual Libyan-Sudanese-Egyptian border, records the importation of incense and other goods from the land of Yam (Northwest Sudan? Ennedi?) and from other territories. These goods were imported through the Western Desert trails that crossed the oasis of Dakhla (Cooper 2012; Darnell 2008; Moreno García 2017a). In his inscriptions, Mentuhotep II boasted of the submission of foreign lands. An inscription of a contemporary official found in Wadi Hammamat attests to Mentuhotep II's interest in this area, and another fragment of an inscription mentions the taxation of "all the Eastern land" as well as campaigns (?) against areas of Nubia and Medja (?) (Postel 2008). Mentuhotep II's successor, Mentuhotep III, dispatched the first maritime expedition of the Middle Kingdom to the land of Punt, while Mentuhotep IV sent expeditions to the harbour of Ain Sukhna. With the incorporation/conquest of the Heracleopolitan kingdom, Mentuhotep II finally succeeded in controlling both the lower Nile (between Nubia and the Mediterranean) and the alternative routes by land (through the trails of the Western Desert) and, at least partly, by sea. His kingdom (a reunified Egypt) now became an inescapable mediator in trade activities between inner Africa, the Red Sea, and the Mediterranean.

The inscriptions of some dignitaries who served under Mentuhotep II and the archaeological evidence reveal the importance of long-distance trade in the politics of this king (Moreno García 2017a and 2017b). One of them, Khety, was "overseer of the Two Treasuries" and "overseer of silver and gold, overseer of lapis-lazuli and turquoise." Another official, Dagi, was promoted to the rank of vizier sometime in the final decade of Mentuhotep II's reign and, like the Chief Steward Henu in Year 8 of Mentuhotep III, he was "Overseer of the Double Treasury" and "overseer of the Double House of Gold" (Allen 1996). In his Theban tomb, another official named Khety recorded several missions conducted on behalf of a king Mentuhotep. These missions included securing control over (supplies of?) precious ointments, dispatching mining expeditions to Sinai and other territories, and transporting precious minerals and stones to Egypt, including lapis-lazuli, which is not found in the Near East but is native to the land of Tefreret according to this and later inscriptions (Landgráfová 2011: 54–58). The coffin of the royal concubine Ashayet mentions myrrh and represents three foreign female servants, two of whom were *Medja* (that is to say, they came from the southern Eastern Desert) while the third one was called Ibhatyt, "The one from

Ibhat"—Ibhat being a region in the Nubian Eastern Desert (Moreno García 2017a: 106–9). All this evidence reveals a deep interest in precious metals, semi-precious stones, and aromatic plants, in pursuit of which the governors of Bersheh proved to be invaluable collaborators. Finally, indirect evidence of the importance of international trade comes from a ritual object that appears suddenly around the reign of Mentuhotep II or slightly earlier, the "paddle dolls." These figurines quickly become quite common over a vast territory, from India and Central Asia to the Aegean and Egypt. They have been interpreted as some kind of protective entity that was particularly relevant at sites in which people from different cultures worked and coexisted (mines, trading posts, etc.: Moreno García 2017b).

The monarchy needed resources, and some inscriptions echo both the effort to rebuild the tax-system and the effort to establish control over the strategic crossroads through which foreign commodities passed into Egypt. The great steward Henenu, for instance, proclaimed that "I taxed for him [=the Pharaoh] Thinis of the Thinite province and the Lower Aphroditopolite province," before describing his activities as treasurer of the produce of the (Western) oasis and the assignation of quotas (*nḥb*) of oxen, goats, asses, and other goods to the provinces of Upper Egypt (Hayes 1949). Henenu also organized expeditions against the desert populations, built ships, cut down cedar trees in Lebanon, and opened the roads for the missions of the king. Cattle feature as a valuable possession both before and after the reunification of the country, and cattle breeding was a correspondingly major fiscal concern for the kings (Moreno García 1999). As was true already in early dynastic times, it seems that cattle, gold, and precious goods (arriving from abroad) represented the main basis of the tax system. This is why slightly later officials like Imeny of Beni Hasan boast of the provision of cattle herds with the obligation to return a certain amount as taxes:

> I spent the years as ruler of the Oryx province with all contributions for the king's house being in my charge. I gave gang-overseers to the domains of the herdsmen of the Oryx province and 3000 oxen as their allocation. I was praised for it in the king's house in every year of the cattle tax. I delivered all their dues to the king's house, and there was no shortage

against me in any bureau of his, for the entire Oryx province labored for me in steady stride ... the man who fixes (lit. provides) the contributions in proportion to the barley is [a just] man in God's eyes. (Parkinson 1997: 241).

One inscription of Mentuhotep II states that districts were paying taxes again (Darnell 2008), while an official of Mentuhotep II states that he had spent many years in the "House of Khety" (the Heracleopolitan kingdom) and that the royal domain and all its departments (*pr-nswt 't.f nb(t).f*) were now under his care, so that the royal domain prospered (Clère and Vandier 1948: 44). At the same time, important officials of the recently incorporated Heracleopolitan kingdom collaborated with Mentuhotep II in the reorganization of his kingdom. Ahanakhte of Bersheh was one of them. He became vizier, several of his subordinates occupied important positions in the reunified monarchy, and he described himself as the one who judged between the provinces, who established the boundary cairns of the Hare province, under whose governance "the South was content while the Northland was under his command," and he who unified the Hare province (Brovarski 1981: 18). In other cases, officials named Khety (or with names formed with composite forms of Khety, such as Khetyankh or Khentykhety) probably also came from the north, were integrated in the administrative structure of the kingdom (Vernus 1970), and played an important role as specialists in the management of the kingdom (cf. *infra*). Judging from the inscriptions of this reign, sealbearers, chiefs of the treasury, and great stewards were the main protagonists in the reconstruction of the fiscal foundations of the kingdom under Mentuhotep II (Allen 1996).

Such fiscal interests would explain why Mentuhotep II sought to control the "gateways" of the freshly incorporated Heracleopolitan kingdom, especially since control over trade routes was the basic aim of his policy. Intef son of Tjefi, appointed as "overseer of the fortress of the great gateway," stated that the king sent him to the Heracleopolitan province as "overseer of the fortress" there and as "great leader" on behalf of the king himself; the king also granted him the unique epithet "treasure of earliest time" (Lichtheim 1988: 49–51). The epithet and titles of Intef suggests that his mission in Heracleopolis consisted of monitoring the circulation of goods into the Nile Valley through the area of Heracleopolis, and that such control was exerted by means of a "fortress" (*ḫnrt*). A similar "fortress" (in fact a *ḥwt*) was operative in the Eastern Delta in Heracleopolitan times, at Ezbet Rushdi, when a king Khety erected a *ḥwt* there at the crossroads where Avaris would later be founded (Moreno García 2010: 26). Some officials serving under Mentuhotep II or slightly later were in control of the Heliopolitan province, in the Eastern Delta, a traditional "gateway" into Egypt from at least the middle of the 3ʳᵈ millennium (when an official called Nefernesut was overseer of fortresses there). In year 41 of king Mentuhotep II, one of these officials was "director of the Heliopolitan province" and "vanguard of the Eastern desert" (Fischer 1959: 131 n. 7). At the very end of the 3ʳᵈ millennium BCE, Khetyankh, an official whose name celebrates an Heracleopolitan king ("May (king) Khety live!"), was "great chief" of the same province as well as "overseer of Lower Egypt" and "one who places fear of the [king . . .] who pacifies for him the Bedouin" (Simpson 2001; Somaglino 2015–2016).[7] Finally, around the same time Ip, a general and treasurer of the king, was in charge of the Western Delta (Kom el-Hisn), the Heracleopolitan province, and the Western desert areas (Fischer 1996b). Much effort appears to have been directed toward controlling the traditional routes of access into the Nile Valley through the Western Delta, Heracleopolis, and the area of Wadi Tumilat, as was also the case in the Old Kingdom (Moreno García 2015).

A Failed Tax System?

Concepts like "Kingdom" and "empire" are frequently used in Egyptology, but they are misleading. They convey a powerful imagery of authority, centralization, and control of resources that can appear self-explanatory and conceal completely the actual realities of power. Mentuhotep II achieved the reunification of the country, but we ignore the political circumstances and conditions that made it possible. The decades after his reign were marked by conflict, especially under the reigns of Amenemhat I and Senusret I. Inscriptions from their reigns refer to rebellions in Middle Egypt and the Theban area, and to tensions in the court that culminated in the murder of Amenemhat I. Although pharaohs undertook extensive efforts to reorganize the kingdom (including the delimitation of the borders of provinces and city territories) and the administration (judging from the titles of the functionaries), there are numerous indications of the relative failure of such efforts and of the weakness of the monarchy. It is quite significant, for example, that leaders from Elephantine and Middle Egypt retained significant control over exchanges with foreign territories (as overseers of "gateways" or as leaders of trading and diplomatic missions), while the old network of *ḥwt*-centers of the crown, crucial for purposes of taxation and stockpiling, was never restored (Moreno García 2017a).

Even at the level of the common people, the ideals of economic autonomy and private accumulation of wealth that developed after the collapse of the Old Kingdom appear to continue unabated during the Middle Kingdom. In fact, this was a period in which a "middle class" of wealthy individuals displayed their prosperity in their funerary offerings and in their monuments, as though they had obtained these riches outside of the circuit of reward and remuneration flowing from the king and traditionally restricted to his officials (Richards 2005). The archaeological and papyrological records also confirm the existence of such a social group, who lived in spacious urban houses equipped with facilities like substantial silos. The frequency of the title *nbt-pr* ("lady of the house") and the abundant use of seals by women suggest that they carried on their own business in a period when texts reveal an increasing use of sealed documents in private transactions. Another prominent element in the sources of this period is an emphasis on patronage networks. Wealth and protection circulated through these networks and helped link different social groups without any intervention of the royal administration (Moreno García 2016). As for foreign trade, the expeditions sent to Nubia and the Levant did not lead to the elimination of potential rivals in these areas and the foundation of imperial power. Quite the contrary: Kush became a formidable power in its own right, and the expeditions launched against Lebanon and other areas further north did not secure control over the Cypriot copper trade (the main producer of this metal at the time) or over the trade routes that tied the Mediterranean to Mesopotamia and beyond. Fluvial trade also appears to have been substantial and it was then that the term *dmi* ("harbor"; *dmi n niwt*, "harbour area of a city") began to become synonymous with "city, village."

When considering monumental architecture, the pharaohs of the early 2ⁿᵈ millennium did not leave much by way of impressive temples, pyramids, and palaces, as was done in previous and subsequent periods of Egyptian history. There is certainly nothing that is at all comparable to the extensive mortuary landscapes of places like Old Kingdom Saqqara, Giza, or Abusir, which were centered around the royal pyramids. In the early 2ⁿᵈ millennium, by contrast, some provincial potentates (especially the overseers of foreign "gateways") built tombs for themselves on an impressive, almost royal scale at Asyut, Beni Hasan, Bersheh, and Qaw el-Kebir, which were not matched anywhere else in Egypt. While the record of monumental architecture should be treated with caution (many buildings decayed or were destroyed over the millennia), all of this evidence nevertheless suggests that the resources at the disposal of the kings were not as abundant as in other periods of Egyptian history. This implies in turn that the re-established monarchy was unable to control and tax much wealth that was now held privately, and that the new fiscal organization had to account for powerful local interests that limited its collecting capacities (Moreno García 2017a). In this light, it may be significant that the administrative papyri and inscriptions of the early 18ᵗʰ century BCE refer to new bureaux and administrative departments responsible for levying goods and laborers (including the creation of a network of work-camps called *ḫnrt*; Quirke 1988 and 1990). These renewed efforts to intensify extraction took place at a time when the monarchy was breaking down again and when some parts of the country (and Nubia) began escaping the control of the pharaohs (especially the Eastern Delta). In other words, the tax system was intensified precisely when the resources at the disposal of the kings were becoming scarcer.

As for the operation of the tax system, unlike in the Old Kingdom local notables and potentates now played a major role in collecting taxes and mobilizing workers. This organizational fact perhaps prevented the creation of a network of centers of the crown. It could also be an indication of a shift in the balance of power between the king and the territories he governed on two levels. On the one hand, the king was obliged to recognize that cities and local potentates were the real powers in the provinces, to the point that the pharaohs of the Middle Kingdom never really managed to "break" this structure and establish more direct control. On the other hand, many administrative documents from this period reveal that dignitaries, officials, and individuals (not institutions) sent contingents of workers to the central administration, and that they were often considered as "localities" from an administrative point of view (in some cases their names are accompanied by the term *bw* "locality"). Precedents for this situation can be detected during the very late Old Kingdom, when districts were sometimes considered the "house" of an official, as is clear from the toponymy (Quirke 1991; Andrássy 2009; Moreno García 2013: 1048–49). Conditions appear to have reverted to those that prevailed at the beginning of the Old Kingdom. The titles of Metjen, who lived under the reign of Snofru (2613–2589 BCE), demonstrate the primacy of the royal agricultural centers *ḥwt-ʿ3t* and *ḥwt* in the countryside. In some cases, these centers replaced former territorial units named *pr* ("house"), each one encompassing several localities. Some toponyms in Metjen's inscriptions are named either *ḥwt(-ʿ3t)* or *pr*, and it is likely that these variant names for the same toponym point to the gradual replacement of the *pr* by the *ḥwt(-ʿ3t)*. The ink inscriptions from Djeser's pyramid as well as the names of some districts at the end of the 3rd millennium show that the *pr* toponyms were usually derived from personal names.[8]

A similar impression of decentralized control of resources and laborers emerges from a comparison of the organization of huge expeditions in the Old and Middle Kingdoms. When Weni organized an army for the king in the Old Kingdom period, manpower was provided by high officials, chiefs of temples, governors of *ḥwt*, and local authorities. By contrast, when a huge expedition to the quarries of Wadi Hammamat was organized by Senusret I in the Middle Kingdom period, it was "mayors" (*ḥ3ty-ʿ*) who provided the workers (*ḥsbw*; Obsomer 1995: 693–96). Provincial leaders like Imeny of Beni Hasan proclaimed that they had accompanied their lord at the head of the contingents of their own provinces (Lichtheim 1988: 135–41). It is instructive that when some early New Kingdom viziers described the administrative organization of the country in their tombs, particularly at the local level, they harked back to the Old Kingdom model and referred to the *ḥwt* that had long since disappeared in order to convey the notion of a well-structured local administration. Such anachronistic references could explain the curious revival at the same time (around the reigns of Thutmosis III-Amenhotep II, 1479–1400 BCE) of older titles. These include *ḥry-tp ʿȝ*, "great chief" of a province, a title borne by Iamunefer from the Hare nome (*ḥry-tp ʿȝ n Wnt*: Edwards 1939: pl. 2–3) and by Mentuherkhepeshef from Aphroditopolis (*ḥry-tp ʿȝ n W3ḏt* Davies 1913: pl. 8); the title *ḥry-tp ʿȝ n Ḥr-wr* ("great chief of the locality of Herwer") borne by Djehuty (TT 11, together with priestly titles related to Cusae and Hermopolis: Galán 2014); and the title *ḥry-tp ʿȝ n Šmʿw* ("great chief of Upper Egypt"), borne by Mentuherkhepeshef and by Min (Bryan 1990: 82). Perhaps more curious is the fact that these provincial "great chiefs" came, once again, from the same region (Middle Egypt) and the same provinces that had enjoyed such extensive autonomy during the Middle Kingdom.

Contrary to current assumptions about the exceptional taxation capacities of the pharaonic monarchy, the preceding study demonstrates that the efficiency of this extractive system depended on the balance of power between the royal palace and the provinces, on the balance of power between different political actors, and on the degree of control over the flows of wealth that crossed Egypt through trade. While the monarchy of the 3rd millennium was generally quite stable, the last three centuries or so witnessed the emergence of potentially disruptive conditions that weakened the authority of kings and their capacity to collect taxes. Foreign trade presented new opportunities for taxation. But it also implied the development of local infrastructures in which the collaboration of local powers was indispensable. In the long term, the flourishing of local power weakened the authority of the central monarchy and led to its collapse. When the monarchy was rebuilt at the very end of the 3rd millennium, conditions had changed: there was a more economically independent "middle class," provincial leaders with vast interests in foreign trade continued to dominate key regions, and the Nilotic trade now had to deal with the emergent Nubian monarchy. All of this meant that the fiscal basis of pharaonic rule was significantly curtailed. Despite the apparent continuity of the symbols, ideology, paraphernalia, and artistic patronage of the Egyptian monarchy, the fact is that its economic foundations experienced deep changes over time and had been weakened from around 2150 BCE. This phenomenon was closely related to the ability of Egypt's kings to implement an efficient tax system and to avoid the emergence of competing powers that were able to divert substantial shares of the wealth of Egypt to their own coffers.

NOTES

1 For literary compositions from Mesopotamia and Egypt that evoke social collapse, cf. Cooper 1983; Michalowski 1989; and Enmarch 2008.

2 Kuzucuoğlu and Marro 2007; Cardarelli, Cazzella, Frangipane and Peroni 2009; McAnany and Yoffee 2010; Nigro 2014; Kerner, Dann and Bangsgaard 2015; Meller, Risch, Jung and Arz 2015; and Höflmayer 2017.

3 Moreno García 2017a.

4 This system can be seen, for instance, in the provisioning of the funerary temples of the kings: Posener-Krieger 1976; Posener-Krieger, Verner and Vymazalová 2006.

5 British tax revenues in British India amounted to about 7 percent of GNP in 1872–73, despite the significantly better organization and greater power of the British administration compared to that of the previous Mughal emperors (Guha 2015: 545). In Han China, a "low tax" regime of about 10% of the production of an average peasant family "was actually set at the limits of what was bearable, and perhaps beyond those limits" (Lewis 2015: 291–92). In the Roman Empire taxes were low, around 6–10% of GDP (Hopkins 2002 [1980]: 201–4).

6 Significantly, a parallel title was held by late Old Kingdom Anhki, who was also *imy-r šn-t3 nb* ("overseer of all vegetation"), *imy-r 'bw-r nb nzwt ddw pt qm3 t3* ("overseer of every repast of the king that heaven gives and earth creates"), *imy-r 'bw-r nzwt m st.f nbt* ("overseer of every repast of the king in all his places"), and *imy-r 'wy zmwt nb(t)* ("overseer of the production of every desert"). See Altenmüller 2012.

7 Two officials called Khentykhety-hotep from, perhaps, the early second millennium if not earlier, were active in the oases of Dakhla and Kharga. In some cases, high officials in the oases were in this period represented bearing royal attributes, like their colleagues in Middle Egypt (Baud, Colin and Tallet 1999).

8 For a more detailed discussion, see Moreno García 2006: 117–19 and 2007: 317–21.

WORKS CITED

Allen, James P. 1996. "Some Theban officials of the early Middle Kingdom." In P. der Manuelian (ed.), *Studies in Honor of William Kelly Simpson* (Boston: Museum of Fine Arts), 12–23.

Altenmüller, Hartwig. 2012. "Bemerkungen zum Architrav und zur Scheintür des Felsgrabes des Anchi unter der Südumfassung der Djoseranlage in Saqqara." *Studien zur Altägyptischen Kultur* 41: 1–20, fig. 1–2.

Andrássy, Petra. 2009. "Symbols in the Reisner Papyri." In P. Andrássy, J. Budka and F. Kammerzell (eds.), *Non-textual Marking Systems, Writing and Pseudo Script from*

Prehistory to Modern Times (Göttingen: Seminar für Ägyptologie und Koptologie), 113–22.

Arnold, Dieter. 1976. *Gräber des Alten und Mittleren Reiches in El-Tarif.* Mainz am Rhein: Phillip von Zabern.

Baud, Michel, Frédéric Colin and Pierre Tallet. 1999. "Les gouverneurs de l'oasis de Dakhla au Moyen Empire." *Bulletin de l'Institut Français d'Archéologie Orientale* 99: 1–19.

Biga, Maria Giovanna. 2012. "Tra Menfi e Ebla." In *L'Egitto tra storia e letteratura* (Turin: AdArte), 23–40.

Biga, Maria Giovanna and Allessandro Roccati. 2012. "Tra Egitto e Siria nel III millennio a.C." *Atti della Reale Accademia delle Scienze di Torino. Classe di scienze morali, storiche e filologia* 146: 17–42.

Brovarski, Edward. 1981. "Ahanakht of Bersheh and the Hare Nome in the First Intermediate Period." In W. K. Simpson and W. M. Davis (eds.), *Studies in Ancient Egypt, the Aegean and the Sudan. Essays in Honour of Dows Dunham on the Occasion of His 90th Birthday.* (Boston: Museum of Fine Arts), 14–30.

Bryan, Betsy. 1990. "The tomb owner and his family." In E. Dziobek and M. Maḥmūd Abd al-Rāziq (eds.), *Das Grab des Sobekhotep: Theben Nr. 63* (Mainz: Phillip von Zabern), 81–88.

Cardarelli, Andrea, Alberto Cazzella, Marcella Frangipane, and Renato Peroni (eds.). 2009. *Reasons for Change. "Birth", "Decline" and "Collapse" of Societies between the End of the IV and the Beginning of the I Millennium B.C.* Scienze dell'Antichità 15. Rome: Università degli Studi di Roma "La Sapienza."

Clère, Jean Jacques and Jacques Vandier. 1948. *Textes de la Première Période Intermédiaire et de la XIème dynastie.* Brussels: Fondation Égyptologique Reine Élisabeth.

Cooper, Jerrold S. 1983. *The Curse of Agade.* Baltimore: The Johns Hopkins University Press.

Cooper, Jerrold S. 2012. "Reconsidering the location of Yam." *Journal of the American Research Center in Egypt* 48: 1–22.

Dalfes, H. Nüzhet, George Kukla, and Harvey Weiss (eds.). 1994. *Third Millennium BC Climate Change and Old World Collapse.* Berlin: Springer.

Darnell, John Coleman. 2002. *Theban Desert Road Survey in the Egyptian Western Desert. Volume 1: Gebel Tjauti Rock Inscriptions 1–45 and Wadi el-Ḥôl Rock Inscriptions 1–45.* Chicago: The University of Chicago.

Darnell, John Coleman. 2008. "The Eleventh Dynasty royal inscription from Deir el-Ballas." *Revue d'Égyptologie* 59: 81–110.

Davies, Norman de Garis. 1913. *Five Theban Tombs (being those of Mentuherkhepeshef, User, Daga, Nehemawäy, and Tati).* London: Egypt Exploration Fund.

Davies, W. Vivian. 2014. "Recording Egyptian inscriptions in the Eastern Desert and elsewhere." *Sudan & Nubia* 18: 30–43.

Diego Espinel, Andrés. 2011. *Abriendo los caminos de Punt. Contactos entre Egipto y el ámbito afroárabe durante la Edad del Bronce (ca. 3000 a.C.–1065 a.C.).* Barcelona: Bellaterra.

Diego Espinel, Andrés. 2015–2016. "Bringing treasures and placing fears: Old Kingdom epithets and titles related to activities abroad." *Isimu* 18–19: 103–46.

Diego Espinel, Andrés. 2017. "The scents of Punt (and elsewhere): Trade and functions of snTr and antw during the Old Kingdom." In I. Incordino and P. P. Creasman (eds.), *Flora Trade between Egypt and Africa in Antiquity* (Oxford: Oxbow), 21–47.

Doxey, Denise M. 1998. *Egyptian Non-royal Epithets in the Middle Kingdom: A Social and Historical Analysis.* Leiden: Brill.

Edwards, Iorwerth Eiddon Stephen. 1939. *Hieroglyphic texts from Egyptian stelae, etc., in the British Museum* VIII. London: Harrison and Sons.

Enmarch, Roland. 2008. *A World Upturned. Commentary on and Analysis of The Dialogue of Ipuwer and the Lord of All.* Oxford: Oxford University Press.

Fischer, Henry Georges. 1959. "Some notes on the easternmost nomes of the Delta in the Old and Middle kingdoms." *Journal of Neur Eastern Studies* 18: 129–42.

Fischer, Henry Georges. 1961. "Notes on the Mo'alla inscriptions and some contemporary texts." *Wiener Zeitschrift für die Kunde des Morgenlandes* 57: 59–77.

Fischer, Henry Georges. 1996a. *Varia Nova: Egyptian Studies 3.* New York: The Metropolitan Museum of Art.

Fischer, Henry Georges. 1996b. *The Tomb of 'Ip at El-Saff.* New York: The Metropolitan Museum of Art.

Forstner-Müller, Irene and Dietrich Raue. 2008. "Elephantine and the Levant." In E.-M. Engel, V. Müller, and U. Hartung (eds.), *Zeichen aus dem Sand. Streiflichter aus Ägyptens Geschichte zu Ehren von Günter Dreyer* (Wiesbaden: Harrassowitz), 127–48.

Gabra, Gawdat. 1976. "Preliminary Report on the Stela of Ḥtpi from El-Kab from the Time of Wahankh Inyôtef II." *Mitteilungen des Deutschen Archäologischen Instituts, Abteilungen Kairo* 32: 45–56, pl. 14.

Galán, José Manuel. 2014. "The inscribed burial chamber of Djehuty (TT 11)." In J. M. Galán, B. M. Bryan and P. F. Dorman (eds.), *Creativity and Innovation in the Reign of Hatshepsut.* SAOC 69 (Chicago: The Oriental Institute of the University of Chicago), 247–72.

Goedicke, Hans. 1967. *Königliche Dokumente aus dem Alten Reich.* Wiesbaden: Otto Harrassowitz.

Goedicke, Hans. 1994. "A Cult Inventory of the Eighth Dynasty from Coptos (Cairo JE 43290)." *Mitteilungen des Deutschen Archäologischen Instituts, Abteilungen Kairo* 50: 71–84.

Guha, Sumit. 2015. "Rethinking the economy of Mughal India: Lateral perspectives." *The Journal of the Economic and Social History of the Orient* 58: 532–75.

Hafsaas-Tsakos, Henriette. 2010. "Between Kush and Egypt: the C-Group people of Lower Nubia during the Middle Kingdom and Second Intermediate Period." In W. Godlewski and A. Łajtar (eds.), *Between the Cataracts. Part 2: Session Papers* (Warsaw: Warsaw University Press), 389–96.

Hayes, William C. 1949. "Career of the Great Steward Henenu under Nebhepetrēʿ Mentuhotpe." *Journal of Egyptian Archaeology* 35: 43–49.

Höflmayer, Felix (ed.). 2017. *The Late Third Millennium in the Ancient Near East: Chronology, C14, and Climatic Change*. Chicago: The University of Chicago.

Hopkins, Keith. 2002 [1980]. "Rome, taxes, rents and trade." Reprinted in W. Scheidel and S. von Redden (eds.), *The Ancient Economy* (New York: Routledge), 190–230.

Jursa, Michael and Moreno García, Juan Carlos. 2015. "The Ancient Near East and Egypt." In A. Monson and W. Scheidel (eds.), *Fiscal Regimes and the Political Economy of Premodern States* (Cambridge: Cambridge University Press), 115–65.

Kerner, Susanne, Rachael J. Dann, and Pernille Bangsgaard (eds.). 2015. *Climate and Ancient Societies*. Copenhagen: Museum Tusculanum Press.

Kuraszkiewicz, Kamil O. 2014. "The tomb of Ikhy/Mery in Saqqara and royal expeditions during the Sixth Dynasty." *Études et Travaux* 27: 201–16.

Kuzucuoğlu, Catherine and Catherine Marro (eds.). 2007. *Sociétés humaines et changement climatique à la fin du troisième millénaire: une crise a-t-elle eu lieu en Haute Mésopotamie?* Paris: De Boccard.

Landgráfová, Renata. 2011. *It is My Good Name that You Should Remember. Egyptian Biographical Texts on Middle Kingdom Stelae*. Prague: Czech Institute of Egyptology.

Lewis, Mark E. 2015. "Early imperial China, from the Qin and Han through Tang." In A. Monson and W. Scheidel (eds.), *Fiscal Regimes and the Political Economy of Premodern States* (Cambridge: Cambridge University Press), 282–307.

Lichtheim, Miriam. 1973. *Ancient Egyptian Literature. Volume I: The Old and Middle Kingdoms*. Berkeley: University of California Press.

Lichtheim, Miriam. 1988. *Ancient Egyptian Autobiographies, chiefly of the Middle Kingdom: A Study and an Anthology*. Freiburg-Göttingen: Vandenhoeck und Ruprecht.

Manzo, Andrea. 2017. *Eastern Sudan in its Setting: The Archaeology of a Region far from the Nile Valley*. Oxford: Archaeopress.

Marcolin, Michele and Andrés Diego Espinel. 2011. "The Sixth Dynasty biographic inscriptions of Iny: more pieces to the puzzle." In M. Bárta, F. Coppens and J. Krejčí, (eds.), *Abusir and Saqqara in the Year 2010* (Prague: Czech Institute of Egyptology), 570–615.

Mathieu, Bernard. 2008. "Le lasso d'Hathor. Relecture de la stèle Turin Suppl. 1310." *Göttinger Miszellen* 219: 65–72.

McAnany, Patricia A. and Norman Yoffee (eds.). 2010. *Questioning Collapse: Human Resilience, Ecological Vulnerability, and the Aftermath of Empire*. Cambridge: Cambridge University Press.

Meller, Harald, Roberto Risch, Reinhard Jung, and Helge Wolfgang Arz (eds.). 2015. *2200 BC—A Climatic Breakdown as A Cause for the Collapse of the Old World? Proceedings of the 7th Archaeological Congress of Central Germany*. Halle: Landesmuseum für Vorgeschichte.

Michalowski, Piotr. 1989. *The Lamentation over the Destruction of Sumer and Ur*. Winona Lake: Eisenbrauns.

Monson, Andrew and Walter Scheidel (eds.). *Fiscal Regimes and the Political Economy of Premodern States*. Cambridge: Cambridge University Press.

Moreno García, Juan Carlos. 1999. *"J'ai rempli les pâturages avec des vaches tachetées . . .* Bétail, économie royale et idéologie en Égypte, de l'Ancien au Moyen Empire." *Revue d'Égyptologie* 50: 241–57.

Moreno García, Juan Carlos. 2006. "Les temples provinciaux et leur rôle dans l'agriculture institutionnelle de l'Ancien et du Moyen Empire." In J. C. Moreno García (ed.), *L'agriculture institutionnelle en Égypte ancienne: état de la question et perspectives interdisciplinaires* (Villeneuve d'Ascq: Université Charles-de-Gaulle Lille 3), 93–124.

Moreno García, Juan Carlos. 2007. "The state and the organization of the rural landscape in 3rd millennium BC pharaonic Egypt." In M. Bollig et al. (eds.), *Aridity, Change and Conflict in Africa* (Cologne: Heinrich-Barth-Institut and Universität zu Köln), 313–30.

Moreno García, Juan Carlos. 2010. "War in Old Kingdom Egypt (2686–2125 BCE)." In J. Vidal (ed.), *Studies on War in the Ancient Near East: Collected Essays on Military History* (Münster: Ugarit Verlag), 5–41.

Moreno García, Juan Carlos. 2013. "The territorial administration of the kingdom in the 3rd millennium." In J. C. Moreno García (ed.), *Ancient Egyptian Administration* (Leiden: Brill), 85–151.

Moreno García, Juan Carlos. 2015. Ḥwt j(ḥ)wt the administration of the Western Delta and the 'Libyan question' in the 3rd millennium." *Journal of Egyptian Archaeology* 101: 69–105.

Moreno García, Juan Carlos. 2016. "Social inequality, private accumulation of wealth and new ideological values in late 3rd millennium BCE Egypt." In H. Meller et al. (eds.), *Arm und Reich—Zur Ressourcenverteilung in prähistorischen Gesellschaften* (Halle (Saale): Landesmuseum für Vorgeschichte Halle (Saale)), 491–512.

Moreno García, Juan Carlos. 2017a. "Trade and power in ancient Egypt: Middle Egypt in the late third/early second millennium BC." *Journal of Archaeological Research* 25.2: 87–132.

Moreno García, Juan Carlos. 2017b. "Métaux, textiles et réseaux d'échanges à longue distance entre la fin du IIIe et le début du IIe millénaire: les *"Paddle dolls"*, un indice négligé?" In N. Favry et al. (eds.), *Du Sinaï au Soudan: Itinéraires d'une égyptologue (Mélanges offerts au Professeur Dominique Valbelle)* (Paris: De Boccard), 173–94.

Mostafa, Maha F. 1984–1985. "Erster Vorbericht über einen Ersten Zwischenzeit Text aus Kom el-Koffar. Teil I." *Annales du Service des Antiquités de l'Égypte* 70: 419–29.

Mostafa, Maha F. 1987. "Kom el-Koffar. Teil II: Datierung und historische Interpretation des Textes B." *Annales du Service des Antiquités de l'Égypte* 71: 169–84.

Mostafa, Maha F. 2005. "The Autobiography 'A' and a Related Text (Block 52) from the Tomb of Shemai at Kom el-Koffar/Qift." In K. A. Daoud, S. Bedier, and S. Abd el-Fatah (eds.), *Studies in Honor of Ali Radwan*, Vol. II (Cairo: Conseil Suprême des Antiquités de l'Égypte), 161–95.

Nigro, Lorenzo, ed. 2014. *Overcoming Catastrophes: Essays on disastrous agents characterization and resilience strategies in pre-classical Southern Levant*. Rome: «La Sapienza» Expedition to Palestine and Jordan.

Obsomer, Claude. 1995. *Sésostris Ier. Étude chronologique et historique du règne.* Brussels: Connaissance de l'Égypte ancienne.

Papazian, Hratch. 2016. "The state of Egypt in the Eighth Dynasty." In P. der Manuelian and T. Schneider (eds.), *Towards a new history for the Egyptian Old Kingdom. Perspectives on the Pyramid Age* (Leiden: Brill), 393–428.

Parkinson, Richard B. 1997. *The Tale of Sinuhe and Other Ancient Egyptian Poems 1940–1640 BC.* Oxford: Oxford University Press.

Pérez-Die, Carmen. 2005. "La nécropole de la Première Période Intermédiaire—début du Moyen Empire à Héracléopolis Magna. Nouvelles découvertes et résultats récents (campagne 2001)." In L. Pantalacci and C. Berger-El-Naggar (eds.), *Des Néferkarê aux Montouhotep. Travaux archéologiques en cours sur la fin de la VIe dynastie et la Première Période Intermédiaire* (Lyon: Maison de l'Orient et de la Méditerranée), 239–54.

Posener-Krieger, Paule. 1976. *Les archives du temple funéraire de Néferirkarê-Kakaï (Les Papyrus d'Abousir): Traduction et commentaire.* Cairo: Institut Français d'Archéologie Orientale.

Posener-Krieger, Paule, Miroslav Verner, and Hana Vymazalová. 2006. *The Pyramid Complex of Raneferef: The Papyrus Archive.* Prague: Czech Institute of Egyptology.

Postel, Lilian. 2008. "Une nouvelle mention des campagnes nubiennes de Montouhotep II à Karnak." In L. Gabolde (ed.), *Hommages à Jean-Claude Goyon* (Cairo: Institut Français d'Archéologie Orientale), 329–40.

Quirke, Stephen. 1988. "State and labour in the Middle Kingdom: A reconsideration of the term ẖnrt." *Revue d'Égyptologie* 39: 83–106.

Quirke, Stephen. 1990. *The Administration of Egypt in the Late Middle Kingdom. The Hieratic Documents.* New Malden: SIA Publications.

Quirke, Stephen. 1991. "The egyptological study of placenames." *Discussions in Egyptology* 21: 59–71.

Richards, Janet. 2005. *Society and Death in Ancient Egypt: Mortuary Landscapes of the Middle Kingdom.* Cambridge: Cambridge University Press.

Satzinger, Helmut and Danijela Stefanović. 2014. "The Middle Kingdom xnmsw." *SAK* 41: 341–51.

Simpson, William Kelly. 1986. *Papyrus Reisner IV. Personnel Accounts of the Early Twelfth Dynasty.* Boston: Museum of Fine Arts.

Simpson, William Kelly. 2001. "Studies in the Twelfth Egyptian Dynasty IV: The early Twelfth Dynasty False-Door/Stela of Khety-ankh/Heni from Matariya/Ain Shams (Heliopolis)." *Journal of the American Research Center in Egypt* 38: 9–20.

Somaglino, Claire. 2010. "Les «portes» de l'Égypte de l'Ancien Empire à l'époque Saïte." *Égypte, Afrique et Orient* 59: 3–16.

Somaglino, Claire. 2015–2016. "La stèle de Héni et la géographie de la frange orientale du Delta à l'Ancien et au Moyen Empire." *Bulletin de la Société Française d'Égyptologie* 193–194: 29–51.

Strudwick, Nigel C. 2005. *Texts from the Pyramid Age.* Writings from the Ancient World 16. Atlanta, GA: Society ofBiblical Literature.

Tallet, Pierre. 2018. "Du pain et des céréales pour les équipes royales: le grand papyrus comptable du ouadi el-Jarf (papyrus H)." In A. Bats (ed.), *Les céréales dans le monde antique. Regards croisés sur les stratégies de gestion des cultures, de leur stockage et de leurs modes de consummation*. Nehet 5 (Paris: Centre de Recherches Égyptologiques de la Sorbonne & Université Libre de Bruxelles), 99–117.

Vernus, Pascal. 1970. "Sur une particularité de l'onomastique du Moyen Empire." *Revue d'Égyptologie* 22: 155–69.

Von Pilgrim, Cornelius. 1996. *Elephantine XVIII. Untersuchungen in der Stadt des Mittleren Reiches und der Zweiten Zwischenzeit*. Mainz am Rhein: Philipp von Zabern.

Warden, Leslie Anne. 2014. *Pottery and Economy in Old Kingdom Egypt*. Culture and History of the Ancient Near East 65. Leiden: Brill.

Warden, Leslie Anne. 2016. "Centralized taxation during the Old Kingdom." In P. der Manuelian and T. Schneider (eds.), *Towards a new history for the Egyptian Old Kingdom. Perspectives on the Pyramid Age* (Leiden: Brill), 470–95.

Weiss, Harvey (ed.). 2012. *Seven Generations since the Fall of Akkad*. Wiesbaden: Harrassowitz.

Willems, Harco. 2007. *Dayr al-Barshā. Volume I: The Rock Tombs of Djehutinakht (No. 17K74/1), Khnumnakht (No. 17K74/2), and Iha (No. 17K74/3). With an Essay on the History and Nature of Nomarchal Rule in the Early Middle Kingdom*. Leuven: Peeters.

Willems, Harco. 2014. *Historical and Archaeological Aspects of Egyptian Funerary Culture. Religious Ideas and Ritual Practice in Middle Kingdom Élite Cemeteries*. Culture and History of the Ancient Near East 73. Leiden: Brill.

Žába, Zbyněk. 1974. *The Rock Inscriptions of Lower Nubia. Czechoslovak Concession*. Prague: Czoslovak Institute of Egyptology.

11

Greek Perspectives on Fiscal Administration under Alexander the Great

ANDREW MONSON

Introduction

Alexander's reign represents an important transition for the fiscal systems of Macedon and the ancient Near East. Only after weighing the continuities with Achaemenid Persia and the pre-Hellenistic east against the fiscal innovations of the Greek world can we arrive at a balanced assessment. This chapter takes preliminary steps in that direction by presenting evidence for taxation and tribute in the reign of Alexander and attempting to clear up some misunderstandings in the earlier literature. It focuses on selected passages of Arrian's *Anabasis* and the second book of the Aristotelian *Oikonomika*, as well as on some related inscriptions. The Macedon of Alexander and his father Philip was quite different from Achaemenid Persia in its fiscal organization. They adopted their models to a fair extent from the contemporary world of the Greek *polis*. In the east, Alexander inherited the Achaemenid fiscal administration but even here Greeks were in a position to institute changes.

During the lifetime of Philip and Alexander rising military costs in the Greek world led to numerous experiments devised to increase revenue. After Athens' empire was gone, its confederacy treaty of 379/378 BCE forbade it from levying tribute on any of its allies but allowed special contributions (Greek *syntaxeis*). The term *syntaxis* was deliberately chosen to stress that the cities were not subjects but autonomous allies of Athens. At the same time Athens reformed its system of extraordinary tax levies called *eisphorai* (Thompsen 1964; Brun 1983; Leppin 1995; Christ 2007; Fawcett 2016). The wealthiest citizens and metics were organized into tax paying groups and their total wealth estimated. A specific sum would be divided among the tax payers as a percentage of their property value. Other institutional changes allowed the state to plan its income and expenditure for each coming year. The assembly decided on a budget (*merismos*), which was not comprehensive but distributed most revenues into specific funds. From its inception, the war fund probably received all surpluses but after the creation of the *theōrika* by Eubulus in the 350s surpluses reverted to that fund except in wartime (Rhodes 2013: 219).

The one important Athenian fiscal treatise that survives is Xenophon's fascinating work *Poroi*, or "Ways and Means," written for the Athenian assembly in 355 BCE after its defeat in the Social War. However, Xenophon represents the conservative aristocratic perspective typical of fourth-century Greek philosophy. It was a basic principle, which we also find in Aristotle, that the state should not spend more than it takes in revenue. Public credit is not explicitly mentioned, though it is conceivable that the capital fund (*aphormē*, 3.6; cf. Bresson 2000: 253) envisioned for the investment in slaves could have included it; public loans were certainly one option that Greek *poleis* had at their disposal. Xenophon is sharply critical of raising revenue by exacting contributions from Athens' allies:

> This set me thinking whether by any means the citizens might obtain food entirely from their own soil, which would certainly be the fairest way. I felt that, were this so, they would be relieved of their poverty, and also of the suspicion with which they are regarded by the Greek world. (Xen. *Poroi* 1.1, trans. Marchant 1968)

When Xenophon writes that revenue should be sought from their own state, he means from the state's own proper resources and not the redistribution of wealth by taxing wealthy citizens. His suggestions are limited to raising revenue by traditional means, including the poll tax on foreign residents and harbor or market dues. The central idea of his treatise is an ambitious plan for the silver mines. He proposes a one-time contribution, raising funds from citizens but also foreign benefactors, so that the state can buy thousands of slaves, which it will lease out along with mining concessions in order to earn sufficient revenue to pay all citizens a basic stipend for their subsistence. On this point Schütrumpf's (1982:

30–45, 65–72) interpretation is more persuasive than that of Gauthier (1976: 20–32).

Athens was in severe financial difficulties when Xenophon wrote his treatise. The assembly appointed Eubulus to reorganize the Athenian fiscal administration. He and his associates were consistently elected to hold the main offices for several years. The orator Demosthenes (Dem. 10 *Phil.* 4, 27–28) tells us that the total revenue increased under Eubulus from 130 to 400 talents of silver per year. However, the wars with Macedon proved that Athens needed still more revenue to remain a major power. For twelve years, from 336 to 324 BCE, the Athenians appointed Lycurgus and his associates to the new office of overseer of public finance (*epi tēi dioikēsēi*), an office that would become a rather common feature of Hellenistic *poleis* (Schuler 2005). During these twelve years Athens reportedly spent a staggering sum of 18,900 talents of silver, on average 1,575 talents per year. At the same time Lycurgus and his associates managed to triple Athens' annual revenue, up to 1,200 talents per year, and also took out large public loans from private creditors to finance public spending on infrastructure, the military, and civil society (Rhodes 2013: 203–31; Migeotte 2014: 435–36).

Gabrielsen (2013) suggests that Athens in the fourth century BCE embodies what Schumpeter (1991 [1918]) called the *tax state*. That concept implies not only the state's capacity to raise taxes, which Gabrielsen emphasizes, but also the alignment of its interests with capital formation or economic development. The tax states stand in contrast to *domain states*, where rulers fund their activities from patrimonial revenues while rents of private domains are largely shielded from expropriation (cf. Bonney 1995). It also contrasts with tributary states where rulers rely on intermediaries who provide only indirect access to property and transactions and siphon away potential revenue. Athens does indeed display many characteristics of the tax state. In the *Poroi*, Xenophon seems to recognize that promoting trade could be the means to the end of increasing revenue (Xen. *Poroi* 3.5). Eubulus and Lycurgus probably implemented his ideas about how to increase those revenues from indirect taxes and mining that the polis could legitimately collect.

Yet philosophical critics of Athens such as Xenophon offer no support for the *demos* levying taxes directly on the property of wealthy citizens, which was key to the formation of the tax state in early modern Europe.

His contemporaries were even more explicit in their criticism of Athenian property taxes in the fourth century BCE. Aristotle (*Pol.* 1320a.20) and Isocrates (7.51) both censure radical democracies, particularly Athens, for their oppressive *eisphorai* or property taxes and liturgies on the wealthy. Isocrates' *Areopagitikos*, written at about the same time as Xenophon's *Poroi*, is directed against the Athenian system of taxing or confiscating the wealth of the rich to pay for the poor to participate in the political system. The consequence of such taxes, he argued, would be social unrest. The Athenocentric bias of these authors may mislead us about the legitimacy and prevalence of direct taxes in other Greek city-states, some of which may have levied them regularly (Migeotte 2003), though this was indeed rare in the case of land and immovable property (Pernin 2007; Migeotte 2014: 277). When the Greeks levied property or capitation taxes on citizens they were usually temporary measures approved by the *demos* for wars and emergencies as in Athens, but their procedures were not necessarily the same as Athenian *eisphorai* (see below; cf. Gauthier 1991: 60–68).

What was wrong for Athens, however, was deemed right for non-Greek barbarians. In his idealizing biography of the Persian king Cyrus the Great, Xenophon goes out of his way to praise the centralization of his tax administration:

> (Cyrus) decided, then, that it was out of the question for him to neglect the revenues, for he foresaw that there would necessarily be enormous expenses connected with a vast empire; and on the other hand, he knew that for him to be constantly engaged in giving his personal attention to his manifold possessions would leave him with no time to care for the welfare of the whole realm. As he thus pondered how the business of administration might be successfully conducted and how he still might have the desired leisure, he somehow happened to think of his military organization. (Xen. *Cyr.* 8.1.13–14, trans. Miller 1914)

Cyrus's tax administration would be set up along the lines of his military organization. Xenophon's biography of Cyrus is to a large degree fictional. His aim was to lay out the possibilities for virtuous monarchical rule. The very idea that Cyrus would obtain the leisure to think beyond his own immediate material interests and consider instead the welfare of his kingdom is one of the hallmarks of fourth century BCE Greek political theory. Such Greek thinking about public finance as well as the rise of fiscal experts such as Eubulus and Lycurgus in Athens would arguably have profound influence on Alexander's administration and that of his Hellenistic successors (Davies 2004).

Macedonian Taxation

Athenian politicians during the fourth century gathered considerable practical experience in how to raise revenue, which they put in the service of kings on the fringes of the Greek world, including Macedonia. Book 2 of the Aristotelian *Oikonomika* recounts a story of the Athenian politician Callistratus, who in about the year 360 BCE advised the Macedonian king how he could double his harbor-tax revenue from 20 to 40 talents by allowing more bidders to participate in the tax-farm auction ([Arist.] *Oec.* 2.2.22). Callistratus is just one example of Athenian fiscal experts serving as royal advisors. Another Athenian, Chabrias, went to Egypt at almost the same time, around 362 to 360 BCE, where he helped the rebel king Taos raise revenue for his war with Persia ([Arist.] *Oec.* 2.2.25; Will 1960; Agut-Labordère 2011).

The Argead kings traditionally relied on Macedonians who possessed their own domains for conducting military campaigns. Many obtained their land from the king himself out of spear-won royal land (Faraguna 1998; Mari 2020). In Hellenistic times at least, such gift estates were effectively private and there is no evidence for taxes or rents on them (see below), though they returned to the royal domain when recipients died without heirs (Tziafalias and Helly 2010: 79–84). Hence it was his own patrimonial estate, including silver mines, timber, and regalian revenues such as tolls and harbor duties that probably furnished the king's main revenue aside from war booty. Migeotte (2014: 399) finds no evidence for taxes or tribute levied on subjected Greek cities. Other conquered peoples, however, could be expected to make payments to the king in the name of the Macedonians. The Thracians for example paid tithes (*dekatai*) to the Macedonians (Diod. Sic. 16.71.2) that may have been agricultural taxes (Faraguna 1998: 373), though these should be compared to the *dekatai* previously collected by the tithe collectors (*dekatologoi*) of King Cersebleptes (Dem. 23.177), which modern translators render as "ten-percent customs duties" or "tolls" (Vince 1954: 337–8; Harris 2018: 177). Once in control of the Thessalian League, Philip and Alexander were entitled to the taxes customarily paid to its military leader (Justin 11.3.2; cf. Xen. *Hell.* 6.1.12).

There is one passage in Arrian's account of Alexander's campaigns that modern historians interpret as evidence for land taxation in Macedonia. Arrian describes the privileges that Alexander granted on behalf of the 25 Macedonians killed in the battle of Granicus in 334 BCE: "to their parents and children he gave exemption from taxes in the country and from all other personal services and contributions levied on their properties" (*Anab.* 1.16.5). The "exemption from taxes in the country" (*tōn kata tēn chōran ateleia*) has usually been interpreted as an exemption from rents on royal land (*basilikē chōra*; Berve 1929: 1.224, 306–7; Hatzopoulos 1996: 437). Others cite this passage as evidence that the kings imposed direct taxes on the agricultural surplus of private land throughout Macedonia (Lane Fox 2011: 377–78). Some scholars (Bosworth 1980: 1.126; Faraguna 1998: 373; Millet 2010: 491) entertain both possibilities, but in fact neither of them is convincing. The words *telos* ("tax") and *ateleia* ("tax exemption") are never used for rents on royal land. This could conceivably be an exception, but without corroboration it remains a precarious assumption; *chōra* itself is too common in classical Greek for it to be read as an allusion to royal land. Normally *telē* (pl. of *telos*) refer to indirect taxes sold at auction each year to tax farmers (Chankowski 2007). Royal grants of land in Macedonia by Philip, Alexander, and their successors could be accommpaned by an exemption (*ateleia*) from import and export duties (*SEG* 38.620; 47.940; 47.893; Thonemann 2009) but not specifically from rents. It is significant that Arrian distinguishes in this passage the *ateleia* of taxes in the countryside from *eisphorai* assessed on property (see below).

A more plausible suggestion is that Arrian's passage refers only to customs duties or tolls levied on the overland import and export of goods. We find a similar expression in a passage from the Aristotelian *Oikonomika*:

> Taking these in turn, the first and most important of them is the revenue from agriculture (*apo tēs gēs*), which some call tithe and some

produce-tax . . . and fourth that which arises from taxes on land (*telē kata gēn*) and sales ([Arist.] *Oec.* 2.1.4, trans. Armstrong 1958).

Note the distinction in this text between revenue "from the land" (*apo tēs gēs*) and revenue from overland taxes (*telē kata gēn*) on trade or transit (Chankowski 2007: 308–9; Pernin 2007: 375). The former are clearly agricultural taxes, while the latter are mentioned in the same breath as market taxes and must refer to transit or bridge taxes and the like (Böckh 1886: 1.370; van Groningen 1933: 39; Aperghis 2002: 126; Zoepffel 2006: 553–54). We find the same association of import and export duties with sales taxes in an *ateleia* grant by Cassander to an estate-holder in Macedonia (*SEG* 47.940). Pseudo-Aristotle in *Oec.* 2.2.21 admittedly uses the term *telê* to describe taxes on land and houses in Mende, but there too we find the preposition *apo*, "from the land", for agricultural taxes.

Another Macedonian landholder whose estate was composed of grants from Philip and Alexander also received from Cassander an exemption (*ateleia*) from import and export duties for the goods of his landed property (*tōn epi ktēsei*; *SEG* 38.620.27–31; Hatzopoulos 1988: 22–26; Thonemann 2009: 264–46). This accords with the practice attested in Hellenistic cities where one's liability for customs duties could depend on whether landed property was registered within a city's territory (*I.Milet* 1.3, no. 149.39–44 [§9]; Migeotte 2001). Taxes on the transporation of goods in Macedon appear already in the treaty of Amyntas III and the Chalcidian League, ca. 400–380 BCE (*GHI* 12 in Rhodes and Osborne 2003). An inscription published in 1994 records an agreement between the Greek trading colony (*epoikion*) of Pistiros in Thrace with its overlord the Odrysian king, who swears that "he will levy no taxes on the roads (*telea kata tas hodous*) that lead to Maroneia" (*SEG* 43.486.20–21) The text dates between 358 BCE and Philip II's conquest of that area about fifteen years later. This is probably just a specific example of what are called more generally "taxes on land" (*telē kata gēn*) in the Aristotelian *Oikonomika*, which is synonoumous with Arrian's phrase "exemption from taxes in the country," and refer to indirect taxes.

Arrian's passage (*Anab.* 1.16.5) refers afterwards to personal services (*tōi sōmati leitourgiai*) and property taxes (*kata tas ktēseis hekastōn eisphorai*). Extraordinary levies (*eisphorai*) on property are well known in the classical Greek and Hellenistic world. The fourth-century

Athenian system is only the best known and was not necessarily the model for Macedon (Migeotte 2014: 278–82, 518–24; cf. Bosworth 1980: 126). Later Macedonian rulers demanded *eisphorai* on landed estates (*ktēseis*) in Hellenistic Egypt (*C.Ord.Ptol.* 75–6; cf. *P.Lips.* 2.124). Plutarch (*Aem. Paul.* 28.3) also uses the verb *eispherein* to describe the tax levies on Macedon's four districts under the Antigonid kings (cf. Polyb. 36.17.13 and Diod. Sic. 31.8.3–9), which were conceivably raised as a lump-sum and repartitioned among citizens by property values or some other criteria just as Greek *eisphorai*. Recent attempts to explain the Macedonian *eisphorai* in Arrian as import/export duties or sales taxes are therefore misguided (Hatzopoulos 1996: 439–40; Lane Fox 2011: 377–78).

Personal services (*tōi sōmati leitourgiai*) have been understood as military service (Bosworth 1980: 126, citing Dem. 10.28), but exemption from military service was rare in the Greek world and never a mark of honor (Gauthier 1991: 55–60). When Alexander became king, for example, he relieved the Macedonians of all obligations *except* military service (Justin 11.1.8–10). The alternative suggestion is thus more likely; namely, such liturgies could be identified with the so-called "citizen liturgies" (*politikoi leitourgiai*) in two inscriptions, where they may have constituted periodic labor services or requisitions (Hatzopoulos 1996: 437–39; Tziafalias and Helly 2010: 117; Lane Fox 2011: 377–79; cf. *P.Tebt.* 1.5.181 and 1.124.18 = *C.Ord.Ptol.* 53.181 and 54.18, resp.). Yet no scholar to my knowledge has observed the intriguing link in Arrian's passage between the *leitourgiai* with one's person (*sōma*) and the *eisphorai* assessed on one's properties (*ktēseis*).

This juxtaposition evokes a parallel with the *eisphora*-practices attested beyond Athens. To raise money for war in the fourth century, the Athenians of Potidaia made a new assessment of property values and, for citizens without sufficient property, they fixed the value of each person (*sōma*) at two minas ([Arist.] *Oec.* 2.2.5). Consequently, with an *eisphora* of one twentieth for example, anyone who fell below the property threshold would pay ten drachmas, a money equivalent of his labor value. When the Athenian mercenary commander Chabrias offered King Taos of Egypt advice for his war with Persia, he too proposed emergency levies on the value of one's person (*sōma*) and on the value of one's house ([Arist.] *Oec.* 2.2.25a). Gauthier (1991) persuasively demonstrates the plausibility of these passages by linking them to the phrase *ateleia tou sōmatos* or "fiscal immunity of one's person" in Hellenistic inscriptions from Asia Minor. Several cities there distinguish between the *eisphora* on property and a corresponding levy on one's person (*sōma*), which resembles a capitation tax when paid in money but is perhaps historically or conceptually akin to labor obligations. Although Gauthier does not mention Arrian's passage, I suggest that *ateleia tou sōmatos* is analogous to Arrian's *ateleia* from *tōi sōmati leitourgiai*, which he likewise distinguishes from the *eisphora* on properties (*Anab.* 1.16.5). This is a complex topic that requires more detailed treatment and falls outside the scope of this investigation.

Greek Tax Officials in Alexander's Satrapies

After his conquests Alexander took over the Achaemenid fiscal administration in the east where there was a long tradition of direct taxation (van Driel 2002; Briant 2006; Kleber 2015). Some of this Persian expertise had already made its way to the Greeks, such as the tribute assessments used by Athens (Rauflaub 2009), but the Macedonian conquest made way for more sustained transfers of fiscal know-how. There was, for example, a royal sales tax on slaves in Babylonia, which continued in the Hellenistic period (Stolper 1989), while in Carian cities it was possible to distinguish between individual taxes that were due to the city and those due to the king (*I.Labraunda* 42 = Hornblower 1982, no. M8; cf. Debord 1999: 41–45). Moreover, unlike the gift estates in Macedonia mentioned above, land grants in the Achaemenid empire were assessed regular taxes (*phoroi*) in money or in kind according to the land's value (Briant 2006; Thonemann 2009).

Alexander declared the Greeks in Asia Minor to be *aphorologētos*, which is usually understood to mean "free from tribute" or *phoros*. This was similar to Philip's course of action in Thrace (Diod. Sic. 16.71), where, for example, the city territory of Philippi was distinguished from adjacent royal land cultivated by Thracians who paid *phoros* to the king (*SEG* 34.664 = Hatzopoulos 1996, no. 6; Faraguna 1998: 369–73). In Asia Minor Greek cities still had to make financial contributions to Alexander's campaign called *syntaxeis*, but these were not merely synonymous with *phoroi* as Sherwin-White (1985:

85–86) believed. They were possibly paid by the city itself as a lump sum rather than by individuals (Bosworth 1980: 280–81; see the case of Aspendos below). Schuler (2007) has persuasively argued that *phoros*, especially its plural form *phoroi*, almost never indicates "tribute" as a lump sum in Hellenistic inscriptions from Asia Minor. Instead, *phoroi* were the various royal "taxes" that kings levied within their territory, which also seems to be the case in Arrian's *Anabasis*. For example, in Hellespontine Phyrgia in 334 BCE, "Alexander made Calas satrap of the territory Arsites ruled, ordering the inhabitants to pay the same taxes (*phoroi*) as they used to pay to Darius" (Arr. *Anab.* 1.17.1, trans. from Brunt 1976).

That such taxes (*phoroi*), unlike tribute, were assessed on individuals is further illustrated in Alexander's decree to the city of Priene in 334 BCE:

> Of King Alexander. Of those living at Naulochon, as many as are [Greek]s shall be autonomous and free, holding their [land] and all their houses in the city, and also the territory, just like the Prieneans, [between the sea] and the [hill] of the Sandeis; but the [village of x], and the village of Myrs[- -] and the village of P[- - and their associated] land I recognize as mine, and those living in those villages shall pay the *phoroi*. I exempt the city of the Prieneans from the *syntaxis* (*I.Priene* 1.1–15, ed. and trans. Thonemann 2012).

According to Thonemann's (2012) intrepretation, Naulochos was a city within Priene's territory, which had some Greek inhabitants, to whom Alexander granted the same autonomy and freedom as the citizens of Priene. This would have included freedom from royal taxes (*aphorologētos*). The decree goes on to specify several villages adjacent to Priene's territory, which, Alexander remarks, "I recognize as mine, and those living in them shall pay taxes (*phoroi*)." Priene itself, he adds, is to be exempt from the *syntaxis*. The best illustration of *syntaxis*—even if that term does not appear—is in Arrian's account of Alexander's demand for horses and a money contribution to pay his soldiers from the city of Aspendos on the south coast of Asia Minor. When Aspendos changed course and refused payment, Alexander besieged the city. After its surrender, Arrian tells us:

He demanded their most influential men as hostages, the horses they had previously promised and a hundred talents in place of fifty; they were to be subject to the satrap appointed by him, and pay yearly taxes (*phoroi*) to the Macedonians . . . (Arr. *Anab.* 1.27.4, trans. modified from Brunt 1976).

The city of Aspendos was placed under the satrapal administration and required to pay taxes, not "tribute" as Brunt translates the term *phoroi* here and elsewhere.

At several points in Alexander's campaigns, Arrian mentions the appointment of a high-ranking fiscal officer alongside or above the satrap and the military commanders (Berve 1929: 1.313–17). Xenophon (*Cyr.* 8.1.13–14, quoted above) had attributed a similar centralization of the fiscal administration to Cyrus the Great but satraps in the Persian period appear to have had greater authority over local finances. These new fiscal officers were often Greeks rather than Macedonians. They were not Persians or other non-Greeks despite the fact that Alexander sometimes entrusted them with other offices. Admittedly, we do not have evidence for all satrapies and cannot rule out that non-Greeks were put in charge elsewhere. On the other hand, it is unlikely that Alexander established the same structures. The regions where Arrian mentions the appointment of a fiscal officer happen to be the only regions where Alexander minted coins during his reign, namely, Lydia, Egypt, Phoenicia, Cilicia, Coele-Syria, Babylonia, and all Asia west of the Taurus (Berve 1929: 1.318–19; Le Rider 2003). It is possible that any attempt to separate fiscal powers from other high-ranking officials constituted special precautions in response to local circumstances (Griffith 1964).

The descriptions of those officers' duties are remarkably similar. In Lydia, for example, Alexander appointed a certain Nikias, who was probably a Greek because this name is never attested among Macedonians. He was put in charge "of the assessment and receipt of the taxes" (*tōn de phorōn tēs syntaxeōs te kai apophoras*; Arr. *Anab.* 1.17.7). In Egypt, Alexander broke up the old Persian satrapy into different parts under separate governors: Egypt, Libya, and Arabia. Cleomenes, a Greek from Egypt, was appointed to the so-called Arabian part, to the east of the Nile Delta. Just as Nikias in Lydia, Alexander put Cleomenes in charge of the financial administration of the whole satrapy, which was traditionally divided into about forty districts or nomes governed by nomarchs:

The government of the neighboring country of Libya was given to Apollonios son of Charinos; and that of Arabia round Heroönpolis to Cleomenes from Naucratis. He was instructed to permit the nomarchs to govern their own districts in accordance with the ancient practices but to exact the taxes (*eklegein tous phorous*) from them himself, which they were ordered to pay over (*apopherein*) to him. (Arr. *Anab.* 3.5.4, trans. modified from Brunt 1976)

Once again it seems that the tax administration was overseen by a Greek, in this case one from the Greek trading colony of Naucratis in Egypt. Within a few years, Cleomenes had managed to expand his power and to be recognized as the satrap of Egypt. In the Aristotelian *Oikonomika* we hear about yet another Greek in charge of the Egyptian fiscal administration, during the time when Cleomenes was satrap. This man Ophelas came from the prosperous city of Olynthus, which Philip of Macedon had conquered and razed in 348 BCE. He centralized taxation in Egypt by appointing his own overseers in one of the nomes in the Delta. Other nomarchs offered to increase the level of the taxes (*phoroi*), if he removed the overseer:

Ophelas of Olynthus appointed an officer to superintend the revenues of the province of Athribis. The nomarchs came to him and told him they were willing to pay a much larger amount in taxes; but asked him to remove the present superintendent. Ophellas inquired if they were really able to pay what they promised; on their assuring him that they were, left the superintendent in office and instructed him to demand from them the amount of tax they themselves had assessed. And so, without being chargeable either with discountenancing the officer he had appointed, or with taxing the governors beyond their own estimate, he obtained from the latter many times his previous revenue. ([Arist.] *Oec.* 2.2.35, trans. Armstrong 1958)

Our sources do not explicitly tell us that the Greeks Nikias, Cleomenes, and Ophellas brought any specific fiscal expertise; Cleomenes and Ophellas merely display cunning and ruthlessness. In 331 BCE Alexander appointed two further fiscal officers, this time Macedonians, who had previously been in charge of the treasury during the absence of Alexander's treasurer Harpalus. Koiranos was put in charge of the "the collection of taxes" (*epi tōn phorōn tēi syllogēi*) in Phoencia, while Philoxenos was to tax (*eklegein*) the region of Asia Minor west of the Tauros mountain range (Arr. *Anab.* 3.6.4). These were Macedonians with experience and Alexander's trust, having jointly administered the royal treasury during Harpalus's temporary absence. However, another Greek, Antimenes of Rhodes, may have succeeded Harpalus as treasurer and certainly took on fiscal responsibilities in Babylonia ([Arist.] *Oec.* 2.2.34, 2.2.38; Berve 1929: 2.44–45 no. 89). Arrian also mentions Asklepiodoros son of Philon, whose assignment was "to exact taxes" (*tous phorous eklegein*) in Babylonia just as his counterparts elsewhere (Arr. *Anab.* 3.16.4). These appointments may have been responses to particular circumstances rather than the execution of a general policy, particularly in the case of Philoxenos (cf. Bosworth 1988: 242), but their standardized descriptions suggest a sphere of responsibility that was well defined and conceptually distinct from that of the satraps.

While scholars are right to point out basic continuities in fiscal administration, this change of personnel at the top should make us attentive to the *convergence* of Greek and Achaemenid practices, which is evident already through the fourth century BCE (Descat 2006) but subsequently intensified under Macedonian rule. The satrapal economy is described as an independent sphere in book two of the *Oikonomika*, written by a student of Aristotle probably at the end of the 4th century (van Groningen 1933; Zoepffel 2006). The author distinguishes four types of *oikonomia*: the kingdom, the satrapy, the *polis*, and the private sphere. The royal economy deals with minting coins, overseeing the satrapies, and controlling expenditure (Descat 2003). Not until the satrapal economy do we find a list of the various sources of revenue, for example, from agriculture, mines, customs duties, market taxes, poll taxes, and so on. Tribute is never mentioned and the *phoroi* that we encounter so often in our sources probably refer to the satrapal taxes. The *polis* and private economies are described more briefly in relatively vague terms.

The author's brief introduction on the four types of administration contrasts with the rest of the treatise, which is a compilation of seventy-seven tricks that have been used to raise revenue. Between these two sections the author makes a few interesting comments about the usefulness of his treatise. First, the author asserts, just like Aristotle and Xenophon, that administrators should not let expenditure exceed revenue, especially in the case of private households ([Arist.] *Oec.* 2.1.6). Immediately afterwards he provides advice specifically for those in charge of the satrapal or *polis* economy: "we must inquire what kinds of revenue, at present wholly lacking, are yet potentially existent; what kinds though now small, may with care be increased" ([Arist.] *Oec.* 2.1.7). The premise here is that administrators ought, wherever possible, to try to increase their revenue. The manual's purpose is to provide the reader with a framework for what revenues are appropriate in what spheres. Admittedly, its utility is vitiated by its brevity and triviality but the Aristotelian categorization is normative as much as it is descriptive, implying that the proper division of the subject matter allows the administrator to achieve his end.

The work has always disappointed modern readers looking for a scientific manual of fiscal administration (Finley 1970; Brodersen 2006). The examples are extraordinary cases drawn from sources whose reliability cannot usually be checked. Yet the author himself seems to anticipate and reject the criticism that they could not be put into practice: "These anecdotes seemed to us by no means lacking in utility; being capable from time to time of application by others to the business they themselves had in hand" ([Arist.] *Oec.* 2.1.6–8; trans. Armstrong 1958). The historical perspective is invariably Greek even when it occassionally turns its gaze to the Egyptian or Achaemenid world. What the anecdotes have in common is that their protagonists typically seek to increase revenue rather than reduce expenditure. Frequently, this is achieved by means of deception and dirty tricks. If we suppose that the treatise was as much ethical as practical, in the sense of describing the proper end of the good administrator, then this message and the examples chosen are strikingly appropriate. Stories about the ruthless Cleomenes and Ophellas, among others, would have appealed to the audience of Greek fiscal officers of the Hellenistic kingdoms, successors to those whom Alexander appointed during his campaigns, and their counterparts in the Greek cities (cf. Schuler 2005), to whom the work is quite explicitly offered as advice.

Conclusion

Alexander's Macedonia found itself between two worlds. Unlike in the Achaemenid empire, there were probably no regular taxes on the private domains or gift estates of the Macedonians. The Argead kings depended on their own patrimonial revenues and tolls or customs duties on overland and seaborne transportation of goods. Their main rivals and peers prior to 334 BCE were Balkan petty kings like themselves and above all the Greek city-states, which by the mid-fourth century BCE had developed sophisticated fiscal institutions. Athenian public finance was just one model that peripheral kingdoms and Achaemenid satraps or rebels sought to emulate, but it was by no means typical of all Greek city-states and neither did the latter fail to offer models of their own. Greek-style property taxes (*eisphorai*) in Macedon appear in Arrian's account of Alexander's early reign and would later be used by the Macedonian kings in Egypt to raise money in emergencies.

The Macedonian conquest of the Achaemenid empire accelerated a convergence of fiscal expertise between east and west. There is not space here to assess the impact of Greek monetary and fiscal reforms or what Max Weber describes as the "rationalization" of fiscal administration in the Hellenistic kingdoms, above all in Egypt (Weber 1998: 233), though recent scholarship may go too far in discrediting them. In many respects these changes simply mark an intensification of an ongoing process, but we should not neglect the impact of geographical and social mobility that Alexander's campaigns created. The brief and preliminary remarks about book two of Ps.-Aristotle's *Oikonomika* at the end of the last section serve to draw out some implications of his appointment of fiscal officers alongside satraps in areas around the eastern Mediterranean and Babylonia. Even if they had no wish to disrupt Achaemenid sources of revenue, the installation of a new class of administrators with Greek education and historical memory—perhaps even pretentions of cultural superiority—furnished new models and orientations. As the cost and scale of warfare mounted in the late fourth and third centuries BCE, their successors were under maximum pressure to increase their revenue however possible, even by unscrupulous means, which accords well with the tenor and stated purpose of the *Oikonomika*.

WORKS CITED

Agut-Labordère, Damien. 2001. "L'oracle et l'hoplite: les élites sacerdotales et l'effort de guerre sous les dynasties égyptiennes indigènes." *Journal of the Social and Economic History of the Orient* 54: 627–45.

Armstrong, G. Cyril. 1958. *Aristotle. Oeconomica and Magna Moralia*. Loeb Classical Library. Cambridge: Harvard University Press.

Aperghis, Girgis G. 2002. *The Seleucid Royal Economy*. Cambridge: Cambridge University Press.

Berve, Helmut. 1929. *Das Alexanderreich auf prosopographischer Grundlage*. 2 vols. Munich: Beck.

Böckh, August. 1886. *Die Staatshaushaltung der Athener*. 3rd edition. Berlin: Reimer.

Bonney, Richard. 1995. "Introduction." In R. Bonney (ed.), *Economic Systems and State Finance*. (Oxford: Oxford University Press), 1–18.

Bosworth, Brian. 1980. *Historical Commentary on Arrian's History of Alexander*. Oxford: Oxford University Press.

Bosworth, Brian. 1988. *Conquest and Empire: The Reign of Alexander the Great*. Cambridge: Cambridge University Press.

Bresson, Alain. 2000. *La cité marchande*. Bordeaux: Ausonius.

Briant, Pierre. 2006. "L'Asie mineure en transition." In P. Briant and F. Joannées (eds.), *La transition entre l'empire achéménide et les royaumes hellénistiques* (Paris: Boccard), 309–51.

Brodersen, Kai. 2006. *77 Tricks zur Steigerung der Staatseinnahmen (Oikonomika II)*. Stuttgart: Reclam.

Brun, Patrice. 1983. *Eisphora. Syntaxis. Stratiotika. Recherches sur les finances militaires d'Athènes au IVe siècle av. J.-C*. Paris: Belles Lettres.

Brunt, P. A. 1976. *Arrian*. Loeb Classical Library. Cambridge: Harvard University Press.

Chankowski, V. 2007. "Les catégories du vocabulaire de la fiscalité dans les cités grecques." In J. Andreau and V. Chankowski (eds.), *Vocabulaire et expression de l'économie dans le monde antique* (Bordeaux: Ausonius), 299–331.

Christ, Matthew R. 2007. "The Evolution of the Eisphora in Classical Athens." *Classical Quarterly* 57: 53–69.

Davies, John. 2004. "Athenian Fiscal Expertise and its Influence." *Mediterraneo Antico* 7: 491–512.

Debord, P. 1999. *L'Asie mineure au IVe siècle (412–323 a.C.). Pouvoirs et jeux politiques*. Bordeaux: Boccard.

Descat, Raymond. 2003. "Qu'est-ce que l'économie royale?" In P. Prost (ed.), *L'Orient méditerranéen de la mort d'Alexandre aux campaignes de Pompés* (Rennes: Presses universitaire de Rennes), 149–68.

Descat, Raymond. 2006. "Aspects d'une transition: l'économie du monde égéen (350–300)." In P. Briant and F. Joannès (eds.), *La transition entre l'empire achéménide et les royaumes hellénistiques* (Paris: De Boccard), 353–73.

Faraguna, Michele. 1998. "Aspetti amministrativi e finanziari della monarchia macedone tra IV e III secolo a.c." *Athenaeum* 86: 349–95.

Fawcett, Peter. 2016. "'When I Squeeze You with *Eisphorai*': Taxes and Tax Policy in Classical Athens." *Hesperia* 85: 153–99.

Finley, Moses I. 1970. "Aristotle's *Oeconomicus*." *Classical Review* 20: 315–19.

Gabrielsen, Vincent. 2013. "Finances and Taxes." In H. Beck (ed.), *A Companion to Ancient Greek Government* (Oxford: Blackwell), 332–48.

Gauthier, Philippe. 1976. *Un commentaire historique des* Poroi *de Xénophon*. Paris: Librairie Droz.

Gauthier, Philippe. 1991. "Ἀτέλεια τοῦ σώματος." *Chiron* 21: 49–68.

Griffith, G. T. 1964. "Alexander the Great and an Experiment in Government." *Cambridge Classical Journal* 10: 23–39.

Harris, E.M. 2018. *Demosthenes. Speeches 23–26*. Austin: University of Texas Press.

Hatzopoulos, H. B. 1988. *Une donation du roi Lysimaque*. Paris: De Boccard.

Hatzopoulos, H. B. 1996. *Macedonian Institutions under the Kings*, 2 vols. Athens: National Hellenic Research Foundation.

Hornblower, Simon. 1982. *Mausolus*. Oxford: Oxford University Press.

Kleber, K. 2015. "Taxation in the Achaemenid Empire." *Oxford Handbooks Online*. DOI: 10.1093/oxfordhb/9780199935390.013.34.

Lane Fox, R. 2011. "Philip's and Alexander's Macedon." In R. Lane Fox (ed.), *Brill's Companion to Ancient Macedonia* (Leiden: Brill), 367–91.

Leppin, Hartmut. 1995. "Zur Entwicklung der Verwaltung öffentlicher Gelder im Athen des 4. Jahrhunderts v. Chr." In W. Eder (ed.), *Die athenische Demokratie im 4. Jahrhundert v. Chr* (Stuttgart: Steiner Verlag), 557–71.

Le Rider, G. 2003. *Alexandre le Grand: monnaie, finances et politique*. Paris: Presses universitaires de France.

Marchant, E. C. 1968. *Xenophon. Scripta Minora*. Loeb Classical Library. Cambridge: Harvard University Press.

Mari, M. 2020. "Alexander, King of the Macedonians." In A. Meeus and K. Trampedach (eds.), *Alexander's Empire: The Legitimation of Conquest*. (Stuttgart: Steiner Verlag), 197–217.

Migeotte, Léopold. 2001. "Le traité entre Milet et Pidasa (*Delphinion* 149): les clauses financières." In A. Bresson et R. Descat (eds.), *Les cités d'Asie Mineure Occidentale au IIe siècle a.C.* (Bordeaux: Ausonius), 129–35. Reprinted in *Économie et finances publiques des cités grecques*, vol. 1. Paris: Boccard (2010), 401–8.

Migeotte, Léopold. 2003. "Taxation directe en Grèce ancienne." In G. Thür and F. J. Fernández Nieto (eds.), *Symposion 1999* (Cologne: Böhlau), 297–313.

Migeotte, Léopold. 2014. *Les finances des cités grecques aux periodes classique et hellénistique*. Paris: Belles Lettres.

Miller, Walter. 1919. *Xenophon. Cyropaedia*. Loeb Classical Library. Cambridge: Harvard University Press.

Millett, Paul. 2010. "The Political Economy of Macedonia." In J. Roisman and I. Worthington (eds.), *A Companion to Ancient Macedonia* (Oxford: Blackwell), 472–504.

Pernin, I. 2007. "L'impôt foncier existait-il en Grèce ancienne?" In J. Andreau and V. Chankowski (eds.), *Vocabulaire et expression de l'économie dans le monde antique* (Ausonius: Bordeaux), 369–83.

Raaflaub, Kurt A. 2009. "Learning from the Enemy: Athenian and Persian 'Instruments of Empire.'" In J. Ma, N. Papazarkadas, and R. Parker (eds.), *Interpreting the Athenian Empire* (London: Duckworth), 89–124.

Rhodes, Peter J. 2013. "The Organization of Athenian Public Finance." *Greece & Rome* 60: 203–31.

Rhodes, Peter J., and Robin Osborne. 2003. *Greek Historical Inscriptions, 404–323 BC*. Oxford: Oxford University Press.

Schuler, Christof. 2005. "Die διοίκησις τῆς πόλεως im öffentlichen Finanzwesen der hellenistischen Poleis." *Chrion* 35: 385–403.

Schuler, Christof. 2007. "Tribute und Steuern im hellenistischen Kleinasien." In H. Klinkott, S. Kubisch, and R. Müller-Wollermann (eds.), *Geschenke und Steuern, Zölle und Tribute. Antike Abgabenformen in Anspruch und Wirklichkeit* (Leiden: Brill), 371–405.

Schumpeter, Joseph A. 1991 [1918]. "The Crisis of the Tax State: An Essay in Fiscal Sociology." In J. Schumeter, *The Economics and Sociology of Capitalism* (ed. R. Swedberg; Princeton: Princeton University Press), 99–140.

Schütrumpf, Eckart. 1982. *Xenophon. Vorschläge zur Beschaffung von Geldmitteln oder Über die Staatseinkünfte*. Darmstadt: Wissenschaftliche Buchgemeinschaft.

Sherwin-White, Susan M. 1985. "The Edict of Alexander at Priene: A Reappraisal." *Journal of Hellenic Studies* 105: 69–89.

Stolper, Matthew W. 1989. "Registration and Taxation of Slave Sales in Achaemenid Babylonia." *Zeitschrift für Assyriologie* 79: 80–101.

Thompsen, Rudi. 1964. *Eisphora: A Study of Direct Taxation in Ancient Athens*. Copenhagen: Gyldendal.

Thonemann, Peter. 2009. "Estates and the Land in Early Hellenistic Asia Minor: The Estate of Krateuas," *Chrion* 39: 363–93.

Thonemann, Peter. 2012. "Alexander, Priene and Naulochon." In P. Martzavou and N. Papazarkadas (eds.), *Epigraphical Approaches to the Post-Classical Polis* (Oxford: Oxford University Press), 23–36.

Tziafalias, Athanassios and Bruno Helly. 2010. "Inscriptions de la Tripolis de Perrhébie: Lettres royales de Démétrios II et Antigone Dôsôn." *Studi ellenistici* 24: 71–125.

van Driel, G. 2002. *Elusive Silver: In Search of a Role for a Market in an Agrarian Environment: Aspects of Mesopotamia's Society*. Istanbul: Nederlands Instituut voor het Nabije Oosten.

van Groningen, B.A. 1933. *Aristote. Le second livre de l'Économique*. Leiden: Sijthoff.

Vince, J. H. 1954. *Demosthenes. Orations, Volume III: Orations 21–36*. Loeb Classical Library. Cambridge, Mass.: Harvard University Press.

Weber, Max. 1998. *The Agrarian Sociology of Ancient Civilizations*. London: Verso.

Will, Édouard. 1960. "Chabrias et les finances de Tachos." *Revue des Études Anciennes* 62: 254–75.

Zoepffel, R. 2006. *Aristoteles. Oikonomika*. Berlin: Akademie Verlag.

12

The *Anabolikon* Tax and the Study of the Linen Industry in Roman Egypt

IRENE SOTO MARÍN

In 1913 a finely woven linen garment now called the Tarkhan Dress and housed in the University College London Petrie Museum of Archaeology was excavated in the Tarkhan cemetery south of Cairo. Radiocarbon dating undertaken at the University of Oxford has recently confirmed that the item dates to between 3482 and 3102 BCE, which would make it 5,000 years old, the oldest surviving example in the world.[1] With evidence for such a long tradition of linen textile production, it is clear that the organization and production of linen was well rooted in the Egyptian economic landscape for millennia before Roman rule. As we will see, by the third century CE, the products of the linen industry in Egypt had become staples in Mediterranean markets and even captured the attention of the imperial offices of Rome. In this study I present the available evidence that can speak to the economic impact of the Egyptian linen trade in the wider Mediterranean world, and I hope to show how studying a particular tax can shed light not only on questions of scale that may be otherwise obscure, but also on an aspect of Rome's fiscal policy during this time, namely the extraction of provincial surplus.

The scale of linen production in Roman Egypt is nearly impossible to calculate. This is also true of textile industries in other areas of the Mediterranean.[2] Unfortunately, archaeological evidence cannot contribute much in this respect.[3] The main obstacle is the fact that textiles, like papyri, rarely survive outside of Egypt. This means that evidence for understanding the export trade or consumption of linen outside of Egypt is immediately limited to literary accounts and epigraphic texts.[4] Some iconographic evidence in the form of sarcophagi and paintings, for example those from Pompeii, may help us to understand the popularity of Egyptian linen in the Roman world. These images, however, do not offer much more information beyond what is already evident in literary sources.[5]

In this study I will first offer a brief historiographical background of the linen industry in Roman Egypt, which is crucial for understanding the structures of its production during the Graeco-Roman period. I hope to show both where the strength of the evidence lies and how it has been approached by previous scholars, and also to shed light on the areas where the papyrological and archaeological evidence has left some lacunae. I will then present the literary evidence available for the trade of linen in the rest of the Roman Empire as our main indicator for its consumption outside of the province. I will then dedicate the last section of this study to a discussion of the *anabolikon* tax and, to a lesser extent, the *vestis militaris* tax, and how both fit into the larger narrative of the economic impact of Egyptian linen and the taxation of surplus in the Roman Empire.

The Historiography of Roman Egypt's Linen Industry

Most of the texts relating to the textile industry in Egypt are tax receipts, contracts, requisitions for the army, and account ledgers.[6] This means that administrators, and not the workers themselves, wrote these texts. Therefore, the daily aspects of the industry are challenging to reconstruct, but we can tell that the industry was highly differentiated and possessed multiple degrees of specialization—from the collection of the raw material to the final tanning and dyeing.[7]

Because of the nature of the documentation, the profession of weaver is perhaps the one most often represented in the papyri. It was weavers who drafted apprentice contracts and leases for looms, and they paid taxes on their trade. This skewed view of the industry means that we actually have little evidence for the other professions on which textile production depended. It has plausibly been argued that it was women who did most of the spinning work, at home, hidden from the public and fiscal eye that created the documentary records.[8] We also now have evidence from the site of Kellis in the Dakhleh Oasis, for example, in which we find women spinners listed in a census declaration dating to the second century CE.[9] In addition to textiles themselves, spindle whorls and loom weights have also been discovered in nearly every domestic structure and in some temple shrines in Kellis dating to the fourth century CE, attesting to household production.[10] The Coptic papyri from House 3 in Kellis, for example, shed light on various interesting aspects of the trade such as fulling, dying, and wage prices.[11] Further papyrological evidence from Kellis indicates that weaving of linen also took place in monasteries, such as *P.Kell.Gr.* 12.16–21: ". . . As I indicated to you concerning my son—-, put him into the monastery, where it (one) teaches him the linen-weaving trade . . ." Similarly, *P.Kell.Gr.* 19a features a slave whose female owner sends her to learn the weaving trade.[12] Archaeological material from excavations at the Monastery of Epiphanios near ancient Thebes corroborates the texts, as remains of fibers, spindle whorls, looms, and even woven goods and garments were found on site.[13]

But production also took place in specialized workshops. A contract for a linen-weaving workshop in Panopolis dated to September 3rd, 355 CE, for example, shows an Aurelius Pasnos son of Alopex leasing a workshop from Aurelios Paulos, a linen-weaver, along with the weaving appliances, including loom frames.[14] Thus, textile production occurred both within households and in workshops, which in fact were often attached to households. The manufacture of textiles was varied and geared towards different markets; perhaps household production supplied domestic need while workshops specialized in producing linen at a larger scale. Private correspondence shows that clients could commission specific garments to be manufactured by a master weaver.[15] What we do not know with certainty is the scale of linen production or exportation during the Roman period.

Peter van Minnen tackled the question of scale and attempted to measure the yearly volume of textile production in Oxyrhynchus based on *P.Oxy.Hels.* 40. He calculated that if the weekly quantities of linen mentioned in the papyrus represented consistent shipments, the number could be extrapolated to suggest 100,000 garments per year for the town of Oxyrhynchus alone. Comparatively speaking, this figure is high. Van Minnen himself notes that medieval Florence produced between 70,000–80,000 cloths per year at the height of its wealth.[16] Accordingly, Wild says that these figures "tease rather than explain." The regularity of the shipments documented in *P. Oxy.Hels.* 40 should, for example, be questioned.[17] It is nevertheless clear from the week's figures that the scale of textile production in one town in Egypt in the third century was significant. Van Minnen concludes that the clothes were being taxed as exports, but it is unclear whether the clothes are being shipped for exportation beyond the nome or only out of the metropolis.[18]

The Edict of Maximum Prices, issued in 301 by the Emperor Diocletian in order to cap price inflation, lists a variety of linen, and specifically Egyptian, textiles. It should be noted that while Egypt certainly occupied a critical position in the manufacture of linen, it is not the only place in the Roman Empire where flax was grown and special linen markets existed, as is illustrated by Pliny's *Natural History* (discussed below). Gaul, Tarsus, Laodicia, Scythopolis, and Byblos all produced specialized linen cloths.[19] The size of the Delta and other marshlands of Egypt, however, allowed it to produce a wide variety of flax and linen throughout the province in exceptionally large quantities, providing a foundation for a much more robust industry. The location of the province within the Indo-Roman trade route paired with the economic role Alexandria played as a Mediterranean port further stimulated the trade in Egyptian linen.

We know that linen was leaving Egypt because of occasional references in textual evidence from the rest of the Empire. There is, for instance, a brief communication on a wooden writing table from Bordeaux mentioning linen spinners who possibly received raw materials by boat from Egypt.[20] Attempts to quantify the scale of this trade are nevertheless beset by uncertainty. If one imagines that the figures from Oxyrhynchus are representative of other textile producing areas in Egypt, there can be no doubt that this was a major industry. General studies on the impact of textile production and the role of flax in the economy of Roman Egypt have attempted to create initial economic models. Mayerson gives an important overview of the changing role of flax and the textile economy during the Roman period, arguing that its profits led to an Egyptian economy centered on textile production by the time of the Geniza archive.[21]

Katherine Blouin's recent analysis of the economy and topography of the Mendesian nome in the Nile Delta shows that the nome specialized in linen production, and Blouin argues for its profitability not only in the hinterlands that produced the raw flax but also for the city dwellers who could then weave it and export it.[22] There is papyrological evidence that unprocessed flax was exported raw out of the province. Although dated between the sixth and seventh century—slightly later than the period under discussion here—*CPR* 7.60 is a report on transactions of tow, the raw material of flax used both for spinning thread and for making ropes. The tow was to be sold in outside markets, a fact apparent in the mention of a storm at sea. The quantities of tow listed are 60 *litrai* (Roman pounds, so about 19.4 kg), which is not a large number, but also not trivial.[23] Blouin also points out the continuing importance of Mendesian flax, apparent from documentary sources dating from the Ptolemaic through the Medieval period.

There is substantial evidence from within Egypt concerning its linen production and the structure of the industry.[24] Evidence of consumption and trade, particularly outside of Egypt, is, however, not as easy to obtain from the papyri. For this we must turn instead to literary sources, which shed light on the perception of the Egyptian linen industry in the Roman Empire.

Literary Evidence for Linen Consumption outside of Egypt

Literary evidence for the consumption of Egyptian textiles and its trade beyond the province is not plentiful. The few passages that exist, though, contain valuable information on how the Egyptian linen industry was perceived in the upper echelons of the Roman administration. In this section I will draw mainly from the *Historia Augusta*, Pliny the Elder's *Historia Naturalis*, and the *Periplus Maris Erythraei*. While the texts may not offer any quantifiable data, I believe they are valuable for showing the impact and reach of the Egyptian linen industry outside of Egypt.

In 1889 Hermann Dessau demonstrated that the *Historia Augusta*, a late Roman collection of biographies of Roman emperors that claims to be the compiled works of six authors writing in the early fourth century, was actually the work of one author writing much later, in 373–383 CE according to Alan Cameron.[25] Since then, numerous explanations, analyses of the texts, and quests to determine what is "authentic" and what is not have been undertaken. While a full discussion of the nature of the text is unnecessary here, it is nevertheless important to acknowledge that the text is problematic.[26] However that may be, the *Historia Augusta* nevertheless preserves a telling reference to the perception of the linen industry at the highest level of the Roman Empire. While the relevant passage is certainly a literary embellishment, it is indicative of the position of Egypt's linen industry in the late fourth century CE, when the text was likely composed. The passage relates the reaction of the emperor Gallienus to various troubles besetting regions of his Empire:

> I am ashamed to relate what Gallienus used often to say at this time, when such things were happening, as though jesting amid the ills of mankind. For when he was told of the revolt of Egypt, he is said to have exclaimed, "What! We cannot do without Egyptian linen!"; and when informed that Asia had been devastated both by the violence of nature and by the inroads of the Scythians, he said, "What! We cannot do without saltpetre!"; and when Gaul was lost, he is reported to have laughed and remarked, "Can the commonwealth be safe without Atrebatic cloaks?" Thus, in short, with regard to all parts of the world, as he lost them, he would jest, as though seeming to have suffered the loss of some article of trifling service . . .[27]

Regardless of the veracity of this anecdote, it implies that a revolt in Egypt portended a halt to the flow of linen, and that this was the first thing that came to mind in such a situation. Egypt was a land of linen, and the importance of the Egyptian linen industry was widely recognized in Rome. A disruption in the supply of Egyptian linen was understood to have Empire-wide repercussions. The intended readers of the *Historia Augusta* would presumably also have understood this economic link, further reinforcing the status of Egyptian linen in the Roman economy.

The author of this passage did not necessarily intend to assign equal importance to the events to which Gallienus is responding. It is clear that he was concerned with the character of Gallienus and his response to events that were detrimental to the stability of the Roman Empire. Indeed, in the same passage the revolt in Egypt is compared to the loss of the entire province of Gaul and to the devastation of all of Asia by the Scythians. Although one cannot take this at face value, it remains striking to see the *Historia Augusta* equating Egypt with the linen industry and the rebellion in Egypt with other major calamities. This, I believe, demonstrates an awareness of the importance of the Egyptian linen industry to the Empire, such that instability in Egypt would have repercussions on the stability of the Empire. Another passage in the *Historia Augusta* concerning Aurelian's reinstitution of the *anabolikon* tax on linen is relevant to the discussion of linen. Because there is substantially more—albeit still limited—papyrological evidence than literary evidence regarding this tax, I will discuss this passage in the section dealing with papyrological evidence for the *anabolikon* later in this study.

Pliny the Elder discusses the geography of linen production and the quality of the linen produced in *Natural History*, composed between 77–79 CE. The first five chapters of Book 19 of his work relate to flax: its nature, how it is grown and prepared, and the regions around the empire where it is produced. Gallic and Germanic wetlands and caves were known to produce it, as well as various regions in Spain; Pliny notes that Spain was known for producing "a linen of the greatest luster."[28] Pliny's account allows us to begin to distinguish the scale and extensive specialization of Egyptian linen production. The author referes to different flax-growing regions of Egypt by listing various types: Tanitic, Butic, Pelusiac, Tentyric.[29] The first three of these descriptive adjectives refer to the branches of the Nile in the Delta, and the regions each one irrigated as well: Tanis, Buto, and Pelusium. Tentyra (known commonly as Dendera, where the famous Temple of Hathor sits) is located near the modern city of Qena in Upper Egypt. This topographical classification is not exhaustive, but it probably includes the best-known flax-growing regions in Egypt. While we have evidence for extensive textile production in Alexandria, Oxyrhynchus, and Antinoopolis, we also know that unfinished garments were sent to Alexandria and Oxyrhynchus for weaving.[30] Pliny therefore appears to be listing flax growing regions rather than textile producing centers.

In another passage in the same text, Pliny complains about the poor quality of Egyptian linen while observing that its production was nevertheless immensely profitable: "The flax of Egypt, though the least strong of all as a tissue, is that from which the greatest profits are derived."[31] Pliny's account does not give a reason for the profitability of Egyptian linen, but it must relate to Egypt's comparative advantage in the cultivation of different kinds of flax and in the production of various textiles. This comparative advantage was enhanced by the scale of

Egyptian production, constituting a solid foundation for a strong and diversified industry. Pliny's observations again suggest a widespread familiarity with Egyptian linen production in the Roman Empire, at a time several hundred years before the writing of the *Historia Augusta*. They also point to the popularity of and high demand for Egyptian linen outside of Egypt.[32] Three central aspects of linen production (and Egyptian production in particular) can be identified in this passage: it served popular needs, involved mass production, and could be quite profitable, characteristics that are corroborated by other literary and papyrological sources.

The demand for Egyptian textiles was not, however, limited to regions within the Roman Empire. The *Periplus Maris Erythraei*, a first-century CE account presumably written by an Egyptian merchant who sailed from the Red Sea ports of Egypt to various ports along the coast of eastern Africa, southern Arabia, and western India, speaks of a strong demand for textiles and garments from workshops in Roman Egypt.[33]

The author claims, for example, that in the regions of Adulis and Axum there was a strong demand for wraps (*stolai*) produced at Arsinoe in the Fayum, a center known for the production of linen:[34]

> There are imported into these places undressed cloth made in Egypt for the Berbers; robes from Arsinoe; cloaks of poor quality dyed in colors; double-fringed linen mantles . . . The most from Egypt is brought to this market from the month of January to September, that is, from Tybi to Thoth; but seasonally they put to sea about the month of September.[35]

The textiles listed span a variety of types and qualities meant for different economic markets: undressed cloth, cloaks, and mantles. These kinds of textiles have also recently been documented archaeologically.[36] The different kinds of products available in the market met different consumer needs, which serves as further evidence of a highly sophisticated industry. Furthermore, the association with specific regions, such as Arsinoe and Diospolis, echoes (but for different areas) Pliny's geographical description of the types of linen listed in the *Natural History*. The fact that some of the textiles were regarded as being of poor quality perhaps suggests that they were mass produced. This regional differentiation and specialization of textile production within Egypt itself is a key indicator of the scale of the industry and of the demand for different types of Egyptian linen and woolen products outside of the province.

The textiles produced in Egypt were central to a broader trade in luxury products. Egyptian linen passed through its ports to eastern markets. The *Periplus* documents the exportation of Egypt's linen textiles and the importation in exchange of all sorts of upmarket items, including precious stones and textiles made of cotton, silk, and mallow cloth:

> There are exported from these places spikenard, costus, bdellium, ivory, agate and carnelian, lycium, cotton cloth of all kinds, silk cloth, mallow cloth, yarn, long pepper and such other things as are brought here from the various market-towns. Those bound for this market-town from Egypt make the voyage favorably about the month of July, that is Epeiph.[37]

Egyptian linen production was thus part of a textile trade of sufficient scale and quality to help underwrite a vast trade in luxury goods across the Indian Ocean.

One of the important aspects of the literary evidence is the identification of Alexandria as a main textile-trading hub. In his description of the connectivity of the port in Arabia Eudaimon, the merchant-author of the *Periplus* points out the role of Alexandria as a focal point of large-scale commercial connectivity:

> Eudaimon Arabia, a full-fledged city in earlier days, was called Eudaimon when, since vessels from India did not go on to Egypt and those from Egypt did not dare sail to the places further on but came only this far, it used to receive the cargoes of both, just as Alexandria received cargoes from overseas as well as from Egypt . . .[38]

Alexandria's central position in networks of commercial interaction between Rome and lands outside the Empire was facilitated by its location on the Mediterranean coast, its access to the Sudan and regions further south in the African continent via the Nile, and its relative proximity to the Red Sea with its maritime link to the Indian Ocean. Alexandria, the most notable textile production center, was probably also one of the main redistribution centers for unprocessed linen since it is from this Mediterranean metropolis and emporium that outward trade was organized.

To sum up the evidence we have covered thus far, literary texts provide information on: the scale and sophistication of linen production in Alexandria; the high volume of total production in Egypt; the desirability of Egyptian linen to external markets; the significant profits to be made; the diversity of garments produced; and the well-known regional production centers within Egypt that exported to the Red Sea markets, sub-Saharan Africa, and the rest of the Mediterranean. Criticisms of the quality of textiles suggest that the linen market was segmented by quality, reaching different levels of the market. All of these literary descriptions are qualitative and offer no quantitative data useful for economic analysis. Nonetheless, these descriptions are important because they show the reputation of the Egyptian linen industry in external markets, and even a certain dependence on Egyptian textiles. This may also confirm the presence of mass-produced, lower quality goods in exportation, showing that the trade of textiles was not only geared towards luxury products. In the absence of evidence from outside of Egypt to understand the scale of consumption of Egyptian linen, the impact and importance of the industry can be better understood by analyzing the systems the state used to extract revenue from it, namely the *anabolikon* tax. Fortunately, this is where papyri can help.

The *Anabolikon* and the *Vestis Militaris*

The papyrological record in Egypt, which is particularly rich in documentary texts relating to economic activities, offers unique opportunities for the study of taxation. A preliminary search on the digital resource papyri.info, for example, yields over 3,000 records of tax receipts dating to the Roman period. This abundance of papyrological evidence attests to a variety of types of tax: the well-known grain-tax, money taxes on land, taxes on animals, poll taxes, other capitation taxes, taxes on trade, sales tax, and other duties associated with commerce, to name but a few. The plethora of papyrological data allows a systematic assessment of taxation in the region. When focusing on one particular kind of tax, it presents the unique opportunity of linking quotidian local evidence of the collection of taxes in a Roman province to wider imperial legislation and the historical accounts given in literary and legal sources.

There are three documents from the second century CE that mention duties for a tax in money on the production of linen.[39] Such taxes existed since the Hellenistic period, and Blouin has hinted at a continuation of the levies on flax production from the third century BCE until the second century CE, as seen through the papyrological evidence. *P.Stras.* 4.299, dated to the second century CE, mentions a tax on linen production called *timē linokalamē*.[40]

Through the study of the history and nature of a specific tax, it is possible to gain insight into the fiscal goals of the Empire. This applies in the case of the *anabolikon*, a late antique linen tax. The analysis of the *anabolikon* in particular lends itself to understanding the logic of the mechanics of extraction as applied in one instance and on the basis of multiple sources. Combining the literary and papyrological evidence does not present a very coherent picture in this case, but it is nevertheless possible to extract valuable information on the economic rationale informing the fiscal systems of the Roman provinces. In this section, I will argue that the *anabolikon* tax was aimed at maximizing extraction from Egypt's most profitable industry—textiles.

Rostovtzeff first explained the tax according to the etymology of its name:

> 'Αναβάλλειν, from which ἀναβολικόν is derived, probably means, as a *terminus technicus* of taxation, to "deal out," i.e. to deal out a portion of a certain kind of goods for export to Rome and to the other capitals of the Empire, the portion which was "dealt out" being a new additional or an old reformed payment imposed on the producers of raw material (flax and hemp) and on the manufacturers (glass, papyrus).

According to Rostovtzeff, the *anabolicae species* are the products subject to the *anabolicum*, a tax in kind or a delivery of goods whose manufacture had been monopolized by the state in the earlier Ptolemaic period (glass, hemp, papyrus). The *Fachwörterbuch* has defined the tax more generally as an "export tax on Egyptian products."[41]

The papyrological evidence for the *anabolikon* was edited and analyzed by Jennifer Sheridan in 1999. While the literary evidence implies that the tax was imposed on many industries, papyrological evidence makes clear that the *anabolikon* in Egypt was a tax specifically on linen and linen products. Following her analysis of the greater portion of the papyrological data, which dates to the third and fourth centuries, Sheridan concludes that the *anabolikon* was essentially a "late antique linen tax, sometimes paid in cash, and sometimes in kind, which supplied some branch of the government, [presumably the army], with its occasional need for linen garments."[42] The tax seems to have been assessed in a manner similar to the *vestis militaris*, a much better understood Late Antique tax, whose purpose was clearly to clothe the army.

The literary evidence for the *anabolikon* is quite limited, but well known among those acquainted with the Emperor Aurelian. *Historia Augusta* 45 refers to the (re)institution of the *anabolikon* tax by the Emperor: "Aurelian permanently established, for the benefit of the city of Rome, a tax on products from Egypt, specifically on glass, paper, linen, and tow, and the anabolic categories."[43] As Jennifer Sheridan has noted, the passage is problematic in both grammar and content. Sheridan points out that the translation by Ramsey MacMullen implies one tax, but Francois Paschoud's translation in French in 1996 distinguishes two separate actions: the establishment of the tax on Egypt for the benefit of the city of Rome and the making permanent of the *anabolicae species*.[44]

Neither Paschoud's nor MacMullen's reading finds confirmation in the papyrological evidence. There is, for example, no evidence of the tax being paid on glass or papyrus paper; only on linen and tow, though it will be conceded that there is in any case little information available on the taxation of glass and papyrus in general. As for the chronology of the tax, lead seals found in Lyons and dating to the time of Septimius Severus (193–211) inscribed with the word *anabolicum* make clear both that the tax was indeed in place long before Aurelian and that the tax existed outside of Egypt.[45] Papyrological evidence further confirms the existence of the tax before 270 CE. *O.Fay.* 49 (dated to 19 CE), for example, offers evidence for the *adaeratio* of the tax, which means the commutation of tax payments in kind into cash. This shows that the default mode of payment at the time was in kind. There are three further references dating to before 270, two of which also refer to payments of money.[46] *PSI* 8.779, dated to the third century, lists the tax being collected in kind and shows it to be an assessment on the land that produced flax.[47]

Our understanding of the *anabolikon* is further complicated by what is known about a contemporary tax, the *vestis militaris*, a late Roman military clothing tax. The *vestis militaris* seems to have been collected in continuous, small orders, and the fact that records were kept for a long time in family archives indicates the importance of documenting payment and keeping the receipts. Sheridan published the fourth-century *Vestis Militaris Codex*, a documentary codex originally composed either in 324/5 or 325/6, recording the payment of the *vestis militaris* by each *pagus* of the Hermopolite nome.[48] Sheridan subsequently traced the history of the tax and its relationship to major empire-wide changes following the economic reforms of Diocletian in 296 CE. Thus, while there is evidence from as early as the second century CE for the government purchase of Egyptian linen for the army, there is no evidence for this tax itself prior to the fourth century, which could lead to the assumption that the *vestis militaris* developed out of the clothing requisition system of the previous centuries, as the *anabolikon* has been assumed to have done. The existence of the *anabolikon* well into the fifth century, however, makes it clear that the tax co-existed with the *vestis militaris* and must therefore be a separate exaction.

P.Mich. inv. 4004 is a fourth century account of contributions by 26 individuals (among them three women) to the *vestis militaris*. Three entries follow each name, indicating the number of *chlamydes*, *sticharia*, and *pallia* in fractional units. The account includes four toponyms that identify the papyrus as coming from the Oxyrhynchite nome.[49] If we compare this account with that of *SB* 16.12827 (342/3 CE), a detailed *vestis militaris* account that converts payments of clothing into monetary amounts, it is clear that payments for the *vestis militaris* were very small. R. S. Bagnall and K. A. Worp call the amount a "trifle," the equivalent of a payment of one artaba of wheat on an estate of 156 arouras during the middle of the fourth century, or about 39 liters of grain for an area of about 43 hectares.[50] The *vestis* thus represented an ongoing requisition system that clothed the army, and the purpose of the tax seems to have been immediate use on the part of the troops stationed in Egypt rather than shipment of the products to the Imperial capital. Perhaps this was also the case for the *anabolikon*.

Wallace (1938) concluded in his treatise on taxation in Roman Egypt that the *anabolikon* was a special levy made for the Roman armies engaged in actual warfare. Accordingly, the reforms of Aurelian recorded in the *Historia Augusta* represented an insistence on payment in kind, since it was possible for commodity prices to change before the army purchased the goods for which the tax was intended.

Another key consideration must be added to this picture, namely that of the currency situation in Egypt during the third century CE. Egyptian coins at this time were not those used in other areas of the Empire, and their intrinsic value was low. What does this mean for the payment of the *anabolikon*? Although we know that the tax was indeed paid in coin occasionally, Wallace makes an important point by stressing the preference for payment in kind. If we assume that the products were indeed destined for the city of Rome or for the army, then we must conclude that the Roman state was more interested in the actual products extracted than it was in collecting Egyptian currency, since the Egyptian coins of the era could not be exported and thus did little to help with Rome's expenses elsewhere.[51] What then was the purpose of the *anabolikon*? Ultimately, the tax demonstrates the intent of the Roman state to regularize extraction, to some extent, of the surplus linen production of Egypt in order to ensure a minimum threshold of raw material, rather than value, which could be convertible to money. Despite this convertibility, the linen was more likely to be used as is given the high quantity in which it was produced and the precarious monetary situation of Egypt in the third century CE.

Rostovzeff was the first to point out that the products listed in the passage from the *Historia Augusta* were highly valuable for Egyptian trade. Accordingly, Aurelian took from Egypt those products that had a high commercial value and that the Roman state knew Egypt produced in surplus. The evidence from other regions of the Empire of high demand for Egyptian textiles makes it clear that there was an important market for the product. The passage from the *Historia Augusta* might thus be better understood not only as evidence that the *anabolikon* was used to meet the immediate consumption needs of the Roman state, but also as an assertion of the particular importance of linen, papyrus, glass, and hemp to the highest Roman authority—the Emperor.[52] The linen industry was varied and produced a large surplus, which was widely traded around the Mediterranean and beyond.

The existence of the *anabolikon* is illustrative of the extractive Roman perspective on Egypt and its products. Although we have not yet discussed the breadth of papyrological evidence for textile production in detail, seeing Egypt's textile industry through Rome's fiscal eyes in the form of the *anabolikon* and the *vestis militaris*, we can already see what the imperial offices saw: an extractable, useful, and highly profitable surplus.

After the tumultuous last few decades of the third century, the emperor Diocletian launched a series of economic and political reforms intended to stabilize the Empire's revenues and expenditures. Changes to the way that taxes were assessed and collected were integral to these reforms. Diocletian had a particular talent for introducing innovations to old customs, which he exemplified during the reforms. He took the Roman idea of the poll tax and introduced the *caput* system, which concerned not only individuals but also the labor power they represented, taking land into account.[53] Perhaps one of the most well-known papyri of the Late Antique period is *P.Cair.Isid.* 1, the Edict of the Prefect of Egypt, Aristius Optatus, dated to March 16, 297 CE. In the text, we can see how the new system of taxation is designed to maximize predictability and regularity by streamlining extraction:

> Aristius Optatus, the most eminent prefect of Egypt says: Our most provident Emperors, Diocletian and Maximian, the noble Caesars . . . having learned that the levies of the public taxes were being levied capriciously so that some persons were let off lightly while others were overburdened, decided in the interests of their provincials to root out this most evil and ruinous practice and issue a salutary rule to which the taxes would have to conform. Thus, it is possible for all to know the amount levied on each aroura in accordance with the character of the land, and the amount levied on each head of the rural population, and the minimum and maximum ages of liability, from the imperial edict which has been published and the schedule attached thereto, to which I have prefixed for public display the copies of this edict of mine. Accordingly, since in this too they have been treated with the greatest beneficence, let the provincials take care to make their contributions with all speed in conformity with the imperial regulations and in no wise wait for the collector to ex-

ercise compulsion. For it is fitting that each person discharge most zeal-
ously the full burden of loyalty, and if anyone should be detected doing
otherwise after such beneficence, he will risk punishment . . .[54]

The language of the papyrus represents a rhetorical effort to convince
the population that the pursuit of fairness informed the restricting
of the assessment, but it is evident that streamlining collection costs
and maximizing revenue were paramount from the point of view of
the Imperial officials responsible for organizing and implementing tax
collection.

Other papyrological evidence shows the expansion of the bureaucratic system for tax collection during the reign of Diocletian. The
archive of Aurelius Isidorus, a fourth-century Egyptian farmer in the
village of Karanis, demonstrates the ways in which the government instituted a new census and land declaration system.[55] After 297 CE, the
rates of almost all taxes were based on landholding, a cardinal principle
of the wider taxation reforms of Diocletian. Sheridan explains that the
state maintained control over surplus extraction through the *vestis militaris* tax, since it expanded the responsibility for tax collection to local
officials within the villages. The inclusion of these middlemen in supplying clothes to the army essentially institutionalized the tax at a local
level. Papyrological evidence dating to the second century CE shows
direct requisitioning from manufacturers and weavers by the central
government. The emphasis shifted beginning in the third century, as
villages and towns were made responsible for the collection of clothes
or their equivalent in money. The burden of the collection of clothing
therefore gradually fell on the citizens, and given the long period of
debasement and the distrust in the local currency, the proper implementation of the tax required having textiles in kind to be able to pay it,
since it was not a straightforward endeavor to provide their equivalent
value in coin. Towards the middle of the fourth century, the collection
of the *vestis militaris* and the *anabolikon* in coin seems to have occurred
more frequently. This is perhaps attributable to the fact that inflation
and dramatic debasement of coinage appears to have subsided after the
Constantian reform, giving greater (and more stable) purchasing power
to the currency in circulation than was the case in previous decades.[56]
The main difference between the two textile taxes is the type of tex-

tiles they collected. The *vestis militaris* focused on the army's need for woolen garments, which was substantial, while the *anabolikon* focused on linen.

Conclusion

In much the same way that the scale of grain production is evident in the *annona* (a tax in grain meant to supply Rome, the armies, and some other cities with grain and other foodstuffs),[57] the *anabolikon* and the *esthēs stratiōtikē*—or *vestis militaris*—can serve as an indication of the scale of linen and textile production in Egypt. At Mons Claudianus, for example, archaeological excavations have yielded different types of weaves and patterns of textiles, some of which were associated with the Roman army stationed there.[58] Elizabeth Fentress points to the army's importance as the bulk market for clothing in North Africa.[59] Along with Carrié's analysis of the Edict of Maximum Prices as securing purchasing power for the army, evidence of this kind cements the importance of textiles not only to the markets but also directly to the state, and shows a truly wide spectrum of demand throughout the Mediterranean world. That the army needed, and regularly requisitioned, clothing is not a novel insight.[60] But these two taxes show graphically the *dependence* of the Roman state on Egyptian textile production from the third century onward.

An updated systematic study of these taxes throughout the Graeco-Roman period might reveal a broader trend of taxation within Egypt, which would be of use to future studies of Roman governance and economy.[61] It remains uncertain how typical these taxes were, though we do have evidence of the *vestis militaris* being collected in other provinces, and there are attestations of the word *anabolicum* outside of Egypt, as in the case of the lead seals found in Lyons.[62] Through the *anabolikon* and the *vestis militaris* we see how important the extraction of Egyptian textiles was to Rome's fiscal policy for the province of Egypt. A political revolt in Egypt would indeed have had repercussions on the regular supply of clothing for the army. For the Roman state to meet its textile needs from elsewhere without the proceeds of the *vestis militaris* and the *anabolikon* would have represented a large additional expenditure.

There are still many questions that remain unanswered concerning the fiscal role of the *anabolikon*. Did the tax affect the linen market? Namely, did the existence and requirement of payment in kind of the tax force the linen industry and its workers to produce a certain threshold of material? Is this then an intervention of the Roman state, as it were, in the linen market?[63] The large economic investment in the Eastern Desert trade along with the development of Alexandria's harbors during the first two centuries of Roman rule in Egypt certainly point to the central role the state played in Egypt's commercial enterprises.[64] There is much more that we can learn about the Egyptian economy under Roman rule. It is nonetheless clear that understanding these specific taxes singly sheds light not only on the salient features of regional economic production, but, and perhaps more central to the present volume, the way in which the State saw and sought to extract revenue from large provincial industries. The evidence from Egypt can thus bring us closer to Rome. In the words of Pliny:

> To think that here is a plant which brings Egypt in close proximity to Italy!—so much so, in fact, that Galerius and Balbillus, both of them prefects of Egypt, made the passage to Alexandria from the Straits of Sicily, the one in six days, the other in five![65]

NOTES

1 For the most updated information on the object see UCL's object site at www.ucl.ac.uk/culture/petrie-museum/tarkhan-dress. For the earliest publication, see Landi and Hall 1979.

2 Flohr 2016: 59 has argued that while it may be possible to calculate the consumption of textiles in the Roman economy, we cannot be sure of the production aspect: "The geography of the Italian wool economy that emerges from early imperial literary sources is a geography of trade and transport rather than a geography of production . . ." See also van Minnen 1986 and its discussion later in this chapter.

3 Publications on the actual textiles found in Egypt for the Roman period are numerous and the study of the manufacturing process of the pieces themselves sheds crucial information on the technological and cultural impact of these textiles. For more on the textiles of different areas of antiquity, see the latest compiled volumes on different aspects of the industry in antiquity with updated bibliography by specialists: Droß-Krüpe and Nosch 2016; Cifarelli and Gawlinsky 2017; Gleba and Pásztókai-Szeöke 2013.

4 Most recently on this topic see Burke 2016 and Lupi 2016 on epigraphic sources for religious textile use and trade. See also *IG* 2² 11254, which mentions garment sellers; *IG* 2² 1673, a purchase of 28 *exomides* for public slaves from clothes-sellers and most notably Diocletian's Edict of Maximum Prices which lists numerous textiles. For the latter, see Herz 2016.

5 See Barret 2017. The Nilotic scenes studied by Barret show the production and weaving of textiles by the river, which I believe should be interpreted as household linen production associated with Egypt.

6 Perhaps no other work on the papyrological evidence regarding the Egyptian textile industry has been more influential than Ewa Wipszycka's *L'Industrie textile dans l'Egypte Romaine*, published in 1965, where she gathered the evidence from the first three centuries CE pertaining to the textile industry in Egypt.

7 The bibliography of John Peter Wild, one of the leading scholars in the study of Roman textiles and a pioneer in the field, is of course of note in this regard. For a complete list of his bibliography up to 2001 see his *Festschrift*, edited by P. Walton Rogers et al. (2014), specifically pages 193–200. More recently he has focused his research on textiles found at the sites of Berenike, Myos Hormos, and Qasr Ibrim. See Wild and Wild 2014a, Wild and Wild 2014b.

8 See Gällnö 2013.

9 Bagnall and Worp 2011.

10 Bowen 1999.

11 *P.Kell.Copt.* 18, 58, 71, 76, 96 in Gardner et al. 1999.
   Livingstone 2009: 73–85, for a discussion of the textiles found at Kellis.

12 Worp 1995: 36–37.

13 MacCoull 1998: 312.

14 McGing 1990.

15 Bogensperger 2016: 260–61.

16 van Minnen 1986: 92. Droß-Krüpe also makes the point that by the medieval period textile spinning technology would have been able to double the production of thread, so 100,000 is even more implausible given the available technology at the time. Droß-Krüpe 2011: 79, referring to Wild 2003: 41–43: "Bedenkt man, dass für ein Stück Stoff von einem Meter Breite und zwei Metern Länge je nach Webtechnik zwischen 3.000 und 9.000 m Garn (für Kette und Schuss) notwendig waren, wird eindrucksvoll deutlich welche Expansionmöglichkeit sich in der textilherstellung durch die Verbreitung des Spinnrades auftate."

17 Wild 2003: 37–45. Wild nonetheless offers important context for the garments mentioned in the Edict of Maximum prices. Using the prices listed in the Edict, for example, Wild concludes that a wool tunic from Laodicea would be more expensive to buy over the counter than to make at home, with a price at 1,350 denarii.

18 van Minnen 1986: 91.

19 Erim et al. 1970: 132.

20 Curchin 1985: 34–35.

21 Mayerson 1997. While the narrative is interesting in itself, the article was intended merely to give an idea of the contrast between the Roman period and the Geniza Archive. The Geniza archive is substantially later, however, and there is therefore a gap in the Late Roman period that is not covered in the article.

22 Blouin 2014: 237 presents *P.Oxy.* 66.4534, a papyrus from the fourth century CE, in which a weaver pays rent by weaving flax rather than paying in currency. She argues that this reflects the desirability of the product, especially if the weaver had any difficulty raising cash.

23 *CPR* 7.60.197–99.

24 Droß-Krüpe 2011 has also substantially contributed new approaches and papyrological information for understanding the textile economy in Egypt during the Roman period. Most of her book focuses on aspects of production itself, i.e., the various stages and professions associated with each step. An important contribution of her analysis is the seriation of papyrological texts chronologically and gregraphically, with respect to particular industries. The graphs and tables presented for different professions and regions of Egypt from pages 48–98 are informative for the type of evidence available for each stage of textile production, but the issue remains that the pattern of most representation of a particular profession also comes from regions where more papyri have been found, such as Oxyrhynchus and the Arsinoite nome.

25 For a detailed discussion and intra textual analysis of the text see Chapter 20 in Cameron 2011.

26 For an updated discussion on the different theories as well as an analysis of the sources of the *HA* see Rohrbacher 2013.

27 *HA*, The Two Gallieni, 6.7.

28 Plin. *HN* 19.2.20.

29 Plin. *HN* 19.2.36.

30 See Van Minnen 1986.

31 *NH* 19.2.14

32 The reliability of Pliny the Elder's *Natural History* has been the subject of much recent scholarship. He seems to be regarded as the compiler of a secondary work rather than as an original researcher. For a recent collection of essays on the various aspects of Pliny as a historical writer, see the recent edited volume by Gibson and Morello 2011.

33 See *Periplus Maris Erythraei* 6, translated in Casson 2012.

34 Albaladejo Vivero 2012.

35 *Periplus Maris Erythraei, 6.*

36 Wild and Wild 2014a.

37 *Periplus Maris Erythraei, 49.*

38 *Periplus Maris Erythraei, 26.*

39 *P.Oxy.* 14.2414.11, 16; *P.Ryl.* 2.214.42–43, 63; *SB* 24.16085. See Blouin 2014: 236.

40 Blouin 2014: 237.

41 *Ausfuhrsteuer ägyptischer Erzeugnisse (insbes. Glas, Werg, Papyrus, Linnen)* in Preisigke 1915: 12.

42 Sheridan 1999: 216.

43 Translation in Sheridan 1999: 215. Original *HA* Aurelian 45: *ʃectigal ex Aegypto urbi Romae Aurelianus vitri, chartae, lini, stuppae, atque anabolicas species aeternas constituit.*

44 Sheridan 1999: 215. MacMullen 1958: 184: "Aurelian permanently established for the city of Rome a tax from Egypt glass, paper, linen, tow, and the anabolic categories"; cf. Paschoud 1996: 209: "Aurélien établit, levé en Égypte au benefice de la ville de Rome, un impôt payé sur le verre, le papier, le lin, l'étoupe et, à titre perpetual, des denrées 'anaboliques.'"

45 See Rostovtzeff 1957: 611 on note 26 for specific references to stamps on oil and wine jars.

46 See Sheridan 1999: 211, for a more detailed description of the texts.

47 14 pounds of flax collected on 100 *arourai* of land subject to the tax.

48 See Sheridan 1998.

49 Moss 2009.

50 Bagnall and Worp 1983: 8. See Bagnall 2009 for equivalencies between arourai and artabas and modern measures.

51 For more on the Roman currency system during the third century CE see Estiot 2012.

52 Wypszicka 1965: 19.

53 Williams 1985: 120.

54 Boak and Youtie 1960.

55 *Ibid.*

56 Sheridan 1998, 86: For the Constantian reform see Bagnall and Bransbourg 2019.

57 The most recent overview of the *annona* tax is Erdkamp 2005. Erdkamp discusses the role Egyptian grain played in the Principate: it not only made up the majority of the grain distributed within Rome, it also constantly provided grain to cities in the east and presumably also to troops stationed there. The term *annona* refers to the annual crop yield, but it slowly evolved to mean the tax on land production and the subsidized distribution of grain in the city of Rome or to rations provided to the military. During 133–121 BCE, the Gracchi brothers offered grain at a subsidized price to citizens in the city of Rome, a move that Cicero criticized 75 years later as an attempt to buy the votes of the poor (*Off.* 2.21.72). Versions of the grain subsidy continued until 58 BCE, when the tribune P. Clodius Pulcher converted it into a free handout. Although Augustus boasts in the *Res Gestae* that he paid cash bonuses to those eligible for the dole, Cassius Dio tells us that the emperor actually restricted the recipients of the grain to 250,000 citizens (out of a population of, presumably, a million). See Nicolet 1980: 192–95.

58 Bender Jørgensen 2004.

59 Fentress 1979: 176, 182–85.

60 Carrié 2004, 2012.

61 For some well-known linen taxes in Egypt attested since the Hellenistic period see also Blouin 2014: 236 n94, referring to older literature, namely Wilcken 1899: 266–69; Wallace 1938: 440, 483; Préaux 1939: 94–95.

62 Rostovtzeff 1957: 611 n26.

63 Andrew Wilson has published several extensive articles exploring the textile industry in North Africa and its relation to urban production in the Roman world; see Wilson 2000 and Wilson 2004.

64 Bowman 2010.

65 *NH* 19.1.

WORKS CITED

Albaladejo Vivero, M. 2013. "Textile trade in the Periplus of the Erythraean Sea." In M. Gleba and J. Pásztókai-Szeökc (eds.), *Making textiles in pre-Roman and Roman times: people, places, identities* (Oxford: Oxbow Books), 142–48.

Bagnall, R.S. 2009. "Practical Help." In R. S. Bagnall (ed.), *The Oxford Handbook of Papyrology* (Oxford: Oxford University Press), 179–96.

Bagnall, R. S. and G. Bransbourg 2019. "The Constantian Monetary Revolution." *ISAW Papers* 14. DOI: 2333.1/3n5tb9sc.

Bagnall, R. S. and K. A. Worp. 1983. "Five Papyri on Fourth-Century Money and Prices." *BASP* 20: 1–19.

Bagnall, R. S. and K. A. Worp. 2011. "Family Papers from Second-Century A.D. Kellis." *Chronique d'Égypte* 86: 228–56.

Barret, C. 2017. "Recontextualizing Nilotic Scenes: Interactive Landscapes in the Garden of the Casa dell'Efebo, Pompeii." *American Journal of Archaeology* 121.2: 293–332.

Bender Jørgensen, L. 2004. "Team work on Roman textiles: The Mons Claudianus Textile Project." In G. C. Alfaro, J. P. Wild, and B. Costa. València (ed.), *Textiles y tintes del Mediterraneo en epoca romana: actas del I Symposium Internacional sobre Textiles y Tintes del Mediterraneo en poca Romana (Ibiza, 8 al 10 de noviembre, 2002)* (València: Consell Insular d'Eivissa i Formentera, Universitat de València), 253–63.

Blouin, K. 2014. *Triangular landscapes: Environment, society, and the state in the Nile Delta under Roman rule.* Oxford: Oxford University Press.

Boak, A. E. R. and H. C. Youtie. 1960. *The archive of Aurelius Isidorus in the Egyptian Museum, Cairo, and the University of Michigan (P. Cair. Isidor.).* Ann Arbor: University of Michigan Press.

Bogensperger, I. 2016. "How to Order a Textile in Ancient Times: The Step before Distribution and Trade." In K. Droß-Krüpe and M. L. Nosch (eds.), *Textiles, Trade and Theories: From the Ancient Near East to the Mediterranean* (Münster: Ugarit-Verlag), 159–68.

Bowen, G. E. 1999. "Textiles from Ismant el-Kharab." *Bulletin of the Australian Centre for Egyptology* 10: 7–12.

Bowman, A. K. 2010. "Trade and the Flag—Alexandria, Egypt, and the Imperial House." In D. Robinson and A. Wilson (eds.), *Alexandria and the North-Western*

Delta: Joint Conference Proceedings of Alexandria: City and Harbour (Oxford 2004) and The Trade and Topography of Egypt's North-West Delta: 8th century BC to 8th century AD (Berlin 2006) (Oxford: Oxford University School of Archaeology), 103–9.

Burke, B. 2016. "Phrygian Fibulae as Makers of Textile Dedication in Greek Sanctuaries." In K. Droß-Krüpe and M. L. Nosch (eds.), *Textiles, Trade and Theories: From the Ancient Near East to the Mediterranean* (Münster: Ugarit-Verlag), 159–68.

Cameron, A. 2011. *The last pagans of Rome*. New York: Oxford University Press.

Carrié, J.-M. 2004. "Vitalité de l'industrie textile à la fin de l'Antiquité: considérations économiques et technologiques." *Antiquité Tardive* 12: 13–44.

Carrié, J-M. 2012. "Were Late Roman and Byzantine Economies Market Economies? A Comparative Look at Historiography." In C. Morrisson, Cécile (ed.), *Trade and markets in Byzantium* (Washington: Dumbarton Oaks Research Library and Collection), 13–26.

Casson, L. 2012. *The Periplus Maris Erythraei: Text with Introduction, Translation, and Commentary*. Princeton: Princeton University Press.

Cifarelli, M. and S. Gawlinsky (eds.). 2017. *What shall I say of clothes? Theoretical and methodological approaches to the study of dress in antiquity*. Boston, MA: Archaeological Institute of America.

Curchin, L.A. 1985. "Men of the cloth. Reflections on Roman linen trade based on a new document from Bordeaux." *Liverpool Classical Monthly* 10.3: 34–35.

Dessau, H. 1889. "Über Zeit und Persönlichkeit der Scriptor *Historiae Augustae*." *Hermes* 24.3: 337–92.

Droß-Krüpe, K. 2011. *Wolle—Weber—Wirtschaft: Die Textilproduktion der römischen Kaiserzeit im Spiegel der papyrologischen Überlieferung*. Wiesbaden: Harrassowitz.

Droß-Krüpe, K. and M.-L. Nosch, eds. 2016. *Textiles, Trade, and Theories: From the Ancient Near East to the Mediterranean*. Münster: Ugarit-Verlag.

Erdkamp, P. 2005. *The Grain Market in the Roman Empire: A Social, Political, and Economic Study*. Cambridge: Cambridge University Press.

Erim, K., J. Reynolds, J. Wild and M. Ballance. 1970. "The Copy of Diocletian's Edict on Maximum Prices from Aphrodisias in Caria." *The Journal of Roman Studies* 60: 120–41.

Estiot, S. 2012. "The Later Third Century." In W. E. Metcalf (ed.), *The Oxford handbook of Greek and Roman coinage* (New York: Oxford University Press), 538–60.

Fentress, E. W. B. 1979. *Numidia and the Roman army: Σocial, military and economic aspects of the frontier zone*. Oxford: Oxford University Press.

Flohr, M. 2016. "The Wool Economy of Roman Italy." In K. Droß-Krüpe and M. L. Nosch (eds.), *Textiles, Trade and Theories: From the Ancient Near East to the Mediterranean* (Münster: Ugarit-Verlag), 49–62.

Gällnö, S. 2013. "(In)visible Spinners in the Documentary Papyri from Roman Egypt." In M. Gleba and J. Pásztókai-Szeöke (eds.), *Making textiles in pre-Roman and Roman times: people, places, identities* (Oxford: Oxbow Books), 161–70.

Gardner, I., A. Alcock, W.-P. Funk, C. A. Hope, and G. E. Bowen. 1999. *Coptic Documentary Texts from Kellis: Volume 1*. Oxford: Oxbow Books.

Gibson, R. K., and R. Morello. 2011. *Pliny the Elder: Themes and contexts*. Leiden: Brill.

Gleba, M., and J. Pásztókai-Szeöke. 2013. *Making textiles in pre-Roman and Roman times: People, places, identities*. Oxford: Oxbow Books.

Herz, P. 2016. "Das Preisedikt Diokletians als Quelle des Textihandels." In K. Droß-Krüpe and M. L. Nosch (eds.), *Textiles, Trade and Theories: From the Ancient Near East to the Mediterranean* (Münster: Ugarit-Verlag), 247–58.

Landi, S. and R. M. Hall. 1979. "The Discovery and Conservation of an Ancient Egyptian Linen Tunic." *Studies in Conservation* 24: 141–52.

Livingstone, R. 2009. "Late Antique household textiles from the village of Kellis in the Dakhleh Oasis." In C. Fluck, S. Martinssen-von Falck, and A. de Moor (eds.), *Clothing the house: Furnishing textiles of the 1st millennium AD from Egypt and neighbouring countries: proceedings of the 5th conference of the research group "Textiles from Nile Valley" Antwerp, 6–7 October 2007* (Tielt: Lannoo Publishers), 73–85.

Lupi, E. 2016. "Milesische Wolle in Sybaris: Neudeutung eines Fragments von Timaos (FGrH 566 F 50) und die Frage nach dem Textilhandel zwischen Kleinasien und Süditalian." In K. Droß-Krüpe and M. L. Nosch (eds.), *Textiles, Trade and Theories: From the Ancient Near East to the Mediterranean* (Münster: Ugarit-Verlag), 169–92.

MacCoull, L. S. B. 1998. "Prophethood, Texts, and Artifacts: The Monastery of Epiphanius." *Greek, Roman and Byzantine Studies* 39: 307–24.

MacMullen, R. 1958. "The *anabolicae species*." *Aegyptus* 38: 184–98.

Mayerson, P. 1997. "The Role of Flax in Roman and Fatimid Egypt." *Journal of Near Eastern Studies* 56: 201–7.

McGing, B. C. 1990. "Linen-weaving workshop in Panopolis." *ZPE* 82: 115–21.

Moss, J. Sheridan. 2009. "Two Michigan Papyri." *BASP* 46: 37–57.

Nicolet, C. 1980. *The world of the citizen in republican Rome*. Trans. P. S. Falla. Berkeley: University of California Press.

Paschoud, F. 1996. *Histoire Auguste, Tome V.1: Vies d'Aurélien, Tacite*. Paris: Les Belles Lettres.

Préaux, C. 1939. *L' Économie royale des Lagides*. Bruxelles: Fondation égyptologique Reine Elisabeth. Repr. Arno Press (New York, 1979).

Preisigke, F. 1915. *Fachworter des offentlichen Verwaltungsdienstes Agyptens in den griechischen Papyrus-kunden der ptolemaische-romische Zeit*. Göttingen: Vandenhoek & Ruprecht.

Rohrbacher, D. 2013. "The Sources of the *Historia Augusta* Re-examined." *Histos* 7: 146–80.

Rostovtzeff, M. I., 1957. *The social and economic history of the Roman Empire*. Oxford: Clarendon Press.

Sheridan, J. A. 1998. *Columbia Papyri IX: The Vestis Militaris Codex*. American Studies in Papyrology 39. Atlanta: Scholars Press.

Sheridan, J. A. 1999. "The Anabolikon." *ZPE* 124: 211–17.

van Minnen, P. 1986. "The Volume of the Oxyrhynchite Textile Trade." *MBAH* 5: 88–95.

Wallace, S. L. 1938. *Taxation in Egypt from Augustus to Diocletian*. Princeton, N.J.: Princeton University Press.

Walton Rogers, P., L. Bender Jørgensen, A. Rast-Eicher, and J. P. Wild. 2014. *The Roman textile industry and its influence: a birthday tribute to John Peter Wild*. Oxford: Oxbow Books.

Wilcken, Ulrich. 1899. *Griechische ostraka aus Aegypten und Nubien: Ein Beitrag zur antiken Wirtschaftsgeschichte*. Leipzig: Gieseke & Devrient.

Wild, J.-P. 2003. "Facts, Figures and Guesswork in the Roman Textile Industry." In L. Bender Jørgensen, J. Banck-Burgess and A. Rast-Eicher (eds.), *Textilien aus Archäologie und Geschichte. Festschrift für Klaus Tidow* (Neumünster: Wachholtz), 37–45.

Wild, J.-P. and F. Wild. 2014a. "Berenike and textile trade on the Indian Ocean." In K. Dross-Krüpe (ed.), *Textile Trade and Distribution in Antiquity/ Textilhandel und-distribution in der Antike* (Wiesbaden: Harrassowitz), 91–109.

Wild, J.-P. and F. Wild. 2014b. "Qasr Ibrim: new perspectives on the changing textile cultures of Lower Nubia." In E. R. O'Connell (ed.), *Egypt in the First Millennium AD: Perspectives from New Fieldwork, British Museum Publications on Egypt and Sudan 2* (Louvain: Peeters), 71–85.

Williams, S. 1985. *Diocletian and the Roman Recovery*. London: Batsford.

Wilson, A. 2000. "Timgad and textile production." In J. Salmon and D. J. Mattingly (eds.), *Economies beyond agriculture* (London: Routledge), 271–96.

Wilson, A. 2004. "Archaeological evidence for textile production and dyeing in Roman North Africa." In G. C. Alfaro, J. P. Wild, and B. Costa. València (ed.), *Textiles y tintes del Mediterraneo en epoca romana: actas del I Symposium Internacional sobre Textiles y Tintes del Mediterraneo en poca Romana (Ibiza, 8 al 10 de noviembre, 2002)* (València: Consell Insular d'Eivissa i Formentera, Universitat de València), 155–64.

Wipszycka, E. 1965. *L'industrie textile dans l'Egypte romaine*. Wroclaw: Zakład Narodowy im. Ossolińskich.

Worp, K. A. 1995. *Greek Papyri from Kellis I*. Oxford: Oxbow Books.

ABOUT THE CONTRIBUTORS

LORENZO D'ALFONSO is Professor of Ancient Western Asian Archaeology and History at the Institute for the Study of the Ancient World, NYU, and Associate Professor of Ancient Western Asian Archaeology at the University of Pavia. He is the author of a monograph on judicial procedures in Late Bronze Age Syria, has co-edited three edited volumes and published several articles and book sections on the history and archaeology of Syria and Anatolia during the Late Bronze and Iron Ages. Since 2011 he has been the director of excavations at Niğde Kınık Höyük in south Cappadocia (Turkey).

RODERICK CAMPBELL is Associate Professor of East Asian Archaeology and History at the Institute for the Study of the Ancient World, NYU. He is the author of *Archaeology of Bronze Age China: From Erlitou to Anyang* (Cotsen Institute of Archaeology, 2014) and *Violence, Kinship and the Early Chinese State: The Shang and Their World* (Cambridge, 2018), as well as numerous articles on Chinese Bronze Age political and economic topics.

PAM CRABTREE is Professor of Anthropology at New York University. She is the author of *Early Medieval Britain: The Re-birth of Towns in the Post-Roman West* (Cambridge University Press, 2018).

STEVEN GARFINKLE is Professor of Ancient History at Western Washington University. Garfinkle's recent and forthcoming publications include a chapter on "Violence and State Power in Early Mesopotamia" in the *Cambridge World History of Violence* and a chapter on the "The Kingdom of Ur" in the *Oxford Handbook to the Ancient Near East*.

MAXIM KOROLKOV is Assistant Professor at the Institute of Chinese Studies at Heidelberg University and Research Associate at the Institute of Oriental Studies, Russian Academy of Sciences. He is the author of a number of articles on the social, economic, and legal history of pre-imperial and early imperial China. His book *The Imperial Network: The Foundation of Sinitic Empire in Southern East Asia* is forthcoming in 2021 from Routledge.

ALVISE MATESSI is Postdoctoral Fellow at the Research Center for Anatolian Civilizations—ANAMED, Koç University (Istanbul, Turkey).

ANDREW MONSON is Associate Professor of Classics at New York University. He is the author of *From the Ptolemies to the Romans: Political and Economic Change in Egypt* (Cambridge University Press, 2012).

JUAN CARLOS MORENO GARCÍA is a CNRS senior researcher at the Sorbonne University in Paris. Recent publications include *The State in Ancient Egypt: Power, Challenges and Dynamics* (Bloomsbury Academic, 2019), *Dynamics of Production in the Ancient Near East, 1300–500 BC* (Oxbow, 2016), and *Ancient Egyptian Administration* (Brill, 2013).

DIMITRI NAKASSIS is Professor of Classics at the University of Colorado Boulder. He is the author of *Individuals and Society in Mycenaean Pylos* (Brill, 2013) and co-director of the Western Argolid Regional Project (Greece).

RICHARD PAYNE is an Associate Professor in the Department of Near Eastern Languages and Civilizations at the University of Chicago. He is a historian of the Iranian world in late antiquity and the author of *A State of Mixture: Christians, Zoroastrians, and Iranian Political Culture in Late Antiquity* (University of California Press, 2015).

IRENE SOTO MARÍN is Assistant Professor of Classical Studies and Assistant Curator as the Kelsey Museum of Archaeology in the University of Michigan. She has authored articles on the economy of Late Antique Egypt dealing with coin molds, olive oil production, and the ceramic industry, and has also edited and published papyrological texts. She is part of the core team for the NYU excavations at the site of Amheida (ancient Trimithis) in the Dakhleh Oasis of Egypt.

JAMES TAN is Lecturer of Classics and Ancient History at The University of Sydney. He is the author of *Power and Public Finance at Rome, 264–49 BCE* (Oxford University Press, 2017).

JONATHAN VALK is University Lecturer in Assyriology at Leiden University. He is the author of a forthcoming book on Assyrian identity in the second millennium BCE and numerous articles covering state and society in the ancient Near East.

INDEX

Lightning Source UK Ltd.
Milton Keynes UK
UKHW010739151021
392187UK00007B/165/J